Elephants

Elephants

C. A. Spinage, D.Sc

Illustrated by
Larry Norton

T & A D
POYSER
NATURAL
HISTORY

© T & A D Poyser Ltd

First published in 1994 by T & A D Poyser Ltd
24–28 Oval Road, London NW1 7DX

Typeset by Paston Press Ltd, Loddon, Norfolk
Printed and bound in Great Britain by
the University Press, Cambridge

A catalogue record for this book
is available from the British Library

ISBN 0–85661–088–7

Contents

List of colour plates   xi

Acknowledgements   xiii

Introduction   xv

CHAPTER 1 *Mysteries of the Past: The Origins of Elephants*   1

Elephants in England

Elephant relatives

Fossils and fantasies

From fantasy to fact

Cradle of the elephants

Archaic ancestors

The greedy gomphotheres

Immodest minds and mastodons

The mighty mammoth

Enter the elephants

Extinction of the giants

Man, the great exterminator?

CHAPTER 2 *The Elephants: Taxonomy and Distribution*   24

An African mystery

Background to the African elephant

The decline of the African elephant

Background to the Asian elephant

CHAPTER 3   *Nature's Great Masterpiece: Anatomy of
              the Elephant*   41

Curious naturalists
Bridges and backbones
'A head of such huge bignesse'
A case of teeth
The elephant's baggy suit
The feet
The hand of the beast
The guts of a giant
The puzzle of the lungs
The liver

CHAPTER 4   *From Aristotle to Benedict: Physiology and
              Functions*   60

Elephants and LSD
The heat of a thousand men
An animal with two hearts
Elephants in the Arctic
Breathalysers and beer drinkers
An unexplained puzzle
An animal with four stomachs
So capable of understanding
Tears for Timur
The strength of a flea

CHAPTER 5   *Mating and Growing Up: Reproduction
              and Growth*   79

The private life of the elephant
The season of birth
The bull elephant
The cow elephant
Courtship and coquettes
Birth
Life of the calf
Perils of poaching

C_{HAPTER} 6   *Of Size, Sindbad and Cemeteries: Growth
                    and Longevity*   99

The giant of beasts
Not built for eternity
Life's game of chance
Drought, the great leveller
The legacy of Sindbad
Death of a matriarch

C_{HAPTER} 7   *Despicable Worms and Mighty Elephants:
                    Diseases and Parasites*   111

Homes for the humble
The elephant doctors
Piano keys and sudden death
Despicable worms
Of bots and Greek cuckolds
Of flies that bite
Elephant ticks
A peculiar louse
The mystery of the symbionts
Curious and curiouser
Tiny helpers

C_{HAPTER} 8   *Matriarchs and Musth: Social Behaviour of
                    Elephants*   128

Wise old cows
Helping others
Happy families
When elephants gather
The clan and the home range
Lords of the realm
Madness and musth
Elephant incontinence
When giants fight
Rumble-grumble
Tales the ears may tell

CHAPTER 9   *Polyperchon's Predicament: Food and*
             Feeding   153
Lessons from ancient Greece
The Billy Bunter of the bush
The Augean Stables
The food the elephant eats
Sowing as they reap
A life of eating
The mysterious elephants of Elgon
A trunk for a hand

CHAPTER 10   *The Great Debate: Elephants and Trees*   169
Creating havoc
The elephants' effects on trees
Destruction of the baobab
A problem in Asia?
The benefits of elephant tree-bashing
Fighting back

CHAPTER 11   *The Elephant Casebook: Examples of*
             Overpopulation   182
The Uganda problem
The story of Tsavo
The Serengeti story
Influence of lake levels
Botswana – a southern case history

CHAPTER 12   *Did Elephants Once Rule Africa?*
             Population Dynamics and Problems   197
Darwin's deduction
Living with too many elephants
Population dynamics
In balance with nature
The magic of migration
The home range
In conflict with man
Prodigal or prudent proboscideans?

CHAPTER 13   *Ivory, the Teeth of Commerce: The
            Structure and Growth of Tusks*   215
Mighty as the head is mighty
Growth and structure
Elephants and daisy patterns
Elephant forensics
An elephantine Dorian Gray
Conjuring tricks of nature
Mammoth ivory

CHAPTER 14   *The Massacre of the Giants: The Ivory
            Trade*   237
Four thousand years of slaughter
Africa's appalling Aceldama
Where did it all go to?
An Africa overview
Asian ivory
The crash
Why not kill elephants?
The graveyard of greed

CHAPTER 15   *Anachronism or Wasted Asset? The
            Domestication of Elephants*   264
An ancient arms race
Classical controversies
Ancient skills
Elephants in Britain
The myth of intractability
Accidents will happen
Using African elephants
The great elephant experiment
An invaluable animal
A use for African elephants

Appendix 1   *Common and scientific names of plants mentioned in the
              text*   287
Appendix 2   *Gazetteer of parks and reserves*   290
Select Bibliography   292
Index   306

The colour plate section can be found between pages 160–161

List of Colour Plates

1. The elephant's remarkable organ – the trunk.
2. Hurrying to water after a hot day.
3. Drinking in the Chobe River, Botswana.
4. A suspicious cow stands guard.
5. A coating of mud helps heat loss.
6. Shade is very important in the heat of the afternoon.
7. The baby elephant suckles with its mouth, not the trunk.
8. Elephant calves are adventurous. This one wants to lead the way.
9. A calf of about 1 month of age.
10. Small calves are protected within the herd.
11. A calf sleeping while a young cow stands guard.
12. A unique study of a new species of Asian moth which makes an elephant cry and then drinks its tears. *Hypochrosis baenzigeri* from north Thailand.
13. Another of the extraordinary Asian moths from north Thailand, *Tarsolepis elephantorum*.
14. The elephant demonstrates its remarkable reach in gathering food.
15. Fresh elephant droppings provide a rich habitat. Here *Colotis* spp. white butterflies seek its moisture and salts in Kenya.
16. An elephant prefers twigs to delicacies.
17. A desolate landscape. Savuti Marsh, northern Botswana. Elephants are only partly to blame.
18. Elephants destroying a baobab tree in Tsavo Park, Kenya.
19. The soft pith of the baobab is chewed.
20. Bark stripping by elephants of *Daniellia oliveri* in the Central African Republic.
21. Elephants as they were in Selous's time along the Chobe River in northern Botswana.
22. Parking, Hyderabad style.
23. The gentlest of creatures. An elephant with unconcerned impala.
24. Poached ivory at Bangassou, Central African Republic. The French soldier appears to be negotiating with the ivory collector.
25. Loading up the spoils. Bangassou.

Acknowledgements

I am particularly grateful to Dr. Hans Bänziger for generously allowing me to use his remarkable photographs of tear-drinking moths. Also to Philip Powell and The University Museum, Oxford, for the photograph of the Paviland pendant and permission to reproduce it. Also to Dr. Caroline Grigson and the Odontological Museum of the Royal College of Surgeons of England for the photograph of the spear head inside a tusk and for permission to reproduce it; also the Trustees of the Hunterian Museum for kind permission to reproduce the photograph of a musket ball in an elephant's tusk. Thanks also go to Dr. Dick Squires for allowing me to reproduce the photograph of Chit Sayah from his grandfather's collection. I also wish to thank Dr. Hezy Shoshani for information concerning the musculature of the elephant's trunk, and James Brooks for information concerning literature on parasites. Many others have contributed information when asked and to these I am equally grateful; also to the staff of the Natural History Library and the Zoological Society of London Library who supplied my photocopy wants so efficiently. Finally to Larry Norton for contributing his excellent illustrations and last, but not least, to the editor, Dr. Andrew Richford of Academic Press, for having faith in the project at a time when it seemed that there was an over-population of elephant books rather than of elephants.

Introduction

Five tons of adult bull African elephant lay prostrate on the ground, oblivious under the effects of a morphine drug 1000 times more potent than morphine itself, its Lilliputian-like tormenters clambering over its inert hulk, drawing chalk lines over its mountainous carcase and sticking temperature probes into the veins standing out on the back of its giant ears like an atlas picture of the rivers of Africa.

'Every time an elephant flaps its ears, it cools the temperature of its blood by one half of a degree,' one of the scientists announced to the curious onlookers.

'In that case,' remarked a sceptic, *sotto voce*, 'it should be a block of ice in half an hour.'

We restrained our laughter, but the sceptic has been proved wrong. That the ears do play a part in cooling the blood of the African elephant is just one of the many discoveries to be made about elephants in recent years. But should not the size of the ears have given some clue to the much more exciting finding that elephants can communicate over large distances by ultra low frequency sound, inaudible to the human ear? Something the ancient Greeks may have suspected.

Elephants have fascinated man since ancient times, but we are only just beginning to learn what really makes them tick. Due to the monumental researches of Henry Fairfield Osborn, former Director of the American Museum of Natural History in New York, until very recent years we knew more about fossil elephants than we did about their living relatives. It was not until the early 1950s, almost 300 years after Allan Mullen dissected an Asian elephant that died in a fire in Dublin, that research began on the living African elephant, with Perry's pioneering studies on reproduction. An enormous wave of research then followed in the 1960s which has continued to the present and a great deal of information has been gathered from culling schemes. Now we know more about the African elephant than we do about the Asian, despite the latter's value to man and his long association with it stretching back to antiquity. More is known today about the African elephant than about any other large undomesticated African mammal. Scientists have not failed to point out that many aspects of the elephant's life history parallel those of man.

Despite the fascination of man from earliest times for this the largest terrestrial mammal, it has been one of the most persecuted beasts upon earth.

Man's cruelty towards it has shown no bounds and it is remarkable it has survived to the present in the numbers that it has. Whether it will continue to do so for much longer is a matter of doubt. Never has the situation looked so bleak for the survival of the larger forms of wildlife, particularly the elephant.

The first 'books' on the elephant, written, so we are told, on elephants in north east Africa, were already lost by the time of Aelian in the second century AD. Since those first accounts from about 400 BC, there has been an intermittent stream which in the past two years has become a flood. But I make no apology for this addition, which covers the parts that others do not and embodies the latest discoveries, as well as showing how much some people already knew about elephants before the new age of scientific investigation which burgeoned in the 1960s.

Chapter 1

MYSTERIES OF THE PAST: THE ORIGINS OF ELEPHANTS

> ... beasts which, living, terrify,
> Become mere toys and knick-knacks when they die.
>
> *Petronius Arbiter, d. AD 66*

ELEPHANTS IN ENGLAND

IN the late afternoon, when the searing heat of the day at last begins to give respite, hundreds of elephants trundle down to the river. The measured, determined tread of the family groups headed by the old matriarch, her trunk swinging in unison with her lumbering gait, others holding their trunks erect like huge wavering periscopes, breaks into disorder just before the lifegiving river is reached. Suddenly the youngsters, heedless of maternal discipline, impetuously break ranks and rush headlong to the cooling water. After a particularly tiring day even the staid matriarch may be infected by their enthusiasm and abandon her careful footfalls to hurry those last few yards. As more and more elephants appear, the reedy islands in the placid river become crowded to overflowing with hundreds upon hundreds of excited elephants, their great curved black shining backs hosed down with trunkfuls of water and then splattered with black mud, glistening in the last red rays of the setting sun like monstrous antediluvian leviathans wallowing in some primeval swamp at the dawn of life. Never was there such a sight as this in the whole of the past century.

This is Africa's Chobe River in northern Botswana, lifeline to the parched elephants of the Kalahari's grim sandy wastes, where the great hunter-naturalist F.C. Selous in this very same place, almost 120 years before, considered that the sight of a hundred or so elephants was something remarkable to behold. In the 1960s you could see the same great herds in Kenya, Uganda, Tanzania or Zambia; before the poacher's merciless holocaust reduced their numbers to a remnant of their former glory.

Barely 10 000 years ago such sights as that witnessed today at Chobe may not have been uncommon in England, when mastodons, mammoths and other great elephants trod the earth in countless numbers from the New World to the utmost corners of Siberia. It may seem a far cry from the dry dusts of Africa to the shaggycoated woolly elephants which roamed the hills and dales of England and drank the waters of the Thames, the Wye and the Humber; but although these giants have gone, many of the plants which provided their food remain.

The plant life of that far-off era was richer and more mixed, with many species no longer found. But there was the oak, the ash and the pine and the thorny bush of the hawthorn, familiar to us today in the English countryside.

How did the spiky hawthorn get its thorns? Did it evolve them as a defence against elephant browsers, remaining to remind us as Britain's most ubiquitous living anachronism of the Pleistocene age, still sporting its spiny protection aeons after the elephants, mammoths and other great browsers which induced its defences have vanished?

When it became cold, the same trees, bushes and grasses persisted but the English countryside became more open and the woolly mammoth needed its long hair to keep itself warm. Some have argued that this creature could only have inhabited temperate to warm–temperate climates; but although it is unlikely to have been an animal of the ice and snow, not only because there would not have been enough food in an icebound habitat, its adaptations are those of an animal able to withstand moderately cold temperatures.

In this misty past, when hippopotamus sported in Trafalgar Square and elephants roamed the site of London Docks, a straight-tusked elephant, *Elephas antiquus*, died at a waterhole in Essex. Several hundred years later, when a cold period intervened in Britain's climate, a woolly mammoth died in the self-same spot. In 1964 their remains were unearthed, the one lying on top of the other.

But the story begins far from Britain's shores when, nearly 70 million years after the last great dinosaurs had disappeared from the face of the earth, a new race of mighty giants almost succeeded in taking their place as its rulers. The world had become a drier, colder and harsher place and it demanded new adaptations to conquer it.

The dinosaurs died a slow death spanning several million years and the last ones were probably still on earth when the first distant ancestors of this new race of giants made their debut. We are not absolutely sure of their origins, but it seems most likely they were creatures known as condylarths.

Typified by *Phenacodus*, a thickset, doglike creature with a donkey's head and stubby hooves, the condylarths emerged in the Palaeocene, the 'dawn of the new age', some 60 million years ago. *Phenacodus*, our earliest clue to the origin of elephants, was not a proboscidean, as elephants are called, it was only on the line which gave rise to them, sharing certain features such as the arrangement of the bones in the wrist and ankle. From this remote past came the race to be known as the paenungulates or 'near-hoofed animals', which gave rise to the proboscideans.

'Between them (the eyes) projects a great nose, thin and crooked, which men call the proboscis,' wrote the ancient Greek Oppian 2000 years ago, giving them the name by which they are known to us today. This appellation does not mean 'nosy creatures' but 'means of providing food'. It is easier to call them proboscideans.

ELEPHANT RELATIVES

The closest-looking animal to the ancestral condylarth alive today, which modern immunological studies suggest has close affinity to the Asian elephant, is Africa's aardvark. Of nightmarish appearance, with trumpetlike snout and great donkey's ears, naked body and long, powerful claws, this strange termite-eating nocturnal creature is recognized as a 'living fossil'. Sole survivor of its lineage, it shows little change since it diverged from its closest relatives.

Its position is far from resolved, but all agree that it is one of the most ancient of mammal lines. Some of its characteristics suggest relation to the bat–hedgehog branch, others to the ungulates, but its closest relatives are the paenungulates.

Cuvier, the great French naturalist who astonished the world at the beginning of the 19th century by his discovery of huge extinct creatures in the Paris area, had classified the hyrax, an animal little larger than a guinea-pig previously thought of as a rodent, with the rhinoceroses, calling them 'little running rhinoceroses'. Later he considered the elephant its nearest ally.

Curious as it may seem, next to the aquatic manatees and dugongs, this little creature *is* the elephant's closest relative. Most recent research, using molecular biology techniques such as immunology and amino acid sequences of the blood's haemoglobin, as well as detailed bone studies, upholds Cuvier's view.

The closest cousin to the elephant is another unlikely candidate, the aquatic *Sirenia*, represented today by the marine dugong and manatee. These creatures branched from the main line of evolution before the hyrax in the early Eocene. Allied to the living dugongs was the marine Steller's sea cow, exterminated in the 18th century.

The haemoglobin amino acid sequence shows the closeness of elephants to the dugongs and manatees, followed by the hyraces and then the aardvark. Thus these unlikely-looking bedmates all represent a closely related branch of mammals, contrasting with the widely separated ungulates, suggesting that they did not share a common ancestry. The ungulates or hoofed mammals and the whales, on the other hand, shared a common ancestor with the carnivores and the pangolin. But elephants and their strange cousins are close to the ancient mammals and represent a unique line of mammalian evolution.

FOSSILS AND FANTASIES

Elephant fossils have been recovered from most of Europe and virtually every geographic region of North America. 'The abundance of elephants' teeth found buried in different parts of the world, and many of those parts such as no elephant is ever known to have lived in, have given amazement to naturalists,' read a 19th century encyclopaedia.

More than giving amazement to naturalists, they provided the core of the controversies surrounding the theory of creation. In 1690, during excavations in Gray's Inn Lane, London, John Bagford discovered an elephant's tooth. Elephant remains had been known for centuries before this and were regarded as relics of the Roman occupation or remains of animals drowned in the Flood. A belief was also widespread that fossil bones were the remains of giant people, a fiction dating from Roman times.

In Britain in 1171 a river bank collapsed revealing the bones of a 'man' who 'must have been fifty feet high'. The ancient chronicler Ralph of Coggeshall, perhaps with an admixture of Saint Augustine (AD 354–430) who claimed to have seen the grinder of a man so large that a hundred ordinary-sized teeth might be made from it, tells us that in King Richard's time two teeth were found on the beach in Essex of a 'certain giant of such huge bignesse that two hundred such teeth as men have now-a-daies might be cut out of them. These I saw at Coggeshall and not without wondering'.

Often such teeth and bones were kept as relics in churches, sometimes attributed to saints.

But John Bagford's find was much more significant than most, for in the same deposit he found a flint implement. This could surely not be manmade as God had created Adam on the 23rd of March in the year 4004 BC, as everyone knew. The Bible tells us what happened thereafter. Then in 1860, almost 200 years later, a Frenchman, Boucher de Perthes, made known his discoveries of mammoth remains and flint instruments in the gravels of the Somme at Abbeville. Cuvier, who everyone including Napoleon listened to, asserted that the mammoth and the vast assemblage of living forms contemporary with it had been destroyed in a universal flood before that of Noah and man was the product of the last period of creation. Man could not have lived side by side with mammoths.

After 15 years of dispute it had to be admitted that man had lived in the antediluvian 'epoch of creation'. Indeed, he had lived side by side with mammoths and before the end of the century numerous paintings and engravings made by Stone Age man were to be found in caves in southern Europe depicting mammoths 'with astonishing exactitude'.

FROM FANTASY TO FACT

Cuvier, despite his orthodox beliefs, made a special study of the elephant and its fossil remains. He showed that the Asian and the African, formerly grouped as one, were distinct species. He then went on to demonstrate from the tooth structure that the mammoth was more closely related to the Asian elephant than to the African and that mastodons were allied to elephants. His work on fossil elephants was not surpassed until 1939–1942 when Henry Fairfield Osborn, curator of the American Museum of Natural History in New York, produced his mammoth work on elephant evolution, *Monograph of the Proboscidea*. With the horses, elephants possess the most well-known fossil history that we have, because apart from their abundance as a race their large teeth and bones have naturally survived better than those of many other species.

Since teeth are the most commonly found remains, differences between fossil elephants are based primarily on tooth width, the number of cones or enamel plates and the spacing of the plates along the tooth's length. More than 3100 individual mammoth remains (not counting mastodon remains) from over 1500 localities are known from the New World alone. Osborn described 352 separate species altogether from New World and Old World fossils and was able to determine the lineage of elephants from their earliest known ancestor to the present day.

In the 1960s a wealth of fossils of *Elephantidae* and other proboscidea were discovered in sub-Saharan Africa, much of it in Kenya. This has enabled the lines of evolution to be boiled down to a more manageable five genera of *Elephantidae* and 25 species. Today we divide the Order *Proboscidea* into five suborders: *Mammutoidea*, *Gomphotheroidea*, *Moeritheroidea*, *Barytheroidea* and *Deinotheroidea*. The order showed enormous past diversity, making its mark as a major part of the tertiary and quaternary age of mammals which flourished 10 million years ago. But all, except members of the family *Elephantidae* of the *Gomphotheroidea*, are now extinct.

CRADLE OF THE ELEPHANTS

Until very recently it was believed that the *Proboscidea* originated in Africa. A gomphothere ancestor, *Primelephas*, which had its lower jaw greatly reduced in length and only a small pair of widely separated tusks, gave rise in the late Miocene to the earliest recognized elephant and ancestor of the modern elephant and the mammoths. But discoveries of new material in India and Pakistan from older geological strata, dating from late–early to early mid-

Eocene compared to the late Eocene to early Oligocene in Africa, suggest the origin was not in Africa but Eurasia. The habitat was similar, near the shores of the ancient Tethys Sea, the great inland sea which stretched from the western Mediterranean to India.

During the Cainozoic, or third great geological epoch, proboscideans lived on all of the continents of the world with the exceptions of Australia, Antarctica and some islands. They ranged from sea level to high altitudes such as in the Andes, where the Andean mastodon *Cuvieronius andium* was found.

Africa was the centre of evolution and dispersal of these creatures. They may not have originated there but it was to their liking and Africa became the great cradle of evolution of the elephants. It is here that we find the early members of closely related groups: the moeritheres, barytheres, sirenians and hyracoids. It is here that we can trace the origins of all of the families in the order, with the single exception of a family known as stegodonts, animals which, despite similar teeth and elephantlike characteristics, are no longer regarded as true 'elephants'. They were a specialized group, probably derived from mastodons, and evolved in parallel with the true elephants.

ARCHAIC ANCESTORS

About 60 million years ago in the epoch termed the Palaeocene, the oldest fossil records of the earliest paenungulates appear, But the living creatures could have occurred in the Upper Cretaceous before this. These fossils show that by the early Eocene a nondescript amphibious animal had appeared in the swamp regions of northern Africa, then bounding the great sea of Tethys. Found nowhere else, this short stout creature, standing about 60 cm high at the shoulder, was an undoubted proboscidean. Although it had no long snout, perhaps in Kipling's words 'He had only a blackish bulgy nose, as big as a boot, that he could wriggle about from side to side; but he couldn't pick up things with it'.

Small and piglike, but with the eyes placed high on the head almost like a hippopotamus and with its second upper incisor teeth much enlarged, it was called *Moeritherium*, the 'wild beast of Moeris', after Lake Moeris near El Fayyum in Upper Egypt, 100 km south of Cairo. Here its remains were found in the 25 million-year-old Miocene strata. Five species have been described from this region.

A far cry from an elephant if you do not have Kipling's imagination, the moeritheres were at least partly amphibious, perhaps wholly so. After a brief existence they became extinct in the Oligocene leaving no known descendants. Some scientists have suggested that perhaps too much weight is accorded to apparent similarities shown in this animal with those that we would expect an elephant ancestor to have had: the somewhat enlarged incisor teeth and a femur and foot looking like those of a little elephant. But the majority of recent workers consider *Moeritherium* to be a *bona fide* proboscidean, forming one of the five families of the paenungulates; although some Asian species of probosci-

TABLE 1.1 *The geological time scale.*

Era	Epoch	Years from beginning
Cenozoic	Recent	10 000
	Pleistocene	2 million
	Pliocene	10 million
	Miocene	25 million
	Oligocene	38 million
	Eocene	54 million
	Palaeocene	65 million
Mesozoic	Cretaceous	136 million
	Jurassic	195 million
	Triassic	225 million
Palaeozoic	Permian	280 million
	Carboniferous	345 million
	Devonian	395 million
	Silurian	440 million
	Ordovician	500 million
	Cambrian	570 million
Proterozoic		1700 million
Archaeozoic		3000 million
Azoic		4500 million

Ages are approximate and mostly follow the maxima given in the British Museum (Natural History) Department of Palaeontology Explanatory Leaflet No: P6 (1971) *The Dating of Geological Time*

dean are slightly older than the African moeritheres, so the latter are no longer considered to have been on the direct ancestral line of proboscideans.

Recent studies show striking similarities of the moeritheres to an ancient amphibious group the *Desmostylia*, from the Miocene and Pliocene of eastern Tethys and the Pacific. From skeletal characteristics using bones not likely to be modified greatly because of a similar function in most mammals, such as the stylohyoideum of the throat, a peculiar aquatic mammal of the Miocene epoch which occurred on both sides of the north Pacific, *Desmostylus*, appears to have been closely related to the group. It had upper canines forming tusks, rather like the aquatic dugong, and prominent lower incisors. Its molar teeth suggest it may have fed on shellfish. The relationship of these early creatures was probably *Sirenia* (the dugongs)-*Desmostylia–Proboscidea–Hyracoidea–Embrithopoda–Dinocerata*.

In Africa the record reaches back to the Oligocene, 27 to 38 million years ago, with the *Embrithopoda* or 'heavy-footed ones'. These archaic monsters are represented by a single grotesque beast *Arsinoitherium*, 'the wild beast of Arsinoe', named after Queen Arsinoe wife of Ptolemy II. More like a rhinoceros than an elephant, it was as large as an elephant but lacked trunk or tusks. At the end of its nose it bore a massive pair of bony horn cores fused at the base, looking like a double rhinoceros horn. A narrow muzzle indicates that it was a

TABLE 1.2   *Classification of elephants (partly after Maglio (1973) and Shoshani (1986)).*

Order Proboscidea

Suborder	*Family*	*Subfamily*	*Genus*
Moeritherioidea	Moeritheriidae		Moeritherium
Barytherioidea	Barytheriidae		Barytherium
Deinotherioidea	Deinotheriidae		Deinotherium
Elephantoidea	Mammutidae		Mammut, Zygolophodon
	Stegodontidae		Stegodon, Stegolophodon
	Gomphotheriidae		
		Phiominae	Phiomia, Palaeomastodon
		Trilophodontinae	Trilophodon
		Tetralophodontinae	Tetralophodon, Morillia
		Anancinae	Anancus, Pentalophodon
		Eubelodontinae	Eubelodon, Cuvieronius
		Serridentinae	Serridentinus, Trobelodon, Platybelodon
		Rhynchorostrinae	Rhynchotherium, Aybelodon
		Amebelodontinae	Amebelodon
	Elephantidae		
		Stegotetrabelodontinae	Stegotetrabelodon
		Elephantinae	Primelephas, Loxodonta Elephas Mammuthus

browser, but its teeth and certain resemblances in the skull suggest an affinity with the hyrax rather than with any other known creature.

Equally grotesque were the *Dinocerata*, or 'terrible horns', beasts of bizarre and ungainly appearance, typically with three pairs of bony horns or knobs on the skull. One pair was situated on the end of the broad, hippopotamus-like snout; the second on the forehead and the third at the back of the head. The upper canines were enlarged, sabre-like teeth, which fitted over a flange in the lower jaw. Starting small, *Dinocerata* culminated in an animal the size of the white rhinoceros.

Another branch of the family tree with origins contemporaneous with the wild beast of Moeris were horrifying-looking monsters called dinotheres, or 'terrible wild beasts'. The most distinctive feature of these elephant-like animals was the downwardly pointed tusks they carried in the lower jaws, looking like the teeth of some great sabre-toothed tiger, except that dinotheres were not carnivorous. Their remains have been found in river, lake and marine sediments, associated with a variety of both terrestrial and aquatic animals.

Although dinotheres could have exploited an aquatic habitat the skeleton is that of a land animal. Their teeth were composed of anterior cutting and posterior shearing elements indicative of the relatively soft diet of a browser; unlike the crushing and shearing mechanism of elephants. The skull structure shows that dinotheres could rotate the head more than can an elephant and move the head down on the neck. Some think it had a long trunk, others think the trunk was short and tapir-like.

The presence of enamel on newly erupted tusks and its absence on older ones suggests that it wore off just as in modern elephants, but it is unlikely that the tusks were used for digging as the animal would have had to kneel to do so. More probably they were used for tearing at thicket vegetation and as a purchase for a short trunk to hold food against. A limitation on large size would tend to predispose against a function as in modern elephants, of most importance in establishing dominance, more frightening to another dinothere than to any other animal.

Best known among these monsters was *Deinotherium giganteum*, or 'terrible huge wild beast', now named *D. bozasi* or 'Bozas's terrible wild beast' after Vicomte Bourge de Bozas's mission which found its remains in Ethiopia in 1903. Other remains had been unearthed long before this and the Reverend Dr William Buckland, Dean of Westminster, who earned immortality as the identifier of fossil coprolites, proposed the theory in 1835 that it had been an aquatic mammal which used its downwardly pointing tusks to anchor itself to the river bank while sleeping!

But the downwardly pointing tusks in the lower jaw were an inefficient mechanical arrangement, since their weight had to be borne solely by the cheek muscles, soon giving the owner jaw-ache if they became too heavy. The backwardly directed curvature in the later and larger species meant that the dinotheres would not dislocate their lower jaw when tearing at vegetation, for the backward movement would force the jaws together. Despite this inefficient weight arrangement, dinotheres had graviportal or 'weight carrying' skeletons and grew as large as a modern elephant. They persisted in Africa until the Pleistocene when they ousted the barytheres, the predominant large browsers which also sheared their food.

The dinotheres' specialized mode of feeding may have limited the range of habitats they could exploit, making them less successful migrants than elephants and causing them to fail to penetrate eastern Asia and North America. They did succeed in invading Europe, although becoming extinct there before the Pleistocene and before the end of the Pliocene in Eurasia. *D. giganteum* had cursorial or running adaptations consistent with a change from dense swamp habitats to those of more open savannah-type. The extinction of *D. bosazi* in East Africa when the open habitat faunas became dominant suggests it was not adapted to this less exuberant type of environment. But they didn't do too badly, for they had a longer geologic record than the *Elephantidae* have had to date, spanning a period of over 20 million years compared to the latter's 13 million.

THE GREEDY GOMPHOTHERES

The family *Elephantidae* derived from the descendants of a creature which probably looked much like *Moeritherium*, very similar to modern hyraces, but had a tendency to grow larger and larger. Unlike other grazing and browsing animals which did the same, their neck vertebrae did not lengthen accordingly, otherwise they could not have grown tusks without getting a pain in the neck. So, like some Victorian cautionary tale for greedy boys, as they grew bigger and bigger their mouths became further and further from the ground – and their source of food. So they compensated for this by their nose and upper lip becoming longer and longer, as well as the lower jaw and the incisor teeth, in order to keep in touch with the ground.

But there was an obvious danger in having a lengthened lower jaw for prodding at food on the ground. If they slipped they would get much worse than a pain in the neck. So the lower jaw shortened, leaving the end of the snout unsupported – it became a trunk.

Shortly after this Kiplingesque solution developed to produce the proboscids, these nosey creatures divided into two major groups, the gomphotheres and the mastodons or mammutids. True proboscideans of the genus *Palaeomastodon* were recorded in the late Eocene of northern Africa and it was probably this genus which gave rise by side branching to both the gomphotheres and the mastodons in the early Miocene.

The first of these groups, the gomphotheres or 'bolted-together-toothed wild beasts', had triple-crested or trilophodont teeth for crushing and shearing. The first gomphothere-like animals from the late Eocene of North Africa already showed highly evolved proboscidean features, suggesting a long prior evolutionary history before the first true gomphotheres appeared in the mid to late Oligocene, 25 to 30 million years ago. Mastodon-like proboscideans, they showed the greatest variety, producing such creatures as the shovel-tuskers and beak-tusked rhynchotheres. With the exception of the shortjawed ones, their teeth remained remarkably uniform and the mechanism of mastication fairly constant, as they experimented with greatly lengthened lower jaws, tusks both upper and lower and a nose probably something like that of a tapir, relatively short but prehensile.

The earliest, *Phiomia*, literally 'the lake province one' and *Palaeomastodon* or 'ancient mastodon', did not have distinctive elephant-like features, but by the beginning of the Miocene a large number of different forms had appeared and the most progressive lines migrated throughout Eurasia and America. By the Pleistocene there were three genera in South America.

A very diverse family, their fossils have been found in every continent except Australia and Antarctica. Several very specialized forms apart, they had a single pair of incisor teeth developed in the lower jaw and sometimes also a pair in the upper. The wide-ranging *Gomphotherium* [*Tetrabelodon*] *angustidens* possessed long, slightly downcurving upper incisor tusks and relatively short chisel-like cutting incisors in a lengthened lower jaw, which made the total length of the lower jaw the same as that of the tusks.

Some gomphotheres were so greedy that a trunk was not enough and tusks in the lower jaw were flattened, producing the 'shovel-tuskers', looking like animated earth-movers, strange animals like platybelodon and amebelodon which literally shovelled food into their mouths. The popular theory was that they scooped up aquatic vegetation, but they were big creatures and aquatic vegetation is a poor sort of food due to the large volume of air space in it to give buoyancy, so perhaps they used them on land after all. But rather than using the tusks as shovels, perhaps they cropped vegetation with them just as hippopotamuses do today with their broad horny lips. However they got their food it was a successful method, for they flourished in Asia and North America but had a limited history in Africa, although it seems likely they originated there in Oligocene times.

Like the hawthorn bush with its spiky protection, the large forest palm *Scheelea rostrata* of South American forests may reflect the past rather than the present, having developed the thick wall of its nut as a protection against crushing by gomphothere molars. Some 39 species of trees and large shrubs in the lowland deciduous forest of Costa Rica have similar fruit and seed traits which seem only explicable by the fact that they must have evolved a protection against large browsing animals which are now extinct. The fruits are like those eaten by elephants in Africa today, in which the elephant acts as an important agent in dispersal of the seeds.

IMMODEST MINDS AND MASTODONS

The mastodons, of the family *Mammutidae*, were allied to the true elephants rather than to the mammoths. They were distinguished by conelike cusps on their teeth which Cuvier, being a Frenchman, naturally likened to a woman's breasts and so named them 'breast-teeth' from the Greek word for breast. Such simple cusps as the mastodons possessed signify a browsing diet, used for chopping vegetation rather than shearing and grinding it.

In the middle of the 18th century it was believed that mastodons were carnivorous, a view shared by William Hunter, the pre-eminent British surgeon who, in an address to the Royal Society in 1768, thanked heaven that such a formidable large and widespread beast was extinct.

Some mastodons reached 4.3 m at the shoulder, but others may have been only a metre high. The more recent had a single pair of large long straight upper tusks, with the lower ones greatly reduced. Their heads were large but they had shorter limbs than the elephants proper.

Stegomastodon in South America, literally 'roof-toothed' mastodon because of the shape of the ridges on its teeth, showed dental adaptations for grazing.

Cuvieronius, or 'Cuvier's', lived up to less than 12 000 years ago in Central America. Weighing an estimated $2\frac{1}{4}$–$3\frac{1}{2}$ tonnes it was more closely related to the North American mastodons than to the North American mammoths. *Cuvieronius* ate fruits and browsed, whereas mammoths grazed and browsed.

Ancestors of the American mastodon first appear in the fossil record in the early to mid-Oligocene, 30–35 million years ago, before the gomphotheres arose. The first fossils found in America, some teeth and a thigh bone on the banks of the Hudson River in 1705, were of the American mastodon, *Mammut americanum*, but attributed by their finder to a gigantic race of men. Since then almost complete skeletons have been recovered, some even bearing fragments of hide and long, reddish-brown hair, although the original colour was probably black. One skeleton unearthed in Michigan in 1968 was dated to 10 200±170 years; but they may have survived until as recently as 8000 years ago.

Mastodons reached South America in the Pleistocene at the time that they died out in Africa. In South America they were gone by 11 800 years ago, although other weird giants continued for another 3000 years: the great armoured tortoiselike *Glyptodon*; *Macrauchenia* like a cross between a camel and a tapir; and the huge sloth *Mylodon*, of which a mummified carcase has survived in a cave.

Mastodons were great wanderers. It is thought they returned to their ancestral home of Africa from Eurasia, preceding the more modern *Elephas antiquus* of Africa and southern Europe. Immunological tests on fragments of dried flesh have confirmed that the American mastodon was closely related to the *Elephantidae*.

The mean age at death based on African elephant age determination techniques of three American mastodon samples of 15, 25 and 30 specimens was closely similar at just over 25 years. The oldest animal was 50. These figures suggest a similar life expectancy to modern elephants in the wild.

THE MIGHTY MAMMOTH

The mammoths get their name not from any fancied semblance to a woman's breasts but from a Siberian corruption of the Arabic Mehemot, itself a corruption of Behemoth, the Siberian word being mamont or mamut. Others consider this derivation unconvincing.

The first reference to frozen mammoths is found in an ancient Chinese work the *Shen i king*, or 'Book of Wondrous Tales', written probably between 120 and 87 BC. It was almost a thousand years later when 10th century Arab geographers wrote of a huge strange animal found underground in Great Bulgaria on the Volga River.

As the tusks were found in the ground, it was believed that they came from a burrowing animal like some gigantic mole. The Chinese themselves believed the mammoth to be a giant underground rat which, like some Peter Sellers's parody, they called *fyn schu* – 'the mouse that hides'. Aixinjuelo Xuanhua described it in the Emperor Kangxi's 'Inquiry on the Physical Law in Leisure' written sometime between AD 1654 and 1722:

> The northern plain near the sea in Russia is the coldest place. There is a kind of beast, which like a mouse, is big as an elephant, crawls in tunnels, and dies as it meets the sun or the moon light. Its teeth are like an elephant's, white, soft and smooth with no crackles. The native people often find it on the river bank . . . . Its Russian name is Momentuowa.

Mammoths first appeared in Africa at the beginning of the Pliocene, 10 million years ago. Although going on to spectacular evolution in Eurasia and North America, by the early Pleistocene the line had disappeared from the African continent. Its main centre of radiation was Eurasia, where it was subjected to a greater fluctuation of climatic conditions than any other group of elephants. From here the earliest form, the southern mammoth *Mammuthus meridionalis*, spread as far afield as North America in the early Pleistocene epoch about 1.8 million years ago. The woolly mammoth *M. primigenius* did not follow it there until the late Pleistocene.

Both mammoths and mastodons probably had similar life histories and social behaviour to the living elephants. Although more primitive than *Gomphotherium*, *Mammuthus* was the most advanced genus among the elephants in its dental and cranial features. It had very high-crowned molars with a complex grinding surface and a high domed forehead to accommodate the musculature of the trunk and the huge weight of the tusks. Some mammoths also had paired fingerlike extensions at the tip of the trunk as well as lateral winglike extensions, which may have aided grass gathering. This would have fitted with the molar pattern which is that of a grazer rather than a browser.

Standing over 4 m at the shoulder compared with the African elephant's 3–4, the mid-Pleistocene Armenian mammoth *M. armenicus* from Europe was the largest known of all proboscideans. Despite its name, the imperial mammoth *M. imperator* was slightly smaller, estimated to have weighed 5–7 tonnes and averaging 3.7 m at the shoulder.

Best known was the woolly mammoth, *M. primigenius*, which existed in Europe and North America until beyond the end of the last glacial period less than 50 000 years ago and is represented in the cave drawings of European Stone Age man. Samples of frozen muscle and clotted blood from three Siberian specimens have been dated each to 11 450, 34 400 and 35 000 years ago.

Inaptly named *primigenius* or 'first born', the woolly mammoth was the most highly advanced of the mammoths and more advanced in many features than either of the living elephants. It is well known as several complete frozen specimens have been found in the permafrost of the Arctic tundra of Siberia since the first reported by Evert Ysbrand Ides, a Dutchman who accompanied an envoy sent by Peter the Great to China in 1692. On his way through Siberia Ides met a collector of fossil ivory who told him that he had once seen the head of a mammoth projecting from the frozen ground, but the inside had decayed.

In 1977 a bulldozer operator of a gold-prospecting co-operative working on the shores of the Kirgiljach river in north-eastern Siberia unearthed a complete woolly mammoth bull calf. Standing just over 1 m high in life, he was estimated to have been about six months old when he died.

Adult woolly mammoths stood about 3–3.5 m high and probably weighed 4–5 tonnes, even 6. They were covered in long bristly hair with a dense yellowish-brown matted underwool, a mane and also wool on the trunk. The skin was not as thick as the thickest of living elephants; although there may have been a thick layer of subcutaneous fat up to 9 cm in places, a seasonal fat hump on the back and possibly on top of the head, but some question this. Similar to the African elephant there were two 'fingers' at the end of the trunk. The human-shaped ears were about one-fifth smaller than those of the Asian elephant. Mammoths had short legs but the back did not slope as much as is generally portrayed, an error copied from cave artists. The number of digits was reduced to four. Several recovered carcases have been found to have horny excrescences, like extra nails, on the hind feet. These could result from walking on soft ground; the weight being borne on the front feet, they are less likely to develop overgrowths.

The woolly mammoth's distribution corresponded largely with the present treeless tundra environment which borders the Arctic Ocean and the taiga, the boreal coniferous forest of the cold north; covering the maximum extent of the Pleistocene glaciations and the glacial or near-glacial environments. The great Victorian geologist Sir Charles Lyell posed the question in 1835 that if it preferred a northern climate, then by what food was the mammoth sustained and why did it not still survive near to the Arctic circle? Recent Russian studies suggest it was adapted to the treeless grasslands, richer in plant variety than wooded tundra, which has a sparse understorey of moss and shrubs with an absence of grass. Wrangel Island (Ostrova Vrangelya), where the last mammoths are believed to have survived, has a ground flora of steppe-tundra three times richer than elsewhere due to a local continental climate resulting in a relative abundance of sunny days.

One suggestion to explain the woolly coat is that it was to stop the mammoth losing heat after drinking ice-cold water, but at low temperatures its water intake would be much less than that of living elephants and its woolly coat would also help it to conserve water that would otherwise be lost through the skin by evaporation. Another possibility is that it had nothing to do with the animal's physiology, but served as a protection against the unbearable myriads of mosquitoes and other biting flies which occur in spring and summer in the north.

A persistent myth is that the woolly mammoths which met with sudden death were frozen solid before decay of even the stomach contents had set in to any great extent. In fact all of the carcases recovered had partly rotted after death and much of the flesh was putrid. Although some was sufficiently preserved to be eaten by dogs, there is only one alleged case of a person eating some. Dying at the end of summer or in the autumn, their remains were frozen in the ensuing winter.

A carcase excavated in 1948 in the Tamyr Peninsula was found in association with branches of willow and dwarf birch, indicating a less severe climate as the willow now occurs 800 km to the south. The forest zone must have reached much farther north and mammoths probably migrated out of this forest still farther north in spring and summer, moving out onto the open tundra, perhaps to escape the attentions of bloodsucking flies just as reindeer do today. On their return, trekking south in the autumn along the river valleys, they may have often died falling through weak ice or caught in flash floods.

Illustrations of mammoths invariably depict them with huge tusks curving outwards and then spiralling in on themselves, but Bassett Digby, an adventurous American journalist who examined 1000 tusks in Siberia in the 1920s, claimed that less than 1 in 10 formed a third of a circle and less than 1 in 20 a semicircle. The tusks tend to curve inwards slightly, those of young bulls curving upwards more strongly than those of the cow, which were thinner and straighter. A tusk of 2.97 m in length Digby referred to as a 'monster', while a pair greater than 3.96 m and weighing 75.9 and 84.6 kg was considered to be of record size. The longest recorded is 5 m, and it has been estimated that the biggest would have weighed almost 130 kg each.

One of the most popular theories advanced to explain such long curved tusks was that they were used as a kind of snow plough to push snow away from the underlying vegetation. Wear, found even on young mammoth tusks, is on the upper side and a recent interpretation of this flattened wear zone at the tips is that mammoths may have used their tusks for peeling off tree bark in summer and breaking ice in crevices in winter. But if the tips of the tusks were close together such wear could result simply from the action of pulling the trunk over them. To my mind the most likely explanation for the curvature was to reduce injury from fighting. In a temperate habitat breeding would have been strictly seasonal, resulting in an annual period of rut with vigorous inter-bull competition. Like spiral kudu horns curved tusks would limit their effectiveness as stabbing weapons, leading to ritualized fighting and minimizing fatal conflict. In Nebraska the fossils of two mammoths have been found with the tusks interlocked. In Africa there are several examples of antelopes and buffalo dying from their horns interlocking.

Be that as it may, what most fail to realize is that if the African elephant had not been hunted ruthlessly for its tusks for the past 150 years, then African elephants with great curving tusks reaching to the ground and without any apparent use would be a not uncommon sight today. Most mammoth tusks were well within the potential growth limits of the tusks of the living African elephant. A sample collected in the 1920s was given as ranging from 1.2 to 3.2 m in length, not so very different from good African elephant tusks. The most common length was 1.2 to 2.4 m.

Of 90 bull and 97 cow frozen tusks collected in the 1980s, the bull tusks ranged in length from 1.48 to 3.62 m with a mean of 2.5 and weighed 11.1–88 kg with a mean of 46.35. Those of the cow were 1.0–2.47 m with a mean of 1.6 and weighed 4.6–19.7 kg with a mean of 9.9. A similar ratio of bull to cow dimensions that one might find in African elephant tusks. The biggest pair of bull tusks measured 3.66 and 3.8 m left and right and weighed 74 kg each; estimated from discoloured bands on the surface to have come from an animal aged 65 years. The biggest pair of cow tusks measured 2.47 m and weighed 19.5 kg each, also from an animal estimated to have been 65.

Eighteenth century American Indians believed mammoths still existed but although the imperial mammoth was alive in Canada 10 600 years ago, only a small number of mammoths survived in Europe as late as about 12 000 years ago. The woolly mammoth was rare or absent in Europe after 13 000 years and in north central Eurasia all mammoths had become extinct 1000 years before this. In China they disappeared 20 000 years ago, but in Siberia they survived until perhaps 7000 years ago and a dwarfed population isolated on Wrangel Island until as recently as 3500 years ago.

ENTER THE ELEPHANTS

Elephants and stegodonts had tall teeth with parallel bands of enamel providing a fore-and-aft shearing effect. In other words, rather than just chomping leaves and fruits they could grind their food and make use of the much more abrasive, but plentiful grass.

A 'shearing index' shows that the teeth of the Asian elephant were three times more efficient than those of the African, but *M. primigenius* had the most effective of all, greater than five times more than those of the living African elephant.

Differing from mastodons in this respect, the striking feature about the elephants was their modification of the tooth eruption pattern to use only one complete tooth in the jaw at a time, allowing increase in molar size without lengthening the jaw. At the same time the milk teeth increased in size and duration at the expense of the premolars, which disappeared in all but the earliest elephants.

Both the elephants and stegodonts independently lost their lower tusks early on, developing them in the upper jaw. This was a much more successful arrangement from a mechanical point of view, doing away with jaw-ache and allowing huge increases in weight to be borne. Together with development of the trunk, which was probably longer than in gomphotheres, there was no holding them back and coupled with a large brain, these features led to an almost explosive radiation, replacing most of the gomphothere groups and dominating the Pleistocene faunas of Africa, Asia and North America. Radiating in the later Cainozoic era (the Cainozoic was from about 65 million years ago to the present), by the middle of the Pleistocene the go-ahead elephants had become nearly worldwide in distribution, failing only to penetrate South America and reach Australia and Antarctica.

Anancus kenyensis, the Kenyan 'straight-tusked' elephant, a Kenyan gomphothere, was contemporary with the earliest elephants but became extinct at the beginning of the Pleistocene and with it disappeared the entire family of gomphotheres in sub-Saharan Africa.

During a second wave of emigration from Africa in the early Pliocene, one relative of *Elephas* (or some prefer to call it *Palaeoloxodon*) passed via Bethlehem, where its remains have been found, and on into southern Asia where it gave rise to the subsequent Asiatic radiation.

The *Elephas–Mammuthus* line evolved 1.4 times faster than *Loxodonta*, the African elephant, and in the past 4.5 million years 5.3 times faster in tooth complexity, *Loxodonta* being the most conservative genus with regard to its dental characteristics because its teeth had no need to change. Early forms of *Loxodonta* which appeared about 4 million years ago showed changes in the centre of gravity of the jaw and the height of the skull associated with development of the trunk, which took place somewhat later in other elephant lineages. So the African elephant is not primitive in the structural sense, rather it is highly specialized in some respects and its skull does not reflect that of an ancestral type. But calculated rates of evolution may change as more material is discovered and the earliest records are pushed farther back into the Eocene.

EXTINCTION OF THE GIANTS

In the later Pleistocene epoch, after a remarkable success in which elephants dominated most of the large herbivore faunas of the world, a striking decline set in leaving us with only the two extant species, *Elephas* the Asian and *Loxodonta* the African. Their scientific names are of prosaic origin: *Elephas* was the Greek word for an elephant first used by Herodotus in the 5th century BC, derived from the Hebrew or Phoenician *eleph*, meaning an ox. *Loxodonta* means 'oblique teeth', after the structure of the diamond-shaped enamel pattern of its teeth.

Shortly after the origin of the family *Elephantidae* in the Pliocene, only a few species were present at any one time but the turnover rate was high as new types appeared through speciation. With the emergence of the subfamily *Elephantinae*, comprising the extinct genera *Primelephas* and *Mammuthus* and the extant *Loxodonta* and *Elephas*, the true elephants, the turnover rate continued high. The number of new species increased and their average length of existence increased but was still relatively short. The late Pliocene and early Pleistocene witnessed a major geographic expansion of range and the number of new types continued to increase without extinctions, the turnover rate becoming low as the species underwent stabilizing selection. Species duration was high and changes in shape and appearance were slow.

In the mid-Pleistocene they underwent a second phase of accelerated evolution and radiation with a spectacular increase in number of species and a rapid turnover rate, so that average species' existence fell rapidly. In the late Pleistocene shortlived forms were the rule with rate of change in shape and appearance very great. Whereas in the family's early history average species' duration had been half a million years, in the late Pliocene and early Pleistocene this averaged 1½ to 2 million years, but fell again to half a million in the late Pleistocene. And whereas throughout most of the history of the family the rate of termination of lines was 0–1 species per million years, in the later Pleistocene this rose to a loss of eight species per million years with the termination of all but the two lines, one in Africa and the other in Asia.

This decline of a family which had spanned about 13 million years was not due to senescence of the lineage, but rather active diversification. The number of species increased continuously, especially in the Pleistocene when the total number doubled during the last million-year period. Overall about 3–4 new elephant types arose per million years for the first half of the family's history, followed by a retardation in the late Pliocene and an increase in disappearances due to transition from one form to another.

Unlike in the northern continents, where competition between *Elephas* and *Mammuthus* coupled with onset of the glaciations may have hastened decline, the order *Proboscidea* showed a gradual fading-out of species over a long period, but by the late Pleistocene *Elephas* was extinct in Africa also.

The more or less sudden final decline could suggest some external cause and man has been proposed as playing a role. However, to suppose that primitive Stone Age man with his simple weapons and the low density at which he then existed could have exterminated such mighty creatures in the millions of square kilometres over which they roamed is stretching the imagination too far.

Excavations at Predmost in Moravia revealed the remains of over 800 mammoths together with numerous human artefacts of palaeolithic man. But what time span did this collection cover? Certainly more than several hundred years, not a very high rate of offtake after all, if offtake it was. One opinion is that found bones were dragged together to make shelters in a treeless environment.

We know Stone Age man did hunt the mammoth and the mastodon with his primitive weapons and possibly to some effect, making use of pit traps. Stone arrow heads of the North American palaeo-Indian culture known as Clovis, which dates from 11 500–11 000 years ago, have been found in association with mammoth and mastodon remains at several sites dated to about 11 200 years. But the sites contain the remains of only a few animals, 15 at most, hardly deserving of the name 'mass killings' with which they have been endowed.

North American palaeo-Indians butchered mammoths and mastodons which they found or hunted, the remains of one of the latter in Michigan dating back 10 395 years, and there are indications that they roasted the meat. Growth lines in the tusks and teeth suggest that natural deaths in North America occurred near the end of winter or very early in spring; but the butchered animals died in mid to late autumn, suggesting perhaps that the palaeo-Indians laid in a store of dried meat for the winter, or it was a period of drought for the animals. In either case absence of mammoths and mastodons in the winter perhaps meant that they migrated elsewhere.

But modern studies around present-day waterholes in Zimbabwe have shown that trampling underfoot by other elephants of the remains of those which have died previously causes breakages and scratches on the bones which look like cuts or splintering made with instruments. So marks on mammoth bones which have been attributed to tool-using man may not be due to that at all. Early hunters would have found mammoths and mastodons easy prey at waterholes in times of drought, but like as not the animals were going to die anyway and their remains may well have been scavenged.

Mammoths and mastodons would have visited waterholes just as living elephants do. Whenever there is a drought in Africa elephants die at their favoured waterholes which have dried up and it is the younger ones which die first, just as many of the Pleistocene mammoth bone accumulations are of young animals. This process recurs repeatedly until such time as geological or climatic change results in the disappearance of the waterhole; the greater the accumulation of bones, then the longer has the waterhole persisted. This explains why the woolly mammoth remains in Essex were found on top of the straight-tusked elephant, although several hundred or even thousand years had intervened between the two deaths.

At the Hot Springs site in South Dakota, more than 30 Columbian mammoths were trapped in a hot spring, but the debris in which they were found represented an accumulation of 300–500 years. Many more remains were found in Friesenhahn Cave in Texas, a den of the great scimitar cat *Dinobastis* (*Homotherium*), which had dragged parts of several hundred immature elephants to its lair. At least 31 mammoths died at Boney Springs, Missouri, apparently from drought and starvation, but over how long a period of time? In two years over 190 elephants died at one waterhole in Zimbabwe. In Africa we do not speak of 'mass mortality' unless the death toll reaches hundreds or even thousands. At the Rancho La Brea tar pits in California, whereas earlier authors wrote in lurid terms of the death struggles of mass entrapments of animals in the tar, more reasoned analysis suggests that in spite of the thousands of remains, of which but few are of elephants, at most only one unfortunate elephant died there each year. It was a relatively rare event when the total period of over 25 000 years which the accumulations represent is taken into consideration.

But as Howorth argued in 1887 in his book *The Mammoth and the Flood*, interesting as the concentrations of remains are, the miring of hapless creatures in bogs, falling into crevasses and other treacherous causes of death, they do not explain the extinction of almost the whole race of elephants and their kin from the Arctic Sea to south of the equator.

In Siberia the story is different, for although occurrences are more sporadic to the south, in the north there are vast mammoth golgothas of incredible proportions, such as the first of the New Siberia Islands (Bolshoi Lyakhov) where the whole soil was described as appearing to consist of mammoth remains. Some later writers claim these earlier accounts were exaggerated and that deposits are mostly along the south coast, mixed with other large mammal remains. The bones, piled in countless thousands, showed no sign of rolling by water, movement by glacial moraines or gnawing by carnivores. Mammoth remains of young and old accumulated in dense numbers, evidence perhaps of compression on a massive scale to avoid rising waters resulting from the melting of glaciers. When the ice starts to melt in the spring, large animals like the mammoth would be unable to cross it and would find themselves trapped. This could explain why these islands had such dense concentrations of bones. Before so much was ransacked by ivory hunters, it was reported that the soil of Siberia teemed with bones and tusks. Tusks, bones, pieces of frozen mammoth (and perhaps complete ones) still appear every spring, but the fresh material quickly rots or is scavenged.

A little over 2 million years ago at the end of the Pliocene, the climate in the northern hemisphere changed dramatically. Summer temperatures rose but at the same time winters became more severe. Under such conditions species diversity declines, for animals which cannot tolerate cold winters can no longer live side by side with those which cannot tolerate hot summers and autumn resources are needed for animals to lay down fat deposits to see them through winter. Larger animals relied on a long growing season and diverse vegetation to provide a balanced diet, which was no longer provided. A change of climate may also have meant that being able to give birth when conditions were favourable for survival of the young was no longer assured.

Up until the Pleistocene epoch spanning the 2 million or so years to 10 000 years ago, the vegetation of Eurasia and North America showed greater mixing and complexity, with much less marked seasonality. In North America, conifers, broadleaf hardwoods and grasses all existed together forming an open parkland interspersed with bogs and marshes, which stretched in a broad belt from the Appalachians to the Rockies. This complex probably also occurred in Siberia where remnants exist today.

The present prairie grasslands of North America were the result of these complex associations breaking up and the deserts, prairies and deciduous forest expanding. The grass composition changed from predominantly those known as C3 species to C4 species, tougher, less digestible and less nutritious. Herbivores which depended upon C3 grasses became extinct in North America or survived reduced in size. Grazers like the mammoth, horse and bison had coexisted with browsers such as mastodon, ground sloth, tapir and deer, together with mixed feeders like caribou and musk-ox. The resultant uniformity of vegetation meant a less diverse animal life as it became difficult for herbivores to satisfy their needs at different seasons, especially when the seasons had become more extreme.

In North America the ice retreated north of the Great Lakes and early pioneering plant communities of spruce woodland and tundra were replaced briefly by pine and then deciduous species. Large areas to the north in Canada became inundated from melting ice and by the time the area had drained and began to support spruce forests again, the mastodons were already gone. Together with the Atlantic coastal region, the Great Lakes region provides the largest concentration of mastodon remains in the New World, underlining the area's former importance.

From the associated pollen evidence, it appears that the late Pleistocene mastodons of eastern North America were mostly solitary forest dwellers which died out in a woodland environment of pine and spruce, with lesser amounts of hardwood species. Apparently adapted to a pine-dominated vegetation, as the coniferous islands vanished, so did the mastodons. They may have been mixed browsers, concentrating on bark, leaves and small branches of deciduous trees and shrubs. The changes probably resulted in a decrease in diversity of browse, which was disadvantageous to them, unable to turn to grass as the African elephant can.

Although the imperial, Columbian and woolly mammoths overlapped in time, the cause of their extinction, wherever it took place, was probably due to an inability to adapt in the face of rapid changes of climate and vegetation. Already inhabiting a marginal environment, it took little to shift the balance against them. We shall see how the living African elephant can lay waste its environment; what must it have been like in Pleistocene times with a plethora of such giants competing for scarce resources in times of want?

The winter landscape of the far north in the last Ice Age was a treeless, cold and virtually snowless plain. But about 15 000 years ago the Ice Age ended suddenly in the space of 15–20 years, the average temperature increasing by 7°C. Winter snows became deeper and winds less, so that shrubs and woodlands began to colonize the area, making it more habitable. But the changes came too late for the mammoths, although there is evidence that the woolly mammoth had begun to adapt by producing a dwarf form, previously thought to be the remains of females. Like the dwarf elephants which evolved on islands in the Mediterranean and dwarf stegodonts on south east Asian islands, so did dwarf mammoths, half the size of their mainland brethren, evolve on islands off the Californian coast and on Wrangel Island near the polar shelf.

Africa did not escape the changes of the Pleistocene and underwent a major alteration in its plant life in response to climatic change at about the same period that changes were taking place in the New World. Because it was the least specialized and could make use of a wide range of vegetation, the elephant as we know it today was the only one which managed to survive in spite of its large size and this probably only in remnant forests in the centre of Africa.

In southern Africa, where elephants are exposed to winter night temperatures well below freezing, during the day the sun soon becomes hot so that they can warm up quickly. This differs from northern climes where winter days remain cold. Furthermore, the habitat in southern Africa has many evergreen shrubs and trees which flourish in the winter, in contrast to temperate regions where winter evergreens are largely unpalatable.

In the cold dry season in Zimbabwe elephants were seen to take twice as much browse as in the wet season and five times as much leafy branches and bark. We need to know more of what mammoths ate in the Ice Age to learn whether food was indeed limiting. Stomach contents of frozen Siberian mammoths have revealed that in summer months the preferred diet was grass together with sedges, herbs, the terminal shoots of shrubs such as willow, birch and alder, and the bark of willow and birch. The 10 000 year old frozen Beresovka young bull mammoth which died in the autumn, as the presence of seeds in its teeth shows, had fed upon wild thyme, sedges, the yellow Alpine poppy, bitter crowfoot, lady's slipper, varieties of gentian and other plants still found today. There was no trace of conifers, but we have no data on the winter diet. In America mammoths also preferred grass but browsed more than mastodons, changing their diet with the seasons. A large deposit of fossilized trampled mammoth dung in a cave in Utah dating from 11 700 years ago suggested a diet of 95%

grass, sedges and rushes. They also ate birch, rose, salt bush, sagebrush, blue spruce, wolfberry and red osier dogwood.

MAN, THE GREAT EXTERMINATOR?

The African elephant was never threatened by man until the advent of relatively sophisticated firearms about 150 years ago. So why should it be supposed that Stone Age man with weapons inferior to those possessed for a millennium by Africans before the introduction of firearms could have been able to wipe out *Elephas* in Africa? This much was evident to some writers over a century ago:

> ... Africa, has been from the remotest historical times peopled by numerous inhabitants, and to these the use of iron seems long to have been known; but until the ivory hunters, with fire-arms, and more recently with rifles and explosive bullets, began to persecute them, the African pachydermata seem to have maintained their numbers. Similarly the civilization of Southern Asia is very ancient, and the use of metals probably dates back there several thousand years; but what have the civilized Asiatics, with the accessories of metal weapons and of the domesticated horse, done towards exterminating the Asiatic pachydermata and great felines? Modern sportsmen, with their destructive weapons, have done more towards this in half a century than has been done during thousands of years of antecedent civilization . . . .
>
> (Wood, 1872)

It can happen if the human population is dense enough, as in China, but this it manifestly was not in Pleistocene times. In America man may have sounded the final death knell to expiring populations, remnants of once great mastodon and mammoth communities struggling to survive in what had become a hostile environment, but he had no part in the cause of their decline nor any part in the great exterminations of northern Europe and throughout the vastness of Siberia. The dwarf mammoths died out on Wrangel Island before man ever reached there. In Africa, while *Elephas* succumbed to extinction on the increasingly arid plains, *Loxodonta* was hiding in the relic forest. When conditions improved, furtive *Loxodonta*, the only genus never to leave Africa, emerged from its forest refuge and overran the continent, free of competition from *Elephas*.

But the late Pleistocene extinctions were all-embracing. All species of large mammal weighing more than one tonne disappeared in the Americas, Europe and Asia between 25 000 and 10 000 years ago. At the same time 41% of known mammals weighing between 5 and 100 kg, and 2% of those weighing less than 5 kg, also vanished. A possible cause was that the large mammals, such as elephants and mammoths, modified the vegetation, making it favourable for the smaller ones. When the large ones disappeared, thickets and forests grew up and many of the smaller species died out. A modern example of such an effect is provided by the Hluhluwe Game Reserve where, after elephants were eliminated by man a century ago, three grazers became extinct and others such as wildebeest and waterbuck declined to low levels.

Climatic change, compression (20 000 years ago the sea level was 140 m lower than today due to the amount of water frozen into ice in the Arctic and Antarctic oceans), the disappearance of 'keystone' species – many factors could have contributed to the extinctions of large and small animals. The question 'What caused the extinction of so many animals at or near the end of the Pleistocene?' is not as difficult to answer as 'What caused the sudden extinction of the incredible number of mammoths in Siberia?', if it was not due to flooding following the melting of glaciers. Always supposing that mammoths are extinct . . . The taiga of Siberia is the largest forest in the world, 30 times the area of Great Britain, practically uninhabited and little explored. But as in North America, this vast forest may have recolonized the area after the last glacial period and after the mammoths had already become extinct. Nevertheless some of the few people who inhabit its wilder places in eastern Siberia have time and time again reported giant footprints, piles of droppings and branches broken off at heights more than 3 m above ground. The footprints and the droppings could be explained by the thawing of ice revealing where mammoths had once passed, the broken branches perhaps are due to storm damage. Yet at the beginning of the Cossack conquest of Siberia in 1580, a Cossack, Yermak Timofeyevitch, reported that beyond the Ural mountains he met 'a large hairy elephant'. According to local people it was valued as food and known as the 'mountain of meat'. Was he referring to a frozen mammoth or a living one?

Whatever the truth of the extinctions, we must remember they took place only some 10 000 years ago. The relic fauna has hardly had time to adapt and diversify to new conditions. Had not man come onto the scene perhaps the earth would have witnessed another explosion in radiation and diversification of animal forms, and strange new hardy elephants may once more have invaded the shores of Britain.

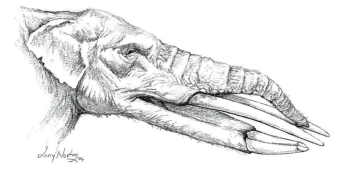

Chapter 2

THE ELEPHANTS: TAXONOMY AND DISTRIBUTION

The elephant, who surely of all creation must have the very worst trousers-maker.

Charles Dickens

AN AFRICAN MYSTERY

WE know less about the mysteries of the past of the living African elephant and where it came from than we do of the ancestry of many extinct species. In the late Miocene of Africa, perhaps 20 million years ago, the earliest African elephantine group with the lengthy name of stegotetrabelodontines, or 'covered-four-pointed teeth', were the dominant elephant forms. They were characterized by a pair of close-together, long narrow tusks in both jaws; the lower ones were some 2 m in length and about 9 cm in diameter. These strange-looking pointed-jaw creatures with their pincerlike tusks were completely replaced by the elephants in the early Pliocene.

The immediate ancestor of the modern African elephant was probably *Loxodonta adaurora*. Larger than the former, it was intermediate in type between stegotetrabelodon and gomphotherium. A species which never left Africa, it flourished from 4.5 to 2 million years ago and then disappeared in the early Pleistocene. It was more than a million years after *L. adaurora* had vanished before the living African elephant, *Loxodonta africana*, appeared. Playing an elephantine game of 'dead men's boots', almost another million years passed before it may have emerged from a forest refuge to fill a large niche vacated by the more specialized *Elephas* with its grassgrinding teeth. At the time of the last glaciation in the northern hemisphere, about 35 000 years ago, *Elephas* suddenly disappeared in Africa.

Remains of a specialized *Loxodonta* and of *Elephas* have been found in northern Africa together with remains of present-day species such as hyaena, giraffe, lion and gazelle, but in southern Africa the two elephants have never been found together.

About 12 000 years ago there were warmer moist conditions in Africa, following a cold dry period which reached its climax about 13 000–8000 years before. This improvement in climate led to a great increase of the forest about 8000 years ago, which would have been favourable for the expansion of forest-dwelling elephants. Alternatively, the radiation of *Loxodonta* may have been related to an earlier degradation of the forest or even to a dry period which followed 7000 years ago. The living forest elephant, *L. a. cyclotis*, is a truly forest animal which might approximate to the original stock and the forest may have harboured it in its depths long after *Elephas* had become the dominant Pleistocene elephant of the open savannahs.

Loxodonta remained exclusively African in distribution. The earliest representatives in the mid-Pliocene in eastern and southern Africa were already well differentiated and it has changed very little up to the present. Its tooth structure is no more evolved today than that of the early Pleistocene species of *Elephas* or *Mammuthus*. *L. atlantica*, which persisted until the mid-Pleistocene, was larger than its modern counterpart and had more complex teeth.

Only three species of African elephant are recognized today: the living *L. africana* and two extinct species, *L. adaurora* and *L. atlantica*.

The presently Asian genus, *Elephas*, appeared in both Africa and Asia in the mid-Pleistocene and may have inhabited Mesopotamia until as late as 800 BC. This latter supposition is based on the fact that the last record of the Assyrians hunting elephants is that of Assurbanipal who slew 30 about 859 BC. Although the kingdom reached its zenith 100 years later, there is no further record of elephant hunts.

The African species, *E. recki* from Olduvai Gorge in Tanzania, already showed more complex molars than those of *Loxodonta*. It is called 'Reck's elephant' after the German professor Hans Reck who, while chasing butterflies in Olduvai Gorge before the First World War, stumbled over some fossils and thus discovered the important Olduvai fossil site. *E. recki*, and its descendant *E. iolensis* with teeth similarly adapted for grazing, remained the most common species in East African fossil deposits. Contemporaneous with man, remains have been found at early Stone Age sites. Both elephants flourished for 3 million years until about 33 000 BC, when the lineage suddenly became extinct in Africa, dying out in Europe at about the same time.

One early Pleistocene offshoot of the African *E. recki*, known as *namadicus*, the 'wandering elephant', appeared abruptly in Europe and Asia. It also reached the island of Malta. Here it gave rise to two dwarf forms; *E. melitensis* standing 1.5 m at the shoulder and *E. falconeri*, no higher than just under 1 m. These existed side by side with *E. namadicus*, persisting until half a million years ago. *E. namadicus* gave rise to dwarf species on other Mediterranean islands also: Crete, Cyprus, Sardinia and Sicily.

These dwarves showed paedomorphic or childlike characteristics. Their skulls lacked a frontal crest for the attachment of muscles of a great trunk; they had large orbits, small tusks, a rounded cranium like baby elephants and fewer plates of enamel in their teeth than *namadicus* possessed.

In Asia *Elephas* persisted as the Asian elephant *E. maximus*, radiating as far east as Borneo and found today in India, Burma, Malaysia, Thailand, Sumatra, Borneo and China.

Cuvier, we saw, first regarded the African and the Asian elephants as being of separate genera and realized that *Mammuthus* was also distinct. Recent immunology tests confirm this but at the same time show that the Asian and African elephants are sufficiently close to one another to warrant a subfamily within the family *Elephantidae*. Only one known hybrid between them has been recorded, born at the Chester Zoo in England in 1979. It lived no longer than ten days, succumbing to an infection.

BACKGROUND TO THE AFRICAN ELEPHANT

Carl Linnaeus, the Swedish botanist and zoologist whose method of classification of the living realm using two names, generic and specific, is still used today, in his first catalogue of animals in 1754 had named only one elephant, *Elephas indicus* or the Indian elephant. But in 1758 he changed the name to *Elephas maximus*, 'the biggest elephant', so that both Asian and African species would be included. Then in 1797 a German naturalist Blumenbach quite rightly distinguished *E. asiaticus* and *E. africanus*, the Asian and the African elephant respectively, basing his distinction on the difference in tooth patterns. Cuvier then considered the latter to be sufficiently distinct on account of its teeth that in 1798 he erected the new genus *Loxodonta* for the African elephant.

The specimen of African elephant molar which led Blumenbach originally to separate the two elephants was never subsequently traced, so in 1926 another German taxonomist arbitrarily designated the Orange River region in South Africa as the type locality. This was so that the name *E. capensis*, assigned by Cuvier in 1798 to a specimen from there shot by the French traveller Le Vaillant in 1784, might be synonymous with the type locality. Taxonomists consider it very important to locate the spot from which the first described specimen of an animal came, but in the case of the elephant this remains unknown for both Asian and African species.

Now found in no more than one third of the continent of Africa, within recent history the African elephant ranged continent-wide south of the Sahara desert. Still distributed throughout much of this region, its occurrence has become greatly fragmented.

In North Africa it was found at the foot of the Atlas Mountains, where it became extinct about 1400 years ago. Pliny the Elder (AD 23–79) reported it to occur in Libya and present-day northern Morocco: 'The city of Sale lies in the vicinity of isolated spaces. Herds of elephants infest them' and: 'Some authors report that in the mountains of Mauretania (northern Algeria and Morocco) herds will come down when the full moon is shining to the banks of a river named Amilis' (probably the present-day Melloulou river).

The Carthaginian voyager Hanno in 500 BC reported elephants on the seashore at Cape Spartel near Tangier and Aristotle refers to their occurrence near to the Pillars of Hercules; but by the 4th century there were none left in Mauretania.

In north-east Africa, in the area where the Ptolemies had hunted them 800 years before, the envoy of Justinian to the ruler of Axumite Ethiopia in AD 533 reported 5000 at one point on the road between Adulis and Axum – but we can take a nought off that figure. Large numbers existed about AD 70 on the plateau above present-day Massawa in Eritrea, but all elephants were exterminated in Eritrea by the beginning of this century.

Low rainfall would have meant that there were not many in North Africa at this time and man simply hastened the end of a population inhabiting an environment that had already become marginal for it.

In the 19th century the elephant was brought to the brink of extinction in southern Africa but managed to maintain a tenuous hold. Today the most southerly population on the continent is found at Knysna on the southern coast, at the meeting point of the Afromontane and Indian Ocean belts of forest. From an estimated 500–600 in 1876, today only three are known to remain. The Duke of Edinburgh shot a large Knysna elephant bull in 1867 at 25 yards range. A sketch made at the time of the hunt shows a herd in an open valley, illustrating that they were not confined to the forest. Elephants persist in forests because of the refuge which they afford, rather than the food.

Almost ubiquitous in its tastes, the African elephant is found wherever rainfall is greater than 200 mm per year, the highest densities being found between a rainfall of 450–1200 and declining in numbers when it is greater than 1900. For comparison, the average rainfall for England and Wales is a little over 900 and for Scotland it is 1400, so Scotland is too wet for the African elephant's liking.

It occupies habitats ranging from the equatorial rainforest of the Congo Basin and West African coastal region, through savannah woodlands to semi-desert conditions in Namibia and Mali. And it ranges up to the *Hagenia* and giant *Ericaceae* zone, 2745 m high on the Rwenzori Mountains and up to the snowline of Mt Kenya.

In Namibia's Kaokoveld it manages to live where rainfall is only 150 mm per year at a low density of approximately one to every 100 sq. km, finding its water from the few springs and beneath the sand in seasonal watercourses, although the 300–400 present in 1970 had been reduced to less than 34 in 1991 by poaching. At the other extreme, in Tanzania's Lake Manyara Park at one time it lived at a density of 5.5 to the sq. km, the highest year-round density recorded. This was despite a rainfall of only 915 mm and was due to the lush vegetation produced by the groundwater which sinks down from the fringing escarpment.

Today the greatest numbers of African elephant are found in the savannah woodland region stretching through central to eastern Africa, together with the forests of Zaïre. In 1979 the total population in Africa was roughly estimated to be 1.3 million and it may have been more. In the following ten years poaching is believed to have reduced this total to 650 000. Kenya's population alone declined by 85% during this period.

Concern has been expressed for its future survival, as due to overhunting the annual yield of ivory in 1989 was estimated to be approximately three times the maximum sustainable yield. Such destruction has already occurred once before at the end of the last century, but it did not reach the same proportions as the present wave and was spread over a longer period of time.

In 1987 the range of the African elephant was estimated to cover 5.9 million sq. km, an area 24 times the size of the United Kingdom or much more than half of the area of the United States. Of this, 5% of the elephants occurred in West Africa, 46% in central Africa, 25% in East Africa and 24% in southern Africa. It is believed that only ten years before, in 1979, its range covered 7.3 million sq. km, an area approximately the size of Australia. The contraction in range during this brief period was due more to illegal hunting than to any other cause such as loss of habitat to expanding human settlement.

Lydekker's fancies

Some regard the African elephant as comprising two subspecies: *L. africana africana*, the savannah or bush elephant, and *L. a. cyclotis*, the forest elephant, the latter first named by Matschie in 1900.

The forest elephant is distinguished by its small size, up to 2.5 m tall at the shoulder in the bull and 2.1 m in the cow, with weights of 2.7–6 tonnes. It has characteristic rounded ears, unlike the 'map of Africa' shape of the bush elephant, and almost straight, downwardly pointing tusks.

The old theory for its downwardly pointing tusks was that they would not hinder it walking through its forest environment. Modern theorists favour the explanation that because the forest elephant lives at low densities, it does not have the frequency of violent encounters that savannah elephants might indulge in. It cannot use its tusks effectively as stabbing weapons because they point downwards, unlike the savannah elephant in which the bulls fight between themselves for the cows, if needs be, using their upwardly curving tusks to stab at each other. This must imply that in the forest elephant they are more for decorative use, like the gaudy plumage of cock birds. Indeed, it is in the bull forest elephant alone that we find the long thin tusks reaching almost to the ground.

FIG. 2.1   *Distribution of elephants in Africa, circa 1979 (after I. Douglas-Hamilton, 1979).*

The forest and the bush elephant appear to interbreed, or an intermediate type exists, for forest-like animals are seen in many bush elephant populations, such as existed in the Queen Elizabeth Park, far from the nearest true forest population. Intermediates are also known from the northern Central African Republic, 800 km distant from the nearest forest race. At waterholes scattered deep in the rainforest in the south west of this country, close to the Sangha River, bush elephants and true forest elephants alternate in their visits, indicative of the overlap in range that exists between the races.

While some Victorian parvenus purchased peerages and others paid genealogists to invent family trees of distinguished ancestors, hunters sought immortality in the apogee of the Victorian era by striving to have animals named after them. The naming of races became rather like the award of honours; you could have a race named after you if you were first to register it with a museum or perhaps if you had been particularly generous in some way, for example by financing a collecting expedition. This resulted in a profusion of races of the African elephant being identified, seemingly distinguished by the distorted shape of the dried ears which the hunters brought back to Europe. Altogether 17 races or subspecies have been described, of which the British Museum taxonomist Lydekker named eight in a paper titled 'The ears as a race-character in the African Elephant'. He was quickly set upon by other scientists eager to point out that the shape of an elephant's ears was more or less whatever the taxidermist wanted them to be. But even in the living animal ear shape can vary from individual to individual in the same group.

Osborn, from his study of fossil forms, enlarged the number of subspecies to 18.

Nevertheless, studies of the genetic relationships of elephants in South Africa have shown that they are remarkably inbred, tending to breed within the home range that they are born into. 'Fingerprinting' of elephants from their blood, technically known as identification or profiling of the biochemical polymorphism of serum transferrins, and the study of haemoglobin types, two techniques now used to identify murderers, have shown that the elephants of the Kruger Park, estimated to number only ten in 1905, are genetically very homogeneous and certainly belong to the same gene pool despite immigration from Mozambique up until 1974. From a sample of 109 animals only one type of haemoglobin was found.

The elephants of Addo were also found to be genetically very similar to those in Kruger. The Addo population has been isolated since 1919, when there were only 16, and the Kruger population since 1974. Animals from both populations were found to be the most inbred of all wild or domestic animals studied.

In Uganda, complete family groups taken in cropping operations have been found to have the same degree of tusk curvature. Such conservatism could well lead to regional characteristics developing and some scientists consider that six races are valid, four of the bush elephant and two of the forest elephant.

The bush elephant comprises *L. a. africana* (Blumenbach, 1797), the bush elephant proper, which includes the formerly designated races of *angolensis*, *capensis*, *mocambicus*, *selousi*, *toxotis* and *zukowskyi*. *Capensis* was the oldest of these, named in 1798 by Cuvier. *Angolensis* and *mocambicus* also speak for themselves as to provenance. *Selousi* was named after a specimen collected by Selous in Mashonaland (present day Zimbabwe); *toxotis*, or 'bow-ear', from the Addo bush in the south eastern Cape, and *Zukowskyi*'s from the Kaokoveld in south west Africa. *L. a. africana* is found in South Africa, Namibia, Botswana, Mozambique, Zimbabwe, Angola, Zambia and southern Zaïre.

L. a. knochenhaueri (Matschie, 1900), the Maasai elephant, is considered to occur in Tanzania, Kenya, south western Somalia and most of Uganda. This race includes two of Lydekker's fancies, *cavendishi* from L. Rudolf and *peeli* from the Aberdares in Kenya.

L. a. orleansi (Lydekker, 1907) has the smallest range, a remnant existing in western Ethiopia. Formerly it occurred also in northern Somalia.

L. a. oxyotis (Matschie, 1900), 'pointed ears', the savannah elephant, has the widest range after *africana* proper. It occurs across the continent north of the tropical forest, in southern and western Ethiopia and the Sudan, the Central African Republic, northern Cameroun, Chad, northern Nigeria, through Burkina Faso to northern Sierra Leone. This race also includes *rothschildi* from the south of L. Chad.

The forest elephant race is considered to comprise two races: *L. a. cyclotis* (Matschie, 1900) and the extinct *L. a. pharaohensis* Deraniyagala, 1948. The forest elephant, which occupies essentially the lowland tropical forest zone, also extends into parts of the northern savannah zone in Guinea and Senegambia and into the Sudanese arid zone in southern Mauretania. This race includes *albertensis*, *cottoni* and *fransseni* from Zaïre and *pumilio* from Congo Brazzaville.

The classification of *L. a. pharaohensis*, 'Pharaoh's elephant', as belonging to the forest race is even more speculative than the alleged distinctiveness of the other elephant races, since the references to the small size of this extinct northern elephant are historical ones relating to captive elephants which were probably half-grown.

Believing in dwarves

Like believing in fairies, some people believe in dwarves because they want to. Stories of a dwarf elephant in the lowland forest which even has the doubtful scientific name of *L. a. pumilio* (Noack, 1906) still persist, despite three quarters of a century of denial. I have heard a Frenchman swear that he had seen them in Gabon, where indeed the hunting law distinguishes between them and the forest elephant. Hunting licences are cheaper for the alleged dwarf elephant than they are for the forest elephant. So the pygmy elephant exists in law, even if not in fact, for the existence of such an animal has never been demonstrated.

Sir Arnold Hodson, Governor of Sierra Leone, sent six alleged pygmy elephant skulls to the British Museum and the explorer Major P.H.G. Powell-Cotton sent two from the Cameroons. All were found to be skulls of immature forest elephants.

In 1938 Hodson, then Governor of the Gold Coast, sent a specimen from British Togoland of which Guy Dollman of the British Museum of Natural History commented in a letter to *The Times* newspaper:

> This is the first record of the forest elephant occurring in the Gold Coast. There is no question about the specimen representing a pygmy race, being simply a young individual of the forest elephant, as is shown by its ivory and molar teeth. The former is typical of what was formerly known as 'pygmy elephant ivory', the tusks measuring only about $19\frac{3}{4}$ inches in total length and having a

circumference of only 6⅛ inches. The molar teeth in wear would appear to represent the last milk molar and the first molar, or the first molar and the second molar. From the evidence of the sutures of the skull it is obviously the cranium of an animal which is only half grown ....

The 'type' specimen on which the name was erected was a live animal in the possession of Carl Hagenbeck, the famous German animal trainer and dealer, who had obtained it from the French Congo in 1905. He estimated its age at about six years, but it was probably less. The tusks were 1.2 cm long. Noack, however, described it the following year as a pygmy race, which probably put the price up significantly and it was sold to the New York Zoological Society. Here, at 11 years of age it was still only 1.5 m tall, weighing 750 kg. When it died in 1915 it was still not fully grown. Its tusks were now 60 cm beyond the gum, it weighed 1227 kg and stood 2 m high at the shoulder – within the size range of a forest elephant. So like Topsy, it just grew and perhaps would have become the same size as any other elephant.

The mysterious wakawaka

Even less credibility is accorded to the possible occurrence of a small aquatic elephant which a French hunter tried to lay claim to. In 1911 Monsieur Le Petit wrote to one of the French zoological authorities concerning a mysterious animal of the lakes of west central Africa, known to the natives as the 'water elephant'. Le Petit claimed to have seen a group of five of these small elephants at a distance of about 450 m, describing them as having remarkably short ears and trunks, necks relatively longer than usual and no tusks. They plunged into a lake and with only the tops of their heads and the tips of their trunks exposed – as is customary with elephants swimming out of their depth – they swam out towards open water and were lost to view. So was born the 'water elephant'.

Shortly after this was reported a Belgian army officer, Lieutenant Franssen, was requested by the Belgian natural history museum to try to secure a specimen of this strange beast. The officer found that near Bongo in the Belgian Congo the natives had a name for it – *wakawaka*. Eventually he was able to shoot a wakawaka at a place called M'Paa, but at great personal cost as he died shortly afterwards of fever. He had, however, measured its height as 1.66 m at the shoulder, photographed the body and recovered its skin and skeleton. In his memory the animal was then named *E. africanus fransseni*, but there was nothing in the brief description – it had tusks projecting 43 cm from the gum – to indicate that it was other than an ordinary immature forest elephant. No doubt Edward Lear could have found a better name for it than Franssen's dwarf elephant.

THE DECLINE OF THE AFRICAN ELEPHANT

The decline of the modern African elephant began about the middle of the last century with the surge in demand for ivory. By the end of the last century people were already very concerned, although if the truth be known there was probably well over a million elephants still in existence.

In 1903 the naturalist-hunter H.A. Bryden published an article 'The decline of the South African elephant' in which he traced the decline of the elephant in South Africa due to hunting for ivory. Elephants on South Africa's Orange River were gone between 1770 and 1795, on the Harts River between 1795 and 1810, the Molopo River between 1810 and 1820 and from eastern Botswana between 1820 and 1850. This is attributed to the arrival of white traders, the distribution of firearms and the fact that they could haul out up to $1\frac{1}{2}$ tonnes of ivory at a time on ox wagons. The traveller William Burchell in 1812 had noted that the Bangwaketse in the east of Botswana brought ivory to sell to the Griquas or half-castes and the following year the missionary John Campbell counted 24 wagons at Griqua Town on the Orange River, wagons which were used for hunting and trading and particularly for the carriage of ivory.

A protagonist of this traditional view has argued that this was a period of considerable turmoil in southern Africa which resulted in large-scale displacements of African tribes and it was their settlement in new areas which drove out or destroyed the elephants, rather than the commerce in ivory. But in Botswana, where elephants were entirely eliminated in the southern part of the country in the space of 80 years, people displaced by the internecine strife in southern Africa did not occupy the areas where elephants were being slaughtered.

The number of elephants on the Orange River in South Africa was already reported to have fallen drastically by 1805, due to the use of guns by the Griquas. This was 17 years before a force of 50 000 men tried unsuccessfully to conquer Kuruman, just outside Botswana.

It has also been pointed out that the Cape population of elephants would always have been relatively small, well under 27 000 animals, because much of the habitat would be unsuitable for them and therefore their early reduction to near-extinction at the Cape was inevitable. Likewise, the low rainfall in North Africa must have meant that the elephants there were at the limits of their range, so it was not surprising that they were the first to go.

Until 1899 elephants roamed where the city of Nairobi now stands. Fifty years later they were unknown within a radius of 70 km, but while it is obvious that man and elephants are not compatible, the ivory trade and the demand for ivory caused and causes the decline. That is not to say that if there had not been a demand for ivory, with Africa's burgeoning human populations elephants would not have been controlled to make way for people.

BACKGROUND TO THE ASIAN ELEPHANT

John Ray, the 17th century son of a blacksmith who became a distinguished Cambridge scholar, laid the foundations of modern zoology in his work *Synopsis animalium quadrupedum*, published in 1693. In this he gave the generic name *Elephas* to a young Sri Lankan elephant that he had seen in the zoo in Florence. Linnaeus, as we saw, then christened it with the misnomer

E. maximus. A misnomer since it is smaller than the African elephant and many extinct ones, but it was an old belief that the Asian elephant, and in particular that from Sri Lanka, was bigger than other elephants, especially the African.

Following Ray's original naming the broad type locality is Sri Lanka, where it also occurs as a fossil. It is therefore more appropriate to call it the Asian elephant, rather than Indian as is often the case. Although Deraniyagala, a former Director of the Ceylon National Museums, considered that there were eight or even nine living races of this elephant, only three are now recognized, if any. These three are: *Elephas maximus maximus* inhabiting Sri Lanka, *E. m. indicus* in India and Indochina and *E. m. sumatranus* in Sumatra.

The Sri Lankan elephant is considered to be larger and more pugnacious than the Indian, a fact first noted by Onescritus, an officer of Alexander the Great, in the 3rd century BC. Megasthenes, Greek ambassador to Chandra Gupta I of India, also noted its larger size at the same period. The Greek military writer Aelian mentions the fact in AD 44 and also that they were exported in special boats beginning about 200 BC.

There has probably been interbreeding with the elephant of mainland India as tuskers were sometimes imported for ceremonial. In 483 BC the bride of King Vijaya brought with her a number of elephants from southern India as a part of her dowry and much later, in the 6th century AD, the Alexandrian traveller Cosmas Indicopleustes recorded that Ceylon had an important import as well as export trade in elephants.

The 5th–6th century BC Sanskrit *Gaja Sastra* ('Elephant Lore') subdivided the Indian animal into numerous races restricted to different areas: races for Persia, Kashmir, Afghanistan and Punjab. Mahouts have traditionally identified different races based on criteria of shape, size, colour, voice, behaviour, strength, body odour, diet and liability to certain diseases. Late 18th century Bengal government contracts stipulated that the government should not be supplied with any elephants captured north of Chittagong province. This was because those to the south in Burma were considered to be of superior breed. Other alleged racial differences in strength were also recorded. The smaller size of the elephant of mainland India tends to increase as one moves eastwards, while tusklessness is uncommon in Sumatran bulls but most advanced in Sri Lankan and Thailand animals.

Asian elephants born in European zoos are larger on average than those imported from India so diet and the amount of work that the elephant does can all influence its size.

Sinhala mahouts distinguish the Sri Lankan tuskers (Atha) from those which bear only tushes (Aliya) as stepping outward with the hind legs when walking, flapping their ears more frequently, possessing a shriller and more trumpetlike voice, a more pronounced nasal bump and a weaker trunk and skull. The tuskers are most common in certain areas, so there may be something to it after all. But it is largely a question of where to draw the line between what should be regarded as a race and what should not. A race is an inbreeding group distinctive in some characteristic or characteristics. Thus although traditionally regarded as differing from each other the differences are so esoteric as to offer little justification

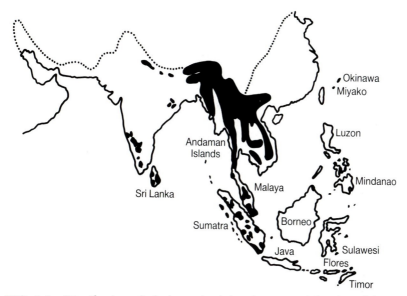

FIG. 2.2 *Distribution of elephants in Asia, circa 1978. The dotted line marks the limits of the range in historic times (in part after Olivier, 1978).*

for separating most of the races of Asian elephant, but it would be a fruitful field for behavioural and genetic inquiry by the curious naturalist.

Depigmentation, causing unsightly leprous-looking pink blotches on the skin, is also considered to be a racial character, most strongly marked in southern Indian and Sri Lankan elephants. The famous 'white' elephants of Siam, for which no less than five kings lost their lives and estates in battles to possess them, were usually nothing more than these blotched animals. Rarely were they true albinos. Legend has it that so covetous was the Burmese Pegu king Aleager of the king of Siam's white elephant that he laid siege to the city of Siam for 22 months before overcoming and sacking it in 1564, the king of Siam committing suicide.

Lydekker, who was so fond of creating African elephant races, considered that there was probably only one race of Asian elephant; but then the ears were too small to be obviously variable in contour.

From war elephant to wild remnant

Once found throughout much of Asia from the Tigris-Euphrates in Syria, through Iran, India, south and south east Asia, into China northwards to the Yangtze-Kiang rivers, even at the beginning of this century there were thought to be only 100 000 wild Asian elephants left in existence. By 1989 this had fallen to some 34 000 to 56 000, living in an area of 436 000 sq. km or an area less than half of the size of Tanzania, but scattered among 13 countries. They have disappeared entirely from Syria and Iraq, Java and most of China.

The Indian subcontinent itself is 13% the size of Africa, but has only 2% of the number of elephants. In 1989 the total population was estimated at 17 000–22 000 or as many as at one time could be found in many a single national park in Africa. Even today, the 11 000 sq. km Chobe National Park in northern Botswana has as many elephants in it as the total number of Asian elephants remaining in the world.

In the 9th century King Rami of India was said to appear at the head of 50 000 elephants in war, more than twice the whole number remaining today in India, but this was undoubtedly a gross exaggeration. The great Mongol ruler Kublai Khan in the 13th century was said to possess 5000 at Beijing, although this was more likely to be 500.

Today there are probably less than a dozen populations which number more than 1000 individuals, most existing in herds of less than 200. In addition to the populations in south, central, north west and north east India, remnant wild populations exist in Sri Lanka (3000), Burma (6560, perhaps more), China (450 in southern Yunnan province), Thailand (3000–4500), Malaysian Peninsula (1000), Laos, Kampuchea and Vietnam (5000 altogether), Borneo, which may be a feral population of *E. m. indicus* arising from introduced animals (500–2000) and Sumatra (300). As late as 1985 there were thought to be 2800–4800 in Sumatra, but these have declined rapidly in number due to forest exploitation taking away their habitat.

In 1935 10 000 were estimated to occur in Burma and an attempt was made to reduce them to 4000–5000. A total of 3288 had been killed by March 1941 and 1286 captured, leaving an estimated 5500. The population has therefore held up well, forming the most significant population of the Asian elephant remaining. Its range has not altered appreciably since the beginning of the century, the herds being mainly confined to five mountain ranges. But when the extent of the forested area is taken into account, an area of over 387 000 sq. km or more than 1½ times the size of Uganda, the low density at which the Asian elephant exists in its undisturbed habitat can be appreciated.

In addition to these wild populations there are an estimated 16 000 in captivity of which most are in Burma (5400 compared with at least 6000 prior to the Second World War) followed by Thailand with 4800, 3000 in India and a few hundreds in other Asian countries.

In northern India since about the 1st century AD there has been progressive desiccation, particularly in Pakistan and the west Gangetic plains, which has made the habitat more unsuitable for elephants. A few thousand years ago elephants roamed over all but the most arid parts of the Indian subcontinent; even in the 5th–6th centuries BC the *Gaja Sastra* mentioned them as occurring countrywide. In the 4th century AD they were still found in the dry tracts of Punjab and Saurashtra.

The Moghul Emperors of the 16th–17th centuries provide us with some information on later abundance; thus the Emperor Barbur (1526–1530) noted that elephants inhabited the district of Kalpi, an area of deep ravines in Uttar Pradesh on the right bank of the Jumna river, and became more and more numerous as one proceeded east. They were captured in the forests of Narwar about 1600 and in the Panchmahals a few years later. These locations represent the westernmost distribution in the 16th–17th centuries. The populations in central India from western Madhya Pradesh at about longitude 74°E to about 81°E were wiped out in Moghul times, but the distribution as in late Moghul times remained the same until the 19th century. In Mysore the country became depopulated from the wars between the British and Tipu Sahib between 1790 to 1799 and became overrun with so many elephants that the British sent in troops to shoot them. Regular culling began in 1805 until the numbers were brought under control.

In 1874 they were distributed from the Himalayan foothills of Bhutan west to Dehra Dun; in central India from Bengal to Mahdya Pradesh and south nearly to the Godavary river, and had only 'recently' disappeared from the Rajmahal hills. Now their range has shrunk to three distinct regions: the hilly tracts of the Western and Eastern Ghats in the south, the eastern fringes of the forests in the centre and the foothills of the Himalayas and the hills of the north eastern states where the populations are broken up and isolated. Nearly half of the total number is now found in the forests of southern India.

Fragmented into five separate populations, there is one in north west India, two in southern India and one each in central and eastern India. The southern population is the most numerous with about 6000 divided into eight groups, of which the largest group is one of 2000 occurring in 5000 sq. km in the southern Eastern Ghats.

Little more than a century ago Sanderson considered that there was no diminution in the numbers of Indian elephants:

> ... whilst in Southern India elephants have become so numerous of late years that the rifle will have to be again called into requisition to protect the ryots from their depredations ... It cannot but be a matter of hearty congratulation to all interested in so fine and harmless an animal that there is no chance of the sad fate that is pursuing his African congener, and leading to his rapid extinction, affecting the Asiatic elephant.

Prior to 1873, when the Elephant Preservation Act came into force in the Madras Presidency, the government offered rewards for the killing of elephants to control crop damage; and in Sri Lanka, to make way for the tea plantations, the numbers shot approached those shot in later years in some African countries. A total of 3500 was destroyed in the Northern Province of Sri Lanka in 1846–1848 and 2000 in the Southern Province from 1851 to 1855.

But unlike the African elephant, it is not poaching which has caused the major decline of the Asian elephant, perhaps because the cow is tuskless and not all bulls have tusks; nor the fact that they have been continually captured for the past 4000 years with an estimated 100 000 captured in Asia in the past century. Surprisingly also, in spite of India's huge human population, double the size of that of Africa but squeezed into one tenth of the area, competition for land with consequent loss of elephant habitat has not come from peasant settlement. In southern India the elephant's range has shrunk only by about a fifth to one quarter in the past century, a much slower rate of attrition than that which has taken place in much of less populated Africa. The main threat has come from large-scale development schemes. In India hydro-electric schemes inundating vast areas of former forest habitat adjacent to rivers; the forestry practice of clear-felling and the replacement of forests with coffee, tea, rubber and cardamom plantations, are most to blame.

In north-west India the large-scale clearing of forests in Nepal along the Indian border has resulted in only some 60 elephants being left. An isolated herd of 21 exists in the central region of southern Nepal, while in the extreme east and west, parts of larger Indian populations totalling perhaps 15–20 and 25 head in Nepal move in and out. In 1977 the population in the east numbered 50 animals, but after a crop raiding rampage in which they killed four people, five were shot and subsequent control appears to have reduced their numbers still further.

In Bangladesh about 150 elephants remained in 1980, mostly in the Chittagong Hills, with a further 60 non-resident animals moving into Burma and India, whereas the majority of forests had harboured elephants here up until 1950. In Sri Lanka it is estimated that there could have been some 12 000 present until the onslaught of the 19th century, reducing their numbers to an estimated 1500 in 1951. In Burma, loss of habitat is not a problem and hunting for ivory, skin and meat is widespread. But of all countries, the populations here appear to have remained relatively stable in numbers.

From plain to forest

The Asian elephant inhabits a wider range of rainfall conditions than does the African, from a rainfall of less than 400 mm per year in the centre of the Indian peninsula to over 8000 in the Western Ghats. Rainfall over 2500 gives rise to tropical wet evergreen forest, but this is only inhabited by a few isolated groups of elephants, the highest density being found in southern India under 600–2000 mm of rainfall in moist deciduous to dry deciduous to scrub forest vegetation. Like the African elephant the preferred habitat is moist and dry deciduous woodland but they also inhabit dry thorn forest, swamps and open grasslands.

One of the least known areas of the Indian subcontinent is the sub-Himalayan region, where relatively large numbers of elephants move regularly between southern Bhutan and Assam. This is a high rainfall area characterized by moist deciduous forest, dry deciduous riverine forest, semi-evergreen and evergreen forest and particularly vast bamboo brakes. There are authentic records of elephants travelling up to the snowline on the mountains.

Some of the herds in north-west India cross the border into Nepal, while others in the north-east also cross into Bhutan. After the 1880s Bhutan War, the ensuing treaty between India and Bhutan declared the entire sub-Himalayan area straddling the boundary as elephant territory and stipulated that Bhutan would receive half of all royalties from elephants captured on the Indian side. Assam and Bengal claim to still honour this treaty.

In China they have usually been destroyed as vermin, no cultural or religious context ever having been accorded to them except among the Dai people, where 450 still exist in Xishuangbanna reserves. Elephants were probably exterminated in the Yellow River valley in the Shang Dynasty (1776–1122 BC), but only one reference to hunting has been found, Chou Kung, who died in 1125 BC, having driven away tigers, leopards, rhinoceroses and elephants 'to the great joy of the people'. Farmers and elephants have never made good bedfellows, and as the peasant farmers pursued their inexorable advance south from origins in northern China in the Yellow River valley, so they either eliminated the elephants or drove them before them, possibly until about 3000 years ago.

By the middle of the first millennium BC the elephant was already restricted to the Yangtze valley, extending from far west Szechwan to the sea. Some are believed to have survived in the Yangtze valley until at least the end of the 10th century, but most were exterminated to provide tribute in ivory exacted by the emperors of the Chou, Ch'in, Han and subsequent periods (1122 BC–AD 221 onwards). In AD 962 they were reported near Hanyang in Hupeh province, subsisting on the crops of the people. The following year some were killed in Hunan province and again in the same place the next year. In AD 966 elephants appeared in Liyang, near Hangchow. In the western region they survived in the province of Szechwan until at least 206 BC to AD 220, some being captured and sent to the court of the Han emperor at Ch'ang-an where they were kept in a zoo. They are said to have still existed in the region between Canton and Shanghai until AD 1263. Today perhaps only 220 now survive in the extreme south west of Yunnan province, 20 of them in the Nangun River Nature Reserve and the rest in Xishuangbanna, part of the large northern population in Burma; a total of less than 500.

Little is known about their numbers in Burma where, occupying forested hill tracts, they are still widely distributed, more common in the north than in the south. In Thailand they exist mainly in a thin band along the western border with Burma, but there are some patches elsewhere. They are widely distributed in Laos in the south and also occur along the north east border with Vietnam. In Kampuchea there are some in the west and others along the eastern border with Vietnam. They were still plentiful in Tonkin and neighbouring Yunnan in the 7th century, when they were hunted for their flesh which was considered to be a great delicacy. It is perhaps significant that in these countries today it is along the joint borders, the 'no man's land', that elephants mainly still exist.

In peninsular Malaysia they are widely distributed in two blocks of small, fragmented populations, one in the north and one in the south. Estimates of population numbers have varied widely here from some 600 to as many as 6000, but 800 is thought to be nearest the mark.

The oldest elephant distribution map known is that for Sri Lanka drawn up by Ptolemy in AD 175. He marked the feeding grounds of the elephant as in the Ruhuna district in the south-east, one of their present strongholds. Yet another map, made much later by Petrus Plancius in 1650, depicts feeding grounds in the north-west. Today the elephant is still distributed over a wide area of the country from the north-west through the dry eastern zone in a broad belt down to the south east coast.

In Sumatra, where it occupies wet evergreen forest, it is distributed throughout the island in isolated populations, while in Borneo it is restricted to the north-east tip of the island, namely eastern Sabah and a small area of overlap into Indonesia's northern East Kalimantan province. Borneo's population may be feral, descendants of those given to the Sultan of Sulu in 1750 by the East India Company and later released. But there were domestic elephants at Brunei in 1521 and trade in ivory with China in the Middle Ages. Added to which Pleistocene fossils of the Asian elephant have been found here.

Elephants coexisted with man on Java until at least 1000 BC and probably into historic times, the Chinese importing ivory from there also. In prehistoric times elephants existed in the north and south Philippines (Luzon and Mindanao), on Sulawesi and on Miyako and Okinawa Is. off east Asia. Stegodonts existed on Indonesia's Flores and Timor islands. In other words, elephants reached the extreme eastern limit of the zoogeographical Oriental Region but, like other mammals, failed to reach the Australasian Region.

There are also 20–30 feral elephants in the Andaman Is., descendants of 80 animals taken over for logging operations and turned loose in the early 1960s. In their newfound freedom they are rather antagonistic towards the human inhabitants with whom they come into increasing conflict. Completely adapted to their island life, they swim across the sea from one island to another. One 7 year old disappeared and was traced 12 years later on one of the islands 320 km from where he was last seen, a journey which at times must have involved swimming for up to 2 km in the sea.

Pliny wrote in his *Natural History*: 'The Indians employ the smaller breed, which they call the bastard elephant, for ploughing'. Strangely enough, no one has ever speculated upon this 'smaller breed' of Indian elephant, even though the Belgians used the smaller African forest elephant for ploughing. Why should the Indians have had a particular name for it if it did not exist? Was it in fact an island race from one of the Indian Ocean islands, now extinct?

With only a 30 000 year history behind it, the living African elephant is younger than mankind. Primitive man was already well established when it made its debut. It was doomed before it started in the competition between man and beast which was to ensue, even if it has taken man 30 000 years to win.

Chapter 3

NATURE'S GREAT MASTERPIECE: ANATOMY OF THE ELEPHANT

Baked elephant's foot, cooked in the skin, and scooped out like a Stilton cheese, was formerly considered a dainty, but most of those who have tasted it of late years express their disapproval.

R. Lydekker, 1894

However tired you may be, you must, at least, take the two front feet.

E. L. Walker, 1923

CURIOUS NATURALISTS

DISSECTING an elephant is a formidable task, but the ancient Greeks did it. The first authoritative recorded dissection was provided by the Greek physician Claudius Galen. Five hundred years before this, Aristotle, who lived from 384 to 322 BC, gave us one of the first examples of comparative anatomy, so beloved of school and university examiners today. Unlike Galen it is not clear whether Aristotle actually dissected an elephant himself or whether he based his work on the accounts of others. Some think he may have dissected one or more of the 15 which were captured at the battle of Gaugamela in 331 BC.

One of the earliest descriptions of a specimen since Greek and Roman times is a quaint account of its head written in 1554 by Sir George Barnes, one-time Lord Mayor of London and a merchant trading to Guinea:

> At this last voyage was brought from Guinea the head of an Elephant, of such huge bignesse, that onely the bones or cranew therof, beside the nether jaw and great tusks, weighed about two hundred weight, and was as much as I could well lift from the ground: insomuch that considering also herewith the weight of two such great teeth, the nether jaw with the lesse teeth, the tongue, the great hanging eares, the bigge and long snout or troonke, with all the flesh, braines, and skinne, with all other parts belonging to the whole head, in my judgement it could weigh litle lesse than five hundred weight. This head divers have seene in the house of the worthy marchant sir Andrew Judde, where also I saw it, and beheld it, not onely with my bodily eyes, but much more with the eyes of my mind and spirit, considering by the worke, the cunning and wisedome of the workemaister: without which consideration, the sight of such strange and wonderful things may rather seeme curiosities, then profitable contemplations.

Two of the oldest surviving museum zoological specimens known are said to be half of a skull of a young African elephant aged about three years and an adult femur. Undoubtedly also from Guinea, these were among curiosities collected by the Tradescants between 1620 and 1662 and displayed at their house in south Lambeth, London. They now rest in Oxford's University College Museum.

Some years later we hear of the first dissection since Galen's time, that of an elephant which died in a fire at the Dublin Zoo in 1681 and was dissected by Dr A. Mullen, 'very brief both in the Anatomy and Osteology, and the Figures not very exact', according to Mr Patrick Blair, Surgeon &c. Blair examined an Asian cow elephant which died at Dundee in 1706. In a communication to the Royal Society in 1710 he explained:

> The Elephant, tho' an Animal so considerable for its Bignes and Strength, so remarkable for its extraordinary Endowments and stupendous Actions (if I may so call them,) that it has become the Subject of the most Curious Naturalists of all Ages, and been admired by all those who beheld it; yet has its Body been hitherto very little subjected to Anatomical Enquiries. This induc'd Me (when April 27, 1706. the last Elephant that was in Britain died near this Place) to bestow some pains in viewing its Parts at the Opening . . .

Other dissections followed, among which was that of the elephant Chuni destroyed at Mr Cross's menagerie at Exeter 'Change in 1826, of which the smell was already so offensive after four days that the Sheriff of London ominously informed Mr Cross on Saturday evening that if the body was not removed 'he will hear from me on Monday in a way that he will not like'. *The Times* newspaper reported:

> On Saturday night a number of butchers were employed in flaying the skin. By ten o'clock on Sunday morning they had completed their operation, and it was removed to the residence of a Mr Davis who had purchased it of Mr Cross for £50.
> At 11 o'clock on Sunday morning, Mr Brookes, ... and other surgeons were present.
> Mr Ryals, a naturalist of some repute, was the operator, under the directions of Messers Brookes and Morgan ...The professional gentlemen who were present, after the removal of the flesh declared they never viewed a more beautiful anatomical display ... At ten o'clock on Sunday night the dissection was completed. Not fewer than four tons of flesh were carted away during the day, and the stench in the neighbourhood was very offensive ...

About 1867 a young elephant 'carefully preserved' in a barrel of spirits was sent from Sri Lanka to Professor Owen at the British Museum for dissection. The first complete skeleton to be sent to Britain, of an adult bull from Sri Lanka in 1872, was packed in two rum puncheons: 'There is nothing better than a cask for packing bones'.

For some 8000 years the African elephant has stalked the earth as the largest terrestrial mammal. Closely followed in size by its Asian counterpart, the largest of these great beasts is almost one third in weight of the maximum limit of size which physical forces permit, approximately 20 tonnes. Massive and unperturbed, the African bull paces ponderously along in a curious heaving motion, like a ship riding a swell. His speed is about 10 kph and if he breaks into a shuffling trot he can move at 20–24 kph.

If danger threatens this bucolic giant is transformed into a mighty terror. Ears erect like giant sails, when he charges, at a speed of up to 30 kph (some claim at up to almost 40), it is like a man-o'-war under full sail, with a span of almost 4 m across. The poet Donne was not in error when he described the elephant as 'Nature's great masterpeece'.

Sir Samuel Baker described his perfect Asian elephant in 1890. No one has yet described the perfect African elephant and although the two are often confused, when compared side by side the differences are obvious. The Asian has a much more roly-poly appearance whereas the African has a low, rounded forehead, very large ears in line with or higher than the top of the skull, tusks in both sexes and both an upper and a lower 'finger' on the end of the trunk. Its back is concave between the shoulders and the hips, the backbone having a double curvature, highest at the shoulder and over the lumbar region instead of in the centre of the back as in the Asian elephant. This is because the dorsal spines, decreasing in length from the centre backwards in the Asian elephant, in the African decrease in length behind the shoulder, forming a saddle in the middle of the animal's back and thus making it much more suitable for carrying a load. In the mammoth the back tended to slope towards the rump, the head being the highest point. The head is the highest point in the Asian elephant, with the back either almost straight or convex, although the Burmese recognize four different types of back curve, and it sags in old animals.

The anatomy of an elephant shows a number of primitive or unspecialized features. Its most specialized are in the head in the form of the trunk, teeth and structure and mode of articulation of bones in the skull. To enter into details of the anatomy would be out of place in other than a textbook and I shall limit my description to some of the more notable aspects connected with its graviportal or weight-bearing adaptations and its large size.

BRIDGES AND BACKBONES

Just as an aircraft designer looks to birds and flying insects to explain principles of flight, so an elephant's construction can tell an engineer how weight can be most economically supported in a moving body. In proportion to the animal's size the skeleton is heavy, increasing more than proportionally to an increase in body weight and weighing about 16.5% of the elephant's total live weight. This percentage compares with about 10% in cattle and similar ruminants. Its primitive features are the retention of a large number of vertebrae; a large number of ribs; the absence or reduction on the femur of the third trochanter which provides the anchorage for the superficial gluteus muscle, giving the elephant its baggy bottom which Charles Dickens noted, unlike the prominent muscles of the buttocks in man; and five digits to each foot. In one or two extinct forms, including the Siberian mammoth, there was a tendency to lose one of the digits.

Elephants have seven neck vertebrae, this number being constant in all mammals. The total number of the remaining vertebrae can vary from 49 to 64 in the Asian and 52 to 62 in the African, but perhaps if sufficient specimens were counted we would find the range to encompass both elephants. Variation is found in the tail, where the number of bones ranges from 24 to 34 in the Asian and 26 to 31 in the African.

Unlike other herbivores, as the elephant grew in height the neck vertebrae did not lengthen. On the contrary they became fused as relatively flattened discs, thus able to withstand the weight of the elephant's head with its tusks but making the trunk even more important because of the limited movement that the elephant can make with its head. The 24 thoracic vertebrae which follow have high dorsal spines to which the muscles of the back of the head are attached and 20–21 of them have broad ribs, so that much of the body is covered by a rib cage. The lumbar region has only three or four sacral vertebrae, but the foetus may have up to six, two or more disappearing before birth. With its variable number in the tail the elephant has a maximum of 69 vertebrae, compared with our own 33.

The clavicle or 'collar bone' disappeared, as in the ungulates, and the relatively massive shoulder blades, providing support as they do for the large muscle attachments of the forelimbs, assumed a vertical position. Due to the curvature of the back it shares with man an almost vertical pelvis, greatly expanded, unlike that of other ungulates in which it is parallel to the ground. This leads to the arrangement of the genital organs which caused so much puzzlement to the ancients.

The elephant evolved to carry its great weight by the limbs becoming columnar, thick and upright, long in the upper part and short in the distal. The greater part of the marrow cavities in the limb bones have disappeared and are replaced by spongy bone, a lacelike network giving great strength with lightness. Mammoths had more massive bones, but their legs were shorter. Between the legs the backbone forms a curved arch or cantilever like the Firth of Forth bridge, stressed between the massive fore and hind limbs supporting it like four great pillars, planted on huge pedestal-like feet, with the bones adopting a semi-digitigrade stance. That is, surprising as it may seem, the elephant half walks on the tips of its toes. But the bones are supported by a huge fleshy elastic cushion of yellow-looking fat contained in a fibrous matrix, giving the elephant an appearance of being flatfooted. Technically it is known as semiplantigrade. The bones of the wrist and ankle do not interlock as in most mammals but are arranged in two rows, one on top of the other, and thus tend to separate under pressure. To avert this they are bound together by very strong ligaments.

One attribute which assisted elephants to attain their large size is the curious fact that the forelimbs are preadapted to withstand stress by the radius and ulna being permanently twisted on one another, the prone position as adopted in our own forearm when we place the palm of the hand flat on a table. This gives the forelimb great rigidity. When weight is placed on them, the forelimbs take nearly 60% of the weight of the body, there is no 'play' in the radius and ulna on the carpal bones. In the bovids these two bones fuse in parallel to form the cannon bone but the carpal bones are offset.

This arrangement does not mean that the elephant cannot 'bend its knees', as the ancients thought, leading to the fallacy repeated in almost every medieval bestiary that once an elephant fell down, it could not get up again. Sir Thomas Browne in 1646 in his *Vulgar Errors*, dismissed this as an absurdity and observed that Aristotle had done so a thousand years before:

> ... the hint and ground of this opinion might be the grosse and somewhat cylindrical composure of the legs of the elephant, and the equality and less perceptible disposure of the joynts, especially in the forelegs of the animal, they appearing, when he standeth, like pillars of flesh.

Aristotle wrote: '... the elephant is not constructed as some have said, but is able to sit down and bend its legs'. He referred to the fallacy as an 'old erroneous account'; perhaps a dig at Ctesias.

Agatarchides (*circa* 200–140 BC) for his part dismissed the story of the hunters who were alleged to find trees which elephants had a habit of leaning against, then sawing halfway through the trunk so that when an unsuspecting elephant came along and paused for a rest against the tree, it would break and the elephant fall over, unable to get up again. Agatarchides noted that the only true thing about this story was that because of repeated leaning against a tree it became bruised and covered with dirt. But bull African elephants will lean against trees to rest during the day and strangely enough, 18th century American Indians who believed the mammoth still existed also believed that it did not lie down but leant against trees to sleep.

What is true is that the knees are near to the ground so that an elephant cannot fall onto its knees as a horse sometimes does. An elephant also cannot move its limbs out sideways from the body. The arrangement does not permit this in the forelimbs, which are stronger than the hind, and in the latter powerful groups of muscles restrict any such movement. Lying on its side an elephant cannot simply bend its legs under its body to rise, but rocks from side to side, heaving itself first into an upright position. It then rises rather like a horse, using its forelegs first.

It is true that elephants kept lying too long on their sides are unable to get up again, the great weight paralysing the nerves. Once an elephant goes down due to exhaustion or sickness it has only a 1 in 4 chance of getting onto its feet again unaided and any method of keeping it upright improves its chances of survival. Burmese handlers resort to the cruel expedient of putting chili-juice into its eye, the pain literally keeping the elephant hopping about.

Hardly surprisingly the elephant can neither jump, trot, canter or gallop but it is quite able to kick both forwards and backwards with great force; as one writer put it, 'high enough to kick off a bowler hat'. Although it cannot jump, a large elephant can clear an obstruction as high as 1.2 m in its stride. Movement is restricted to a walk, the straightness of the limbs giving it the peculiar heaving motion. The Asian elephant, by reason of its shorter gait, is slower than the African but it can move at up to 24–32 kph. To move fast, because of its great bulk the elephant holds its back rigid and flexes its legs relatively little, swinging them stiffly through small arcs. The African elephant is winded in about 450–550 m but soon recovers. When frightened it can travel up to 145 km between daylight and dark.

The larger the animal the less weight it can move and the energetic cost of walking is increased markedly. This is not offset by reduction of movement in elephants as might be expected because of the considerable distance covered by the pace, and the stresses on the bones, muscles and tendons of the legs when an elephant runs are in fact the same as in smaller ungulates.

The epiphyses, the cartilaginous layers between the ends of the long bones and the articulations, which allow the bones to grow in length, fuse by about 32 years in the cow African elephant and over 40 in the bull or at about the same time that the last molar comes into wear. The last long bone epiphyses to fuse are those of the 'forearm' or radius. A few other epiphyses fuse later, but growth has effectively ceased by this age, a process which terminates in most mammals soon after puberty.

Most do not associate the elephant with possessing a long tail, but it is relatively longer than that of most other herbivores, up to 1.5 m total length, flattened laterally at the end which has a fringe of stiff hairs. Wild Asian elephants bite off one another's tails, especially while swimming when an elephant may grip the tail of the animal in front with its teeth and sometimes bite too hard. Baby elephants can panic when swimming and bite off their mothers' tails in this manner. If it is short in an African elephant then this is more likely to have resulted from a hyena attack on the calf, although no such attacks have been witnessed.

'A Head of Such Huge Bignesse'

Many a novice hunter has died through a lack of understanding of the anatomy of the elephant's skull, for the massive forehead holds not the brain, as the unwary might suppose, but is composed of an extraordinary development of enormously inflated sponge-like cancellous bone, formed of a multitude of cavities between the two surfaces of the bone. Separated by postcard-thin walls, these provide size with great lightness. After birth the braincase increases but little in size but the exterior surface of the skull must be of considerable surface area to support the trunk and provide space for the attachment of muscles of sufficient size to control it and wield the skull, heavily weighted as it may be by the tusks. This leads to the extraordinary development of air cells, or 'pneumatic sinuses', between the tables of nearly all of the bones of the cranium, separating them in some instances by as much as 30 cm or more. The cranial cavity housing the brain occupies only a small part of this mass in the adult, situated behind the eyes in line with the auditory canal.

In very old elephants a process of pneumatic osteolysis or dissolution of the bone surrounding the air spaces takes place. Whether this is a structural remodelling of the skull or whether it is due to the increasing calcium imbalance characteristic of ageing in all mammals is not known. Any bone that can be economized upon is absorbed, leaving a paper-thin surface in places where there is no stress, keeping the skull as light as possible as the tusks now increase rapidly in weight. This creates the markedly hourglass shape of the face in old elephants, with gaunt, sunken temples.

The skull of the African elephant lacks the dorsal bulges and the dished forehead of the Asian. The African cow has a relatively flattened skull in front which comes to an angular point on the forehead, whereas that of the bull is rounded. This allows the sexes to be easily distinguished in the field. That of the Asian is taller in proportion with the forehead highly domed and its lower jaw is also deeper in proportion. The relatively flattened nature or squashed face makes a pivot of the skull to balance the trunk.

The nasal passages enter the skull just above the level of the eyes, so that under the skin of the trunk there is a hollow between the elephant's eyes which the elephant can bulge, possibly by inflating with air or dilating it by muscular movement. In most ungulates the nasal passages are filled with lacelike, baglike scrolled bones known as turbinals, which warm and clean the air drawn in over their surfaces. These bones are rudimentary in the elephant, the nasal passages being quite free as the part of the turbinals is played by the lining of the trunk.

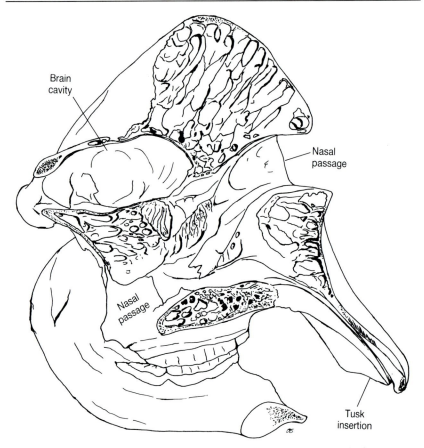

FIG. 3.1 *Sagittal section through the skull of an African elephant.*

Tusks

The conspicuous tusks of the elephant are its elongated upper second incisor teeth. The upper first incisors and the canines are absent and the lower jaw has no incisors at all, being short with the two halves fused at the front so that the elephant is the only mammal besides the primates to possess a chin. It has only a short tongue, therefore a diastema, the space between the end of the jaw and the molar teeth so characteristic of other herbivores, is absent.

The tusks are of sufficient significance to warrant a chapter of their own (Chapter 13).

A CASE OF TEETH

All mammalian teeth are composed of three hard calcified substances: cement, the softest component; enamel, the hardest substance in the body; and dentine, intermediate in hardness, which forms the bulk of the tooth. Within the tooth is a cavity filled with the pulp. Wrongly termed the nerve, although richly endowed with nerves, the pulp comprises mainly connective tissue covered with odontoblastic or tooth-forming cells, the cells which continue to produce dentine almost throughout life, gradually filling the pulp cavity.

The cement anchors the tooth in the jaw but in complex teeth it also fills the spaces between the cones of which the tooth is composed. Teeth of the earlier mastodons which were composed of separate cones, looking rather like pig's teeth, lacked cement, although a little appeared in later ones. All mammoths, on the other hand, had their teeth encased in cement like elephants but the earliest browsing forms had low-crowned teeth covered with thick enamel. More specialized forms evolved high-crowned teeth with thin enamel, providing sharper cutting edges to deal with grass but also wearing down more quickly.

John Corse, who was in charge of elephant capture in Tipperah, Bengal, at the end of the 18th century, aptly described the elephant's tooth as a 'case of teeth'. Most mammalian teeth consist of arrangements of several cones fused together but of single origin, that is, arising from a single tooth germ. This is carried to its greatest extreme in the teeth of elephants which are composed of numerous parallel rows of plates or laminae or lamellae, but nonetheless the tooth has its origin in a single enamel organ, suggesting its origin is from a single tooth. The lamellae are really like flattened cones. These provide a surface of alternating enamel–cement–enamel–dentine, of which the enamel, being the hardest substance, stands up, forming cutting edges. In the Asian elephant the pattern is more compact than in the African; the lamellae are not diamondshaped in cross-section but squashed flat, forming a more effective rasping surface with twice the number in the last three molars, associated with the tendency found in other herbivores of a closer pattern indicating a predominantly grazing habit, grass wearing down the teeth more quickly than browse. Despite its grazer's teeth, the Asian elephant is considered to be primarily a forest animal. Those of the woolly mammoth were similar.

The elephant can only move its jaws forwards and backwards on one another and there is little sideways movement like a cow chewing the cud, so the ridges act as two rasps grating upon one another. These are made more effective by the teeth being slightly curved along their lengths.

But there is more to the elephant's specialized dentition than simply the complex nature of the individual tooth; it is the modification of the general mammalian tooth eruption pattern which is perhaps of greater significance. Aristotle observed that the elephant had four teeth on either side but it was John Corse in 1799, in a communication to the Royal Society, who first described the unique mode of succession of the elephant's teeth.

The elephant needs an adequate grinding surface for the vast amount of food that it must process in its lifetime but because of its short jaw allied to the structure of its skull, it is unable to accommodate all of its teeth in the jaw at once or if it did so, they would have to be so small that they would last for only a short part of its potential lifespan. Most mammalian teeth, including our own, gradually move forwards during life pushed by growth of the bone behind, in our own case the teeth meeting in the middle. This maintains a unified grinding surface.

The elephant uses this inherent phenomenon in a unique way. When born it has four developing teeth in each side of the jaws. A small first tooth and a second tooth erupt almost together after birth, the anterior end of a third following soon after, while the fourth is still below the gum. As a tooth wears it is pushed forwards, the front end wearing into a shelf as the roots are absorbed. This shelf eventually breaks off and finally the remaining fragment of tooth is pushed out. The absorption of tooth roots is a phenomenon which takes place in old age or injury in all mammals.

After the first and second teeth are discarded, parts of two adjacent teeth or one almost complete tooth are in wear in each half of the jaw at any one time, until there is only the great 6th molar left, weighing almost 4 kg and with a maximum grinding length of 21 cm and width of over 7 cm. Once this massive tooth, which is in wear for some two fifths of the animal's life, is finished the elephant can no longer masticate its food and dies at the age of about 60.

Sometimes a small seventh tooth is present. It was found in 1 in 100 elephants in Murchison Falls Park, but only 1 in 1236 in the Luangwa Valley. In Tsavo I found one present as a simple cone, like a small tusk, but it had not cut the gum.

John Corse observed the chronology of the first four teeth in the Asian elephant fairly accurately. The first cuts the gum at six weeks and all four are in use by $8\frac{1}{2}$ weeks. The second comes into wear at two years, the third at five, the fourth at 9–10, the fifth at 20 and the sixth and final one at 30–40. A series from animals which had died in the London Zoo was exhibited to Fellows of the Zoological Society in 1918, particular attention being drawn to the teeth of a cow which had died when she was known to be about 50. If the 6th molar had come into use at the age of 40, then she had lost more than a third of the laminae in ten years. On this basis it was deduced that she would have been toothless before the age of 70.

The African elephant appears to have an identical time scale of eruption, but confusion is caused by some giving the estimated age of eruption of a particular tooth while others give the age at which it becomes defunct. The African elephant loses its first molar at 1–2 years; the second at 3–4; the third at 9–10; the fourth at 19–25 and the fifth at about 43. The sixth molar begins to erupt at about 30 and is finished by 65. In 1936 the fragments of two shed teeth of the London Zoo's young African Jumbo II, estimated to be about four years old, were picked up from the floor of its stall, but they are seldom recovered in this way.

The number of lamellae or enamel loops has been studied by palaeontologists for over a century, but was first related to the age of elephants in 1947. In the first three molars the number of lamellae is distinct: 3:4 for the 1st molar; 6:8 for the 2nd and 7:12 for the 3rd, for the African and Asian elephant respectively. Numbers in the 4th–6th molars overlap between teeth and so are unreliable as a guide, but are approximately 7:12, 8:16 and 10:24, for African and Asian respectively. A 'laminary index' obtained by dividing the number of lamellae by the length of the erupted crown of the tooth is no better as a guide to age.

To look at an elephant's droppings one would not think that it had very effective teeth composed, as the droppings are, of hastily chopped leaves and twigs, often undigested and easily recognizable. This gobbling of food is due to the speed with which it must pass through the body, the elephant simply does not have time to chew its food. In spite of the complex nature of the Asian elephant's tooth, with its rasplike grinding surface, it hardly grinds its food at all. Its jaw movement is that of a crusher, the jaws moving up and down crushing only what falls directly beneath the teeth. When the American physiologist Francis Benedict fed strips of old car rubber inner tube measuring 4×20 cm to the Asian elephant Jap, many pieces passed through the gut undamaged. Some were very much chopped up and some presumably so much so that they were never found again. This led Benedict to speculate whether the feeding habits of the elephant had not changed profoundly since the line evolved its specialized dental apparatus. He concluded that the grinding surface of the elephant's tooth seemingly played a wholly insignificant role in its life. But the surfaces become worn down readily enough, so the complex nature of the tooth enables the elephant to meet the demands placed upon it, occasioned by the sheer volume that passes through the mouth. If the elephant ground its food or chopped it up any more than it does, then the teeth would wear down more rapidly than they do and be insufficient to sustain it through its normal life span.

The elephant can suffer an almighty toothache. Almost one tenth of elephants dying naturally in Murchison Falls Park were found to have swollen jaws with massive tooth root abscesses, some as big as a grapefruit with a sinus draining pus to the outside. Also found in elephants in Tsavo, tooth abscesses are particularly common in older cows. Their presence is generally attributed to poor nutrition, but stress due to overcrowding has also been proposed. Often they have been the cause of captive elephants being put down because of fits of bad temper.

THE ELEPHANT'S BAGGY SUIT

Elephants, together with rhinoceroses and hippopotamuses, are known as 'pachyderms' or thickskinned animals. The skin is of great thickness and toughness in parts, characterized by its wrinkled and furrowed appearance like the bark of some great old oak tree, but surprisingly sensitive. Elephants need to bathe regularly and rub their skins otherwise they become scurfy and get skin irritation. If you load an Asian elephant's back for too long it soon becomes sore. The skin of the African elephant is more wrinkled than that of the Asian and it has been suggested that the fissures may be important in retaining moisture. This wrinkling means that the actual surface area of the underlying layer may be as much as doubled in places.

The horny outer layer or epidermis, which is only about $1\frac{1}{2}$ mm in thickness, overlies the dermis which is up to 25 mm in parts. The thinnest skin is on the trunk, breast, legs, ears and in the groin. The dermis is linked to the underlying or subcutaneous tissue by columnar pillars or 'studs', instead of simple projections or papillae as in most other mammals. The total surface area of the skin of a 2 tonne 46 year old Asian cow elephant is about 12 sq. m; that of a big African bull would be much more.

A Frenchman, C. Perrault, made the first known study of the elephant's skin in 1681 from the dissection of an elephant which had belonged to Louis XIV and lived at Versailles for 13 years. It was a forest elephant from the Congo, sent by command of the King of Portugal. The whole French Academy of Sciences was present at the dissection, conducted by Perrault and two others.

But it was Smith in 1890 who noted that the skin was 'notoriously sensitive' due to numerous nerve endings in the dermis. Asian handlers use a kind of acupuncture knowledge to control their elephants; knowing which are the most sensitive points on the skin, they prick them with their goad or ankus. Some 114 points on the bull and about 28 in the cow have been located, the lower number in the cow not meaning that she is less sensitive but that she is more easily controlled.

The Asian elephant is covered with a yellowish or reddish-brown hair at birth, but this is generally lost later. However, some elephants might be more hairy than they appear for circus elephants in America have their hair singed in the spring, except in the ears where it is clipped, since this is considered to make them look better. It was observed to grow about 20 mm in length in several months on the body and almost 40 mm in the ears, but growth may have been stimulated by the treatment and the climate.

The African elephant also has reddish soft hair at birth, which it loses at six months of age, to be replaced by stiff black bristles.

The long tail hairs are usually black in appearance, but occasionally white or pigmentless hairs are present, considered as great charms by elephant hunters. The trunk is covered with sensory hairs.

Neither sweat nor sebaceous glands have been found in the elephant's skin. Dampness apparent on the backs of Asian elephants after they have been ridden with a cover over them, and on the back of the ears in the African elephant, are due to water loss through the skin and not sweat glands. The mammoth also lacked sweat and sebaceous glands. This would have meant that the hairy coat of the woolly mammoth would have become soaked whenever it came into contact with water and, in an Arctic climate, frozen to the skin. But samples of hair from a mastodon found in Wisconsin show possible water-repellent adaptations that have been interpreted as semi-aquatic. The stout outer or 'guard' hairs are hollow as in the African elephant, but there was a very fine and wavy underfur like that of the otter or beaver. Perhaps this was related to the lack of sebaceous glands.

Also lacking in elephants, as they were in the woolly mammoth, are hair erector muscles, the little muscle attached to the base of each hair which can erect the hair to control the animal's temperature, or, in the case of fright, make one's hair stand on end!

THE FEET

How many toes does an elephant have? is an old poser. All elephants in fact have five digits in both fore and hind feet, but there are usually five toenails to each forefoot and only four to the hind in the Asian elephant, as in the mammoth and the African forest elephant. In the African bush elephant there are usually four to each forefoot and three to the hind. This arrangement is genetic and is found in the foetus, but sometimes differences are found simply because nails have been lost. The nails are large and flat, embedded against the rounded foot.

The shape of the forefoot is round as it takes most of the weight, while that of the hindfoot is elliptical because the equivalent of the 'big toe' is greatly reduced. If weight was not a consideration the relative lengths of the digits suggest that if evolution were to continue, a trend to four toes in the African elephant, as found in the hippopotamus, and three in the Asian elephant, as found in the rhinoceros, would take place.

Elephants are well known for the extreme silence with which they can move. This is because the foot bones rest on a great pad of spongy material which acts as a built-in shock absorber, forming an internal cushion like a lightly inflated tyre. When the elephant rests its weight on the foot it splays out, distributing the weight evenly. The elastic cushion forms a convex bulge to the underside when the foot is raised off the ground, but when in contact it smothers any objects beneath it and provides the elephant with the advantage that any noise, like a stick cracking, is muffled and it can move with catlike stealth. Its nature also allows the elephant to walk in deep mud without difficulty, for when it withdraws its foot the circumference becomes smaller, so suction is reduced.

The horny plantar region is deeply fissured and expert trackers can identify individual elephants from the pattern that it makes on the ground. At one time every trained elephant in former Indo-China was known by its feet and elephant thieves were adept at changing the pattern by cutting the sole. When it moves the elephant 'paces', placing its hindfeet on the spot vacated by the fore, so the tracks almost overlap.

In spite of their apparently tough nature, an elephant's feet are among the most sensitive parts of its body. Some African hunters recognized it as the elephant's 'Achilles' heel'; following up behind an elephant they would shoot an arrow into the sole of the hindfoot as it raised it while walking, thus bringing the elephant to a halt. Others, less daring, placed camouflaged sharpened stakes on elephant footpaths, crippling the elephant when it trod upon them.

It has long been a rule of thumb concerning domestic Asian elephants that the height of a fullgrown animal is almost exactly twice the circumference of the forefoot and the forefoot has long been used by hunters as a measure of an elephant's size, referred to as early as 1591 by Filippo Pigafetta as known to natives in Zaïre. In the cow it does not increase in size after 25 years, but a straight line relationship in the bull with body size confirms the hunters' contention. But it is only an *average* relationship, which is why some hunters dispute it.

The length of the hind footprint can be used to estimate the age of a cow elephant up to 15 years with some accuracy and in the bull beyond this age as the foot continues to grow in size.

In captive elephants the greatest problem is their feet, the horny sole becoming cracked and overgrown from lack of wear, especially if the elephant is kept on damp or soft ground. The same applies to the nails which become split, ingrown or overgrown and exercise on hard ground is essential or regular pedicure is necessary.

THE HAND OF THE BEAST

The ancient Greeks realized the importance to the elephant of its trunk in feeding: 'In the elephant the nostril is very large and strong, and it answers to the purpose of a hand, for the animal can extend it, and with it take its food, and convey it to its mouth . . .' wrote Aristotle. Oppian (*circa* AD 200) referred to it as 'the hand of the beast'.

The trunk of the African elephant is said to be considerably weaker than that of its Asian counterpart, perhaps allied to the fact that the Asian has tended to dispense with the use of tusks, and it is less extensible. In other words the Asian elephant can stretch its trunk further.

Strong or weak, the trunk has been described as a 'fantastic appendage' with which its possessor can smell humans at a great distance, signal with it, trumpet with it, snorkel, drink, bathe and dust itself with it, select choice food morsels or break branches up to 20 cm in diameter, use it as a vacuum cleaner or as a weapon to strike with. A wild elephant has been seen to pick up a twig with it and scratch its leg and both elephants can throw stones with it quite accurately. An elephant can lift about 4.5% of its own weight with it or 270 kg in an adult bull. An adult Asian elephant can hold over 10 litres of water in it. Just as importantly, an elephant breathes through its trunk although it can use its mouth as well. Its psychological importance to the elephant is demonstrated by the fact that if the trunk was secured, Sri Lankan elephant trainers could break in a wild elephant within a week.

It is important in tactile relationships and is used by the cow in helping her calf, in courtship and in signalling.

But the trunk's uniqueness lies in the fact that it has no skeleton; the nasal cartilage does not extend into it so it is literally like a piece of rubber. Yet the muscles are able to twist it in all manner of directions. How does it do this? We do not really know. It puzzled Dr Mullen in 1681:

> . . . by what means he was able to shoot it [the trunk] out, from a foot, upon any sudden occasion, to five feet long, and that with extraordinary force, I cannot clearly perceive . . . we do not find any part without a bone except this, that is spontaneously protruded or prolonged, and so kept for some time.

A later author was to write in 1881:

> The simplest popular view of the matter is to say that when the trunk is shortened it is thickened; and when it is lengthened it is rendered thin: and the only difference between these operations, and the production of the same changes in an elastic tube of Indian rubber, consists in the moving force of the trunk being in the organ itself, and distributed amongst the almost infinite number of

muscles which that organ contains. In this way, the force is
multiplied by the action of the will of the animal upon a vast
number of points; and although the bellying of a few muscles may
scarcely produce any visible motion, the repetition of the same
action by many thousand muscles will effect that sudden extension
which appeared so wonderful to the Dublin anatomist. The difficulty there may have been in comprehending the peculiarity of the
trunk is not surprising, when we consider that the instrument is
altogether constructed upon principles different from common
muscular action; and that the power of the mechanism is balanced
by an almost infinite number of these small muscles, not more than
the twelfth of an inch in thickness.

Notwithstanding these comments it has been suggested that the trunk
operates as a type of closed hydraulic system, the muscles contracting on fluid.
Pumping fluid into one side would cause that side to expand and the emptied
side to contract. This is at the cellular level and there are no obvious fluid-filled
spaces in the trunk.

Cuvier estimated the trunk to contain 40 000 muscles. The entire human body
has only 639 and in fact the elephant's trunk has no more than the nasal region of
a dog, that is to say, six pairs of major muscles. But these are subdivided into
over 100 000 muscle units, so in a sense Cuvier was right. They are divided into
two sets of pairs: longitudinal, which run almost the length of the trunk; and
radiating and transverse. The first group is mostly superficial. In four segments
they lie on top, underneath and along each side. The anterior pair, termed the
levators, which raise the trunk, begin at the frontal bone and extend the length of
trunk into the fingerlike tip. Those on the underside, termed the depressores,
curl the trunk up but do not reach into the extremity. On either side are
latitudinal bands which bend the trunk from side to side. Underneath these
longitudinal muscles are the deeper transverse ones which probably create the
more complex movements.

An elephant also tests smells with its trunk, placing the tip inside its mouth
after contact with an object, to transfer the smell to a small opening in the palate
which leads to the organ known as Jacobson's organ, an accessory organ of
smell found in all vertebrates.

The trunk is particularly important in greeting, elephants placing the tips into
one another's mouths. Although some might see this as a gesture akin to kissing
in our own species, it may relate more to an appeasement gesture as in wolves
and dogs rolling onto their backs and exposing their most vulnerable parts.
Although there are several recorded instances of elephants which have lost the
end of the trunk in a snare surviving, the trunk is the elephant's most sensitive
possession and it shows its confidence in another by placing the tip into its
mouth where it could be easily bitten off.

In using the extremity the Asian elephant, having only one 'finger', relies
more on grasp, bending the end of the trunk round an object. The African
pinches objects between an upper 'finger' and an extended lower 'lip' which is
not muscular like the 'finger'. The Asian elephant can also pinch an object
between its 'finger' and the lower 'lip'.

THE GUTS OF A GIANT

Our first description of an elephant's insides comes from Aristotle. Describing its alimentary tract he wrote:

> The elephant's intestine is formed of parts so put together as to give the appearance of four stomachs. Its viscera resemble those of a hog, but are of course much larger. The liver, for instance, is four times as large as that of an ox. The spleen however is of small size considering the bulk of the animal.

The 'four stomachs' to which he was referring were the stomach, caecum, colon and small intestine. The stomach is simple, up to 140 cm in length and 40 cm in diameter, with an empty weight of up to 45 kg. The sacculated caecum is not especially large relative to other parts of the gut although it has a circumference of up to 1.8 m. It resembles that of the *Sirenia* rather than that of any other mammal. The colon is uncompartmentalized. The intestines are simple and short for the size of the animal, essentially the same length as those of the horse, sheep and goat. In the African elephant they total up to 18 m of which the large intestine measures 6 m and the small 12 m. In an Asian elephant the large intestine has been measured as 12–13 m long and the small 16–22 m; providing a ratio of small to large intestine averaging about 1.7:1 compared to 1.3:1 in the African.

Whereas the elephant's tract is roughly three times the length of the body, that of the horse is 12 and the cow 20. This means food must remain in the tract for a shorter length of time compared with these other animals. The length of time of fermentation by the gut flora which break down the food, apparently in the hind end of the tract as opposed to the rumen of ruminants, must be shorter and the action lessened. Therefore a low utilization rate per unit weight of food is compensated for by a rapid passage time allowing a high intake; a hasty skimming off of the cream, as it were. The total weight of gut contents amounts to only 7–12% of body weight, compared to 40% in a ruminant like the steer.

If the recorded difference in length of the intestinal tract between the Asian and African elephant is real and not due to stretching in the former during measuring, then passage time in the African must be even faster than it is in the Asian. This may be related to the difference in tooth structure, the African elephant chopping up its food even less and therefore being obliged to pass through more. It could thus be erroneous to extrapolate energy functions from the Asian elephant to the African.

Fermentation of food by protozoa and bacteria occurs throughout most of the tract except in the stomach, the caecum being the first important site. The colon is the main area of digestive and absorptive activity. Sugars and starches are found in excess in the upper parts where they are partially fermented to lactic acid. Fermentation of the soluble sugars is completed in the caecum. The colon is a site of continued fermentation of starch, soluble polysaccharides, cellulose and protein.

The stomach and intestine are bathed in several gallons of clear fluid and it is probably this fluid which elephant hunters used to drink, not fluid from the stomach itself as is generally supposed. Such fluid is present in all mammals.

THE PUZZLE OF THE LUNGS

The lungs are relatively primitive in that they are bilobed but almost unique in that there is no pleural cavity, a feature shared only with the Malayan tapir. Unlike those of other mammals they are not suspended in the thorax but adhere to the inside of the chest wall and to the diaphragm, fused by a thick layer of tough connective tissue. Separate in the foetus as in other mammals, fusion takes place by the time that it is born.

Lungs are elastic structures usually held against the inner surface of the ribs and diaphragm by surface tension, a partial vacuum in the pleural cavity ensuring that they remain distended. If the chest wall is pierced air enters and the lungs collapse. We draw in air by altering the size of the pleural cavity through expanding our rib cage, so that the increased size of the cavity creates a bigger vacuum. The lungs then expand to fill this, thus drawing in air. But the elephant breathes by moving its diaphragm, to which a large area of the lungs is attached, rather than by expanding its rib cage. This works well if the animal is standing but not if it is lying on its side and lying elephants have a much faster heart beat than when standing.

The support of the lungs that we find in the elephant is not due to their large size, as such an arrangement is not found in the rhinoceros or hippopotamus, and that largest of all mammals, the blue whale, has only minor adhesions. So if it is not due to the large size of the lungs, why should the elephant have this peculiar arrangement? It seems it is connected with its ability to inhale water through the trunk, which it does with the mouth open, an average of 4 litres being inhaled to a height of at least 2 m. This would serve to create a considerable negative pressure in part of the bronchial tree. But it also blows the water down its trunk and into its mouth, while swallowing at the same time.

So the elephant does not suck with its trunk by using its tongue and cheeks as we would do; it must be using its chest and the muscles of the diaphragm. A man can suck water up to a height of about 6 m using tongue and cheeks and a very long straw! But if he uses his chest and diaphragm muscles then he can only achieve about one tenth of this. Using the latter means the elephant is more efficient at sucking than a man for it raises the water some 2 m or more and not in a column but in a cone which may start with a diameter of about 4 cm at the tip and widen to more than twice this at its widest point, a total capacity of almost 6 litres. Dr Roger Short of Cambridge University, who studied this problem, considered that the adhesion of the lungs to the diaphragm was not apparently instrumental in creating this large power of suction, but that it may be important in helping prevent the collapse of the lungs due to the combined effects of the weight of the lungs and the large vacuum, or high negative pressure, the elephant can generate. The elephant lacks the circular cartilaginous rings which other

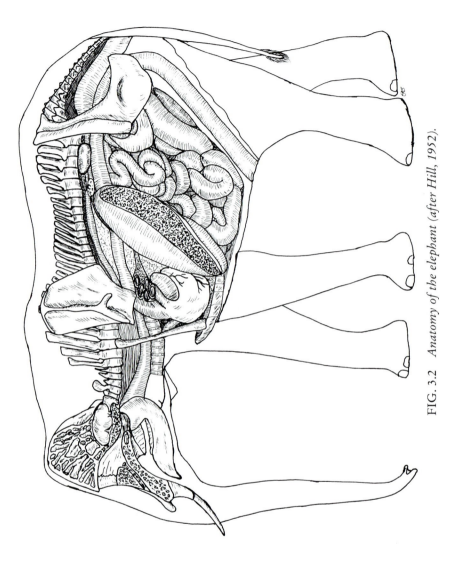

FIG. 3.2   Anatomy of the elephant (after Hill, 1952).

mammals have to support the bronchiole tubes to prevent their collapse, presumably because the lungs are supported.

If you look into an elephant's mouth you cannot see down its throat as you can in man and there is no uvula, the fleshy flap hanging from the upper palate at the back. The mouth connects with the throat by a narrow, sphincterlike slit so although it may hold its mouth open when it sucks up water, it can apparently at the same time close its throat.

THE LIVER

Aristotle noted there was no gall bladder, but that a bilelike fluid ran out from the place where it was attached in other animals. Some years later, in 300 BC, the Athenian physician Mnesitheus is said to have dissected an elephant at Alexandria and confirmed the gall bladder's absence. A gall bladder is of no use to an animal which is passing food through its gut almost continuously, as its purpose is to store bile between meals and then discharge it when food is present.

In the African bull the liver can weigh up to almost 70 kg. Its simple bilobed nature is one of the elephant's primitive features.

A bile duct is present and gall stones are not uncommon in it in wild animals. In an isolated Uganda population, one in every five examined had gall stones, with one carrying up to three quarters of a kilogram. The largest stone weighed 430 g. Another examined in Kenya was carrying an astonishing $5\frac{1}{2}$ kg. Gall stones have also been found in mammoth remains.

Chapter 4

FROM ARISTOTLE TO BENEDICT: PHYSIOLOGY AND FUNCTIONS

Since all of my nineteen baby elephants died, my four years of work at Lake Chad might be considered a complete loss.

H. Oberjohann, 1953

ELEPHANTS AND LSD

MORE than a century ago physiologists were asking whether an elephant, because of its Brobdingnagian dimensions, showed any striking differences in its metabolism from other animals, particularly with respect to heat insulation and regulation: 'What are the specific modifications implied by a weight of perhaps three tons? [In fact an elephant can weigh well over twice this.] How nearly do the existing species approach the limits of size fixed by mechanical laws and by the physiological properties of animal tissues?' were questions being asked in 1875.

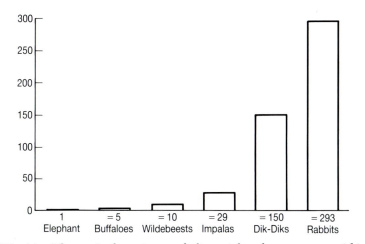

FIG. 4.1 *The equivalents in metabolic weight of one average African elephant weighing 4790 kg.*

It was not until 1935 that Francis Benedict in the United States conducted the first detailed physiological experiments on an elephant; a 40 year old, 3.6 tonne long-suffering Asian cow called Jap. No one has attempted it since, although we still have mostly only preliminary findings from this single domesticated Asian elephant, fed on hay, to answer many of our questions.

It is a fundamental law of physics that each time the surface area of a body doubles, the volume trebles. Metabolic rate, the rate at which energy changes take place in a body, is a regular function of body size and is close to the power of three quarters. That is, for every unit of increase in mass, say 1 kg, the metabolic rate decreases by one quarter.

The effects of this scaling were underlined in a disastrous experiment. Some workers in America who wished to study an Asian elephant in musth decided to inject it with the drug LSD. Using the amount required to enrage a 2.6 kg cat they multiplied this up according to the weight of the elephant to arrive at a dosage of 297 mg (a milligram is one-thousandth part of a gram). Since a human takes about 0.2 mg for a 'trip', this was therefore the equivalent of about 1500 trips. Upon receiving this dose the elephant immediately started trumpeting and running around, went into convulsions and collapsed and died within five minutes. The 'scientists' concluded that the elephant was particularly sensitive to LSD.

However, had they extrapolated from the weight of the cat using metabolic weight, the dosage would have been only 80 mg. And if they had considered the weight of the brain alone and extrapolated from man, whose 1.4 kg brain requires only 0.2 mg, then the 3 kg brain of an elephant would require only 0.4 mg, which happens to be about the dosage used with the morphine drug M99 to immobilize elephants. They had overdosed the unfortunate beast by almost 750 times.

THE HEAT OF A THOUSAND MEN

The relationship between size and bodily functions is at once both advantageous and disadvantageous to a large animal like the elephant. It means that as its body has a relatively small surface area in relation to its bulk over which to take up heat from the environment, it will not heat up quickly in its tropical surroundings. But conversely, once it has warmed up it cannot lose heat quickly. Thus it is important for such a large animal not to become overheated.

How does the elephant deal with this problem? It was assumed that the large ears of the African elephant were for the purpose of assisting in the cooling of its body. Nobody asked why the Asian elephant managed to do with much smaller and thicker ears inhabiting just as hot an environment. The Asian elephant does not like heat and always seeks the shade, collapsing if forced to work too long in the sun. When out in the sun it will cover its head with debris. Its African congener, on the other hand, is quite happy to feed in the hottest sun, although in the most arid parts of Namibia's Kaokoveld desert the desert-adapted elephants chew the leathery leaves of the ebony tree and spread them over their head and ears like Asian elephants. The domesticated forest elephants in the Belgian Congo also covered their own heads with leaves and mud if they were worked in the sun at midday.

Benedict believed it to be inconceivable that a large hairless animal, unprotected by fur, should require any special temperature regulating device in its ears. With severe muscular work the temperature of the blood in the ears increases considerably, but he did not consider that the ear movements could play any great role in regulation. In fact, the 2 m long trunk plays some role in heat loss, its temperature being lower than that of the expired air.

The deep body temperature of the African elephant measured immediately after death is about 36.1–36.8°C, with an average of 36.4°C, close to that of man, 36.9°C. It occupies an intermediate position between those animals which show wide fluctuations in temperature associated with water conservation (prevention of sweating), as in the camel, and those with a relatively constant body temperature, like the hippopotamus which keeps its temperature constant by staying in the water as much as possible during the heat of the day.

The elephant's dark grey colour absorbs up to 85% of the energy striking it and free-roaming semi-domesticated elephants at Tsavo, a hot semi-arid area, showed that with a daytime temperature rising to about 35°C at midday the elephant gained as much as 90% of its heat load from the environment and only 10% came from its body metabolism. Of the 90% some 43 came from the sun, 30% was reflected from the ground when not covered with vegetation and the remaining 17% was reflected from vegetation or objects in the environment. Now, the elephant cannot sweat because it has no sweat glands and neither does it pant, so how does it lose this heat?

First, because it does not have sweat glands this does not mean that an elephant cannot lose water through its skin. Preliminary studies on water loss from the skin of the front of the ear of an African elephant in an ambient temperature of about 26°C showed that it lost at least ten times that which a man loses from his thigh, and from the back of the ear this rose to 70 times. It also lost more water through the skin of the flank than from the front of the ear. But when he perspires a man greatly exceeds the elephant's rate of loss through the skin. Flapping the ears creates a current of air over the body equivalent to a breeze of only about 2 knots. This is greater over the ear surface itself and there would be considerable turbulence around the ear margins, but clearly this is not of great significance.

The horny outer layer of the skin is thickest on the trunk and thin on the flank. Tough as it is, it has to be kept moist by the diffusion of water from within the body otherwise it becomes stiff. This lubricating moisture evaporates when it reaches the outer surface of the horny layer and its rate of diffusion to the surface increases with increased skin temperature or with raised humidity, in the latter case because the damper and more flexible the horny layer, then the more permeable it becomes. As long as it is moist, thickness of the horny layer is no barrier to water loss by diffusion. The wrinkling of the skin means that the surface area available for diffusion under the horny layer may be almost doubled.

As a result of this diffusion a young 1.2 tonne elephant loses about 2.5 litres of water every hour under average temperatures. An adult bull would probably lose about twice this quantity and so must drink at least 120 litres a day to balance this loss. All in all, it is estimated that about three quarters of the elephant's heat loss requirements *could* be met by this loss of water through the skin and the elephant has therefore no necessity for sweat glands. Indeed, if it did have sweat glands water would be lost too quickly.

The amount lost by diffusion through the skin by the average-sized elephant requires as much heat to evaporate it as would be sufficient to bring almost 30 litres of water to the boil every hour. But this evaporative water loss amounts to only 7% of the total heat lost and the rate of diffusion of water through the skin remains constant throughout the day, despite an increase in ambient temperature. Benedict calculated that Jap lost some 20% of the total heat given off in vaporization of water from the body. This compares with 25% in another hairless animal – man.

The number of breaths per minute of the Tsavo elephants remained constant at 10–12 regardless of the time of day or the temperature, which was the same number as Jap's. Some 3% of heat was lost from the skin by air currents, but the greatest loss was 80% radiated to plants and other cooler objects. Hence standing in the shade is important. The remaining 10% was not dissipated but stored in the body, raising the temperature by 2.1°C during a typical day, less than half of the maximum of about 5°C that could be withstood without collapse. This stored heat was then lost by radiation in the evening when the temperature became cooler or by bathing and wallowing.

Wallowing and spraying with water are thus important cooling mechanisms at the end of a hot day and not carried out just for fun. These activities also promote hydration of the horny skin layer and thus can increase water diffusion outwards through the skin.

Experiments with a pig, a non-sweating hairless animal, revealed that when its flank was soaked with water the evaporative water loss from the skin increased by up to 20 times, but fell back after about 15 minutes. When its flank was smeared with mud the same increase occurred, but in this case it lasted for two hours. So we can see the advantages to the elephant of plastering itself with mud, for this cools the body for much longer than a dousing with water alone.

When Jap's body was just ticking over quietly, the basal heat production produced by the energy exchanges (that 10% of the heat load) was 2060 calories per sq. m of surface area per day. With a total surface area of 24 sq. m this was equivalent to the body heat produced by 30 men. Benedict calculated that the heat produced in a barn in Florida which housed 34 elephants was equivalent to that produced by 1000 men. The maximum heat output of 74 500 calories was when the ambient temperature was 21.5°C.

The resting or basal metabolic rate was about 13 calories per kg of body weight per day, amounting to an average of 45 800 calories per day all told. Since a mature African bull elephant would weigh almost twice as much as Jap, the production of heat would be much higher and it would need to lose correspondingly more water vapour from the skin.

Despite the apparently enormous heat output of an elephant, the larger the animal the less heat per unit weight is produced. Thus Jap's resting heat production per kg of bodyweight of 13 calories compares with 170 for a 20 g mouse, 116 for a 2 kg rabbit or 25 for a 64 kg man.

If we take as an example the 50 000 elephants in northern Botswana, these are producing as much heat per day as 1.5 million men, more than half as much again as the total human population of Botswana present in 1981. However, the elephants range over 80 000 sq. km, so the heat production per sq. km of land area amounts to the equivalent of only 20 men, an entirely negligible amount.

Although an elephant weighs 2000 times as much as a rabbit, its heat output is less than one quarter. If the elephant had the same metabolic rate as the rabbit its surface temperature would be above boiling point. But the smaller animal must produce more heat to keep pace with its surface loss, as it has a greater surface area relative to its volume. So a mouse will eat half of its body weight in a day to provide sufficient energy to produce this heat.

Heat loss at the surface is related to the rate of oxygen uptake in the lungs, for the energy reaction which produces metabolic heat can take place only as fast as oxygen is supplied. Diffusion of the oxygen through the walls of the capillaries, the rate of absorption of food through the walls of the intestines and the speed of the blood's circulation are all factors which contribute. The small ratio of surface area to body volume ensures a reduced rate of heat gain and a large reserve of water for evaporative cooling. Thus large animals are more resistant to drought regardless of temperature, because of their absolutely larger stores of water within the body and the fact that evaporative water loss, together with the water lost in respiration, rises more slowly with body mass than does sustainable water loss. Thus large species are better suited to hot, dry climates.

But in hot humid climates large size may be a disadvantage as evaporative cooling is less effective. Thus if the ears of the elephant play any part in evaporative cooling, the smaller ears of the Asiatic elephant may reflect the

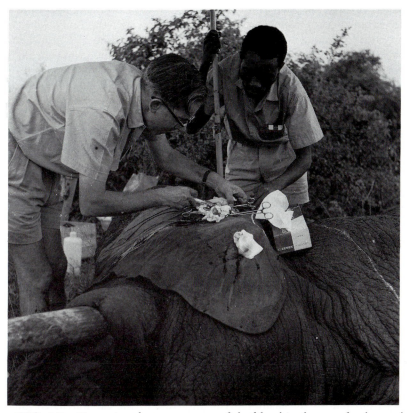

FIG. 4.2   *Measuring the temperature of the blood in the ear of a drugged elephant.*

method's ineffectiveness in the more humid regions that the Asian elephant inhabits. In the humid rainforests of Malaysia, the elephant may have to reduce activity in the hot season and in the hottest part of the day. Its low density in such forest may be due not to a paucity of food, but to physiological limitations.

In south east Sri Lanka bulls showed a peak of activity at about 8 am in the morning, before the day had warmed up. Activity then declined towards midday to be followed by a second peak from about 4 to 5 pm in the evening. The cows showed a peak at about 10 am in the morning followed by another peak from about 3.30 pm up until 6 pm, but sometimes there was also a smaller peak at midday from about 1 to 2 pm.

A hairless animal like man can lose heat by increasing the blood flow to the skin over most of the body, but this is not so in an elephant. Only the ears have a significant network of blood vessels close enough to the surface for this, although the skin is much more vascular than is generally supposed and biting flies easily draw blood. But to lose heat to the environment the surface of the ear must be hotter than the environment yet measurements have shown that it is cooler at midday, especially on the back, and lower than the temperature of other external parts which is singularly uniform over the body. The ear temperature measured only 21–23°C compared with up to 26–27°C elsewhere.

By 6 pm the vessels of the ear had dilated and the flow of blood increased. The temperature was now higher than that of the general body surface and the environment, resulting in heat transfer to the environment taking place, the network of blood vessels now acting like a radiator instead of as a wet towel hung out to dry.

So the African elephant's ears do assist it in cooling, both by exposing a large evaporative cooling surface to the air and by exposing the blood vessels to a large surface area. In the African elephant the combined surface area of both sides of the ears amounts to about one fifth of the animal's total body surface area.

During the morning an African elephant does not flap its ears very often, but during the hot midday period it may flap them up to 23 times a minute. In rain it generally ceases to flap them and instead holds them against the side of the body. When the temperature drops the arteries of the ear constrict, reducing the blood flow.

Asian elephants increase their rate of ear flapping when the cloud cover decreases or the wind speed drops. In a strong following wind Asian bulls will often just hold their ears out. Since rate of evaporative heat loss depends upon the humidity of the surrounding air, it is most effective in hot, dry areas, and least in humid forest. Large ears would probably be of little use as a cooling mechanism to an elephant in the Malaysian forest.

Some all too brief experiments were conducted with a free-living young bull at Lake Manyara by inserting probes into its ear and monitoring the temperature changes of the blood by radiotelemetry. The temperature of the venous blood from one of the main veins in the back of the ear fluctuated fairly narrowly between 35.4°C and 35.8°C, but arterial blood being pumped into the ear was usually no less than 3°C higher. When the elephant climbed a steep escarpment the temperature of the arterial blood rose within 15 minutes to an astonishing 44.8°C, higher than that recorded for any other surviving mammal. (The highest recorded in humans is 44.4°C in a very sick woman who recovered.) The temperature of the elephant's venous blood remained steady; thus the ear was cooling it by 5.6°C. Clearly this overheated blood was not reaching the brain otherwise collapse would have taken place. We have a lot to learn concerning the causes of such rapid increases in blood temperature, where it takes place and how it is that it does not damage vital organs.

AN ANIMAL WITH TWO HEARTS

The volume of blood passing through the two ears of the African elephant is some 18 litres per minute, far more than is necessary for the ordinary metabolism of the tissues of the ear. It means that the total 360 litres of an average elephant is passed through the ears in 20 minutes at resting metabolism.

The arteries of the ear derive from the carotid and the veins enter the jugular vein, a relatively short journey from the heart. The heated blood is therefore coming from the posterior vena cava, the great vein which runs the length of the body collecting up blood from all of the other veins and discharging into the heart. This blood is then pumped out in its heated state mixed with blood recharged with oxygen from the lungs, probably therefore lowering the overall temperature. Some then goes to the ear via the carotid artery, but the greater volume goes to the great dorsal aorta supplying most of the body. However, that flowing to the ears is returned to the heart fairly quickly after cooling to mix once more with the heated blood, so that the major volume being pumped into the dorsal aorta is partly cooled.

The veins have proportionately much thicker walls than other species, for some vessels may be up to $3\frac{1}{2}$ m in length and would require a very high blood pressure to prevent the collapse of their walls if they were thin. Because of their size the junctions between arteries are often supported by ridges of elastic fibres or muscle cells, which may become calcified in older elephants.

An elephant's heart does not have the usual mammalian shape but appears like two hearts stuck together, bilobed at its extremity and with paired anterior venae cavae. This led the ancients to believe that it had two hearts: one evinced ferocity, the other gentleness. An elephant with two hearts was shot in southern Africa about 1870, one of the two being smaller than the other. The bilobed heart is regarded as a primitive feature but perhaps its retention in the elephant, together with the paired anterior venae cavae, are an adaptive feature connected with the cooling circulation. The heart of the woolly mammoth was apparently larger than that of extant elephants, allegedly an adaptation to a cold climate.

In a large African bull the heart can weigh up to almost 30 kg, the size increasing by approximately 5 g for every kg of total body weight. It represents about 0.5% of the total bodyweight compared with man's 0.6%.

The heart beat of the Asian elephant is about 31–34 beats per minute, after exercise rising to about 37 and to 46 if lying on the side. This is much lower than that recorded by Gilchrist in India in 1851, who commented '49 is the average healthy pulsation of the heart'; increasing up to 100 per minute after exercise. But this must have been measured on nervous elephants, for Benedict noted that the heart rate increases almost instantly if the elephant becomes apprehensive. Like some shy Victorian maiden, any procedure out of the ordinary, such as the approach of a stranger, even a change in attention or interest, could give Jap palpitations, sending up her heart rate. The average minimum in the standing elephant is about 28 and it is about 10 beats per minute higher when lying down. In man the normal rate is about 70.

Jap's metabolic rate measured in terms of oxygen uptake was 210 litres of oxygen per hour, compared to 13 in man. The volume of the lungs is directly related to body weight, comprising about 6.3% of the total. This translates into the amount of air held in the lungs as about 310 litres and the maximum amount breathed in and out at any one time about 50. Only about 70% of the air entering the respiratory processes is discharged through the trunk.

The large volume of the elephant poses problems in the transport of oxygen. To help overcome this it has the largest red blood corpuscles in the mammalian kingdom, measuring about 9.25 microns (a micron is one millionth part of a metre) in diameter. Only the South American giant anteater has corpuscles of similar size. The blood count, similar in both African and Asian elephants, is consequently lower than that of almost all other mammals. It is not known where an elephant produces most of its replacement blood cells for there is little marrow in the long bones, the usual major sites of production. Other sites of production could be in the cranium, ribs, sternum and vertebrae, as in man.

The next largest mammalian corpuscles are those of the jackal at 7.8 microns, while those of man are 6.7–7.7. But the elephant's are dwarfed by those of the African lungfish, 41 microns in diameter! The large size of the elephant's may be related to the high oxygen affinity to haemoglobin; the larger the animal the higher the oxygen affinity due to the slower metabolic rate. That is, it does not give up its oxygen easily. So as the largest land mammal the elephant's haemoglobin gives it up at a lower oxygen pressure than all other mammals. The effect of acid on haemoglobin is to reduce its affinity for oxygen, driving off the oxygen which therefore increases in the arterial blood. So an elephant does not become 'blown' as quickly as a smaller animal in which the effect is greater because of its higher metabolic rate and therefore higher production of acid.

The myoglobins, the proteins found in muscle fibres which store and carry oxygen for doing the work of the muscle and which also bind carbon monoxide, differ in elephants from most other mammals. Elephant myoglobin, which is pink in colour and not dark red as in other animals, resists the breakdown and release of the oxygen to a greater extent than other myoglobins, so the muscles do not lose it as quickly as those of other mammals. That means that it can be replenished more slowly. But it is up to eight times more sensitive to carbon monoxide. An elephant could be gassed relatively much more quickly with carbon monoxide fumes than could a man.

Elephants stressed during capture will die and others often die within the first six months in captivity, attributed to a 'broken heart'. Such deaths are probably due to 'straining', the heart muscles being damaged by not being replenished with oxygen quickly enough during unusual activity.

ELEPHANTS IN THE ARCTIC

Being hairless the elephant has no insulation against cold but its large size means that it loses heat relatively slowly. But as with gaining heat, so the converse works with cold and the bigger the animal the lower the critical temperature, that is, the environmental temperature at which it does not increase heat production to combat cold. But if an elephant becomes chilled then it cannot warm up quickly again and death is likely to ensue. Cases of collapse from hypothermia in the cold wet season are not uncommon with working elephants in Burma, usually taking place at night.

Instructions for dealing with this, in a little book on elephant care issued in 1945, make no mention of lighting a fire near to the animal to warm it up but recommend rubbing with warm earth, oil or pig's fat, adding 'Brandy or rum

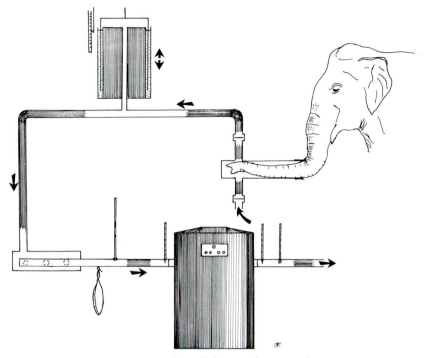

FIG. 4.3 *Benedict's breathalyser (after Benedict, 1936).*

and strychnine pills are useful'. If the elephant refused to stand after three or four hours of treatment then it was recommended a chicken was killed and the fresh blood rubbed in its nostrils and mouth as the smell of fresh blood arouses elephants. Since the chilling would be deep inside the elephant, rubbing warm potions onto its skin would hardly be likely to be very effective.

In 1905 a menagerie elephant in Sweden was taken to Ström in the Arctic Circle at 64° latitude where the temperature was −12 to −20°C. The elephant, dressed in a coat of reindeer skins and provided with boots, returned from this experience with only slight frostbite to its privates and recovered completely. Elephants have been recorded at over 3000 m on Mt Kilimanjaro and at the snowline on Mt Kenya at 4500 m. Night-time temperatures in West Africa can drop almost to freezing in elephant habitat and in much of southern Africa where elephants once roamed many degrees below freezing are experienced. In 1972 elephants in Hwange Park were subjected to subzero temperatures sometimes falling as low as −14.4°C for four months, and maintained condition.

BREATHALYSERS AND BEER DRINKERS

Using a special sort of 'breathalyser' fixed to the end of her trunk, Benedict found that of Jap's total water loss, 47% was lost via the lungs during respiration. The rest was from the skin, faeces and urine. This amounted to 22 kg in weight of water lost from the lungs and skin.

Jap discharged an average of $5\frac{1}{2}$ litres of urine at a time, with a maximum of $10\frac{1}{2}$. The daily total was about 50, or 13.6 cc for each kg of bodyweight. She also passed more than 2 kg of dissolved solids in the urine, of which 160 g were common salt.

Like expert beer drinkers who relax the throat and simply pour the beer down, an elephant does not appear to swallow when it drinks. Water is sucked up through the trunk and then squirted into the open mouth and throat. A 37 year old Asian bull elephant drank 212 litres of water at one go, comprising 25 trunkfuls. This is probably as much as an average elephant would usually drink in one day. Most drink only about once in 24 hours but up to 300 litres at one time may be consumed. In the Queen Elizabeth Park where the elephants are surrounded by easily accessible water, they would sometimes go for three days without drinking. At yet other times they would drink three times a day for three days in succession, but most of the time they drank slightly more frequently than once every 24 hours.

Despite the large water requirement, elephants which became trapped in a fenced ranch in an arid area of Kenya were able to survive for over 14 days without water, two aged 2–3 years dying on the 15th and 17th days. Desert-dwelling elephants in Mali often drink only once in three days, despite living in a near-desert environment with little shade. Those inhabiting Namibia's harsh Skeleton Coast may go four days without drinking.

In Uganda in the lands bordering the Nile, the elephants had no regular drinking pattern and their movements were very localized. This is in contrast to the arid regions of Kenya's Tsavo Park where they had a regular routine of drinking at night in the Galana River and feeding during the day 15 km away. They also conserved water and energy by resting from 10 am in the morning until 3 pm in the afternoon in the dry season, remaining in shade if they could find any.

AN UNEXPLAINED PUZZLE

In an emergency elephants resort to a unique aid to cooling, showering their head, ears and back with water that they suck out of the mouth with the trunk and spray over themselves. This was known to the early hunters in South Africa who pursued elephants on horseback and Sparrman writing in 1775 believed it was kept in reserve in the trunk. It was mentioned in the 16th century by the Persian Abul Fazl in an account of the elephant stables of the Emperor Akbar: '... an elephant frequently with his trunk takes water out of his stomach and sprinkles himself with it ...'.

Tennent wrote in 1859:

> The fact of his being enabled to retain a quantity of water and discharge it at pleasure has been long known to every observer of the habits of the animal ... [And of elephants that had just been captured] ... inserting the extremity of the trunk in their mouths,

they withdrew a quantity of water, which they discharged over their backs, repeating the operation again and again ... I was astonished at the quantity of water thus applied ... Seeing that the herd had now been twenty-four hours without access to water of any kind,...the supply of moisture an elephant is capable of containing in the receptacle attached to his stomach must be very considerable.

Yet despite these references it was regarded as a fable until well into the 1960s. I witnessed it in 1965 when an immobilized cow elephant started to become overheated lying on her side in the sun. Small calves whose mothers had died were seen doing it in Tsavo during drought, spraying themselves repeatedly as they became heat-stressed standing by the carcases of their dead mothers.

Anatomists from the 19th century to the present day are unable to comprehend where the water comes from, although there is plenty of liquid in the stomach and perhaps it is able to exert sufficient suction with the trunk to draw up some of this.

From an examination of drawings of dissections made about 1750 by the Dutch scientist Petrus Camper, anatomist, surgeon, gynaecologist, hygienist, expert in medical law and veterinary surgery, and Sir Everard Home in 1828, Professor Owen, counted as Britain's greatest comparative anatomist, appeared to imply that the caecum might be a water reservoir. An anonymous writer in 1850 thought the folds of the cardiac end of the stomach, figured by Camper from his dissection of an Asian elephant which died in the Paris *Jardin des Plantes*, held water. But Camper never stated any such thing, simply remarking that the folds seemed to be a type of special division. These folds are considered to be too shallow to hold any significant quantity of water and the pharyngeal or throat pouch can only hold less than a gallon.

An Asian elephant dissected in 1847 was reported to have a small muscle between its windpipe and its oesophagus, which it was suggested might be an aid in retrieving water from the stomach or perhaps to help in dilating the windpipe during expiration of air from the lungs. The muscle was not found again until 1980 and then only in 1 in 3 elephants examined.

AN ANIMAL WITH FOUR STOMACHS

A scientist posed the question: 'Does a 5000 kg elephant bull eat one thousand times as much food per day as a 5 kg dik-dik?' The answer is no, for the daily food intake of the dik-dik is about 175–200 g, representing 3.5–4% of its body weight. For an elephant to achieve the same proportion it would have to feed for up to four times as long as it does. The day is not long enough for it to do this, since it feeds for more than 12 hours as it is. It can get by with only 50 kg of dry weight of food per day or about 1% of its body weight. A 4 g shrew, on the other hand, eats one half of its own body weight in food per day and requires some 100 times the supply of oxygen and nutrients that a 4 tonne elephant does per unit weight.

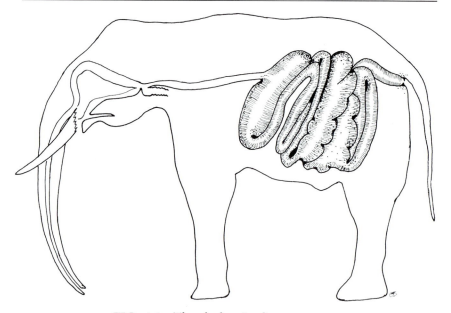

FIG. 4.4   *The elephant's alimentary tract.*

Why should this be so? The answer was made clear in the experiment with LSD. Like the ratio of the surface area of a cube to its volume, the basal or maintenance energy requirements of a wide range of mammals has been found to vary according to the three quarters power of body size, or near enough. Hence the basic maintenance requirements of an elephant should be only 180 times that of the dik-dik and not 1000. Larger animals can support their lower specific metabolic or energy requirements by either eating less food per day, or by eating food of a lower quality, or by a combination of both.

In spite of the fact that the specific metabolic rate decreases with increasing body size, that is, the rate of energy turnover becomes slower, gut capacity remains a constant fraction of body size in a wide range of African herbivores, including the elephant. This means that the larger ungulates should be able to tolerate a lower minimum dietary quality than smaller species because they can take in more food, but they also tend to eat less food per day as a proportion of their size than do small herbivores. The elephant makes use of this low dietary option, being able to eat both grass and woody vegetation, either the one or the other of which tends to be of low quality when the elephant is selecting the alternative. Because its nutritional requirements per unit weight for mainten-ance are lower than those for smaller and shorter lived species, a habitat can support higher numbers of elephants than it can of, say, impalas. For whereas 100 impalas may be equivalent in weight to an average elephant, the same elephant's metabolic requirements are equal to only a little more than one quarter of this number.

Generally the elephant's forage is very woody or stemmy with a low protein content, but it is also fermented inefficiently with a high loss of methane gas and a low breakdown of cellulose by the gut bacteria. So, not being a ruminant, it cannot do well on limited quantities of high fibre food; it must pass as much volume through as possible, breaking down the soluble sugars in its simple stomach and fermenting the fibre in the caecum. The digestibility of hay is about 44% in the elephant compared with the cow's 60%, sheep's 61% and horse's 53%, when fed on the same type of hay. Thus the elephant is not very efficient in its digestion. But the forage that it ingests in a semi-arid area like Tsavo has an organic matter digestibility of 55–65%, with a chemical composition roughly equivalent to good English meadow hay, although much higher in calcium.

Scientists prefer to make their calculations in terms of dry weight, for obviously the weight of fresh vegetation varies according to the amount of moisture which it contains. Weight of the stomach fill also does not take account of the large quantities of water elephants take in and we must remember that it is the rate at which the food passes through the body, not the size of the stomach fill itself, which is important.

An Asian elephant needs 108 g of dry plant matter per day per kg of metabolic body weight and 6 g of digestible crude protein. This means that a large 6.7 tonne bull elephant would require a total of almost 67 kg per day including nearly 4 kg of protein. This is similar to calculations arrived at for the African elephant, translating into about 167 kg of fresh forage of which about one third is used for maintenance. This consumption represents some 10–22% of the amount of vegetation produced in a given habitat.

Due to the high intake of forage many plant poisons are assimilated into the bloodstream before they can be broken down into less harmful substances, so the elephant tends to select plants which depend mainly upon structural defences – thorns and tough sheaths – rather than chemical toxins. But yet it cannot make as much use of a high fibre diet as can a ruminant. Variety is therefore important, supplementing its more toxic fibrous diet of the leaves and shoots of trees and shrubs with a grass diet low in toxins.

But it takes a great deal of poison to affect an elephant, as was discovered in Geneva in 1820 when an attempt was made to put down a 22 year old Asian bull which had begun to chase its attendants due to musth. First it was administered 3 oz of prussic acid in 10 oz of brandy with no effect, so this was followed by 3 oz of arsenic mixed with honey and sugar, also without effect. Finally they resorted to a cannonball through the head at close range with instantaneous effect.

By placing his strips of old car rubber inner tube inside loaves of bread Benedict, in his experiments with patient Jap, observed a passage time between ingestion of food and its excretion to be from 21 to 54.5 hours. When oranges were fed to a semi-wild elephant at Tsavo, the first peel was excreted at 11 hours and all had been passed by 19. More recently, two 11 year old African cow elephants at Knowsley Safari Park were studied by feeding them beetroot, which they probably found more to their taste than pieces of old inner tube. The colour from the beetroot appeared in the droppings in 21–46 hours. Other workers with African elephants have found the average retention time of food in the gut to be 33 hours. Food passage time varies with quality of the food and in round figures we may say food begins to pass out after about 12 hours and that it is all eliminated by about 50.

The 150 kg of fresh green food that an elephant takes in each day produce an enormous quantity of methane gas. Benedict calculated that it amounted to 767 litres but more recent workers have calculated it to be about 1859, equivalent to 73.4 megajoules of energy. This represents a loss of 27% of its digestible energy, compared with only 5–12% in ruminants. Energy from the digested food which would otherwise be used by the elephant is used to produce the methane. The amount wasted is equal to that required to burn an average gas fire for ten hours. Put another way, at present-day British prices the elephant wastes 32.62 pence of gas per day. A population of 50 000 elephants, such as that in northern Botswana, is therefore wasting the equivalent of £16 312 per day, a staggering £6 million a year!

Roughly one quarter of this passes out through the trunk and the rest through the anus. Despite what Aristotle said, the elephant is thus not a belcher like a ruminant. The methane which passes out through the trunk as it breathes is absorbed by the body fluids and carried to the lungs where it diffuses into the air. The same cannot be said of the remaining 1400 litres which pass out, unquietly, as gas.

So Capable of Understanding

'There is not any creature so capable of understanding as an Elephant. They are apt to learne, remember, meditate, and conceive such things as a man can hardly perform,' wrote Edward Topsell in 1607. Aristotle referred to the elephant as 'the beast that passeth all others in wit and mind'. Is the elephant as intelligent as the ancients believed? Is it true that an elephant never forgets?

Next to the sperm and blue whales, with a brain volume of 6.5 litres the elephant possesses the largest brain of any living creature. In its cerebral development and anatomical complexity the brain is second only to the primates. That of the African bull weighs up to 6 kg, that of the cow being smaller. The olfactory lobes are large as is the cerebellum or motor region.

Despite its absolute size it is relatively small in relation to body size when compared with that of man or the higher apes. An elephant weighing 75 times the weight of a man has a brain weighing only twice as much. At birth it is 35% of the adult weight, compared with 26% in man and 90% in most other mammals. The weight of the brain of a near-term 115 kg bull foetus has been recorded as 4.1 kg; thus the ratio of brain to body weight at birth changes from 1:30 to 1:1000 in the mature bull. This compares with man's 1:50 or less in the adult.

The elephant's capacity for intelligence and bodily co-ordination is surpassed only by the higher primates and it shares several traits in the anatomy of its brain with man. It has a large cerebral cortex, the 'grey matter' which controls much of the animal's activities, and a large neopallium, the area associated with memory, but the cerebral hemispheres do not cover the cerebellum as they do in man and other primates, regarded as a very advanced feature.

Although the ancients believed that the elephant possessed vast intelligence and memory, G.P. Sanderson, the head of the government elephant-catching station at Mysore in India in the last century, from his wide experience with domesticated Asian elephants did not consider that it was particularly intelligent. It was quick to learn but wanting in originality. Cuvier did not think that its sagacity equalled that of a dog and some other species of carnivore but William Hornaday, Director of the New York Zoo, in 1922 classed the Asian elephant as the most intelligent animal after the chimpanzee and orang-utan, placing it above the horse and the dog.

As circus trainers well know, once an elephant does learn something then it does not forget it. It is said that timber elephants never forget the command to sit down. In one authenticated case in India a trained cow escaped and lived wild for 14 years until she was seen by a catching party. Noting that she appeared unafraid, one of the party shouted out the command to sit down and she promptly did so! He then ran up and seized her by the ear, climbed onto her back and rode her home with her calf following behind as if she had never been out of harness.

By the time it is 25 years old, a well-trained Asian elephant should be able to understand 24 separate words of command, as well as the signals from its handler. Altogether it can learn up to about 100 words and phrases of command, in addition to prods with the bull hook and kicks or pressure from the mahout's feet.

In 1957 a German psychologist conducted a learning experiment with a five year old Asian elephant. The experiment was designed to find out if the elephant could identify different symbols and remember them. This was achieved by painting the symbols, for example a circle and a square, on the lids of each of two wooden boxes. The box marked with the square contained food, that marked with the circle was empty. After 330 tries the elephant learnt the difference. Further pairs of symbols were then used, which the elephant mastered more and more quickly, until for the 4th pair it took only ten tries. Eventually the elephant was able to master 20 pairs, making very few mistakes.

A year later the test was repeated with 13 of the pairs, the elephant scoring between 73% and 100%. The only difficulty with the experiment was that sometimes the elephant became frustrated and simply ran at the boxes and smashed them up. It found that to be a much easier way to get at the food.

The right tusk of an elephant is usually more worn than the left indicating that elephants tend to be 'right-handed', although observations on zoo elephants have suggested that an elephant prefers to twist its trunk to the left when using it, rather than to the right. The worn tusk is often referred to as the 'servant' as opposed to the 'master' tusk. Pliny's theory was that 'they spare the point of one so that it may not be blunt for fighting and use the other as an implement for digging roots and thrusting massive objects forward'. But the difference has deeper reasons than that.

Bushman elephant hunters in Botswana assert that if one is charged by an elephant in a tight corner, one's best chance of escape is to run *at* the elephant and pass it on its left side for, being right-handed it cannot turn to the left quickly. But if you run past on its right side then it will swing round and have you. Remember, if trying this, that his left is your right. Not that I am seriously suggesting that any reader *should* try; rather one should take the advice of William Bosman, written in 1705: '. . . we resolved never for the future to come so near an elephant; to which I would not advise any man who hath the least tenderness for his life'.

The American circus elephant trainer 'Slim' Lewis recommended that a dangerous elephant, especially a bull tusker, should always be approached from the left-hand side; a remarkable confirmation of Bushman wisdom.

Elephants usually lie down on their left side both to sleep and to die, no doubt so that they may still be in a position to get up quickly, attacking to their right if needs be. Even mammoths have been found to have died lying on the left side.

TEARS FOR TIMUR

Elephants have poor visual discernment, relying on movement in detecting objects. The size of the eyeball is almost identical with that of man and thus small for such a large creature. But only a small part of the retina of an eye is used so an eye does not increase in size in proportion to the body. The pupil and the iris are round and the iris usually hazel-coloured. The elephant and the wild pig are the only ungulates with a round pupil, normally associated with forest or shade-adapted animals and regarded as a primitive feature. This gives elephants a limited angle of vision, but they can see forwards better than sideways or to the rear. Their eyesight seems poor in bright light, but good in deep forest cover and on dull days, when it is said the slightest of movements can be detected at up to 45 m. They are not very good, however, at discerning shapes and can be approached very closely if one moves slowly enough. There is little evidence of colour perception but they dislike red.

Although elephants shed tears there is no functional tear gland. The tears come from another relatively well-developed gland termed the Harderian gland, the function of which is to moisten the third eyelid or nictitating membrane. Unlike that of a cat this nictitating membrane does not cover the whole eye.

At the ancient battle of Delhi in 1398, Prince Timur is said to have captured 3000 elephants from his opponent Prince Mohammed (it was probably 300), which wept at the defeat of their master. But it is alleged that the weeping was caused by Timur ordering snuff to be rubbed into their eyes.

Some claim nevertheless that elephants do cry. 'Slim' Lewis alleges that when he punished a young cow Asian elephant which could not learn her tricks, the elephant lay down on her side 'tears streaming down her face and sobs racking her huge body'. When Randall Moore's big tame bull African elephant died of salmonella infection, one of its young cow companions was found the next day

FIG. 4.5   *Only elephants, primates and pigs have a round pupil.*

to have tears running down the sides of her face which continued for two days. But when Andrew Sparrman related that a wounded elephant when it cannot escape 'will in a manner weep, the tears running down its cheeks', this was undoubtedly a reference to the temporal gland secreting when an elephant is excited.

Jap's respiration rate of ten breaths per minute when standing fell to 4–5 per minute when lying asleep, suggesting that the decrease in metabolism in the sleeping animal is about 50% of that when awake, compared with about 10% in man. Elephants close their eyes in sleep, captive elephants sleeping for 2–4 hours at night, although healthy wild Asian elephants only go into deep sleep for about half an hour lying down, but doze on their feet for an hour before this. In the wild deep sleep takes place in the early hours of the morning, between about 4 and 7 am. At this time they sleep deeply and can even be heard snoring loudly. There is usually also a shorter rest period in the early afternoon to shelter from the heat of the day, when the calves may sleep again but the adults just doze.

Aristotle corrected the erroneous belief that elephants only slept while standing. At night most lie down to sleep but calves often lie down and sleep during the day when the family group is standing resting. Even big bulls sometimes lie down and have a nap.

FIG. 4.6   *A rare sight of a bull elephant sleeping during the day, using a termite mound as a cushion.*

THE STRENGTH OF A FLEA

It comes as a surprise to many to learn that the elephant is not a strong animal when its size is taken into consideration. Weight for weight a man is estimated to be one tenth stronger than an elephant and a horse one quarter stronger than a man. So some 84 ten stone men would be required to do the work of one 6 tonne elephant and not 94; or six horses and not seven. This is because of the scaling effect of body size and the heavier skeleton that the elephant must move.

At the end of the last century the peculiar interest of Lord Rothschild led him to observe 'performing' fleas at a circus moving objects many times their own weight. He was greatly impressed with their apparently enormous strength and considered the feat equivalent to a man dragging two full-sized elephants round a cricket ground. But later, when scaling and body size were understood, it was pointed out that the feat of the performing fleas could be more accurately compared to a man dragging two sheep round a cricket ground because, as the body of an animal becomes smaller so the relative, but not the absolute, power of a muscle increases. The great strength of the flea is therefore more apparent than real.

Chapter 5

MATING AND GROWING UP: REPRODUCTION AND GROWTH

The penis should not be despised. In a large male elephant, as most rogues are, the skin can be made into quite a useful golf bag.

E.L. Walker, 1923

THE PRIVATE LIFE OF THE ELEPHANT

I DO not think that anyone would despise the phallic propensity of the elephant, even if they are not golfers, although Aristotle considered that its 27 kg was disproportionately small compared to the size of the animal. But then, logic has never been a strong point as far as man's observations upon the sexual anatomy of the elephant have been concerned. In spite of the fact that about 350 BC Aristotle had asserted: 'The female has the pudendum in the same position as the udder of the sheep, and when excited with desire, it is lifted outwards, so as to be ready for copulation with the male . . .', and that the cow elephant 'bends down and divides her legs, and the male mounts upon her'; medieval writers preferred the assertion that the genitals were put on backwards. Thus elephants were obliged to mate back to back, for being excessively modest they preferred to look the other way while about it. Even then, stated the scribes, the male was such a chaste creature that he had no desire for offspring.

These ancient beliefs are not surprising when it is realized how seldom mating is observed in the wild. Even Aristotle was aware of this: 'The difficulty of seeing copulation causes this difference of opinion respecting the period of gestation'. This is not because the bull has no desire for offspring, but because the cow may only come into heat once in every 3–5, or even more, years. The period of heat may last for no longer than two days although the maximum may be ten. The African elephant then comes into heat again about every 16 days and in the Asian 18–27 day cycles have been recorded. But if mating is successful and she conceives it will be at least another three years before she mates again and this will only happen about ten times in her lifetime. Thus without continually watching elephants the chances of seeing mating taking place are slim. I witnessed it only once during more than 30 years in Africa, but naturally those that study elephants fulltime have had their pruriency with respect to the private life of the elephant rewarded more often.

John Corse wrote in 1790: 'The mode of connection between the male and female is now ascertained beyond the possibility of a doubt ... in a manner exactly similar to the conjugation of the horse with a mare'. Lt Col. G.H.Evans, one-time head of the veterinary department in Burma, finally settled the argument in 1910:

> The question as to the manner in which fecundation of the female is brought about was set at rest at Thayetmyo [Burma], where two elephants were observed in the act and in the position common to quadrupeds, but in order to place the matter beyond the possibility of contradiction, Mr Porter, Schoolmaster of the Bedford Regiment, took an excellent photograph; the trunks and tails came out rather indistinctly; this, Mr Porter afterwards informed me, was due to the fact that they were in constant and rapid motion.

Quite so.

Elephants were bred in ancient Rome, or at least calved there, and despite an early Indian superstition that it was unlucky, the Moghul Emperor Akbar bred them in the late 16th century. But although Asian elephants have been kept in captivity since ancient times, they do not breed very well when confined. This was explained as a refusal on their part to provide slaves for the use of man, but may be more probably due to the fact that if a young captive bull starts to show a natural interest in a cow, he is immediately discouraged by his mahout. Eventually the bulls learn that they must not take an interest in the opposite sex and abandon all thought of it. What the mahout in effect does is to replace the role of the dominant bull in musth, which is able to suppress musth in lower ranking bulls. This is perhaps not the answer which Charles Darwin expected when he wrote in his *Origin of Species*:

He who is able to explain why the elephant, and a multitude of other animals, are incapable of breeding when kept under only partial confinement in their native country, will be able to explain the primary cause of hybrids being so generally sterile.

No, the apparent sterility of the captive elephant does not help at all to illustrate Darwin's poser, for overworking them can also be a cause. Where working elephants are turned loose into the jungle to feed at night, as in Burma, then they do reproduce successfully.

Sparrman commented on the inability to make captive Asian elephants mate, even though the bull may be in rut, not realizing that the cow must also be on heat before she would allow it. But he had an ingenious theory to explain the impasse:

> In all probability, therefore, this repugnance in a point which nature, on the other side, visibly encourages all her creatures, proceeds from the peculiar make of the elephant, rendering it partly unfit for the performance of these rites; an impediment which nature, perhaps, found it necessary to set up against the too great increase of these gigantic animals; as, were it otherwise, by defoliating and laying waste the whole extent of the warmer climates, they would bring destruction upon their own species. [And]
> Elephants (excepting some males, which, being either too old or too young to contend with their stronger rivals, are hunted away by them) always keep in herds; so that while some few are, perhaps, prevented by the jealousy of others from copulating in the early part of life . . .

Aristotle was surprisingly well informed about elephant reproduction, stating that the bull was ready again for mating at the end of three years (it of course being the cow which was ready again). He also considered that reproduction was seasonal, taking place in the spring. The cow reached puberty at ten years of age, 15 at the latest, and the bull at five or six. Gestation length was two years, but he quotes others as believing it was from 18 months to three years.

Having got his estimates of puberty pretty close he then goes on to say that they begin to mate at 20 years, which is average for the captive Asian elephant.

The length of gestation for African elephants in zoos is 660 days. That observed in wild African elephants at Amboseli averaged 656 days in the range 652–660 days. In the Asian elephant it is shorter by about ten days.

It was probably Perrault's description in 1681 of the reproductive anatomy of the cow African elephant which died at Versailles which led Sparrman to refer to the 'peculiar make of the elephant', for the female opening is not close to the anus as in other mammals, but in front of the hind legs and forwardly directed. So the male organ has to be proportionately long to reach there and also S-shaped to counter the forwardly directed position. The arrangement in the cow is occasioned by the near vertical position of the pelvic girdle, but if the female opening was under the tail then the bull during mating would have to place much of his weight on the cow's back and a bull elephant can weigh three times as much as a cow. As it is he has to lean backwards onto his own hind legs and so little weight is placed upon her. In fact, the bull's organ never enters the vagina, but only the elongated urino-genital canal.

THE SEASON OF BIRTH

The first modern scientific studies on the reproduction of elephants were conducted by Perry from 1947 to 1950 in Uganda. It was formerly thought that elephants bred throughout the year in Africa, but this was subsequently shown in many cases to be due to an error in predicting conception and birth dates from estimated age of the foetus. The cube root of the weight of the foetus (that is, the value which multiplied by itself three times gives the weight, which reduces it to a linear measurement) in a wide range of mammalian species has been shown to increase, on average, in a straight line as the foetus grows. This relationship has been used to predict the time of conception or birth from a known foetal weight. However there is a lag period when the cell is dividing but not of measurable weight, which has been roughly estimated at one tenth of the pregnancy period when pregnancy lasts more than 400 days.

Studies in Zimbabwe indicated the lag period for the elephant was longer than for other species and a factor of 21% was probably more correct, followed by a faster rate of growth of the foetus. Also the weight at birth was probably closer to 106 kg than 120, more in line with the recorded weights of Asian elephant calves. When predictions of conception or birth were made using this revised formula, small foetuses were dated two months earlier and a distinct seasonality was revealed. Breeding appeared to be associated with rainfall on a month to month basis and was restricted to the wet season. In Zimbabwe this occurs from October to May with the main rains in December to March. If applied to the Uganda populations a much more distinct seasonal pattern would probably be revealed there.

Like many other herbivores, elephants react to the wet seasons. The fresh growth of grass tends to bring the cows into heat, especially after a period of dry years, and the large aggregations which sometimes take place at the beginning of the wet seasons result in synchronized mating. This dependence on rainfall tends to make populations breed at the same time, although this is less likely in Uganda near to the equator.

By virtue of the 22 months pregnancy which follows, the earliest calves are born about two months before the rains bring on the fresh growth. The result is that by the time their demands for milk are vigorous there is plenty of green grass for the cow to produce milk, grass being more important in this respect than browse.

A 1787 Dutch account in Sri Lanka noted that all cow elephants calved at the same season. In Burma it is said that most calves are born between March and May. In India Sanderson reported that most were born in September to November, with a few in other months. This would imply a peak towards the end of the rains, whereas one would have expected mating to have taken place in

June to July with calving in about March to April. Others have questioned the existence of any seasonal peak in India.

THE BULL ELEPHANT

Aristotle knew what some hunters are unaware of even today, that the testes of the elephant are intra-abdominal, situated close to the kidneys. Neither the reason for the abdominal position nor how temperature regulation is effected have been satisfactorily explained but the reason for their intra-abdominal position may be the same reason that the cow's breasts are between her forelegs – because the hind end of the elephant is too close to the ground for comfort. Even so their 6 kg weight is relatively small compared with some mammals, representing only about 0.1% of the body weight. In man it is even less, about 0.08%; and in the domestic bull it is almost 1.25%, in the dog almost 2% and in the rat almost 9%.

The bull African elephant's reproductive tract is similar to that of the Asian, differing from that of other mammals by lacking any apparent cooling mechanism. Other mammals have a network of blood vessels surrounding the testes which are designed to keep them at a relatively constant temperature below that of the body. It also lacks any obvious epididymis, the finely coiled tube at the top of the testis where the sperms are stored as they are produced. There is a tube of course (the Wolffian duct) and it is some 50 m long but relatively primitive in nature and not coiled like that of other mammals.

It holds a vast number of sperms, estimated at some 250 quadrillion (a million multiplied by itself four times), almost $2\frac{1}{2}$ times the number found in the ram. The ducts carry only immotile sperm at the distal end, but an alkaline salt solution is sufficient to induce movement. The sperms are similar in size, appearance and structure to those of ungulates.

The testes which produce this incredible number of sperms grow in size throughout life, reaching more than 3 kg each in weight in a bull of over 40 years of age. Like man and a number of other mammals in this respect, they enlarge in the foetus due to growth of the non-sperm-producing tissue, so that just before birth they are much larger than they are subsequently in the young bull up to puberty, but they shrink rapidly at birth.

Aristotle stated that 'All that Ctesias [400 BC] said about the semen of the elephant is false', namely that it hardened so much that it became like amber. Whatever else which was false that Ctesias, the earliest surviving Greek writer on the elephant, had to say about its reproduction has been lost.

In recent years sperm has been collected from drugged wild African elephants and deep frozen for use in the artificial insemination of zoo elephants, since adult bull elephants are generally not kept by zoos because of the expense and difficulty of handling. The sperm was collected by electroejaculation as in cattle, stored in egg yolk mixed with citrate and frozen. It was found to survive freezing and thawing just as well as cattle sperm.

In 1889 a recalcitrant 35 year old Asian bull elephant belonging to an

American circus, who was 'so vicious as to imperil the lives of his attendants' and furthermore was at an age 'at which refractoriness should yield to obedience and docility', was castrated in an attempt to make him more amenable to these Victorian concepts of good behaviour. The operation took $1\frac{1}{2}$ hours and hardly surprisingly the unfortunate beast only lived for 57 hours after this somewhat drastic remedy for refractoriness. Nonplussed, the veterinarian who performed it considered that it could be done in half an hour with suitable instruments and should then be successful. Evans was to write in 1910:

> With a view to preventing that peculiar sexual disturbance known as *musth*, many attempts have been made to castrate these creatures; but owing to the immense size of the carcase and the peculiar position of the testicles, the operation is necessarily a very formidable and dangerous one.

Nevertheless the only bull kept at the Belgian domestication centre of Gangala-na-Bodio in Zaïre was successfully castrated.

The onset of puberty in the African bull ranges from seven years in healthy populations to as late as 18 years in malnourished ones. Probably 12 years is an average figure and usually most have reached sexual maturity by 15 years. An Asian bull has been known to mate successfully at nine but normally he does not mate until he is 20–25 years of age, since before this he is prevented by older bulls.

THE COW ELEPHANT

The cow elephant shares with whales the phenomenon of possessing multiple corpora lutea or 'white bodies', the bodies in the ovary which produce the egg and the hormone progesterone, essential for the maintenance of pregnancy. Whereas most other species only have one, in the first half of pregnancy the elephant has from two to as many as 26 in one ovary, with an average of almost seven, and they tend to stand out exceptionally prominently on the surface. One set, probably including the one which produces the egg, appears to last throughout pregnancy and for about two months afterwards. Traces may remain for up to four years after the cow has given birth. Nevertheless, only one egg is produced at each cycle for the elephant is what is termed a 'monovular polyoestrous' animal, one which produces a single egg but has repeated periods of heat. Heat in the African cow lasts 2–6 days, with a possible maximum of ten. In the Indian 2–8 days has been recorded. But to produce the numerous corpora lutea she first undergoes several sterile cycles or 'silent heats', the purpose of which may be to accumulate a certain minimal amount of luteal tissue, the tissue of the corpus luteum, before pregnancy can take place. Unlike other mammals the corpus luteum appears to secrete very little, if any, progesterone and possibly many corpora lutea are required to build up a sufficient volume of this hormone.

In the foetus the ovaries, like the testes in the male, enlarge in the second half of pregnancy so that they may be bigger at birth than in the young cow, but they shrink immediately after birth.

In the African cow puberty is attained from about 9–18 years, with 12 probably the average. The earliest recorded conception is at seven years. In the relatively undisturbed population of Amboseli the earliest first conception was at ten.

In the Asian elephant puberty in the cow is estimated to occur at 16–18 years. A captive bull Asian elephant was observed mating with a four year old cow, but she did not conceive until she was between six and seven. The cow normally attains puberty at a minimum age of about seven and usually all have attained it by 11.

At Amboseli cows have been observed to come into heat every three months if conception does not take place, although the length of the cycle in captive African elephants has been recorded as 16 days and for the Indian elephant 22 days. Conception was successful in 50–70% of the cows in heat at Amboseli, but it is very sensitive to environmental conditions, with drought inhibiting conception.

After the first calving, mating takes place while the cow is still suckling her calf but lactation ceases before the next parturition, the breasts developing noticeably about seven weeks before she gives birth.

The interval between birth and the next conception varies from nine months to about four years, but in an overcrowded population in Uganda this interval had increased to almost seven years. On average elephants at Amboseli gave birth once very five years, but in African elephants in general the average interval between births has been recorded as ranging from $2\frac{3}{4}$ years up to 13.

The calving interval in the Asian elephant is considered to be about 4.7 years, similar to that of the African. The 1787 Dutch manuscript referred to earlier recorded that in Sri Lanka elephants calved every three or four years.

Due to the placenta being of the zonary type, when the cow gives birth this leaves a thin horizontal scar in the uterus which may persist for up to 30 years. By counting the number of these scars in dead animals it is possible to tell the minimum number of calves that the animal has produced.

The reproductively active life of the African cow lasts until about the age of 52, a total period of 40 years. There is a peak in fertility at 18–19 years and it declines markedly after age 40. One cow at Amboseli gave birth at 52 but the calf died within a month; yet another which had not given birth for the previous nine years did so at the advanced age of 58, but again the calf failed to survive. In the Kruger Park 88% of cows older than 50 years in a sample of 42 were pregnant and producing milk, except for one old cow of 60 with only fragments of teeth left which was carrying a 19 month old foetus but was dry. In a Ugandan population the peak in cow fertility was not attained until between 30 and 40 years and from 45 years onwards there was a progressive decline until at the age of 55 the cows could no longer conceive.

COURTSHIP AND COQUETTES

Sanderson in 1878 realized that it is the cow which must be in season before mating can take place, but that it was not marked by any particular signs: 'In approaching a male elephant, a female desirous of his attentions utters certain sounds and courts his society; but only those conversant with elephants would notice this'.

It is indeed difficult to detect heat in the elephant unless you know what you are looking for, but the older cow does have a definite pattern of behaviour averaging four days – similar in duration in both elephants. In early heat the African cow shows highly visible behaviour related to her condition. It begins by singing a song to advertise her state. This siren song begins as slow, deep rumbles, rising gently and becoming stronger and higher in pitch, then sinking to silence again at the end, a series of intense, very low frequency calls. It may continue for half an hour and before long the lascivious singing cow will be surrounded by eager bulls.

The first day or two, with typical female contrariness she is wary of the suitors that she has called up and tries to avoid their approaches, moving in a characteristic manner with her head held high and her eyes wide open, avoiding the bulls trying to test her. These come up to her and placing the tip of their trunks on her genitals, then put it into their mouths to taste for hormones. If pursued by young bulls at this stage she tries to run away from them and protests vigorously against any attempt at mating with a loud, angry, pulsating roar. This has the effect of attracting other, higher ranking bulls who have previously shown little interest in the cow or her singing and who now drive the younger ones off.

At this time the cow will move away from her family group to avoid the bulls who follow her, using a greater stride and speed than normal, sometimes with her tail held out, but nevertheless looking back coquettishly over her shoulder as if to see if a bull is following. Indeed, her behaviour at this time may be designed to draw the bulls' attention to her. Usually only one bull follows and she moves in a half circle and comes back to her group again. But the pursuit may become a chase. Making a show of modesty the cow runs away, but like any coquette she does not run as fast from a bull in musth as she does from a young bull. When, if more than one bull is following her, the fastest running bull catches up and places his trunk on her back, having behaved at least with all decent propriety, like a playground game of tag these elephantine gambols cease and she stops. He then attempts to mount and she may run on again. When she finally stands he then mounts using his head and tusks as a lever, rearing up and placing his forefeet on her rump but sinking onto his hind legs. The cow then backs onto him and, as Aristotle noted, opens her legs. Actual mating then takes about 45 seconds and may be accompanied by deep groans from the bull.

On the three or four days in the peak of her heat she becomes guarded by bulls in musth and shows her liking for these older bulls by keeping close to them and standing when they attempt to mate with her. The dominant guarding bull only mounts her infrequently, all told about three times in 24 hours. Towards the end of her heat the dominant musth bull loses interest and leaves her to be guarded by lower ranking bulls. Bulls aged 35 and upwards accounted for almost nine tenths of observations of guarding behaviour.

When a bull succeeds in mating the cow then she may boast of the event loudly by calling repeatedly, giving utterance to two or more loud, low bellows, which may be repeated for up to 30 minutes and can probably be heard by other elephants at distances of several kilometres. When she announces a successful mating in this way it can elicit great excitement among members of the cow's own family. If they are present, they rush over to her, rumbling, screaming, trumpeting, urinating, defaecating and secreting from their temporal glands, in a contagious frenzy which has been termed 'mating pandemonium'. She herself may rub her head against the bull's shoulder.

The cow's calls attract more bulls to the scene which may result in a large bull finding her, whom she accepts as her suitor for anything from a few hours to as long as three days. One bull was seen to remain with a cow for over 18 hours, the cow keeping as close to him as possible so that she could feed and drink without harassment by other would-be suitors. Mating did not take place again until the next morning, 12 hours later, and this time the cow did not first run away. As before, when mating was announced by the cow, the family again raced over in great excitement.

By this time eight other bulls were present and if one got too close the musth bull would lunge at him, sending him running away with a groaning sound. When any tried to approach the cow she moved close to her lover. They stayed together for two more days mating only once more. By the fourth day the musth bull was beginning to lose interest and although the cow tried to keep him close to her he eventually let the other bulls separate her from him and then left. The other bulls then rushed in to try their luck and the cow ran from them but eventually gave herself to one large bull who mated with her. By the following morning all had lost interest and she returned to her calf.

The young and inexperienced cows who do not ally themselves to one bull get chased and harassed throughout their period of heat, often being repeatedly mated by a series of bulls of all ages. They learn by experience that it is best to stick to one partner who will defend them against the others, as being chased for 3–4 days is an exhausting experience. If they can attract and stay with a large musth bull then they can avoid this harassment for at least part of the time.

The young bulls do less chasing than would be expected from their numbers in the population and when they do so they are likely to be unsuccessful in mounting the cow. It is the large bulls which are the most successful at catching and mating.

Sometimes there is no form of courtship behaviour, the bull's movements being slow and the cow remaining passive during mounting. In one case a bored cow continued feeding while mating took place.

Sometimes a cow shows a little more enthusiasm by butting heads with the bull and entwining her trunk with his, and in yet other cases appears to show a preference for a bull by joining in his attack on another suitor. When a bull repeatedly attempted to mount a small cow which fled from him, he chased her for two minutes until another cow came up and chased him off. But more often other elephants, including other bulls, appear to take no notice and remain passive, even when mating takes place in the middle of large herds.

In some cases rather more romantic activity takes place, such as the bull caressing the cow with his trunk, putting the tip of his trunk into the cow's mouth and then gently butting the cow. It seems that the elephants of Amboseli, where most observations have been made, lack this finesse and even less so at Manyara where the cow generally remains silent after mating.

When I witnessed mating in Uganda, for the greater part of the time the cow and the attendant bulls were almost completely inactive, standing about or idly feeding. These long periods of inactivity were interspersed with short periods of intense activity when the cow was usually chased in a circle and then mounted, four mountings taking place in less than two hours.

Behaviour in the Asian elephant is similar except that prior to mating the couple may stand head to head with their mouths open attempting a clumsy form of elephantine French kissing, trying to make mouth to mouth contact while at the same time pawing one another by intertwining their trunks. They may also circle, examining each other's privates. The bull also often presses his chin on the cow's back or shoulders, sometimes trying to give her love bites in the neck region. This often leads to a little more coquettishness on the part of the cow who walks off, the bull following with his trunk on her back until she stops and he consummates the act. This more refined form of courtship apart, mounting and mating are the same in both elephants. Although some gentle head-to-head sparring occasionally occurs in African elephants, circling and biting have never been seen. But Asian elephants are otherwise less demonstrative and the cow has only been recorded as showing 'some excitement' after mating by trumpeting softly, flapping her ears or whisking her tail. The bull just moves off and remains silent.

It is believed that antagonism of the matriarch to the younger cows in her family group when she is in heat may prevent them from coming into heat until she herself has been satisfied. As a result they are likely to breed later than the dominant and therefore older cows. It is the matriarch who leads the family group from the dry season home range to the best rainy season areas, where the majority of mating takes place, and thus benefits from first pickings from the bulls.

The author of a 12th century bestiary, repeating Pliny and wistfully moralizing, stated that elephants 'never quarrel about their wives, for adultery is unknown to them'. This monkish scribe would have been disappointed to learn that, on the contrary, it is what scientists term a 'highly competitive polygynous system', meaning that the bulls fight for the cows which mate with many more than one. At first there is no competition, but as the cow's heat progresses so a large bull assumes mastery and drives other lesser bulls away. Thus the chances of the calves of the same mother having the same father are probably rather slim due to the 4–5 year birth interval, the death rate of large bulls and the fact that it is usually only the musth bulls which mate successfully with a cow and they are sexually active for only a few months in the year.

Elephant mating then is a rather passive, unexciting affair, for there is no defence of territories or excessive combat. This takes place elsewhere and most bull elephants already know their place so that only a limited amount of challenging for a cow takes place, consisting of head butting and clashing of tusks. Such halfheartedness is not always the case and bloody and horrendous fights can take place between competing bulls probably in musth, as described later. In one non-violent incident, a frustrated subdominant bull was seen to give vent to his petulance by bellowing and rolling on the ground.

The cow mates with the highest ranking bull in any given situation and may receive several bulls in her 2–4 day period of heat as other bulls arrive on the scene and displace the former ones. How effective these other matings are is not known; whether, for instance, it is only the mating at the peak of heat, just before its termination, that is likely to be successful, in which case conception is likely to be monopolized by a dominant bull. For many years this situation existed at Amboseli, but in Ruaha where breeding is seasonal it was calculated in one area there were 195 mature bulls for every cow on heat. Thus there would be much competition for the cow's favours and a continual turnover of the most successful bulls.

BIRTH

The weight of the calf at birth is about 106 kg but it has been put as high as 120 for the bull, the cow not exceeding about 100, and it stands some 0.85 m at the shoulder. In captive Asian elephants in America, the weight of the calf at birth ranged from 70.5–102.3 kg for a bull and one cow calf weighed 109 kg. These mothers conceived at about seven years of age.

The weight at birth equals about 3.5% of the weight of the mother, compared with 6–7% in man and sometimes more than 10% in some domestic animals and smaller ungulates, such as the medium-sized antelopes. Thus there is a lower peak investment in reproduction relative to the maintenance of the mother's energy requirements, but the lifetime investment in the young is probably similar. Total metabolic or energy cost of reproduction is directly proportional to maternal size, so the net effect is a reduction in reproductive effort as size increases. But calf survival is high compared with smaller species and the period of maternal care is longer so the cow must, on average, look after more calves for a longer period and thus produce more milk in her lifetime, even though the rate of milk production is less of a burden.

Twins occasionally occur, comprising about 1% of births in both species, although out of 85 births in Namibia almost 5% were twins, including one pair due to two eggs; a more common type of twinning in man than the splitting of one egg. The two offspring are seldom reared, one usually dying within a few months. There is one record of triplets in a shot elephant.

Birth is quick because the birth canal is almost vertical in position and the baby is small in relation to the mother's body size. But it is not always easy and labour may take four hours, while the remains have been found of a cow which died giving birth.

But if few have witnessed the mating of elephants, then even fewer have been present at a birth. This led to the old beliefs that the cows retreated to 'calving grounds' or that birth took place at night. Such observations as have been made on the African elephant in the wild show that the mother-to-be does not go off on her own to give birth, although at Amboseli half of the cows left their families for a few days to two months in dry years after giving birth but in wet years less than 10% did so, and then only for a day or less.

Before giving birth the mother-to-be's behaviour is almost unchanged. A cow in labour may repeatedly walk backwards a few paces, kneel on the hindlegs bringing her stomach close to the ground, lie down and get up again, between continuing to feed. One cow behaving thus was in a group of other cows and calves who during this time took no notice and births may be ignored by the rest of the herd. But here suddenly there was considerable commotion with much rumbling and some trumpeting as the group gathered round a newborn baby which had suddenly appeared on the ground.

Once the calf appeared the mother and the other largest cow in the group began to remove the foetal membranes which covered it, using trunk, tusks and forefeet with great delicacy, but this may be done by the mother alone and is not always gentle. The rest of the group continued to show excitement, with prolonged rumbling and standing with ears spread and heads held erect in the alert position, while some raised their trunks and extended them in the direction of the calf to scent it. Two elephants faced outwards as if on guard. But this only lasted for about ten minutes and they resumed feeding and drinking as if nothing untoward had happened.

After removing the foetal membranes the mother tried to stimulate the baby to move and get onto its feet, prodding it with trunk, tusks and forefoot, even grasping the baby's head and lifting it from the ground with her trunk and tusks. One or two of the other cows assisted from time to time. Some 20 minutes later the baby managed to stand up but promptly fell down again and it was not until another ten minutes had passed that it could stand without falling over, find its mother's breasts and suckle for 1–2 minutes.

Other calves have been seen to get up in 12 minutes, but are unable to stay up until after some 37. One bull calf was walking fairly steadily within minutes of birth and was so adventurous that the mother had to keep restraining him with her trunk. Some have been seen to walk at 40 minutes, others at about an hour.

The mother meanwhile occasionally scraped the ground with her forefoot and from time to time blew sand over herself with her trunk, which is believed to be a comfort behaviour, perhaps like stroking herself. She then seized pieces of the foetal membranes with her trunk, waved them about and ate several. Other elephants also seized pieces and waved them about but did not eat them. By this time most of the rest of the group had wandered on and only one other cow and a young bull remained. While the mother went and drank the cow looked after the baby, fussing over it and touching it repeatedly with her trunk. After an hour the family moved slowly away with the baby moving somewhat unsteadily between them.

A fairly old cow seen to give birth was closely attended by another cow who warned off any others which came too close. After the birth the mother would not let any other elephants near. The calf was seen to be covered with soil soon after birth, but the mother did not appear to consciously cover it, although in another case the cow did scuff earth onto the wet calf. She blew earth over herself several times. It was $3\frac{1}{4}$ hours before the calf suckled. While in labour the cow produced a copious discharge from her temporal glands.

When a cow gave birth to twins in the Kruger Park she appeared first to prepare a soft patch of earth by scraping with her forefeet, onto which patch the calves were deposited. The slime which covered the newborn animals was cleaned off with sand by the cow. The total sequence of the two births took half an hour, with 20 minutes between the appearances of the two calves.

If it does not occur at the same time that the calf appears, the afterbirth is expelled up to two hours following the birth and may be rubbed into the ground with the forefoot. Among other ungulates the eating of the afterbirth and the careful removal of all traces of the birth are believed to be designed to prevent predators being attracted to the event. In the African elephant, where there is little danger from predators due to the elephant's ability to defend itself, this may be simply an inherent behaviour from the elephant's ancestry, no longer serving any real purpose.

Birth is similar in the Asian elephant. In an incident observed in the Yala Game Reserve in Sri Lanka a cow, one of a herd of nine, which from her behaviour was probably a first-time mother, began repeatedly to lie down. After the fluid escaped she lay prone for half an hour, straining and waving her trunk, then, spreading her hind legs, the head and forelegs of the calf appeared. She stood up, knelt and then lay down again and the calf emerged. The cow walked off ten paces, rolled on the gound and expelled the afterbirth. Eating part of it she trampled on the rest. Meanwhile the calf was left abandoned wriggling on the ground. Another elephant came up, picked it up and put it down and rumbled. Others approached, each examining the calf with feet and trunk and throwing sand on it for half an hour. By this time the calf was dry and stood up and attempted to suckle the other elephants, at which point the mother came up, knelt with her head touching the ground and the calf reached her teats and suckled. The mother then got up, picked up the calf and tucking it under her chin walked off surrounded by the rest of the herd.

J.H. Williams of 'Elephant Bill' fame believed that during the first month the dam would carry the calf in her trunk if disturbed, having seen one pick up its calf in this manner. He noted that when a small calf was present in a wild herd which ran off, there were no tracks of the calf to be seen. Carrying of the calf by the dam has only rarely been recorded in the African elephant. Hunters in South Africa in the last century sometimes reported it and in recent times an African game scout in northern Uganda saw an elephant pick up a newly born calf which was lying immobile on the road and carry it off on her tusks, held against them by her trunk.

Another difference between the species as recorded by J.H. Williams in Burma was that the would-be mother allegedly went to a certain defensible spot to give birth, protected by the rest of the herd. It may well be that the considerable threat from tigers induces this behaviour as he believed:

> The noise is terrifying. The herd will remain in the neighbourhood of the maternity ward for some weeks, until the new arrival can keep up with the pace of a grazing herd. The ward may cover an area of a square mile, and during the day the herd will graze all over it, surrounding the mother and her newly born calf, and closing their ranks around her at night.

LIFE OF THE CALF

The first thing that the calf tries to do when it stands is to find the teats. It can have difficulty in reaching the dam's breast if she is a large animal, a situation which could conceivably lead to a lowered survival rate with more indifferent cows who do not stand long enough for the calf to satisfy itself. With an inexperienced mother, finding the teats can take over four hours.

The new calf suckles frequently, using its mouth and not its trunk, as Aristotle correctly observed. Attempts to suckle are most frequent in the first six months and then decline, but the bull calves are selfish brats, suckling on average every 37 minutes to the cow calf's 50, each bout lasting about $1\frac{1}{2}$ minutes.

This frequent suckling, unlike antelopes which may only suckle their young a maximum of twice in 24 hours, is probably related to volume. As the calf requires about 15 litres a day the mother's mammary glands would have to be too large to provide this amount all at once. Mothers rarely encourage the calf to find the nipple, but are very tolerant of the calf's demands. One great big overgrown girl suckled until she was eight years old at Amboseli, having some difficulty because of her height and her protruding tusks. Another dam has been seen patiently allowing her calf of three years old to suckle on one teat and the previous calf of seven years old to suckle on the other at the same time. In Sri Lanka small calves have been seen to suckle both their dams and other cows in the group. Rarely is an orphaned calf allowed to suckle by another cow and probably only when the cow has lost her own calf.

Sanderson knew of only one instance of an Asian working elephant cow allowing an orphan to suckle along with her own calf. Orphaned calves are not usually accepted by other mothers and when a calf tries to suckle a cow which is not its mother she will usually reject it aggressively if she is feeding one of her own, but exceptions do occur. Some cows are very tolerant and will allow other calves in the group to suckle them. One calf has been seen to suckle from its grandmother. Calves from birth to three months try most often to suckle other cows, the bull calves more than cow calves. Growing faster than its sisters, the bull calf always tries to suckle more often than the cow and demands more milk, screaming petulantly if the mother moves away while it is sucking.

As in antelopes, the calf is nursed until just before the next birth is due, when the mother's mammary glands cease to produce milk in preparation for the production of colostrum for the next birth. Nursing averages five years, ranging from three to eight, due to the fact that the interval between one calf being born and the next is variable, conception being influenced by environmental conditions. The shortest time between two births that has been observed is 35 months. After the next birth some calves return to suckle with the new calf, which antelope mothers never permit.

During its first three years it is the calf which usually stops suckling, but with bull calves from the age of $3\frac{1}{2}$–$4\frac{1}{2}$ years it is more often the mother which terminates it.

The earliest analysis of elephant's milk was performed in 1882, but analyses of milk have little meaning unless they are related to the stage of growth of the calf as the consistency changes, becoming weaker as suckling progresses. Thus the assertion of Benedict in 1936 that it had the consistency almost of cream, with 17.5–22.1% fat, probably relates to a very early stage.

For the first few days of its life, although it can walk, albeit rather shakily, stumbling over any branch that is in its way and having to be guided by its mother's trunk, the calf is almost helpless, finding its mother apparently by smell, touch and sound. It doesn't seem to know what to do with its trunk; finding it uncontrollable, it sometimes sucks it like a baby sucking its thumb. After the first week it begins to pick things up with it but drinking is more difficult to master. Although it tries to drink through it from an age of three months onwards, it takes about a year to do this successfully.

The mother makes soft noises to the calf and if it should cry out all the cows in the immediate vicinity rush over to it, but it is not until it gets older that the mother will allow other cows to deal with it.

The long period of mother–calf attachment creates an exceptionally strong maternal bond, the depth of which was vividly demonstrated to me when I accompanied a park warden to shoot an injured calf. The calf, about 18 months of age, had had its left forefoot caught in a wire snare, which as usual had cut through to the bone just at the ankle, turning the foot into a swollen, festering mass. The calf was gallantly hobbling along behind its patient mother, while the rest of the herd fed slowly ahead. Although older animals often survive this frequent trauma there seemed little hope for the calf so it was decided to put it out of its misery. Unfortunately the shot was botched, hitting the calf in the lungs.

The calf was bowled over by the shot and the dam, screaming with alarm, instantly rushed to its rescue. Trumpeting with rage she frantically pushed the calf to its feet and tried to lead it away. Lolling against her legs, it staggered a few paces and collapsed again. Tusks streaked with its blood, the mother desperately tried to raise it until helpless, she stood over it as it lay there. Then, just after it died, she raised her trunk high into the air and gave vent to a penetrating wail of anguish. And it was a wail, not a trumpet, which echoed forlornly over the countryside. My flesh tingled, I had never heard anything like it before, pitiful in its desperate intensity and poignant with sorrow. After standing over the dead body for about half an hour the grief-stricken cow then turned and slowly followed after her departed comrades.

Other incidents of the strength of the maternal attachment are a cow elephant in Uganda carrying around the putrefied corpse of a calf on her tusks, while another remained by the side of her dead calf for four days.

The calf is completely dependent upon its mother for the first three months of life. It then starts trying to take vegetation and at between three and four months swallows some grass, sometimes even kneeling and biting it off. The young calf imitates its mother in feeding and often investigates what she has taken by putting its trunk to her mouth. Occasionally this extends to withdrawing some of its mother's food and eating it. By the age of six months it is taking a significant amount and at two years spends as much time feeding on vegetation as an adult.

African calves are unable to survive on their own before two years of age. The youngest orphaned calf known to have survived was 26 months at the time of its mother's death. In Burma orphaned domestic elephant calves were suckled by Burmese women, who considered it a great privilege. I cannot imagine that this incongruous association went on for very long.

Mothers, whether African or Asian, rarely allow familiarities by other cows with their young. But African elephants will rally immediately to a calf which calls for help and will not readily abandon one whose mother has been killed. Eleanor, a tame cow elephant at Tsavo, when she was 12 years old and still unmated showed great solicitousness and possessiveness towards any orphaned calves which were brought to her, but this would vanish immediately when another calf arrived and she promptly lost all interest in her former charge.

Perhaps because she supplies it with milk, a dam who has dug a hole for herself in the bed of a sand river to drink water seeping into it will keep the calf from it until she is herself satisfied and then usually just walks off, leaving the calf no time to drink its fill. It is not uncommon for another family unit which has been waiting for the first cow to finish to arrive and push away waiting calves before they have had a chance to drink at all. This could contribute to a lowered survival rate of calves in drought years. An alleged exception to this seemingly callous indifference relates to the desert-adapted elephants inhabiting Namibia's Skeleton Coast, which in the dry season excavate pipes in the dry sandy river beds. If the water in the pipes is too deep down for small elephants to reach, then it is alleged the adults squirt water into their mouths. In the Tsavo area Daphne Sheldrick found that bulls showed an amazing tolerance towards small calves at waterholes in the sand and often allowed several calves to drink with them at the same time.

The calf keeps close to its mother, within 2 m on average, until it is eight years old, when the cow will already have another offspring some 1.8 m high following her. Like Dickens's good Little Dorrit, juvenile and adolescent cows comfort, assist and protect all other calves in a family unit, even if they are not

FIG. 5.1 *Cow elephants retrieving a calf from a pitfall. An artist's impression based on an incident in Botswana, 1894.*

their brothers and sisters. A calf or juvenile always has at least one other elephant close to it when it is in the family group, usually closer than its mother. Such closeness is random; most tend to be cows but there does not seem to be a particular companion.

Calves of the matriarchs get themselves into less trouble than those of younger mothers, falling into holes, tripping over logs, getting stuck in the mud or in water, straying up to 10 m away from the mother, being alarmed by predators or seriously annoying other elephants. All lead to cries for help in the form of a low rumble or a loud bellow, which elicits a dramatic reaction from the adults who come to the calf's rescue. When serious danger is suspected the calves are protected in a ring of the older cows facing outwards; otherwise the juvenile cows from the family group tend to assist the calf, usually being closely related to it and more often a big sister than an auntie. Young calves have a greater survival rate from such assistance.

The habit of Asian elephant calves of a few months of age of scrambling onto the mother's shoulders when swimming, although well able to swim themselves, has not been reported among African elephants.

Disciplining young calves consists of poking, trunk slaps, shoves and threats, usually by the mother and rarely by other elephants, only young bulls or

FIG. 5.2   *Elephants in the open making a defensive ring.*

independent adult bulls. Generally the behaviour towards the calves depends upon individual temperament. Some cows are very intolerant towards new calves and one has been seen to snatch up a two month old calf in its trunk, hurl it to the ground and trample it to death.

Play among calves consists of head to head sparring, trunk wrestling, mounting one another, chasing and rolling on one another. The calves are more vigorous in this than older youngsters and indulge longer, anything from 20 to 50 seconds. The elephants reared by David and Daphne Sheldrick in Tsavo Park, which were allowed complete freedom of movement during the day, indulged in extraordinary play activities with other species.

Perhaps the most remarkable was that of the 2 m tall bull Samson with the young black rhinoceros Rufus. Samson would kneel down before Rufus who would then charge, butting the amused Samson with his horn, Samson warding off the blow with his trunk and then wrapping it round the rhino's neck in a vicelike grip. Rufus, with much angry puffing and struggling, extricated himself and repeated the attack, eventually giving up and walking away. Samson would then walk in front of him and lie down and the game would start all over again. The elephant had other elephant companions and his life was restricted in no way likely to produce abnormal behaviour, yet in the wild these two species avoid each other like the plague. How animal ethologists, those who study behaviour as a science, would explain this behaviour and the lack of it in the wild, I have no idea.

Whenever any new elephant calves were brought in, they were immediately accepted by the other elephants, who fussed over them attentively. At one time the number totalled four. As the oldest, Samson always took the lead and when walking in single file the others followed a set order.

At the first drops of rain these elephants would display great excitement; although they always had an ample supply of drinking water the prospect of an abundance of fresh green food caused much boisterousness. They would rush around trumpeting, charging through the bush and, kneeling down, pound the earth as if goring an enemy, roll on their sides and fling mud over themselves. No doubt their wild compatriots behave in the same manner, as the onset of rain excites many wild animals to unusual exhibitions. Samson would also sometimes go around pushing trees over as a part of the display of excitement.

Hunters long ago reported the presence of 'aunties', cows in the family group which help to look after the young calves and often attend a cow when she gives birth. Even so calves less than two years of age have no chance of surviving without their mother, for other cows will not adopt them despite the fact that they may sometimes allow other calves to suckle as well as their own. The aunties tend to be family members but are not always sisters. Where there are no aunties mortality is higher in the first two years of life for calves than where there are such 'allomothers' in the behaviourists' jargon. Yet calves less than two have the least interactions with aunties, while those between two and four, when they are likely to be weaned from their mothers, have the most. The calves of young mothers have a higher rate of contacts with other elephants than do those of more experienced ones. Mothers of 25–40 years of age are more successful at raising their calves during the critical first four years of life than are younger or older mothers.

Calf deaths are high in the first year of life; rates of 36% have been reported in Uganda, but after the first year mortality is low. Under normal conditions the adult sex ratio is only slightly biased in favour of cows and is equal at birth, but in dry years more bull than cow calves die, possibly because they grow faster than the cow and therefore require more food. They are also weaned at an older age and when a cow raises a bull calf then the period until her next calf is longer by several months, because there is more drain on her energy reserves due to the greater amount of milk that the bull calf requires. The mother therefore invests more in a son than she does in a daughter.

Why should this be so? By ensuring that the son can grow fast at an early age it will ensure his ultimate mating success, because size is an important factor. The bigger bulls are the ones who mate with the most cows. The daughter is going to mate anyway, whether she is big or little.

Whereas the daughter dutifully remains in the family unit with her mother, the son is driven away at the age of about 15 and must fend for himself. At Amboseli this took place from nine to 19 years with 14 as the average. The young bull is driven away by the adult cows whom he increasingly begins to importune, by his mother or by a bull when the mother comes into heat.

PERILS OF POACHING

In some heavily poached national parks in Kenya and Tanzania there were less than 20% of bulls of 15 years or older in 1989 population estimates. Breeding bulls represented 5% or less, compared with an expected 22% as found in the relatively unpoached Amboseli population. A lack of mature bulls resulting from killing them for their ivory could accelerate declines in population numbers, compounding the effect of killing the bulls alone.

During the two days that conception is believed to occur during her period of heat, the probability that a cow will find a sexually mature bull, especially one in musth, decreases as the number of such bulls declines. Thus whereas at Amboseli a third of adult bulls came into musth each year and the probability that a cow would conceive during any particular period of heat was estimated at only $\frac{1}{2}$%, in heavily poached populations with many fewer adult bulls, the chances become even less, so recruitment is slowed up.

Furthermore, mate searching success is influenced by elephant grouping patterns, which vary with the type of habitat. Thus in the more open areas where elephants respond to heavy poaching pressure by aggregating in larger than normal groups, conception rates may be less affected by poaching than they might be in those areas, such as the Selous and the Luangwa Valley populations, where the elephants do not aggregate because of the nature of the woodland habitat.

At Amboseli it has been shown that three quarters of the families are led by a cow who is more than 30 years old but in Tsavo East in 1989, just over one third of 32 families observed were orphans or had no adult cow in the group. In Tsavo West the figure was almost half of 28 groups and in Tanzania's Mikumi Park, it was almost three quarters of 69 groups.

The destruction of family relationships and bond groups which form the basis of elephant society, and the loss of stored knowledge which this entails, must have far-reaching consequences. The young elephants in such groups will grow up as yobs if nothing else. But in the Tarangire Park, although there were no bulls older than 30 years and only six in the 25–30 age group in 1989 due to heavy poaching in the 1970s, the population had a high recruitment rate, suggesting that young bulls can mate successfully after all in the absence of competition from mature bulls and the cows accept them for want of something better.

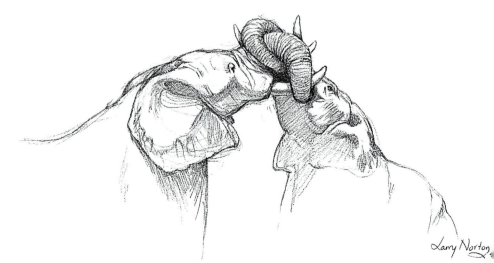

Larry Norton

Chapter 6

OF SIZE, SINDBAD AND CEMETERIES: GROWTH AND LONGEVITY

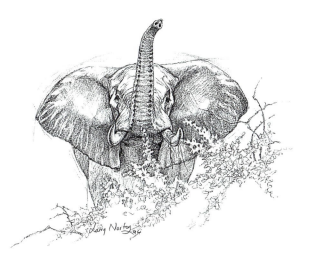

... at last he fell down; after which they immediately cut off his snout, which was so hard and tough that it cost the Negroes thirty strokes before they could separate it, which must be very painful to the elephant, since it made him roar; which was the only noise I heard him make: ... this elephant sufferd above three hundred shot to be made at him, without any sign of being enraged or resistance ...

William Bosman, 1705

THE GIANT OF BEASTS

WELL might Oppian write: 'These beasts have a bulk such as on the earth no other wild beast yet hath worn. Seeing an Elephant thou wouldst say that a huge mountain-peak or a dread cloud, fraught with storm for hapless mortals, was travelling on the land'. No less impressed than Oppian, generations of schoolchildren have marvelled at the size of the mighty stuffed African bull elephant in London's Natural History Museum, and well they might, for, shot in Malawi in the 1920s, it is believed to have been stretched a foot to make it the 3.45 m at the shoulder it now stands.

This chimera apart, almost twice the height of an average man, the shoulder height of a standing adult bull African elephant is just over 3 m, and he weighs the equivalent of more than 70 adult men. In Uganda and Zambia it has been measured as 3.2 m, and the Kruger Park lays claim to elephants of up to 3.4 m. The cow is slightly smaller at about 2.7 m, but up to 2.9 m has been recorded.

The shoulder height is approximately the highest point of an African elephant, but the centre of the back in the Asian elephant can be some 8% higher than the shoulder.

The weight of an adult bull was found to be 5.5–6 tonnes in Uganda and Zambia, but a captive zoo animal from Tanzania weighed 6.6 at an age of 25 years and was thus still growing. A comparison of the growth rate with wild elephants in Zambia of Diksie, a cow elephant in the London Zoo, showed that the wild elephants had a considerably slower rate of growth, but this may be due to exercise. The cow has been estimated at 2.5–2.8 tonnes with a maximum recorded of 3.2 from Uganda and Zambia but again, a captive cow of only 16 years of age had reached 3.2.

It is problematical to weigh an elephant and most of the weights recorded for wild elephants are estimates derived from weighing the hind leg, which is assumed to have a constant ratio to the weight of the animal as a whole, but may well tend to produce underestimates of the true value since it can only predict the *average* weight of an animal for that particular weight of hind leg. There was once a suggestion of using a balloon to weigh the carcases of cropped elephants, but this never came to anything.

The biggest African elephant known is claimed to be a bull shot in Angola in 1955, alleged to have been 4 m at the shoulder and to have had an estimated weight of 10 tonnes. This specimen has been mounted and now stands in the Smithsonian Museum, where it is known as the Fenykoevi elephant after the man who shot it.

Asian bull elephants have a maximum recorded height of 3.2 m and a weight of 5.4 tonnes. For the cow maxima are 2.54 m and 4.16 tonnes. Average shoulder heights are 2.7 and 2.35 m for bull and cow respectively. Sanderson claimed there was never such a thing as a 10 feet high (3.04 m) elephant in India, that such reports were the result of throwing a tape over the shoulders from one side to the other and halving the measurement. But hunters dispute this, claiming to have measured 10 feet high elephants and some even taller.

The African forest elephant kept in domestication in the Congo was found to be 75 cm high at birth and to increase by 7–8 cm in height each year, taking 12–13 years to reach a shoulder height of 1.6 m. A general guide to the baby African elephant's age is that it can pass under the front legs of its mother until it is one year old, when the baby savannah elephant is 1.1–1.15 m high.

Both sexes grow throughout life, but growth in size of the African cow starts to level off after puberty at from 10–15 years, thereafter becoming very slow. At the age of 20 years the bull, which then exceeds the height of the cow by 30 cm, appears to undergo a secondary growth 'spurt' over the next five years, as does the Asian bull.

At the age of 25 the bull is almost twice the size of the cow. The average potential bull shoulder height at 60 is 55 cm, almost one fifth taller than the cow, and his weight is potentially 2 tonnes or one third heavier.

Growth in body length as well as height continues, so that the age of bull elephants can be approximately determined from aerial photographs. In the bull the head becomes increasingly large in relation to body size to accommodate the increasing size and weight of the tusks. In both sexes the forehead broadens with age, making the temporal gland region appear more sunken, and in the bull the shape of the face changes dramatically, assuming an hourglass shape. By 35–40 years the bull has a broad forehead and eye region, the face then narrowing to widen again at the tusk gums.

NOT BUILT FOR ETERNITY

Man has always been intrigued by the possible life span of the elephant. In 1938 *The Times* newspaper carried a lengthy correspondence on the subject when H. Macnaghten of the Bombay Burma Trading Company reported that the company had kept elephants for over 50 years and the ages of 1700 working elephants were known. Of these, 8.4% were aged 55–65 years and 1.4% were older than 65.

This prompted a letter from a descendant of Lord Clive who referred to an elephant allegedly ridden by Lord Clive at Plassey in 1757 and which died at Meerut in 1879. Its last public appearance was claimed to have been in 1877 when it headed a procession of 2000 elephants at the Durbar proclaiming Queen Victoria Empress of India. His tusks were worn to within 6 inches of the gum and wooden ones had been screwed in. As evidence of his age he was reported as walking like 'a very old man'. When he died he was given a soldier's funeral. This letter was followed by another from a correspondent claiming to have ridden, early in 1887, the elephant known as 'Warren Hastings' which had been ridden by the Governor through Calcutta in 1773, when it was judged to have been over 30 years of age. The correspondent reported a person claiming to have fed this elephant in 1891 at Barrackpore, where the government had an official document certifying it to be the elephant that had been ridden by the proconsul Warren Hastings, who was known by the Indians as 'Horrible stink sahib', although not in the official document. It was last reported at about 150 years old. But a further letter, from one who had been a young subaltern at Fort Chunar on the Ganges in 1886, claimed that the said elephant had killed its mahout and the writer of the letter had been responsible for signing its death warrant.

Although it is possible that the odd elephant may live to a great age, these were all similar examples to that of 'Ajax', the giant elephant captured by Alexander the Great in 326 BC in his battle against the Indian prince Porus. Ajax was allegedly seen by a traveller in India 350 years later bearing gold rings on its tusks upon which was inscribed in Greek, 'Alexander the son of Zeus dedicated Ajax to the sun'. Another example was 'Alice', Jumbo's former companion at the London Zoo, which it was claimed was still alive in Australia's Sydney Zoo in 1938, aged 152 years. In fact the real Alice had been sold to the United States in 1886 and died a year later in a fire at Barnum's Circus. The same name was simply passed on from one elephant to another. In 1982 an Asian cow circus elephant in Australia was said to have died at the age of 86, just about the life span of two circus elephants.

The real life span of elephants had been guessed at with some precision from antiquity, the cautious Aristotle noting that 'some say' that it lives for 200 years, others 300 years, but, he stated, it arrives at 'perfection' at the age of 60. Sanderson, a fount of early information on the elephant, noted one which was 76 years old and still working with no appearance of age although past her prime, and thus thought that a life span of 150 years was possible. Indian and Sri Lankan accounts generally give 100 years as the age at death, but that some lived to 120. Tennent considered its life span was about the same as that of man – 70 years.

Apart from Sanderson's claim, an Indian elephant has been known to live to 69 years in an Australian zoo. Frank Beddard of the London Zoo caustically summed it all up in 1902: 'In spite of their longevity, however, elephants, unlike Rome, have not been built for eternity'.

Elephants are believed to live in the wild for about 50 years, but have a probable potential life span of 65. No captive African elephant has lived for longer than 44 and captive working Asian elephants live for 50 to 60, with the maximum recorded being 67 (Sanderson's record being discounted). For the Siberian mammoth the maximum age inferred from the tusks has been estimated at 73 years, but some may have lived to 80, always assuming that the interpretation is correct.

LIFE'S GAME OF CHANCE

As in man, the mortality rate for much of an elephant's life span after it has passed the weaning stage is nearly constant, ranging from about 5.1% to 6.6%. After 50 years there is a steep rise in the rate due to the wearing away of the last molar tooth. Elephants usually die of old age in the dry season, for when this tooth fragment has been reduced to about 7 × 10 cm in area its surface is almost smooth and the elephant can no longer shear dry food effectively.

Those bull elephants that reach this stage are frequently driven to trying to feed on soft aquatic plants which have little food value, so they often die in the water, sometimes from becoming bogged down in their weakened state. But the old matriarch will try to keep up with her family group until she drops. Her

FIG. 6.1 *Elephants in their undisturbed state. Uganda, 1956.*

family would not leave her even if she tried to wander off so it is rare to find an old cow on her own.

There are few elephant populations in Africa today where there is no hunting and the true picture of natural mortality can be seen but one such population was that inhabiting Amboseli between the 1950s and 1980s. Here the mortality of calves from various natural causes was observed in wet years to be 7.5% (of the total number) up to one year of age and 15% by $2\frac{1}{2}$ years. On average one fifth of calves died in the first two years of life, but then the proportion fell to 12% for the next 2–5 years. In dry years, when the mothers may have had difficulty in providing enough milk as well as the calves possibly suffering heat stress, calf mortality was much higher. Then one quarter of the number of bulls born died in the first year, although only one tenth of the cows did. As bull calves suckle more frequently this may relate to the difference in survival.

When food became scarce young mothers with their first calf were seen to be the first to split from the family group, but the matriarch is the one most likely to find the best resources, so the action of the young mother could contribute to a lessened chance of survival on the part of her offspring. By $2\frac{1}{2}$ years just over one half of the bull calves had died compared with one third of cows. Above this age the mortality rate drops to much the same as that of the adults.

In Tsavo Park the collection of tusks from elephants which had died naturally in the years 1959 to 1970, before the great massacres took place, showed that almost one tenth of the bulls were more than 30 years old and just one tenth were aged from 15 to 30. For cows, almost one fifth were older than 25; thus cows were living longer than bulls. An estimated one third of calves of both sexes died before they were one year old, falling to one tenth from the ages of 1–5 years. Thereafter the annual mortality of bulls from 6 to 25 years of age was the same as that of cows from 6 to 45, namely 2–3% each year.

In the adjacent but less arid Tsavo West Park, calves born after the peak of the long rains were more likely to die than were those born earlier. The former also tended to be born to young cows, which gave birth later than the older ones. For calves born during the short rains there were very few deaths and no difference between those born early on and those born later. At Manyara it was estimated that only one tenth died in their first year and then only 3–4% each year thereafter. Once past the weaning stage the number of animals dying each year is much the same for most elephants until old age. Prior to the slaughter of the 1970s, adult elephants wherever they were did not experience much change in the rate of survival, even under crowded conditions.

The only predator other than man which elephants have to fear in Africa is the lion, which succeeds in taking calves from time to time and even elephants up to 12 years of age. In Asia the tiger is a much more aggressive predator than the African lion, estimated in Burma in 1950 to take one quarter of all elephant calves.

Elephants die from many causes other than predation: disease, accidents, fighting, starvation, drought, stress, heat stress, drowning, snake bite and congenital malformation. One case of a dead foetus has been recorded, but as with African ungulates this is rare. In Botswana the death of young elephants from eating a poisonous plant called *mogau* (*Dichapetalum* spp.) is not uncommon.

Although there is at least one authenticated case of a four year old elephant dying from snake bite, many cases of sudden death reported in Asian working elephants as being from this cause are probably due to heart failure or diseases such as surra or anthrax. A snake is considered to have insufficient venom to kill a fullgrown elephant.

Other causes of death are fracture of the long bones, the animals usually weakening and dying within a month although rare cases of recovery have been recorded, getting stuck in the mud, drowning and falling down steep slopes. Elephants may also die from being struck by lightning and in Uganda two victims of this were found dead side by side in identical positions. Death from falling trees has also been recorded and elephants have been crushed by baobabs falling on them that they have been destroying. Asian elephants are greatly alarmed by the sound of falling trees and can be driven by playing recordings of the sound through loudspeakers; a modern refinement of the traditional method of driving them by ringing bells, beating pots and pans and creating a general hullabaloo.

DROUGHT, THE GREAT LEVELLER

Successful elephant reproduction requires adequate food, water and shade, both during the cow's pregnancy and during the period after birth when she is suckling the calf. Animals killed in Hwange Park, which experiences marked seasonality, confirmed the importance of fluctuations in rainfall causing variations in the age structure of populations. At Amboseli during the drought year of 1977, more than three quarters of the population of calves under one year of age died, but only a handful did so in 1980, another dry year. Continual rainfall variation implies that the age structure of elephant populations will always be changing, affecting survival through the availabilities of dry season water and food, infant deaths and inhibition of conception in famine stressed cows. So the age structure of an elephant population in non-equatorial regions is unlikely to be stable; it will show many ups and downs related to past climate, albeit with a two year lag behind climatic events.

Studies ranging from Uganda and Kenya to Namibia suggest that low rainfall before or during the normal season of conception might lower fertility and coupled with this, exceptionally hot and dry seasons might affect calf survival in the first year of life. But any relationship with climatic events is likely to be masked, for although a bad year, or a series of bad years, might be followed by exceptionally good conditions, this would not result in a high conception rate or high natality because a large proportion of the cows would be pregnant.

In Ruaha Park most natural deaths took place in the dry season. When conditions were such that more elephants died than usual, then this was made up by a higher proportion of young animals. In 1976 when there was a much longer and more severe dry season than in the surrounding years, the youngest animals with no tusks or tusks up to 2 kg in weight died, and the proportion of tusks recovered weighing less than 6 kg, equivalent to a bull aged less than 18 years or a cow aged less than 36, rose sharply.

During unusually dry conditions in 1970–1971 an estimated 5900 elephants died in Tsavo East out of the total population of 20 000–25 000 in the area, or 15% of the estimated total of 40 000 for the whole ecosystem. Most of the mortality was among cows and young animals up to five years of age, almost three quarters of this comprising mature cows and calves under three years. Only one-tenth were adult bulls. High calf mortality continued up to 1974 due to the fact that the surviving elephants tended to return to the same impoverished areas each consecutive dry season.

Amboseli suffered from the drought in 1975–1976, during which years reproductive activity almost ceased. Only five conceptions took place in two years. Then in 1976 nearly half of the year's calf crop died. Of those that died half were less than two months old, the other half 5–6 months. The newborn animals probably died from lack of milk, both quantity and quality in terms of nutrients falling significantly when the mother is subject to drought conditions; the others because they would have been starting to eat green food. Calves of 4–5 years also died, perhaps representing those which had been recently weaned. Significantly more bull than cow calves died, maybe because the mothers could not produce the greater amount of milk they require.

From 1973 to 1978 the total population at Amboseli declined each year, one third of the calves dying in the first year of life. Puberty was not reached until 16–17 years and the calving interval was lengthened to more than six years. The

FIG. 6.2   *Suffering from the drought. An old cow elephant seeks the shade of a gulley. Note the prominent backbone, the hip bone and the ribs sticking out. Tsavo, 1971.*

cows virtually stopped reproducing for two years and there were no births for 16 months. Although the elephants were in relatively poor condition they were not starving. But then from 1979 to 1983 the population responded by increasing each year by an average of 6.6%, giving an overall increase for the ten year period of 3.4% per year, providing a net gain to the total population size of 17.2%.

In Zimbabwe 1982 was the driest wet season for 65 years. Up to 134 elephants were recorded dying within 4 sq. km around a natural waterhole which provided a dwindling water supply through seepage. Another 66 died the following year which was also dry. In the first year most of the deaths were of 2–8 year olds but in the second year most of the deaths occurred among adult cows who were lactating, very old or with herds and, unlike the bulls, unwilling to move far looking for alternative sources of water. The youngest animals died closest to the water supply, older animals tending to wander away from it and die. The cause of death was not thirst but starvation, all available food within reach of the water supply having been consumed.

When water becomes scarce the older animals crowd out the younger ones and display unusual aggression, even mothers to their young. The younger animals are obliged to wait their turn to drink, a long drawn-out process as the adults wait for water to seep slowly into the hole that they may have dug. Then when the older animals have drunk their fill and move away to feed, the young get left behind. Unable to find enough forage in the vicinity of the water the young animals gravitate back to the water and die. As in Tsavo Park, most of the dead animals had full or partly full stomachs but the contents were mainly woody, of low nutrient quality and digestibility. Fidelity to the dry season ranges was so great in Tsavo that during the drought of 1970–1971 elephants died of starvation near the Galana River only 15 km from food sources.

Not only starvation may be the cause of increased death in times of drought, but heat stress as well. Elephants during the heat of the day crowding under the remaining shade of a single tree in Tsavo East Park were once a familiar sight. In north east Zimbabwe, close to the Zambezi River, the elephants seek shade during the heat of the day, resting in the apple-ring thorn tree woodland. In deciduous thicket, particularly mopane woodland where shade is sparse, they crowd under any available shade, such as a large baobab.

During drought, when there is competition for scarce water supplies, much fighting can take place around waterholes and elephants frequently break off pieces of their tusks. Similar fractured pieces of mammoth and mastodon tusks have been found in Pleistocene fossil bone assemblages in such countries as North America, Belgium, Crete and Spain, suggesting, contrary to the belief that they were pieces chipped from tusks by Stone Age men to use as weapons, that these groups of mammoth and mastodon bones were also the result of animals dying at waterholes during a drought period and competing for water in the same way as their modern counterparts.

THE LEGACY OF SINDBAD

The finding of so few old dead animals on land led to the myth that there were elephant graveyards, secret places where all the old elephants went to die and where hunters would find massive hoards of huge ivory! The myth appears to have arisen in ancient India where it was claimed a secret valley existed to which elephants went to die. This became widely popularized in the story of Sindbad the Sailor in the 9th century *Thousand and One Nights*. Sanderson rightly dismissed the idea. Relatively few animals will survive to very old age, for as with all species there is a steady attrition in numbers throughout life.

In 1959 a total of 188 dead elephants was found in the Uganda national parks, but probably many of these died of bullet wounds from control operations conducted outside the park boundaries. One remote area north of the Nile in the Murchison Falls Park was particularly favoured by aged bull elephants in the 1950s and later. Keeping an eye on the biggest of them, in the space of about four years the warden found the bodies of four which had died naturally. The tusks weighed from 31.8 kg, with the largest, whose teeth were completely worn away, having tusks of 71.7 and 66 kg, but these patriarchs did not all die in the same spot.

In the north of Tsavo East Park, the remote Tiva River in the 1960s harboured what was described as 'an astonishing number' of old bulls carrying tusks greater than 50 kg each. Mt Marsabit in northern Kenya, for the 40 years prior to 1980, was also known as a haunt of very large tuskers. In addition to the famous Ahmed there was also Mohamed and Abdul. Ivory from dead animals found here between 1962 and 1969 also showed a preponderance of older tusks.

The nearest to an 'elephant cemetery' reported was that found in 1902 by the explorer P.H.G. Powell-Cotton in Turkana, northern Kenya, south-west of Pelekech mountain:

> Here I was surprised to find the whole countryside scattered with remains [of elephants], the fitful sun . . . lighting up glistening bones in every direction . . .
> This place was well known to the Turkana, who regularly visited it to carry off the tusks. However, before we left the district my men found several small ones.

The most likely explanation for this concentration of bones was that the animals died there in times of drought. Probably in normal seasons the only source of water in a wide area, the elephants ate out the food supply around the pools and died of starvation or the pools dried out and they were too exhausted to move elsewhere. It is significant that he found *small* tusks.

DEATH OF A MATRIARCH

Few have witnessed the natural death of a wild elephant, but there is one remarkable story of the death of an aged matriarch seen actually taking place in the Serengeti Park. The observer came across an old cow which appeared to be sick and as he watched her head fell forward, she swayed back and forth and then fell to the ground. The rest of the family group quickly gathered around her trumpeting and rumbling. One young bull tried repeatedly to lift her by putting his tusks under her and straining with all his might. There being no response he tried stuffing vegetation into her mouth and this also having no effect he then tried to mount her. The others stood around touching her and caressing her with their trunks. One calf got down and tried to suckle. Eventually the group started moving away until only one cow and her calf were left with the dead body. Facing away the cow reached back from time to time and touched the body with a hind foot. Finally she left and slowly followed the others.

Many years ago a correspondent to the *Daily Telegraph* newspaper related how in Kenya he had watched two cows helping along a third which fell down from time to time and had to be assisted to its feet again. Eventually it fell down to be left alone after much commotion on the part of its two companions and, approaching the body, he found it to be that of a cow which had apparently collapsed and died of old age.

During the deaths in Tsavo, I arrived on the scene just after a matriarch had dropped. She was still alive and could weakly twitch her trunk but already the family group was slowly walking away. Perhaps they had become accustomed to the toll of death in the drought and this accounted for them leaving her before she had finally expired.

FIG. 6.3 *A matriarch lies dying in the drought in Tsavo Park in 1971 as the family group moves away.*

A family group which rallied round a young cow that had collapsed from being darted with an immobilizing drug ceased interest abruptly the moment she died and the matriarch then partly covered the head and shoulders with vegetation. In this case it was probably the cessation of the sound of the heart beat which made the group conscious that death had taken place.

When a group of elephants becomes aware of a skeleton it often elicits great excitement. Crowding around it, raising their tails and half extending their ears, the elephants conduct a bizarre thorough investigation, picking up bones or moving them about with their feet. Sometimes tusks have been carried away and smashed on rocks. A young bull has been seen to carry a pelvic girdle for 70 m, while others distributed ribs and tusks to some distance away, carrying them in their mouths rather than with the trunk.

Dr Douglas-Hamilton watched the reaction to the skin and bones of a dead elephant which he placed near to a well-used elephant track. Of eight groups which passed, six displayed intense curiosity and excitement and the other two simply walked over the bones as if they were not there! Do they then recognize the bones of former group members?

It has been known since ancient times that elephants will cover the dead bodies of other elephants and even of men that they have killed. An Asian elephant buried the remains of a dead buffalo which it had chased a tiger away from. Often this curious behaviour is no more than a gesture of throwing a few branches or foliage on the body, but none the less remarkable for that. The most extraordinary account was related by the late George Adamson of lion fame, which concerned an old, half-blind native woman in northern Kenya. Becoming lost she resigned herself to her fate and when night fell lay down and went to sleep under a tree. A few hours later she was awakened by an elephant sniffing her with its trunk, which was shortly joined by others trumpeting loudly. They all then joined in burying the terrified woman under a huge pile of branches and then left her. Thus well protected from marauding lions and hyaenas she was only released the next morning when a passing herdsman luckily heard her faint cries for help.

But perhaps the most remarkable incident in this respect relates to the cropping of elephants in northern Uganda. The salted dried skins of the ears and the skinned feet were stored in a shed at the base camp. One night elephants broke into the shed and partly buried the skins and feet. What are we supposed to make of such curious behaviour?

Chapter 7

DESPICABLE WORMS
AND MIGHTY
ELEPHANTS:
DISEASES AND
PARASITES

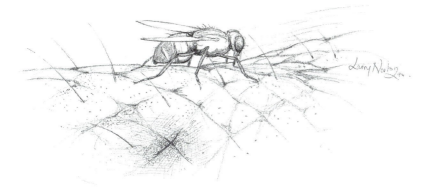

If, however, a leech finds an elephant taking a casual bathe and can creep into its anus, the days of precarious wanderings are over. However successfully and however long a leech maintains this position it will certainly never suck the elephant dry.

Rothschild & Clay, 1952

HOMES FOR THE HUMBLE

I HAVE never found a leech in an elephant's anus, but I will take Miriam Rothschild and Teresa Clay's word for it that it can provide a fine home for a lucky leech. They also favoured the trunk of an elephant according to Pliny who remarked:

> The beast is by their tickling and sucking in his snout almost mad;
> which doth manifestly show the wonderful power of insects; for
> what is there greater than an elephant? and what is there more
> despicable than a horse leech? Yet the greatness and wit of the
> elephant must give way and yield to this Worm.

I can find no other references to leeches occurring in an elephant's trunk either, but it sounds a very plausible happening since they abound in many of the elephants' favoured places.

An elephant provides an ample home for many parasites, both ectoparasites – those that pass a precarious existence on the outside of the body in the leathery cracks and folds of the skin – and endoparasites – those which live more comfortably perhaps inside its capacious body. And there are also the symbionts – creatures which live inside the elephant but which, as it were, live with it and do not parasitize it by sucking its blood or eating its flesh.

The causative organisms of disease – the viruses, bacteria and single-celled animals or protozoa – are all parasites, even though they may kill their host.

The Elephant Doctors

During the previous two centuries several Indian princes employed British veterinarians to look after their elephants and, together with the imperial government's interest in using elephants, this led to four classic works on diseases and parasites in Asian elephants. The first of these was written in 1851 by W. Gilchrist, to be followed by M. Slym in 1873, J. Steel in 1885 and G. Evans in 1910. By Evans's time a whole veterinary science had grown up around elephants, albeit smacking rather of a medieval apothecary than of science but an improvement on methods such as the 18th century Assamese one of throwing a tortoise into a river, always considered a good cure for sickness in elephants. Evans listed 236 'drugs' employed in the treatment of elephants, among which were arsenic, strychnine, datura, henbane, camphor, opium (widely used), sweet spirits of nitre and, we are informed, croton oil (a drastic purgative) which was useful in apoplexy. It was still a common practice in J.H. Williams's time to keep normally uncontrollable elephants quiet with opium. No wonder they went wild when the effects wore off.

Although probably reflecting the state of veterinary science in general at the beginning of this century, the majority of the 'cures' was probably no more effective than the Indian mahout's custom of feeding an elephant a piece of tiger's liver to make it brave, or of pushing down its throat the eyeballs of the great horned owl, torn from the living bird, in order to make the elephant see well at night.

Aristotle was in error when he stated 'The elephant does not appear to suffer from any other infirmity except flatulency'. Anaemia has been found in populations in Uganda, both in the Queen Elizabeth and Murchison Falls Parks. One quarter of the number of captive elephants in the United States suffer from rheumatoid arthritis, believed to be caused by a bacterial organism known as a mycoplasma. Whether this is contracted from humans or whether elephants contract it from the wild is not known. Boil-like bumps on the skin in past times were usually found to be encysted bullets and pellets. Elephant pox has been recorded in Asian and African elephants, characterized by eruptions similar to those of smallpox in man.

As to their flatulence Aristotle wrote:

> Elephants suffer from flatulent diseases, for which reason they can neither evacuate their fluid or solid excrements. If they eat earth they become weak, unless used to such food. If it is accustomed to it, it does no harm. Sometimes the elephant swallows stones. It also suffers from diarrhoea. When attacked with this complaint, they are cured by giving them warm water to drink, and hay dipped in honey to eat; and either of these remedies will stop the disease.

In more modern times studies in East Africa showed that elephants at high densities restricted to national parks apparently had a higher incidence of cardiovascular abnormalities than those inhabiting forest habitats. The main disease was an elephant arteriosclerosis, involving the deposition of calcareous materials and fats on the walls of the aorta, coronary arteries and peripheral muscular arteries. The vessels become narrowed as in man, yet elephants eat no animal fats and probably only a small amount of vegetable oil. A thickening of the blood found in some elephants from the Murchison Falls Park may be associated with this condition or it may be an artefact resulting from shock when the animal is shot. Although some changes in the blood in the dry season in Murchison Falls elephants were possibly due to dehydration, this was thought to be unlikely as the cause of the blood thickening.

It is considered that this spontaneous arteriosclerosis is found only in elephants where they are overpopulated. In Luangwa the lesions increased with age in number and calcification and it has been suggested that unlike arteriosclerosis caused by high cholesterol levels in man, in the elephant it is a repair action to damage caused to the arteries by wear and tear of the pressure of blood through them and death from 'stroke', the blocking of the arteries, must be very rare among wild elephants. There is no simple relationship between arteriosclerosis in the elephant and cholesterol levels in its blood.

PIANO KEYS AND SUDDEN DEATH

No serious viral disease is known to affect elephants but they show positive reactions to most arboviruses for which they have been tested. Arboviruses (the name simply means arthropod-borne viruses), usually transmitted by mosquitoes, are tropical viruses of which we know very little but that they are often fatal to man and domestic animals. Ten per cent of elephants tested in Uganda showed a positive reaction for the yellow fever virus, fatal to man, showing that they had been infected with it. Greater than 70% were positive for the Bunyamwera, West Nile and Wesselsbron viruses. West Nile affects the brain of horses and is fatal, while Wesselsbron causes abortion and death in sheep. What their effects on elephants are we do not know. Antibodies for African horse sickness, fatal to horses, are commonly found in the elephant in East Africa.

Foot-and-mouth disease, a virus disease particularly affecting cattle, was allegedly first identified in Asian elephants in the Afghan campaign in 1839, when one elephant died and several shed the hoof-slipper, the horny sole of the foot. Since then there have been other reports from India up to the present day and a particular strain of foot-and-mouth virus has recently been isolated. In all cases it was alleged that it was contracted from cattle or other infected animals, possibly transmitted indirectly. It is potentially of great importance in countries like Botswana that export beef to the European Common Market, which insists upon the beef coming from foot-and-mouth disease-free zones. Fortunately so far it has not been isolated from the African elephant and the elephant has not been incriminated in the transmission of the African types of virus.

The most serious bacterial disease affecting elephants is anthrax. Evidence of its persistence in the dried spore form is provided by the remarkable case of the piano-key maker in America who died suddenly of anthrax in 1946. A case of 'the biter bit', he contracted the disease from spores present on a tusk that he had been cutting up. Anthrax is common in the soil in most countries and erupts from time to time in many species of animals. It is usually seasonal in occurrence, its development favoured by alkaline warm waters such as are found towards the end of the dry season in many places in the tropics. It is a common cause of death among elephants in Etosha Park, occurring throughout the year with a peak in November towards the end of the hot dry season, when waterholes are drying up. A mystery is that this is contrary to its occurrence in other herbivores in the area, such as zebra, among which deaths peak in the rains in March.

In one outbreak over 200 elephants died, adult bulls succumbing more frequently than cows perhaps because they spend more time at infected waterholes. Considerable numbers of elephants are believed to die in the South and North Luangwa Parks from this cause. In Zaïre prior to the slaughter by poachers, a number of elephants died each year on the flat land to the west of L. Albert, possibly 1000 having died there in the three months from December 1960 to February 1961. Deaths also occurred in the Karuma Falls area of Uganda.

Anthrax was probably the cause of enzootics which have taken place repeatedly in Asia. About 1858 half (150) of the Indian government elephants at Dacca died at the same time that wild elephants were dying, the disease lasting with varying virulence for over ten years. In 1862 a similar outbreak occurred in the Chittagong forests and numbers of wild elephants died from anthrax in Mysore in 1903. In Burma it was considered to be most common among working elephants at the beginning and at the end of the rains, but the Burmese ascribed such deaths to the elephants eating a black hairy caterpillar. From 1935 regular inoculation was practised with much success among Burmese timber elephants.

Captive elephants in the United States are often afflicted by *Salmonella*, which is nearly always fatal. Three different species of the bacterium were isolated from elephants which became sick and died imported into Britain from northern Uganda. A 14 year old 3.3 tonne bull domesticated African elephant roaming freely near Tsavo Park also succumbed to this disease. At the post mortem it was found that the entire intestinal lining had been eroded away by the bacteria. This incident suggests that its occurrence is probably more common as a cause of death among wild elephants than is generally supposed.

Of protozoan or single-celled parasites which live in the blood, anaplasma (gall sickness), babesia or piroplasma (redwater), theileria (east coast fever) and trypanosomes have been found. Elephants from East Africa have also been found infected with a leptospirosis or spirochaete, a microscopic wormlike creature which is widespread in the world and found in many species, including man in which some produce fever. The spirochaetes can be passed out in the urine and remain alive and infective in damp soil or in alkaline water for several weeks.

A form of tick fever or redwater caused by a babesia is well known in Asian elephants. Transmitted by hard ticks, the protozoan invades the blood corpuscles and can cause high fever, anaemia and general weakness. It is probably widespread in African elephants but only one isolation of an unknown species has so far been made, from a sick elephant.

Although small calves may well succumb to the disease there is no authenticated record of an African elephant being susceptible to trypanosomiasis, the disease which causes sleeping sickness in man and fatal nagana in cattle. However, a form of trypanosomiasis known as *surra* common in horses also affects Asian elephants, in which it is known as *thut*. The trypanosome, *Trypanosoma evansi*, is transmitted mechanically by tabanid or 'horse' flies and can cause a form of dropsy in working elephants, fluid accumulating under the skin around the neck, chest, abdomen and legs. It appears to run a chronic course and the elephants usually recover. Wild elephants are probably seldom infected, taking more evasive action from the flies than working elephants can.

There are only two isolated records of finding trypanosomes in the blood of an African elephant, both from Uganda. The first was described by Bruce in 1909 from an elephant shot near L. Albert and the second not until 1970 from an elephant shot near Busoga, provisionally believed to be a subspecies of Bruce's trypanosome, *Trypanosoma brucei*, known as *T. brucei elephantis* or Bruce's elephant trypanosome.

Steel, in his book *A Manual of the Diseases of the Elephant and of his Management and Uses* published in 1885, recorded that the tsetse fly in South Africa 'has proved a serious enemy to the elephants, its poison giving rise to anthracoid symptoms and rapidly fatal results'. Where he got this idea from is hard to tell, unless it was from Rankin's account in 1882 of the Asian elephants walked from the Tanzanian coast to Mpwapa, and which were so bitten by tsetses which 'swarmed' on them that blood 'trickled down their flanks in a constant stream'. Three of the elephants died on the way and trypanosomiasis could well have been the cause, although there was no evidence to this effect. There are no other known published references to tsetse flies affecting elephants other than in Steel's work, although elephants are a major host to tsetse flies in some areas, as near Mombasa in Kenya.

DESPICABLE WORMS

Worms are numerous in elephants, exactly how many different species one cannot say as they are being found all the time. Some 15 have been recorded from the large intestine of the Asian elephant, compared with six in the African. Altogether the Asian elephant has ten more internal parasites so far known than does the African. There are numbers of roundworms, one lives in the coverings of arteries and limb muscles as well as in the bile duct; another minute one lives in the intestines.

In the African elephant strongylid worms, not all of which are bloodsuckers, inhabit the stomach, intestines and caecum. One species of stomach worm causes gastric ulcers. There are three species of hookworm or ancylostomes, voracious bloodsuckers, longer than the strongylids with some males being up to almost 5 cm in length living in the bile duct. *Grammocephalus clathratus* of the African elephant causes inflammation and swelling of the bile duct when it is numerous. In Mkomazi it was found in all elephants older than two months, the calves becoming infected as soon as they began to take in any grass.

A new nematode worm, *Leiperenia moreli*, was found recently in the large intestine of elephants from south eastern Zimbabwe which differs from previously known species found in Uganda and India. The females are viviparous, producing partly developed larvae which mature in the same host, no stage of the life cycle being passed outside the elephant. This lack of a freeliving stage indicates a long evolutionary association and it is interesting that the most closely related genus is found in the hyrax.

No worm is common to both the African and Asian elephants, although the African shares one trichostrongyle, *Murshidia omoensis*, with the black rhinoceros. The Asian elephant has its own species, *Murshidia murshida*. All the worms inhabit the alimentary tract, mostly in the large intestine, except for the hookworm *Grammocephalus* which lives in the bile duct. One species of hookworm which lives in the small intestine of the Asian elephant has been described, named *Bathmostomum sangeri* or Sanger's deep-mouth, after Lord George Sanger of circus fame who had the doubtful distinction of losing a whole herd of performing elephants from the worm.

One type of gapeworm characteristically found in the windpipe of birds and some mammals, and which goes under the lengthy name of *Mammomonogamus loxodontis* in its African host, is found in the respiratory passages, sometimes in hard bundles blocking the smaller ducts. The Asian elephant has its own species, *M. indicus*.

Two spiroid worms occur in the stomach and intestine walls and a number of filariid worms have been recorded from the blood. Filariid worms have microscopic infective larval stages known as microfilariae which are transmitted by bloodsucking insects. Three quarters of a sample of working elephants were found to be infected in Thailand and one third in Sri Lanka, but as microfilariae may show nocturnal periodicity in the blood they are not always easily detected. Suffice to say that such infections appear to be common.

One filariid worm, *Stephanofilaria assamensis*, lives in cauliflower-like nodules which it creates on the heels of the Asian elephant in India. Two species known as *Loxodontofilaria* live under the skin of the African elephant, one from eastern and southern Africa very similar to a species found in the hippopotamus. A similar but distinct species, *L. asiatica*, has been found in the Asian elephant in Burma. In the Asian elephant *Indofilaria pattabiramani* causes skin nodules which repeatedly bleed, but do not seem to cause the elephant undue distress unless they become infected. The infective microfilariae stage of *Dipetalonema* causes a form of hepatitis in the African elephant.

Two large species of flatworms or flukes are known from the African elephant: a liver fluke which lives in the liver and bile duct, formerly known as *Distomum robusta* or big two-mouth but now as *Protofasciola robusta*; and a pear-shaped one living in the large intestine, almost 2 cm in length and formerly known as *Brumptia gigas* or Brumpt's giant but now as *B. bicaudata* or Brumpt's two-tail. The Asian elephant is host to a liver fluke *Fasciola jacksoni* just over a centimetre in length which can cause death in working elephants, and a small pink-coloured fluke which attaches itself by suckers in the large intestine, formerly known as *Amphistoma hawkesii*, or Hawkes's mouth on both sides, but now as *Hawkesius hawkesii*; described as like grains of barley and smaller than the African species. Tapeworm cysts have been found in the liver of Asian elephants but have not so far been recorded from African. The Asian elephant also harbours an adult tapeworm, *Anoplocephala manubriata*.

Both elephants also have their own specific type of bilharzia infection by *Bivitellobilharzia* species.

The idea that salt-licks were a kind of elephants' chemist's shop which they visited for salts to clear out their intestinal worms seems to have originated with Captain Forsyth in 1871 in the book *The Highlands of Central India*. Forsyth wrote:

> Elephants are very liable to intestinal worms. They generally cure themselves, when they get very troublesome, by swallowing from ten to twenty pounds of earth. They always select a red-coloured earth for the purpose. In about twelve hours after, purging commences and all the worms come away.

In fact it is the salt which the elephants seek and if it does clear out some of the worms then that is an unintentional bonus.

OF BOTS AND GREEK CUCKOLDS

In one of his books James Herriot relates the story of Sam Broadbent who could stampede heifers by making the noise of a warble fly. Warble or oestrid flies are troublesome to cattle in the summer, laying their eggs on the hairs. A minute larva hatches from the egg and bores its way through the skin of the animal, working its way through the tissues until it finally comes to rest under the skin on the back. Here it bores a hole through the skin to the outside world and standing on its head breathes through the hole via its hind end and proceeds to grow large. When big enough it pushes its way out backwards and falls to the ground where it pupates.

Cattle somehow appear to associate the attentions of the fly with the irritation that the maggots subsequently cause and can be driven frantic by the fly's buzzing sound, although the flies have no mouth and cannot bite or sting. The ancient Greek goddess Juno, having discovered that her husband Jupiter had fallen in love with Io, sent a warble fly to persecute her rival who had been disguised by Jupiter as a heifer. Io was driven to frantically running about all over the place by its torment until she came to the banks of the Nile, where her shape was restored to her. The Greeks called this fly 'oistros'. Hence some witty scholar steeped in classical lore gave the name 'oestrus' to a female on heat and the flies are known as oestrid flies.

There is another very similar fly known as a bot fly. Stomach bot flies also parasitize horses, zebras and rhinoceroses, but those of the African and Asian elephants are more primitive. The maggot stage is fairly conservative; it is impossible to tell many of them apart, but the flies can show marked differences. They have reduced mouthparts and do not feed, dying after they have laid their eggs or deposited their larvae. Two genera are specific to the African elephant and one infects only the Asian. Like the warble, the bot fly lays its eggs on the hairs of the host but then these are usually taken in by the animal and find their way to the stomach where they develop attached to the stomach wall. When mature, they pass out in the droppings to pupate in the ground.

Whether elephants are driven to behave like Io by warble flies is not known, but they are plagued by not one but several of both kinds, although only one known has maggots which develop under the skin, most living in the elephant's insides.

The type like our own cattle warble is known as the African elephant skin maggot, *Ruttenia loxodontis*, and is found in boils in the skin on the buttocks, stomach flanks, chest, thighs and in the ears. Described so far only from Zaïre, although 'warbles' have been recorded from elephants in East Africa, the larvae appear seasonally under the skin in the dry season from the end of September to the beginning of February. The pupa takes about three weeks to complete its metamorphosis. Another species, *Elephantoloemus indicus* or the Indian plague to elephants, occurs in Asian elephants in Burma where they are reported as being numerous on working elephants:

> The elephants from which these 'bots' were taken literally swarm with swellings in all parts – head, ears and body. The scars of recent eruptions are in some parts of the body so closely pitted as to impart to the skin a honeycomb appearance, showing that thousands of the parasites have burrowed out during the last few months. Curiously enough, only the elephants brought from India

last year are affected . . . In the elephants from which the specimens were taken the numbers were almost incredible.

Probably the same species occurs on elephants in Thailand. The pupa takes about ten days to metamorphose.

Peculiar to the African elephant, living in the throat is a specialized bot of the African elephant throat bot fly, *Pharyngobolus africanus*, restricted to the equatorial forest belt and not found in southern Africa. The first elephant bot to be described, it was found in an African elephant which died in the Vienna Zoo in 1866 and rediscovered 50 years later in the Congo. The female is viviparous, depositing the live larvae near the tip of the trunk or around the eyes. The migration of the maggots into the throat where, fat and white, they are sometimes found in large, squirming numbers, can only be guessed at. The maggots are found in the morning in fresh elephant's droppings quickly burying themselves in the soil. So they are swallowed and passed out through the alimentary tract when ready to pupate, not sneezed out through the trunk as is sometimes supposed. The relatively large fly, about 13–15 mm in length, emerges after about three weeks pupation.

Apparently found in the Siberian woolly mammoth, this parasitic niche does not seem to have been exploited in the Asian elephant, although Evans wrote:

> That bots find lodgement in the pharynx of the elephant in Burma is certain. It is not a rare occurrence for an elephant to suddenly commence a sort of coughing or sneezing and blow bots out of the trunk.

This may be the manner of exit of the stomach bot, which in the African elephant is coughed up.

If you dissect an elephant you may find as many as 1000 large fat maggots up to 2 cm in length fixed to the stomach wall, as did Dr J. Kirk in an elephant shot on the Zambezi River in Livingstone's 1858–1863 expedition. A similar maggot was already known from the Asian elephant as the black elephant stomach bot fly, *Ruttenia (Cobboldia) elephantis*. Also first recorded from the Vienna Zoo, in 1896, the colourful Asian species is about the size of a bee, with an ochraceous-orange head, deep black body and purplish-black wings with white roots. It emerges after a little more than two weeks pupation. It is abundant in the early rains in grassy places and is such a pest that elephants at this time keep as much as possible to heavy cover. The flies attach their eggs to the hairs about the mouth or to the tusks near the gums. When the eggs hatch the larvae probably actively migrate to the mouth or nostrils and then to the gut.

Common in the stomach of the African elephant everywhere, the African species was not given a specific name until it was more fully described from specimens supplied by the German explorer Dr Oscar Neumann (not to be confused with the elephant hunter A.H. Neumann) in 1897 and it was named *Cobboldia loxodontis*, now *Platycobboldia loxodontis*. The adult fly, which is very shortlived, lays its eggs at the base of the elephant's trunk and the maggots find their way into the mouth and are swallowed. When ready to pupate these creatures detach themselves from the stomach wall, to which they have clung by means of hooks around their mouths, and somehow make their way up the elephant's throat, gathering under the elephant's tongue until he coughs them out onto the ground. Here they pupate in the soil for 2–3 weeks, emerging looking like blow flies up to just over a centimetre in length.

One species found in elephants throughout Africa, the blue elephant stomach bot fly, has a metallic blue body and orange head; another, the green elephant stomach bot fly, found from elephants in Zaïre and South Africa, has a metallic green body. A third species, also known only from Zaïre, is not known in the fly stage. Of course entomologists do not mean that the elephants are coloured but the flies.

Three bots, including the species living in the pharynx, have been found in mammoths. The stomach bot *Cobboldia russanovi* with the others, became extinct upon the extinction of the mammoth.

Ugly as they may appear, the elephant stomach bot fly maggots are profoundly interesting, because those of the blue and green bot flies not only live side by side in the same elephant's stomach, restricted to the peaked end where the wall is folded, but these two species of maggot look exactly the same as each other. It is the adult flies which differ. So what do these maggots feed on inside the elephant's stomach? Do they both partake of the same nourishment or do they each have specific preferences? Orthodox theory has it that different species do not occupy the same niche for competition would drive one of them to develop an alternative food resource or alternative way of life. The flies themselves, although very different in appearance, appear to have the same lifestyles, although they may be found to deposit their eggs or larvae in different sites on the elephant. If they have the same food and behave in the same way the theory of natural selection tells us that they should be the same creature; there is no selection for them to be different.

It would be of interest to know whether the bot and the warble which the Asian elephant took with it when it migrated from its African home have evolved faster or more slowly than their African counterparts. Or have they remained the same? And how do those of the woolly mammoth compare? As far as is known the parasites of the two elephants, which are peculiar to them, are host specific and cannot exist on the other elephant. There are just as exciting things to be found out about the elephants' maggots as there are about elephants.

Stranger still is the elephant foot fly, *Neocuterebra squamosa*. Neither a warble fly nor a bot fly, it is placed on its own for the maggot lives in the sole of the elephant's foot. The fly of this creature of such strange habits is dark metallic blue or violet, up to almost $2\frac{1}{2}$ cm in length. It is known only from the Central African Republic, Cameroun, Zaïre and Uganda.

OF FLIES THAT BITE

In AD 337 when Shapur II, King of Persia, was besieging Nisibis in Mesopotamia, it is reported that the bishop St James, leading the defence of the town, sent

FIG. 7.1 *The elephant foot maggot at home in the sole of the foot of an African elephant (Uganda).*

a swarm of gnats to sting the trunks of the attacking elephants. The elephants and beasts of burden were so suddenly and furiously attacked by the swarms as to kill or disable them, causing the siege to be raised. Whether it happened in such a manner or whether simply mosquitoes and malaria overcame them, we shall never know but the latter explanation seems more likely. Nevertheless, in parts of Asia bloodsucking biting flies are very troublesome at certain times of the year, the large horseflies drawing blood readily. After thunderstorms towards the end of the hot season and also during breaks in the monsoon, the flies swarm out of the jungle attacking any animals that they can find.

Elephants become very agitated by these attacks and with ears flapping, tails and trunks swinging, make hurried journeys to escape them. In Africa biting flies do not seem to present such a problem but elephants probably avoid spending much time in very mosquito-infested places. Normally they would drink in daylight when mosquitoes are not abroad, but where harassed they are driven to drinking at night, mosquitoes being a lesser evil than an arrow or a bullet.

Elephants are certainly found where tsetse flies are at their worst and seem to put up with them with equanimity, despite Steel's assertion. The tiny bloodsucking *Stomoxys*, together with similar gnats *Lyperosia* and *Haematobia*, attacks most mammals, as also do the larger tabanids or horse flies and tsetse flies, but although stomoxys have been seen swarming on African elephants they have not been detected taking their blood. It was said that elephants were driven from the shores of L. Chad in the dry season by a fly which flew into their ears, perhaps a reference to stomoxys.

Not content with merely sucking the blood of their hosts, there are at least six curious biting midges in Africa, cousins to the mosquito, which rear their larvae in the dung of animals. All use elephant dung but one, the newly discovered *Culicoides loxodontis*, is specific to elephant dung. So far found only in the Kruger Park, its distribution in Africa is probably much wider. Up to 500 have been reared from 2.5 kg of wet elephant droppings, emerging as midges in 8–10 days. This is as much as we know of their life cycle. Do the midges then rest in vegetation like tsetse flies, zooming out to examine each passing animal to see if it is suitable for a blood meal? Until she is gorged with blood the female cannot develop her eggs so she will not seek elephant droppings until she has fed. Their existence must be increasingly precarious as elephants become scarcer and scarcer.

There was much alarm in the press at the end of the 1980s concerning a different type of fly, a kind of bluebottle known as a screw-worm which lays its eggs on wounds in the skin of animals. The maggots feed on the living flesh and can kill the host. A screw-worm known as the New World screw-worm fly had been imported into north west Libya from South America and became established in 1988, spreading amongst domestic animals. A serious pest of livestock in the Americas, concern was expressed that it might get into the wild game and become impossible to control, so a major campaign was launched using the technique of releasing sterile males to bring it under control. By mid-1991 this appeared to have been successful.

In fact a species of screw-worm was already widespread in tropical Africa and parts of Asia, known as the Old World screw-worm or *Chrysomia bezziana*. It is frequent in cattle and sometimes occurs in man, but the only wild animal known to be infected in Africa is the elephant, which seems to tolerate it. The eggs are laid under the gum at the base of the tusk and when they emerge the maggots erode the ivory causing pitting of the surface. In the Asian elephant it has only been recorded in the cow.

ELEPHANT TICKS

On the outside of the African elephant at least 21 species of hard tick find a home, of which two, *Dermacentor circumguttatus* and *Amblyomma tholloni*, are elephant ticks, the first having been found also on the grey duiker, perhaps an accidental host. Other than these two, the rest parasitize many other animals as well, so they have no particular adaptations for piercing the elephant's thick skin since they find its soft spots easily enough.

A PECULIAR LOUSE

It can be truly said that there are no fleas on an elephant but this is not true of lice. A louse, if it was not firmly attached, might well be rubbed off the elephant's skin or get stuck in the mud when the elephant's several tons roll upon it. Some hardy specimens may effect transference from one host to another at mud wallows. Until the early 1950s it was thought that the African elephant's louse, *Haematomyzus elephantis*, first found on an African elephant in the Rotterdam Zoo in 1869, was unique to the elephant, the Asian elephant having the same species. In Africa it occurs on elephants from the Sudan to the Transvaal but in smaller numbers than on Asian elephants, no more than three per elephant having been found on elephants in Kruger Park, although more may have been hidden in fissures of the skin. Then in the 1950s a louse was discovered in large numbers on a warthog in Uganda which appeared to be almost identical with the elephant's louse, differing from the warthog's own special species, *Haematopinus phacochoeri*. Found only on warthogs in Uganda and subsequently Kenya, more careful examination suggests that this louse is a different species to that occurring on the elephant and it is given the name of *Haematomyzus hopkinsi*.

Elephant and warthog lice are very special types of lice appearing to be intermediate between the two main groups, the *Anoplura* or sucking lice, which suck blood and are found exclusively on mammals, and the *Mallophaga* or biting lice, which occur mostly on birds, feeding upon hair, scurf, sebaceous matter and other detritus. The elephant louse, which is found on the head and in the abdominal regions, feeds on blood but appears to be in a stage of transition between a biting and a sucking louse, with unique piercing mouthparts. The puzzle is, did it evolve first on the elephant or on the warthog? As the louse is unlike any other it seems that it must have evolved on an isolated group of animals, like elephants. But how does the same species come to occur on both African and Asian elephant, two animals which have never been in close contact with one another?

There are some slight similarities in the structure of the breathing tubes, or spiracles, of a more widespread African louse which also occurs on the warthog and those of this specialized louse. So if it did first evolve on the warthog, how did it come to infest the elephant? Perhaps via the medium of mud wallows and in the prehistoric past this would have been more likely to involve *Elephas* which was roaming the African savannas while *Loxodonta* was hidden in the forest, for the warthog is not an animal of the tropical forest. But some overlap at forest edges could have taken place with *Loxodonta*, thus effecting transmission of the louse, just as the forest elephant and the savanna elephant use the same forest wallows today. The fact that it is less common on the African elephant than on the Asian suggests that it was acquired secondarily by one of the two. If lice could be recovered from frozen mammoths they might provide us with a clue or, as is more often the case, raise more questions than provide answers.

Lice are very host specific – they would rather die than feed upon a strange host. The specificity is due to the bacterial symbionts in their gut which break down the blood meal for them and not to any particular delicacy on the part of the louse.

Recently an ear mite, *Loxanoetus lenae*, has been found in an Asian circus elephant originating from Malaya which died in Australia. Until recently ear mites were known only from cattle, waterbuck and Uganda kob antelopes and the Australian wombat. Then in the 1960s large numbers of a new genus in all stages of development were found in the ears of an African elephant in the Kruger Park. It was named *Loxanoetus bassoni* and subsequently found also in the ears of buffalo in Uganda, which had two more species in addition. Later another genus, *Otanoetus wetzeli*, was found in the ears of an elephant in Namibia.

These mites, which can cause intense irritation in the ear and swelling of the bone, are known as slime mites, mites which have their mouthparts peculiarly adapted to a life in wet, organic substrates. Ear wax is one of their delicacies. They are probably spread by phoresis, carried from one host to another on the legs of biting flies that crawl around the ears, such as *Stomoxys* or *Lyperosia*.

THE MYSTERY OF THE SYMBIONTS

Mammals cannot digest cellulose, the complex sugar of which plant cell walls are constructed, and so herbivores must enlist the co-operation of protozoa and bacteria which produce the enzyme cellulase which breaks down cellulose. Herbivores therefore house a unique protozoan fauna in their guts known as ciliates, microscopic blobs of single-celled protoplasm possessed of a mouth, which propel themselves through the fluid of the gut by means of batteries of protoplasmic hairs or cilia. Many freeliving ones exist in either water or damp soil, best known of which is the slipper animalcule or *Paramecium*, but those which inhabit the guts of animals as symbionts or 'animal helpers' live an anaerobic existence, a life without oxygen, which is considered to be a primitive state. They reproduce themselves simply by dividing into two.

Intestinal ciliates are voracious little omnivores, not only ingesting particles of cellulose, chromatophores and other fragments of plant cells, but also bacteria and other protozoa. Two orders occur: the holotrichs which do not have a moustache of cilia around their mouth and the spirotrichs which have a permanently open gullet with the mouth surrounded by cilia.

In the elephant, unlike other hosts, they are found in all parts of the gut with the exception of the stomach and are most numerous in the colon where an estimated 46 million live per litre of gut fluid – and an elephant's gut holds several hundred litres of such fluid. Their numbers may fluctuate seasonally according to the amount of fibre in the diet, spirotrichs favouring a high fibre diet.

Eighteen species have so far been identified from the elephant, of which three were found for the first time in 1978, and three are common to both the African and the Asian elephant. Two species found in elephants from Zaïre have not been found in elephants from the Kruger Park so we may expect that other host and regional specificities exist. None of those found in ruminants has been found in elephants. The latest to be discovered is a new genus, *Pseudoentodinium elephantis*, found in the droppings of a captive Asian elephant.

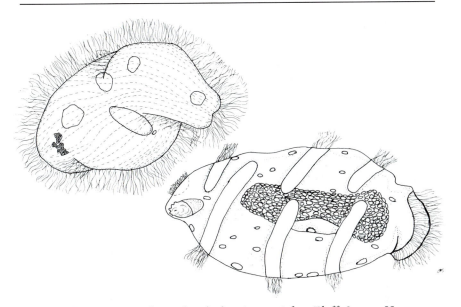

FIG. 7.2   *Protozoa from the elephant's gut (after Eloff & van Hoven, 1980).*

The largest is *Polydinium mysoreum*, its name, 'multi-whirler from Mysore', reminiscent of a dervish dancer. Common to both elephants, it is 3200 microns in length, the largest known and readily visible to the naked eye, but most are less than half of this size.

Essential to the efficient digestion of food in a herbivore, an unsolved mystery is how these intestinal protozoa are transmitted from one host to another. Very few are passed in the droppings and their life outside is of very short duration, especially in the presence of oxygen. In ruminants the transfer is believed to be effected by the parent licking the offspring. In rabbits coprophagy has been suggested, the eating of partially digested faeces by the young, and a similar mechanism has been suggested for elephants. Coprophagy is rare in elephants but there is one report of a matriarch which passed some very liquid dung in which the plant material had been well digested and younger members of the group eagerly and carefully scraped up small samples of the dung using trunk and forefoot and ingested them, later repeating the procedure.

CURIOUS AND CURIOUSER

Creatures which know that the elephant does cry are curious moths which drink the tears of mammals. Not really parasites, they are widespread in parts of Asia and come mainly from three families of nightflying moths: the prominents or *Notodontidae* and the unrelated *Pyralidae* and *Geometridae*, which include

FIG. 7.3   *A bull elephant with its helpers. Cattle egrets waiting for insects to be disturbed.*

moths known as carpets, waves and pugs. The caterpillars of the tear drinkers are unknown but those of the notodontids are capable of ejecting an irritating fluid, while most geometrids resemble twigs and are known as 'loopers' from the way in which they move by curving the body into a loop.

Attracted to any body fluids, from wounds and around the mouth or anus as well as sweat, some also use fresh elephant dung but they are particularly attracted to the eyes, probably because of the salt content. If tears are not present then these extraordinary moths insert the proboscis into the edge of the eyelid or tickle the surface of the eyeball with it until the elephant sheds tears. In this respect they could be said to become true parasites.

Generally brownish in colour some of the animal-loving notodontids are relatively large moths with wingspans of up to 79 mm and long bodies. *Tarsolepis elephantoroum*, a recently discovered species, is distinguished by a forked tuft of hairs on its tail. It is found most frequently on elephants in Laos and Thailand, while in peninsular Malaysia and south west China *T. remicauda* has the same behaviour. Groups of 5–10 have been seen flying around an elephant's head trying to settle and three moths were seen to suck at one eye together for over two minutes. Clinging with its forelegs, the moth beats its wings furiously while sucking. An elephant can become agitated by the flickering around its eyes and often vented its annoyance on the observer.

Semiothisa elephantedestructa is another newly discovered species, so named *elephantedestructa* because when first seen sucking tears from below the eye of an elephant it was then abruptly crushed with an unceremonious swipe of the elephant's trunk. A geometrid moth, it has a wingspan of about 37 mm. One species, *S. inaequilinea*, has been recorded from South Africa although it has not been seen on elephants.

It takes a great deal of zeal to spend one's nights out in the jungle watching elephants and other animals with a flashlight, but that is just what Dr Bänziger did in Thailand to discover this remarkable relationship. The true enthusiast, he even allowed specimens which favour man to tickle his own eyeball and make him cry in the cause of science. Anyone prepared to watch elephants at night in central African forests will no doubt reveal more species with the same habits as their Asian counterparts.

TINY HELPERS

Besieged by an army of external parasites, the elephant receives some relief from their attentions by the assistance of somewhat larger winged creatures; the tick birds, egrets and the piapiac. Tick birds are not common on elephants, perhaps because they irritate them, but they occur to some extent. In northern Uganda their place is taken by a glossy blue-black starling known as the piapiac which is tolerated by the elephant. The little white cattle egret follows along at the elephant's feet seizing insects that it disturbs, but it also jumps up and picks ticks off the elephant's belly. Well, the elephant should be grateful for that.

Chapter 8

MATRIARCHS AND MUSTH: SOCIAL BEHAVIOUR OF ELEPHANTS

Perhaps the barbarous practice of hunting the African elephants for the sake of their teeth, has rendered them more untractable and savage, than they were found to be in former times.

Mungo Park, 1799

WISE OLD COWS

ELEPHANTS possess one of the most advanced and harmonious social organizations known amongst mammals. The basis of this is the matriarch: 'Wise old cows lead elephant herds' as one writer expressed it. William Bazé writing in 1950 of the Asian elephant in Vietnam stated: 'The wild herd, therefore, is ruled by a matriarchy. The oldest females . . . are usually the leaders of the herd'. Three quarters of all elephant groups examined in culling schemes in Kenya and Uganda included a matriarch ranging in age from 38 to 60 years with an average age of 49. These mothers or grandmothers are important in leadership and infant care and when a group is alarmed it always bunches on the matriarch, following her lead. Whether it is the African elephant or the Asian, it is the matriarch which always charges in case of danger and takes the rear position in flight.

That elephants differ from most other mammalian societies, in which it is the male which plays the dominant role in social grouping and defence, has been known for many years, although not generally recognized perhaps because it did not accord with the macho image with which hunters liked to label their quarry. John Corse wrote in 1790 of the Asian elephant: 'a herd in general consists of from about 40 to 100, and is conducted under the direction of one of the oldest and largest females, called the *Palmai* [herd leader], and one of the largest males'. In 1878 Sanderson was to write: 'A herd is invariably led by a female, never a male . . .' He had an ingenious explanation for this:

> . . . they must accomodate the length and time of their marches, and
> the localities in which they rest or feed at different hours, to the
> requirements of their young ones; consequently the guidance of a
> tusker would not suit them.

In this he anticipated by a century Cynthia Moss who spent many years studying the elephants of Amboseli, for she noted that the cow with a new calf was often obliged to move independently of the group as the small calf was unable to keep up.

This tends to nullify the theory that family units evolved primarily as a defence against predators. More probably they result from the bulls' social organization reflecting their incompatability with one another in times of musth. Additionally family units have value as schools of learning with the grandmother as teacher. Young bulls thus stay at school for almost the same length of time as young boys, but then having no Dickens's Wackford Squeers to discipline them, they leave and form their own unruly gangs.

During control operations the significance of the matriarch's role has been underlined. When alarmed the family group crowds closely together while the matriarch tries to identify the threat and then if it is not too close she leads the group away at speed. If one or more of the group is shot, then in cases where there is no small calf she will often defend others that have been shot and has been observed to alternately try to lift two such shot animals or try to cover them with trunkfuls of debris, the latter activity perhaps being an attempt to hide rather than bury them.

But if she herself is shot, then the group mills about in panic and all cohesion is lost. The whole family clusters around her body, often trying to nudge her upright, making it easy for them to be destroyed.

Although the technique of shooting the matriarch first was introduced into culling operations in Uganda at the beginning of the 1960s, its efficacy and the social structure of elephants were already known to the hunter James Chapman in southern Africa a century before. In his *Notes on the Elephant* written in 1856 (which were not published until 1971), he wrote:

FIG. 8.1   *A fine cow elephant in Uganda, showing a temporal gland discharge.*

> Elephants are gregarious and run in herds which separate into families and meet again at certain points. Except for young ones, or one or two who seem to act as an escort, the males are found separate from the females during most of the year... A favourite plan amongst hunters is to drive a troop of cow elephants... When thoroughly knocked up, the hunters drive them, if they can, into a patch of bush or a few trees, where they huddle together, their young ones in the middle. One occasionally ventures to charge, but they are generally all shot down, one after the other, before they can recover breath. Bulls, unlike cows, who combine for mutual defence, cannot be hunted in this way, as they generally disperse in different directions when closely pressed ...

Living together in small family units the oldest cow guards her close relatives, for the basic family is composed of 5–6 related animals. The simplest has an average of three members consisting of a mother and her 1–2 offspring. This forms the fundamental population unit.

African elephant calves are thus born into stable groups of related cows. The daughters remain with these groups perhaps for the rest of their lives as they depend heavily on the co-operative efforts of the group for protection and the wisdom of the matriarch in finding food. They cannot join new groups, being repulsed by the members.

Sons, on the other hand, slowly become independent, not being abruptly driven away as is the case in some ungulate species. At about 14 years of age the young bulls have joined another family group as a step towards independence or have begun to associate with other young bulls. In Sri Lanka the young bulls appear to leave the family unit at puberty, but older juvenile bulls may feed slightly apart from the family unit, often moving in advance of it.

In India Sanderson noted:

> Each herd of elephants is a family in which the animals are nearly allied to each other. Though the different herds do not intermix, escaped tame female elephants, or young males, appear to find no difficulty in obtaining admittance to the herds. (When they were resting, he recorded) ... they usually dispose themselves in small distinct squads of animals which seem to have an affection for each other.

In the African elephant two or three of these families will often spend much time together forming the group size of 5–6, sometimes larger – as many as ten in high density populations. The larger groups continually split up for a few days, joining again later. These kin groups are probably related as a matriarch and her immature offspring, together with one or more mature daughters and their offspring forming an 'extended family'.

Tennent pointed out the relevance of the family in elephant social behaviour when writing of the Asian elephant in Sri Lanka in 1859:

> A *herd* of elephants is a family, not a group whom accident or attachment may have induced to associate together. Similarity of features and caste attest that, among the various individuals which compose it, there is a common lineage and relationship.

Sanderson, while claiming that much of Tennent's book was based upon imagination, apparently agreed with him on this point, for he stated : 'Each herd of elephants is a family in which the animals are nearly allied to each other'.

The matriarch has the wisdom of many years to help and guide the daily and seasonal movements of the group in its search for food, water and mineral resources. This is especially important to bush elephants whose habitat is characterized by highly localized seasonal rainfall. The old cow, grandmother to most of the group, knows from her many years which are the best wet and dry season feeding and watering areas, areas which may be widely spread out within the family group's home range. This wisdom provides her with an almost uncanny knowledge of the habitat. In Tsavo Park the day that a waterhole dried up a family which had visited it regularly failed to appear, but instead watered at another point $3\frac{1}{2}$ km away.

Such aptitude makes the matriarch important to the survival of future generations of elephants as her knowledge is learned by her daughters, who pass it on to their daughters and so on. This means that the areas of the home ranges and the movement patterns of the animals within them are very conservative, remaining the same over long periods of time, even although in drought years there may be drastic changes during the dry seasons. In southern India Sukumar showed that movements in 1981 to 1983 followed exactly the same pattern as that described by Sanderson for the same area in 1878.

The structure of the small groups of the forest elephant is not known, but even here stored knowledge is equally important since they move from one patch of fruiting trees to another scattered over a wide area and they must arrive at the appropriate time.

HELPING OTHERS

On many occasions the matriarch has been seen to stop and try to lift a member of the group which had been shot. Usually the matriarch also assists wounded bulls and hunters' tales of bulls helping wounded bulls were more often than not cases of mistaken gender.

There are few cases of bulls helping bulls. It is usually a case of each one for himself as there is nothing to bond the group together. As Chapman noted, they scatter in all directions when alarmed. It is not to their genetic advantage to help one another, for they are in reproductive competition with each other. The cow, on the other hand, is ensuring that it is her genes which are perpetuated when she helps other members of her family. Of course it would be in a bull's interest to help members of his own family but he leaves it and the chances are that the bulls with which he associates are not related to him.

That elephants knowingly help one another was shown by a bull African elephant in the Rome Zoo which was confined to a cage because its trunk was injured. An Asian cow elephant which had formed an attachment to him stood constantly by the bars of his cage feeling his trunk with her own and when he was not given any hay because of his injury, gave him some of her own, laying it in front of him with her trunk. Animal behaviourists agonize to find explanations which contradict an altruistic motive for such behaviour, that is, that the cow elephant was trying to help the bull elephant. Apparently all species should express the 'selfish gene', their actions selected to benefit themselves.

HAPPY FAMILIES

At Amboseli all of the total population of some 650 elephants knew one another. Forty seven family units were recognized, totalling 525 elephants (bulls above the age of puberty not remaining in the family units). Thirty two of these family units, comprising 253 elephants, formed a subpopulation; nine units within this subpopulation formed a clan of 55 elephants which shared the same range and often came together but did not form close bonds with one another; four units, comprising 20 elephants, formed a bond group of possibly related members, perhaps formed by overlarge families splitting up. The fundamental unit was composed of eight elephants led by a matriarch with three immature offspring and her related children.

In southern India family group size ranged from about five in the wet season to eight in the dry, perhaps the lower wet season figure indicating that the family was more spread out at that time. In Sri Lanka family groups comprised 15–40 animals which remained distinct from others in the same overlapping home range. These groups divided into two types of family unit, one comprising cows nursing calves, the other non-lactating cows and juveniles. These two types of family unit usually feed separately, the cows with nursing calves moving more slowly and over a smaller area than the more mobile cows with older young but both come together near water as members of the 'extended family'. This arrangement may be more evident in thicker vegetation and not so distinct in open country.

An animal like the elephant which is a member of a family unit for 10–20 years while immature can be expected to develop strong social bonds with its mother, brothers and sisters. This is reflected in the way the groups behave, almost invariably copying one another's activities. They all tend to feed, walk, rest, drink and wallow together and usually within a few yards of each other. Spreading out when feeding, they bunch together again when travelling or resting, the bunching accompanied by frequent greeting of one another.

Other groups may be associations of related cows, the original matriarch having left or died, but the most consistently stable association is between the cow and her youngest offspring. The family unit as a whole is not necessarily stable, although in the Manyara population the same animals were always found in the same families. But at Amboseli it was found to vary from family to family, some tending to split up, others to join permanently together. Others were very stable but yet mixed with other groups. The stability or otherwise is most affected by environmental conditions, large aggregations taking place when conditions are good. At Amboseli almost all of the elephants have been seen to come together under such conditions. But other factors which affect the stability of the family unit are the death of the matriarch of a very stable family; the unit becoming too large; the strength of the bonds between its members; the physical condition of an important member and the attempted immigration of a stranger.

Like those good little girls in Victorian stories who stay with their mothers and help raise the rest of the family, young cow elephants do just that. Only the young bulls leave these groups when they reach the age of puberty. They may not depart immediately from the group but hang around near the family for several years before making the final break. They do not meet aggression from the other wandering bulls unless they challenge them over cows or water rights, bulls associate freely with one another when not in musth and with the cows and calves again once they have become too big to be chased away.

No bulls have been seen to have particular attachments to one another but they are rarely very far away from each other. Young ones form small bachelor groups or gangs of roaming youths or they may attach themselves to an older bull, keeping separate from the family herds. In Uganda the average age of bull groups was just over 30 years, covering a wide range of ages from 20 to 49. Several had an old bull many years senior to the rest. The age distribution of solitary bulls is not different to that of the groups.

An individual may associate with related or non-related elephants in groups of various sizes and composition during a single day, but family groups show consistent association patterns with from one to five other family units to which they are probably related. These groups of families have been termed bond groups. Because of their long period of play and learning together, ties between individual family groups may be strongest between calves of similar age with different mothers; consequently the leaders of aggregates of family groups may be cousins rather than sisters when there is no clear matriarch.

Family units also associate loosely in larger gatherings termed clans, seemingly at random. Whether these are structural in the sense that the members are related is only supposition and they may be due to geographical proximity.

Elephants recognize each other at a distance and display great excitement when meeting again after even a short absence. They run together screaming and trumpeting, greeting one another by raising heads in the air and clicking tusks, intertwining trunks and rumbling loudly, flapping ears and holding them in the greeting attitude. They whirl around and rub on one another, backing and urinating. Temporal gland secretion is profuse, running down the sides of the face and into their mouths. Urinating and defaecating accompanied by loud rumbling and trumpeting can last up to ten minutes. Although excited when meeting, constantly reinforcing the group bonds, cows rarely spar.

WHEN ELEPHANTS GATHER

From time to time elephants may form huge gatherings of several hundred individuals. Although generally believed to be due to harassment by man or range compression, early accounts suggest they are of long standing.

In Uganda two types of such gatherings were identified. First those comprising many small herds which showed little co-ordination as a single unit. These numbered usually less than 100 individuals, but concentrations of up to 240 have been seen. They are thought to be random or chance aggregations of the clan, perhaps drawn together to good feeding after rainfall. When disturbed they break up and scatter. Tennent observed this type of association in Sri Lanka at the beginning of last century:

> In the forest several herds sometimes browse in close contiguity, and in their expeditions in search of water they may form a body of possibly one or two hundred; but on the slightest disturbance each distinct herd hastens to re-form within its own particular circle, and to take measures on its own behalf for retreat or defence.

The second type is much larger, with up to 1200 counted together. These tend to show co-ordination, moving as a single unit and not scattering when disturbed but bunching more tightly. In Uganda these were always found in certain areas, the largest over 800 animals. Always near to the periphery of the elephant range, they were never seen in the centre. Their age structure appeared to reflect that of the elephant population as a whole and it is thought they might have resulted from the shooting of matriarchs or breakdown of behavioural mechanisms which would promote dispersion, unable to disperse outwards because of conflict with human settlement, unable to retreat inwards because the home ranges were already occupied or because they had lost the necessary leadership and knowledge of what to do. Hence they wander like lost souls on the edge of the elephant range.

In the areas of high density almost half of the herds numbered more than 100 members, so aggregation seemed not to be due to favourable environmental factors but population density. They just could not get away from one another. Neither were these large herds all family groups; bull herds were mixed with them as well.

However, Kalman Kittenberger, an Hungarian museum collector, wrote in 1929:

> In East Africa, in the Kilimanjaro country, I never saw more than fifteen to twenty elephants in one herd, while in Uganda and in Unyoro more than a hundred will keep together in herds. On January 1st, 1914, in the Lugogo papyrus swamps in Uganda, I saw a herd of at least six hundred elephants. E.C.Akeley must have seen the same herd in the Budongo forest (which lies to the north of Lugogo in Unyoro) and he estimated their numbers as being even higher, saying that there were seven hundred of them.

At the end of the last century two administrative officers in Bunyoro commented on the abundance of elephant, stating that the herds numbered hundreds and in some cases a single herd might number up to 700 animals. Thus large herds in Uganda seem of long standing and not the result of the comparatively recent reduction in elephant range nor of control shooting which was initiated in the mid-1920s.

In the Manovo-Gounda Park herds increased in size in the dry season due to harassment by poachers, poaching still being conducted as it has been for centuries by pursuing the elephants on horseback and spearing them. The cause of the increased herd size, elephants often massing in large herds after pursuit, was due to the dry season facilitating poaching rather than to any climatic response by the elephants to the distribution of water or other resources. In contrast, in the unharassed Amboseli population herd size increased at the onset of the rains and then progessively decreased through the dry season as food reserves diminished and the elephants spread out more to seek them.

In Vietnam, north east of Saigon, up to the 1950s from July to November there was an annual gathering of elephants numbering several thousands on the savannahs bordering the Lagna River. Coming from far and wide, they massed in one great seasonal assembly of intermingled herds attracted by the lush grassland. Clearly here they were focused on one area by the nature of the vegetation.

THE CLAN AND THE HOME RANGE

Family herds share home ranges in clans. Those of the family groups themselves, the areas over which they wander in their daily foraging, occupy only some 14–52 sq. km in the well-watered Lake Manyara Park, whereas in Tsavo Park after the drought which destroyed large numbers of elephants, the family home ranges occupied from 300 sq. km in the better areas to as much as ten times this in the most arid. In southern India the home ranges of family herds covered at least 105 sq. km but in Malaysia they ranged from 60 in secondary forest up to almost three times this in the dense undisturbed forest.

An elephant clan, as Doctor Richard Laws first termed these associations from observations of the Tsavo population, consists typically of several herds or groups which are genetically related occupying a largely exclusive home range. Clans are obvious in the dry season when large numbers of families come together temporarily. Five such clans occupied a forested area of 1130 sq. km in southern India, each clan comprising from 50 to 200 animals. Seasonal movements of the families within a clan are broadly co-ordinated and the movements of the clan distinctive.

In the middle of the last century Asian elephants were reported by Sanderson to occur in herds of 30–50, but 100 was not uncommon. 'When large herds are in localities where fodder is not very plentiful,' he wrote, 'they divide into parties of from ten to twenty; these remain separate, though within two or three miles of each other. But they all take part in any common movement such as a march into another tract of forest.'

Such seasonal clan movements have been seen in Sri Lanka but not in the rainforests of Malaysia. In Sri Lanka they use only relatively small areas of the total range for 1–3 months, remaining dispersed within it. Then the herds gather together and make a relatively long move as a single group to a geographically separate part of the range, the wet season range differing from the dry.

Within the range they have regular trails in the forest used by other animals as well which browse along them so that they become almost bare of vegetation. Scattered within the forest, often at the intersection of two trails and not far from water, are roomy resting areas where the elephants like to stand around together, 50–100 sq. m in extent and bare of understorey vegetation.

In the Kruger Park, despite the fact that this 20 000 sq. km area is now mostly fenced, the population is separated into fairly discrete sexually segregated subpopulations or clans of breeding herds and bull ranges. The clans average 327 members, varying from 80 to 600. They range over 126 to almost 1000 sq. km, with an average home range size of 450, size depending upon the quality of the habitat. This is only a little over twice the size of that of the forest elephant, which in the Ivory Coast is thought to have a home range of about 150–200 sq. km. The forest elephant, however, moves about only in small groups of 3–4 individuals.

Home ranges overlap considerably but are relatively stable over long periods of time for family units. Wet season ranges are smaller than dry season, when the elephants must forage farther afield to meet their requirements. The choice of areas which elephants occupy is influenced by avoidance of man when hunting takes place more than by any other factor and home ranges shrink in size as a consequence. Otherwise habitat preference is a combination of seasonal differences in quantity and quality of food, availability of minerals, the social organization of the population and, least of all, water availability. Rainfall itself has little influence on the overall distribution of elephants, although they react to it in dry areas by moving to where rain has recently fallen.

Clearly in low rainfall areas, or areas where the habitat is degraded or rocky, then elephants must range more widely in their search for food. Likewise the forest elephant, whose diet includes a large proportion of fruits, must search widely in the tropical forest to satisfy its needs as fruits do not grow as abundantly as leaves. The boundaries of these sometimes vast areas, up to 3000 sq. km in Tsavo, seem to be recognized by adjacent clans and are long-lasting, although there may be some overlap at the edges. Within the home range members know the area in detail and it is not by chance that they follow well-worn paths. It is often supposed they may leave their sign on trees with temporal gland exudate but more likely the characteristic smells are a mixture of droppings and urine and skin odours rubbed off on bushes in passing.

LORDS OF THE REALM

In addition to family group ranges bulls have their own ranges. Bull areas in Kruger Park are occupied by from ten to 100 postpubertal bulls; on average 41. Generally covering a wider area than cow clans they have a mean size of 660 sq. km, in the range 200–1700. In southern India three known adult bulls had minimum ranges from 170 to 200 sq. km.

Within the bull range there exists a hierarchical dominance order among the bulls that develops over a period of 20–30 years and it is to these bull ranges that the young bulls come after leaving the maternal group. From the age of 15–45 years they circulate leisurely into and through the adjoining clan ranges fairly regularly, but most return to the bull range of their original choice, although some may settle in new ones. Most members of a bull range will have originated from the nearest clan. When not in musth, a bull of 20–45 years of age is relatively sedentary in his habits and only moves 3–4 km a day.

Young pre-musth bulls are the most adventurous and first to occupy new areas. After the break of seven years of drought in northern Botswana, young bulls of 14–15 years turned up in the northern part of the Central Kalahari Game Reserve where they had not been known for 50 years.

MADNESS AND MUSTH

Musth is a corruption of the Urdu word *mast* meaning intoxicated. Reported in the Asian elephant by Megasthenes in 300 BC, it was not thought to occur in the African species. One of the major discoveries in recent years has been that African elephants do experience musth just like their Asian counterparts.

Charles Darwin referred to it in 1871 in *The Descent of Man*: 'At this period [the rutting-season] the glands on the sides of the face of the male elephant enlarge, and emit a secretion having a strong musky odour'. But it was to take another 110 years before it was reported in the African elephant, first identified in the mid-1970s.

Stories of the danger of Asian elephants in musth, the so-called 'rogue elephants', are so well-known that it is hard to believe it took so long to recognize it in the African elephant, for its symptoms are highly visible. But real behavioural studies only began in the 1960s with the work of Iain Douglas-Hamilton. Of course, he had the advantage that elephants had become accustomed to people in national parks and did not flee at the first scent or sound of man, but even his studies concentrated mostly on cows and their family groups, so that the signs of musth were not evident.

In the Asian elephant, in which musth tends to be of regular annual occurrence, one of its most important indicators is a secretion from the temporal gland, situated just behind the eye. Yet whereas in the Asian elephant this gland only secretes in the bull when he is in musth and in the cow rarely at all except when she is on heat or giving birth, in the African elephant it flows in both bull and cow; indeed, it flows more frequently in the cow, especially in the dry season. It flows in young elephants also and when a single African elephant is separated from its family then it almost always secretes. So it is perhaps not surprising that a possible connection with musth was dismissed as unlikely.

Described as a modified and complicated sweat gland, the temporal gland is apocrine in nature, meaning that it loses a part of the protoplasm of the gland's cells when secreting. In the African elephant it secretes in both sexes from about six months of age, but as the bull gets older he secretes less often and when adult, usually only when in musth. The gland can weigh more than $1\frac{1}{2}$ kg in an adult bull and swells considerably when he is in musth. In the cow it is approximately half this weight. The orifice of the gland of the woolly mammoth had bristles protruding from it but those of the African and Asian elephants lack any hair.

The first chemical analyses of the exudate, from an African bull which had gone out of musth, showed it to consist principally of cholesterol, a common constituent of animal tissues, as were the other compounds which were present. There was no indication of any odour-producing compounds or pheromones. Any odour produced is thought to be by the action of bacteria on the exudate, as with human perspiration.

Stress and excitement stimulate the gland to secrete so one would expect it to be particularly active when a bull is in musth. There has long been discussion on its nature. One worker in 1916 was not far wrong when he suggested that it was a scent gland, while recent workers consider its probable function is communicatory, used in marking, herd member recognition and behaviour such as mating. Elephants rub the gland on tree trunks and on branches, often blocking the orifice with sticks and gravel which African hunters prize as charms.

Apparently unlike the Asian elephant (but let us remember that in the Asian elephant musth has only been observed closely in domestic animals in which attempts are made to suppress it as much as possible), in the African elephant the gland has two types of secretion. One is a watery secretion which evaporates quickly, common to both bulls and cows of all ages and which occurs when the animal is excited. The other, produced only by older bulls, is sticky and stains the side of the face for longer periods. The two secretions are difficult to distinguish on casual inspection, but it is the latter which is characteristic of a bull in musth and the bull will often raise his head high with the mouth open and rub the trunk on the gland area. He also rubs the gland on trees and vegetation, both in and out of musth, but more frequently during the latter. Although it may appear to be secreting copiously this appearance is often caused by the exudate accumulating on the side of the face during musth, looking like a black stain.

ELEPHANT INCONTINENCE

But the most obvious feature of a bull African elephant in musth is his inability to hold his water. Joyce Poole, who discovered the phenomenon of musth in this species, divided the degree of incontinence into ten rates measured against water flowing from a tap, from a dribble to a flood! When it has been in the dribble state for some time the pizzle becomes stained green and is a further aid to recognition by curious biologists.

When this interesting fact was first observed it was thought that the elephants had some kind of dreadful disease which was dubbed 'green penis disease'.

The urine of the musth bull is distinguished by a particular odour, which can also be detected on the urine trails he leaves behind in his incontinent passage. These trails are carefully investigated by both cows and other musth and non-musth bulls, the latter often then avoiding the vicinity. Normally the bull passes water out between the hind legs, but when in musth he sprays the insides of his legs until it is dribbling faster than rate 4, when he no longer urinates. This incontinence does not seem so pronounced in Asian elephants, but nevertheless elephant handlers have always considered that the dangerous state is over once the animal stops dribbling and urine is passed freely.

The bull's incontinence associated with musth means that a large bull loses 345 litres of urine in 24 hours or a small bull about 144 litres, dribbling more urine when walking than when stationary while feeding. This compares with a normal loss of about 70 litres a day, the bull usually passing about 5 litres 14 times a day. Thus the bull in musth must drink more frequently and the physiological cost will be higher in the dry season than in the wet, because water will be harder to come by and more energy is expended fighting in the heat. So we find in fact the higher ranking bulls do come into musth during the wet season, whereas most of the medium ranking ones do so in the dry. But because they stay in musth longer, the high ranking bulls can guard as many cows in heat as could a medium ranking bull in the wet season, when he would have to compete with the high ranking bulls. The majority of low ranking bulls come into musth in the wet season but their periods of musth are short and sporadic and do not present much competition to the high rankers.

Bulls also carry themselves in a characteristic manner when in musth, although this is perhaps less discernible to the casual observer. The head is carried high, well above the shoulders, and at an angle such that the chin looks as

FIG. 8.2   *An incontinent old bull.*

if it is tucked in. The ears are held tensely, spread out and carried high, while the animal adopts a sort of bully-boy swagger, with a controlled swinging motion of its head and tusks. Demonstrations of aggression are kneeling down and tusking the ground and throwing up clods of earth, mud or grass, tusking vegetation and throwing logs, bushes and other objects at other elephants or even motor cars. Such demonstrations are seen occasionally in both sexes of all ages – when young bulls are sparring one may kneel and dig its tusks into the ground in challenge – but they always accompany fights between bulls in musth.

Another characteristic is the 'musth rumble'. This is a low, pulsating call of up to 108 decibels ('average' traffic noise is 60 decibels and a pneumatic drill 2 m away emits a sound of 120 decibels), with fundamental frequencies as low as 14 Hz or cycles per second, which means that the sound is low but powerful. This is performed with an ear wave or ear fold and a loud ear flap marking the end of the call. It is made most frequently when alone, apparently searching for cows. Although also made when the bull is with cows, it is then much less frequent and even less so when guarding a cow on heat.

Musth rumbles are not of sufficient volume to travel more than a few hundred metres, but since bulls in musth crisscross the range searching for cows on heat they may make such calls and listen for others making them in order to avoid collisions which would necessitate fighting. It may be a class of calls composed of several different rumbles, each with a specific meaning which can be used in a variety of different but specific contexts. Even the low frequency sound of an aircraft flying overhead can elicit it.

Large bulls, of 40 years of age and more, call up to three times more frequently than younger ones and this particular type of call has never been recorded from non-musth bulls. When the musth call is made near to cows, adult cows typically answer with a chorus of low frequency calls and may often respond with a specific loud low frequency reply of up to 111 decibels.

Musth is seen throughout the year but at Amboseli, close to the equator where most of the studies have been conducted, it is most frequent in the first seven months following the two rainy seasons. The peak numbers of bulls in musth coincide with the maximum numbers of cows in heat but whereas heat lasts for only a few days, musth may last for several months. It is therefore not seen as a direct response to the cow being in heat, although the latter may stimulate the onset of musth in particular bulls.

Musth appears to be more seasonal in southern than in eastern Africa but its onset in an individual bull is closely synchronized between one year and the next. The exceptions are when a bull is increasing in rank and gradually moving into a reproductively more favourable time of the year, or when a bull is decreasing in rank his periods of musth become shorter and more sporadic in occurrence. No bull younger than 24 years of age has been seen in musth, the average age of first appearance ranging from 26 to 32. Duration is highly variable, from a single day to 127, but it is similar in length for individuals from one year to the next and positively correlated with age.

The oldest bulls, aged 50 and over, come into musth before they associate with cow groups. Then they go out and look for them, remaining in musth for as long as they are with a cow and only drop out of it when they return to the bull area. Younger bulls aged 35–40 join cow groups, actively test cows for heat and compete for them but do not show signs of musth for several weeks. It usually finishes long before they leave the company of the cow groups. Bulls younger still, in the 25–35 year age class, only come into musth after associating with cows for up to one month and they rarely stay in musth for longer than a few days, coming into musth several times in succession.

This peculiar state is associated with heightened levels of the male sex hormone, testosterone, which can increase to 50 times its non-musth level. First analysed in the Asian elephant, it was found that testosterone levels in blood plasma were low, in the range 0.2–1.4 nanograms per ml (nanogram, one thousand millionth part of a gram) when there was no sign of musth, rising to 4.3–13.7 during the onset and up to 65.4 nanograms when a bull was in full musth.

The same was true of elephants in Addo Park. Samples taken from the ear veins of drugged bulls ranged from 3.5 nanograms in the lowest ranking bull without any sign of musth to 19.8 in a bull just terminating musth. Urinary testosterone is also significantly greater in African bulls closer to musth or in musth than for those not in musth.

Among non-musth bulls it is body size which determines the rank of an individual and this reflects his age. In 70 conflicts between two musth bulls the largest won 93% of encounters. When the contest was between a musth bull and a non-musth bull, then the musth bull won 86% of 42 encounters, despite being the smaller of the two.

Although sexually mature by the age of 17 a bull cannot compete successfully for cows until he is at least 30, even although by the age of 25 he will have begun to experience alternating periods of sexual activity in terms of hormonal changes such as musth and associated activity patterns.

In the small Addo Park where there is a very high confined population of some five elephants to every 2 sq. km, no more than one quarter of postpubertal bulls will ever have the chance to mate, so that sexual maturity is no guarantee of success.

In the bull herds the young bulls find their place by frequently challenging the largest bull but the large, dominant bulls never challenge the subadult bulls. It is here the young bulls learn their place in society, as opposed to when they are in the family group sparring with others of their own age, but any rank hierarchy that may emerge is overthrown when a bull comes into musth.

When in musth the bull moves long distances seeking cows in distant clan ranges. One musth bull was recorded moving 224 km in 22 days and another 125 km in 30. They may associate with up to eight clans in less than a month, giving a much greater chance of contacts with reproductively receptive cows as well as promoting outbreeding. It is calculated in the above case that the two bulls could have contacted up to 780 and 378 cows respectively, compared with only 143 and 86 if they had stayed at home. Furthermore, the occupants of a bull range are most likely to have originated from the nearest clans and are therefore likely to be related to their members. By ranging widely chances of inbreeding are lessened. But old bulls, of 50 or more years of age, occupy smaller home ranges although the positions tend to shift with time.

A bull in musth has more success guarding cows in heat and obtaining matings than a non-musth bull, due not only to his enhanced competitive ability through increased aggression but also to cow preference. Musth has been likened to the rutting of deer and antelopes, seasonal periods of heightened sexual activity when the males of the species advertise their state and presence by calling and scent marking. The difference is that whereas rutting is a synchronized activity, musth periods are not, the younger and the oldest animals experiencing it at less advantageous times of the year as regards cows in heat.

This may be due to the fact that dominant musth bulls can depress musth in lower ranking animals and even suppress it entirely. Larger musth bulls have been seen to chase smaller ones, sometimes for several kilometres, until the latter's urine dribbling and temporal gland secretion have been switched off and the smaller bull has adopted a head low, non-musth posture or departed elsewhere. This does not prevent non-musth bulls from mating and they do so until a musth bull arrives on the scene.

For this reason it has been suggested that it is an alternative mating strategy. Being high in terms of physiological cost occasioned by the increased activity of the bull and its potentially disruptive effects on elephant society, it is therefore relatively rare. If it was a regular phenomenon, it is suggested that it would be the only mating strategy. It has not been confirmed that it occurs in all populations, but this may be due to lack of adequate observation. It does serve to promote outbreeding but this could be attained by other social systems.

Another theory is that the bull in musth may be signalling that he places a high value on a cow in heat whereas a non-musth bull, no matter how old or how large, signals that he places a lesser value on her. In other words his male hormone level does not prompt him to the same extent that the heightened level in the musth bull prompts the latter.

In the semi-arid Ruaha Park the behaviour of the bulls appears somewhat different to that recorded elsewhere. Here, at the beginning of the rainy season in mid-November, the adult bulls spend their time feeding on the new growth, apparently storing up energy reserves and ignoring the cow family groups. But six weeks later, in the middle of the rains, behaviour changes and they feed for shorter periods, moving towards any family groups that they come across. At the same time they increase their daily range, now travelling long distances so that they are more likely to meet cows. In effect they now search for cows on heat.

Unlike at Amboseli near the equator, at Ruaha there is a distinct breeding season in the latter half of the rains which continues for half of the year, when the cows are in heat and the bulls also are active. But unlike elsewhere, so far no one has recorded any signs of musth in these bulls.

WHEN GIANTS FIGHT

Because of an increase in aggressiveness and unpredictable behaviour, especially towards other bulls but most of all other musth bulls, the musth bull is found either alone or with cow herds. Usually non-musth bulls avoid him but if fighting occurs between musth bulls it is conducted with a high degree of ritualized movement, consisting of a direct forehead-to-forehead approach accompanied by the clashing of tusks, but nonetheless dangerous. In the Addo Park, where the animals cannot easily avoid one another, seven bulls, four of which were in musth, have been killed by other musth bulls in ten years but two cows were also killed. One musth bull broke a tusk killing a non-musth opponent, then broke the other tusk killing a cow before he was in turn killed by another musth bull.

Serious fights have also been seen in the Kruger Park, but nothing quite so dramatic as the above. In Tsavo, fighting over a cow coming into heat, a bull drove one tusk through the roof of his opponent's mouth, while his other tusk penetrated the chest, lifting his opponent's forelegs off the ground with the force of the blow. As the impaled bull struggled to disengage himself he exposed his flank and was immediately tusked in the side:

After a brief pause, the victor, who was bleeding profusely from several gashes on the trunk and forequarters, walked slowly back to the pool and drank. When he had his fill he returned to the battle site. On viewing the body of his erstwhile challenger, he appeared to be seized by a blind rage, and trumpeting loudly charged, ramming his tusks full length into the dead animal's head ... the infuriated bull managed to turn the body completely over so that it was facing the opposite way ... For the next six hours he mounted guard over the dead elephant, chasing off several groups of elephants coming down to drink and forcing them to detour a considerable distance to the pool.

During a fight between two wild musth bulls in India, one of the combatants broke off part of one tusk in the palate of the other and part of the other tusk in its trunk. In this encounter both animals died.

In Amboseli, out of 20 fights which were observed, two resulted in the death of one of the contestants, one bull was blinded in one eye and several broke tusks during the bouts. Fights lasted up to six hours, carried out during the heat of the day. When not locked in combat, the contestants smashed bushes, tossed logs into the air, tusked the ground and walked up and down in parallel to one another, similar to fighting behaviour seen in antelopes. After such encounters many were visibly heat stressed and made for a wallow or pool immediately after the combat was finished. All of the fights ended by the victor chasing the loser for several kilometres.

Only 31 serious or escalated contests were seen in 14 years' observations at Amboseli, which suggests the signals associated with musth allow individual elephants to make relative assessments of each other. In other words, a bull which is smelling to high heaven is recognized as very determined, so the less odoriferous one gives way. Elephants recognize musth also by voice, so they know with whom they are dealing and retreat to a greater distance from threats by musth bulls than they do from threats by non-musth bulls.

A feature of musth is that a bull rises in the dominance hierarchy and even normally higher ranking bulls will run away from him. Bulls in musth also try to avoid each other when not actively competing for cows on heat since it is wasteful to fight in the absence of mating opportunities. They do this by inspecting the urine trails and by listening for each other's musth rumbles.

A branch of mathematical theory termed 'game theory', applied to biology by Professor J. Maynard Smith, suggests that competing animals should not signal their intention to attack one another as such a signal could be exaggerated without cost. That is, they could bluff. This would lead to evolutionary cheating or in other words, a race of bluffers would develop which would succeed until one called another's bluff. Musth does not appear to fit this logic since it does announce aggressive intent, possibly signalling fighting ability and an intention to monopolize cows on heat. But it has been argued that elephants should clearly signal that they will not fight, by not being in musth, when the benefits derived from winning are relatively less than they would be either at a different time of the year or at a later stage in life. In other words, there is no point in fighting for a cow when she may refuse the bull or in fighting when there are no cows on heat about.

Among elephants the bull's lifetime reproductive success is strongly dependent upon his age as he continues to grow in size throughout life. Thus his success increases as he gets older until size is no longer related to strength.

When a musth bull approaches the cows they present their hindquarters and urinate for his benefit to enable him to test the urine for its hormonal content, as in other herbivores. If one is found on heat mating takes place.

In Sri Lanka adult bulls did not associate with cow herds for longer than a few days, totalling about one quarter to one third of their time. They tended to move like the herds, spending two to several days in one locality and then moving to another. Bull home ranges overlapped and, when not competing for cows in heat, bulls tolerated one another.

Both physical and behavioural characteristics of musth are strikingly similar in both African and Asian elephants. In each it is marked by an onset of the temporal gland swelling and secretion, incontinence (although this does not seem as marked in the Asian elephant) and increasing aggression. Both rub the temporal gland with the trunk and mark vegetation more often with the gland. In both, musth is variable in duration, lasting from a few days to several months, occurring throughout the year but peaking during the wet season, and it has an annual periodicity in its timing. The only significant difference so far recorded is that it appears in the Asian elephant at as young as 11 years but this is in domestic elephants and may be due to nutritional factors. The musth rumble has also not been detected but this may be a lack of interpretation.

Most bulls show a decline in bodily condition during musth and those which suffer most do not come into musth again the following year. Usually, when they get into poor condition they drop out of musth several days after a fight. During musth they spend significantly less time feeding and resting and more time walking and interacting with other elephants, but domestic Asian elephants kept chained and fed normally still lose weight. This may be due to the heightened metabolic rate associated with high male hormone levels.

Tame Asian circus elephants, when they have enough to eat, have been known to stay in musth for 3–4 months. In Asia working elephants are chained and starved, reducing the period sometimes to as little as ten days.

When Chuni first showed signs of musth in 1820, 'those annual paroxysms, wherein the elephant, whether wild or confined, becomes infuriated', Mr Cross attempted to purge his elephant of this undesirable behaviour.

> Mr. Cross . . . resorted to pharmacy, and, in the course of fifty-two hours, succeeded in deceiving his patient into the taking of twenty-four pounds of salts, twenty-four pounds of treacle, six ounces of calomel, an ounce and a half of tartar emetic, and six drams of powder of gamboge [a drastic purgative]. To this he added a bottle of croton oil, the most potent cathartic perhaps in existence; of this

a full dram was administered, which alone is sufficient for at least sixty full doses to the human being; yet, though united with the preceding enormous quantity of other medicine, it operated to no apparent effect.

But there was no increase in violence until six years later and 'a quarter of a pound of calomel was given to him in gruel' – a dose more than enough for 600 men. This failed to produce any effect other than an extreme suspicion of food.

J.H. Williams recommends a much less drastic and apparently effective method for controlling musth – reducing the quantity and quality of food and placing a few drops of nitre in the drinking water. This is seemingly sufficient to calm a bull elephant.

RUMBLE-GRUMBLE

The shrill trumpet of an elephant has thrilled or terrified many an African adventurer. For long it has also been known that elephants 'rumble', hunters having assumed, like Aristotle, that elephants are prone to flatulence. This was extrapolated to the fact that they only make such borborygmic gurgles when contented. It was well-known that at the first cause for suspicion or alarm they abruptly controlled their 'stomach rumbles'.

Sanderson recorded for Asian elephants that they: '... make use of a great variety of sounds in communicating with each other, and in expressing their wants and feelings. Some are uttered by the trunk, some by the throat'. Pleasure was expressed by a continued low squeaking through the trunk 'or an almost inaudible purring sound from the throat'. This was also referred to as a 'chirping' noise and one with which captive elephants often greet their handlers. Dislike, apprehension or threat could be expressed by rapping the end of the trunk smartly on the ground, snorting at the time of impact, creating a booming sound which can be heard at a great distance, used especially when sensing a tiger during a tiger-hunt. The characteristic squeak of greeting made by the Asian elephant, allegedly produced in the trunk, has not been recorded in the African elephant.

Calls of elephants range from higher frequency screams, trumpets, bellows and roars in the range 322–570 Hz down to lower frequency rumbles or growls of 18–28 Hz. The frequency of elephant sounds, like that of any other animal, relates to the degree of excitement or emotion. When calm, elephants emit only low frequency rumbles and growls, the pitch rising to trumpeting, bellowing and screaming when they are alarmed or excited.

A number of different audible low frequency sounds has been classified as the greeting rumble, the contact call and its corollary, the answer, the let's go rumble, the musth rumble, the cow chorus, the postmating call and the mating pandemonium call. Sylvia Sikes, who hunted many elephants, claimed they also make a growling noise before attacking one.

After separation for several hours, elephants of the same family or bond group greet one another again with loud rumbles. The longer the period of separation, the more intense the greeting, with louder rumbles for up to several minutes. A typical sequence at Amboseli was provided by two adult cows of the same bond group, one of which was feeding among an aggregation of several hundred animals. The other arrived and at 20 m from the crowd called, to be immediately answered by her relative, the calls overlapping. She called again and the other rushed out from the crowd, calling with ears lifted and folded, her calf following and also calling. Both cows then urinated and defaecated and rumbled back and forth, using rumbles of 18 up to 25 Hz and back again to 18, while the calls were in the range 61–71 decibels.

When elephants are in one spot feeding, one of them may move to the periphery and, facing away typically with one leg lifted as if ready to go, give vent to a long, unmodulated and, to our ears, soft rumble accompanied by a steady ear flapping repeated every few minutes until the others join her and the group moves off together.

Contact calls and answers are dissimilar to one another but occur in association, generally within the same bond group. The contact call is a relatively soft, unmodulated sound accompanied by steady ear flapping for its duration. Preceded by a listening attitude the answer starts abruptly and loudly and then softens. An elephant trying to contact its family may engage in contact calling and answering for several hours. These calls were in the range 83–88 decibels when up to 2 km apart. But what was interesting about them was that tape recordings printed out as sonographs showed that both types of call were preceded by faint low frequency calls, inaudible to the human ear, which can travel farther than audible sounds.

One of the most remarkable additions to our knowledge of the natural history of elephants to emerge in recent years is that elephants are capable of making very low frequency sounds, inaudible to the human ear, which have the capacity to travel over distances of several kilometres. Very low frequency sounds travel greater distances than high frequency sounds of the same pressure levels and are little affected by passage through woodlands and other obstructions. These low frequencies with high pressure levels should travel for several kilometres before becoming inaudible to receptors of this level of frequency. Elephants are thus aware of many sounds that we are unable to hear.

Although it has long been known that elephants have an acute sense of smell and undoubtedly use it in locating others, communication by infrasound was suspected from studies in the Sengwa area where movements, tracked by radio-collared animals, appeared to be co-ordinated over very long distances. Groups responded to each other's movements even when separated by distances of up to 5 km and when the direction of the wind ruled out any possibility of contact by smell. At Amboseli the proximity of related cows changed from hour to hour from several kilometres apart to being close together.

Theoretically, sounds at up to 115 decibels can carry for 10 km, which could explain why radio-tracked elephant groups in Zimbabwe which were converging towards one another then moved apart when they were within 3–5 km.

Sanderson anticipated this finding a century earlier when he wrote of Asian elephant groups remaining separate, although within two or three miles of each other, but all taking part in any common movement such as a march into another tract of forest. But he thought they kept themselves informed of each other's whereabouts 'chiefly by their fine sense of smell'. But at the end of the 18th century Sir Everard Home had deduced from the anatomy of the ear drum that the elephant, although lacking a 'musical ear', could hear sounds at a greater distance than a man. This was confirmed to him by John Corse who related how a working elephant was always aware of a horse behind it long before its footfalls could be heard by anybody. Also a cow whose calf was kept at home while she was working, on her return could hear the calf call long before it was audible to the people with her.

A calling animal opens its mouth and raises and flaps its ears while rumbling and sometimes just before or after will stand very still with its head and ears lifted as if listening. A group of elephants will often freeze, ears held out, in order to listen to faint, distant sounds.

Oppian was not far off the mark when he wrote:

> It is said that elephants talk to one another, mumbling with their mouths the speech of men. But not to all is the speech of the beasts audible, but only the men who tame them hear it.

It was almost 2000 years later in 1986 that an American biologist watching Asian elephants in Washington Park Zoo, Oregon, detected a throbbing sensation in the air but could hear no sound. Her experience with whales suggested the elephants might be making sounds below the range of human hearing. Using a tape recorder to record the sound, she found that when speeded up ten times the sound became audible.

Humans hear a frequency range of 20–20 000 Hz. Elephants speak to one another, to use Oppian's words, in the range 14–24 Hz, with high sound pressure levels of 85–90 decibels, compared with human conversation of 65. Thus elephants make very low but relatively loud sounds. Bats, at the other extreme, make very high sounds, greater than 20 000 Hz.

The elephant uses a repertoire of low frequency calls and it is the female which is the most vocal. The only terrestrial mammal which communicates by infrasound, it is able to respond to calls up to 4 km away and probably twice this distance. The reason for this was pointed out in 1980 in a letter to the American scientific journal *Science*, although its significance appeared to pass unnoticed at the time. Thus the difference between bats, man and elephants is related to the difference in distance between the two ears and the speed of sound. Small animals which have their ears close together can hear high frequency sounds; the wider apart the two ears become, the lower will be the frequency of sounds that they can detect. The elephant has the most wide apart ears of any land animal.

Experiments were conducted with a relatively small elephant, a seven year old Asian zoo elephant which was trained to receive a glass of orange juice if she pressed the right button with her trunk upon hearing a sound. From this experiment it was found that the *range* of hearing was similar to that of other mammals but it was shifted downwards, so the elephant could not hear sounds above 10.5 kHz at an intensity level of 60 decibels, the range being from 17 Hz to 10.5 kHz; although slightly higher frequencies could be heard at very high intensities. Thus an elephant is less likely to be alarmed by the highpitched scream of a jet aircraft flying overhead than we are but it would be more likely to be alarmed by the thunderous low roar of a Wellington bomber. By the same token elephants can hear thunder at greater distances than any other terrestrial creature and thus move to distant areas where it may have rained.

Sir Everard Home discovered this lowered acoustic capacity in 1823, when he conducted an experiment in the elephant's musical appreciation:

> I got Mr. Broadwood, as a matter of curiosity, to send one of his tuners with a piano-forte to the menageries of wild beasts in Exeter 'Change, that I might know the effect of acute and grave sounds upon the ear of a full-grown elephant. The acute sounds seemed hardly to attract his notice; but as soon as the grave notes were struck, he became all attention, brought forward the large external ear, tried to discover where the sounds came from, remained in the attitude of listening, and after some time made noises by no means of dissatisfaction.

Sir Everard concluded, however, that the elephant was insensible to harmonious modulation and 'destitute of a musical ear'. In contrast, French investigators, who experimented with a bull and a cow elephant in 1798 in the Paris *Jardin des Plantes*, claimed that the song of the revolution, '*Ca Ira*', roused them to a state of excitement. But first they were treated to a rendering of 'Oh, My Tender Musette' which allegedly caused the cow to try and induce the bull to mount her by backing onto him. But at this interesting juncture the music stopped.

Perhaps Sir Everard played the wrong tunes.

As in Oppian's day, Asian elephant handlers pretend to a secret language with which they speak to elephants. An elephant handler in the Basle Zoo in the 1960s claimed to possess this knowledge and was able to stimulate both African and Asian cow elephants to rumble by stroking the udder and 'speaking' to them:

> ... Mr. Behrens began to stroke her and talk to her in 'elephant language', which I could not understand. Within a very few seconds, she lifted her head slightly, straightened her trunk and began rumbling or purring. There was an immediate response by the other five elephants that quickly closed in about us, squeezing us uncomfortably in their midst and forcing us to stop the experiment.

They repeated the experiment with the elephants chained up!

It was discerned that the noise was made in the throat, accompanied by sharp expulsions of air from the trunk. The sound excited the other four cows which pressed close to the rumbling cow and the two bulls became aggressive to one another. But perhaps it was the stimulation of the udder which caused the response.

Although production of the low frequency sound probably has its origin in the vocal cords, it may be amplified by the skin over the hollow between the eyes being vibrated.

Whales communicate over long distances underwater by means of infrasonic sound and they are known to emit clicks, whistles, quacks, buzzing and moaning noises, as well as prolonged 'siren' songs. Humpback whales compose new songs each year, improvising on the old ones. Whether this is innovative or simply due to poor memory we do not know. From what we know of the elephant's memory we would expect its calls to remain the same over long periods of time.

In their remarkable book *Back to Africa*, Randall Moore and Christopher Munnion suggest that elephants may be able to hear whale sounds, as well as those of dolphins. When transporting three African elephants by sea back to their homeland from America, they came across a pod of shortfinned pilot whales which they allege 'could be clearly seen', thus implying that they were some distance from the ship.

> The reaction of the elephants was fascinating. Long before we spotted the pilot whales, Tshombe, Durga and Owalla had their trunks fully extended over the ship's rail, trying to identify the scent of these other, strange mammals. All three were emitting excited guttural sounds and at one stage Owalla let rip with a strident trumpet blast . . . (Later) . . . Owalla startled us with a loud, prolonged trumpet. All three elephants were at the rail, their trunks fully extended towards the ocean . . . these were dolphins, weaving and dipping in perfect formation alongside the ship. The elephants were excited with this new encounter and exchanged deep growls among themselves for a full ten minutes before the school moved on.

Poetic licence or did the elephants really hear the whales and dolphins? They are unlikely to have either seen or scented them.

TALES THE EARS MAY TELL

It was confirmed in the experiments with the glass of orange juice that the elephant used its ear pinnae to locate sounds accurately. So the African elephant with its larger ears should do better at this than the Asian and also, possessed of a bigger head, perhaps hear slightly lower frequency sounds.

But in addition to their aid to hearing the ears also tell a tale. Threats to other bulls – or even to watchers in motor cars – consist of folding the bottom part of the ears, ear waving and rapid flapping. Musth ear signals consist of mostly waving one ear only and thrusting the upper part forward vigorously with the lower trailing after. It is thought that waving the upper part of the ear may be designed to waft the temporal gland scent before it.

Elephants have many other ear signals, such as rapid flaps with head extended, seen between cows threatening one another; ear fold, a general threat; ear fold with head and ears lifted high, used in greeting within a bond group; ear flap slide, signalling an intention to move or change activity; thrusting forward the upper part in bull confrontations, and flapping accompanying different vocalizations. Other threats are shaking the head or holding it high and tossing the trunk. The threatened animal, if it is not willing to respond, either looks away or walks away with head and ears held low.

In the interplay to achieve ranking and dominance in the bull groups, a subadult bull challenges a larger one by approaching him with ears spread and the trunk extended with the tip turned down or with the trunk curved back over the head. If the approach is made with the trunk extended the other may respond likewise until the tips of their trunks nearly touch. If the head and tusks are raised or the trunk curled back or if the tusks are held horizontally, then a brief skirmish follows, but if the trunk is moved to the side without lifting the head, then the challenger retreats. Display of the tusks is probably important in achieving rank. Bulls become sexually aroused when sparring, which has nothing to do with the threat of a musth bull to another. These are often accompanied by the musth rumble and the attacked bull bellows if tusked or groans if chased.

There seems little difference in the threat display of bull and cow. Visual communication relates to the ears probably more than anything else, although the position of the head is also important, holding it up indicating a readiness to challenge. Wild Asian elephants also hold their head erect but after being captured and having their neck trodden on by the mahout they carry their heads low, interpreted as 'becoming dispirited' but in fact it is an inherent gesture of submissiveness. So they were retrained to carry their heads high.

Held out at right angles to the body, the ears indicate a threat in both African and Asian elephants but in the latter in an aggressive approach the trunk is extended forward and the ears may also be bent forward. When threatening, the Asian elephant will also kick the ground with one foot, often raising its leg as high as an angle of 45°. It then collects the loosened earth in its trunk and throws it over its back, lowering the trunk slowly and holding it for a few seconds in the direction of the threat, ears extended. Asiatic elephant trackers use this behaviour to deter the close approach of an elephant by talking normally to it and throwing a handful of dirt into the air, leaving the arm briefly raised. Apparently the elephant recognizes the signal.

When it is intended to push home a charge, both species hold the ears back against the sides of the body and curl their trunks up under them, not in the air. But normally an elephant, whether bull or cow, will try to get away with bluff, erecting the ears, 'standing tall', swishing the head to one side and flapping the ears against the side of it with a loud 'crack'. Twiddling the trunk and swinging one of the front legs backwards and forwards are characteristic of an elephant deciding between attack and retreat. The more marked or more impressive the threat display, then the less likely is an attack. If the object of its attention still does not give way it may make a mock charge, halting if there is still no response and then turning tail or first indulging in 'redirected aggression', attacking bushes or flinging logs, earth and vegetation at the unwelcome object.

In Uganda I saw a young bull elephant give vent to a remarkable display like a trained circus elephant. After the sideways swish of the head, he suddenly knelt on all fours and, lifting one foreleg, pawed the air, mouth open and with trunk curled back over his head, penis extruded. Astonished more than fearful, I still didn't budge, so he got up, backed away and trundled off.

Chapter 9

POLYPERCHON'S
PREDICAMENT:
FOOD AND FEEDING

At night when the keeper was sleeping and Jap became hungry, she would gather up refuse from the floor and throw it at his cot to wake him to go and get hay. If this did not waken him, she would search around until she found a stone. On several occasions stones as large as a hen's egg were removed from his bed, where she had thrown them.

Francis G. Benedict, 1936

LESSONS FROM ANCIENT GREECE

WHEN almost 6000 elephants died during the drought in Tsavo Park in 1970–1971 only two were dissected and it was announced with some puzzlement that their stomachs were full of food. Their stomachs may well have been full of woody vegetation, but what they were not full of was protein, the nitrogenous bodybuilding matter found in green vegetation. A lesson could have been learnt from the Roman Polyperchon who discovered over 2300 years ago in his war against Cassander, King of Macedonia, that elephants must have green food. When Polyperchon enlisted the help of Alexander the Great's mother Olympias, Cassander besieged her in the Greek town of Pydna with Polyperchon's 65 remaining elephants and she was obliged to feed them on sawdust. Hardly surprisingly they all died of starvation.

In Zambia in recent times elephants which died of drought near waterholes were found to have mostly mud in their stomachs and their droppings were nothing more than balls of mud with a few fragments of grass and leaves.

Food quality is high in the wet season, falling to its lowest point in the latter half of the dry. At this time elephants appear to lose condition, more sharply so in bulls than cows, and the hip bones become prominent but the loss of fat may provide some benefits in facilitating body temperature regulation.

Protein in the stomach contents in Uganda varied between 6–14% in the wet season and 5–8% in the dry. Falling to almost half that of the wet season, the dry season amount might be below the level required to maintain the animal. The daily digestible protein requirement for a young growing elephant of 1 tonne weight has been calculated as 0.3 kg, which would mean that it would require about 6% of protein in the food that it eats. The dry season intake in Murchison Park fell below this.

In the Queen Elizabeth Park there was a higher proportion of browse in the diet and the crude protein content was higher than that of elephants in Murchison, which had a predominantly grass diet. But an unexplained anomaly was that the elephants in Queen Elizabeth Park had a higher relative food intake in both seasons than did those in Murchison. As a result the elephants in the latter area showed an increased rate of growth in the wet seasons, higher than that in the Queen Elizabeth Park which remained stable throughout the year as nutrition was adequate in both seasons through a constant higher intake of protein.

Elephants from Murchison showed that the intake of essential fatty acids important in metabolism, vitamin F and linolenic acid, decreased markedly in the dry season in areas where elephants fed mainly on grass, accompanied by a similar decrease in their rate of growth. Elephants had up to five times less vitamin F as a percentage of the total intake of dietary calories than that found to cause deficiency symptoms in a range of experimental animals from rats to man. On the other hand the common palmitic acid, which occurred at high concentrations of 43–46% and which did not vary much with season, was also present in high concentrations of 40–45% in the elephants' fat deposits.

Leafy browse is a better source of protein and vegetable fats than other vegetation, except when grass reaches comparable levels. In the dry season grass is of poor quality but woody vegetation tends to be higher, many shrubs and trees flowering and coming into leaf at this time. In Tsavo there was no good quality browse left within reach of water in the dry season. At the beginning of the wet season the fresh green grass is more nutritious than the mature leaves of trees and shrubs and the elephant takes advantage of this.

Observations in southern India indicate that the Asian elephant is marginally more of a browser than a grazer, despite its more developed tooth structure suggesting the contrary. In an average year it consumes approximately 57% browse and 43% graze. Grass is most important in the diet in the first wet season in May to June, when it averages about 54% of the food intake. As the grass matures the amount taken declines to some 44%, and in the dry season in January to April the intake of browse increases to 70%. These relative seasonal amounts are similar to those of the African elephant studied in semi-arid north-east Uganda.

In Hwange Park from mid-April to mid-November grass constituted less than one tenth of the diet, rising to more than half during mid-December to the end of March, with a peak of up to 98% in February, thus forming the major component of the diet for a period of three months. From July to September the browse is low in protein and the elephant's intake consists only of twigs, bark and roots. Rains fall in late November to early December and the annual grasses show their maximum levels of protein in December, with their lowest in June to July. Thus from July the elephants are existing on a low protein diet until the grass flushes in late September to early October.

The Hwange picture was confirmed in areas surrounding the Kruger Park, where the intake was very woody with a low protein content. Due to the low amount of energy that could be extracted from the food the elephant compensated by an increased intake. But this was not completely effective and the elephant had to rely on its body reserves in the winter and dry season to make up the deficit in its food, maintaining or gaining condition in the rainy season up until late autumn.

In Murchison stomachs averaged 84–95% grass but this was attributable to a scarcity of browse. In the very dry year of 1976 in Ruaha Park, woody browse alone formed over 80% of the diet of cow elephants for more than three months, but this high dependence on woody browse led to a decline in condition and a high rate of mortality in the late dry season.

Most observations of diet have been based on examination of faecal contents or feeding time, which can give misleading results. Faecal contents in the Queen Elizabeth Park suggested an intake of 90% grass in the wet season, but observation of feeding time only 60%. Thus in the open areas of Uganda grass may form 60–90% of the diet all the year around, while in the wooded savannahs of Kenya, Tanzania, Zambia and Zimbabwe, it comprises between 40% and 70% of the feeding time during the wet season, but only 2–40% in the dry. Overall the results suggest that grass forms more than half of the diet in the wet season and as little as 2.5% in the dry.

The Asian elephant in Sri Lanka took almost 90% grass in Ruhuna and in Gal Oya Park only some 50%. In the Malayan forest, although palms are a favoured food, up to one third of feeding time was spent on grass even though it represented only 1% of available food. Bamboo can also be important.

In Africa the elephant's diet seems to be a straightforward relationship with seasonal availability. Grass is not abundant throughout the year in the most favoured elephant habitat and when in fresh flush its high water content means that its intake must be balanced with other food of a more fibrous nature.

The elephant's propensity for roughage was well appreciated by a Superintendent of the Royal Society for the Prevention of Cruelty to Animals, on duty at the London Zoo in 1882 supervising the crating of the famous African elephant Jumbo for his voyage to America. He reported wryly:

> An elderly lady, who appeared to be quite sane, came in a cab at 6.30 am on Friday last, bringing with her six pounds of hothouse grapes, about four pounds of raisins, with apples, oranges, cakes, biscuits and sweets to eat, and wall-flowers and daffodils for Jumbo to smell. She also brought a nice basket for Jumbo to feed out of. Before Jumbo had finished the delicacies, he seized the basket and ate it, ribbons and all, in preference to the grapes. The lady seemed disconcerted, and said to me, 'He is rude and ungrateful'. But I said, 'He is quite rational for he prefers his natural food (twigs) or something like it.' ... She asked, 'Now, what would be a treat to him, do you think?' I said, 'Old birch-brooms.' The lady went away quite crestfallen.

THE BILLY BUNTER OF THE BUSH

At London's Saint Bartholomew Fair in September 1825 Atkins's 'Royal Menagerie' announced an elephant as:

> That colossal animal, the wonderful performing Elephant. Upwards of ten feet high!! Five tons weight!! His consumption of hay, corn, straw, carrots, water, etc. exceeds 800 pounds daily. The elephant, the human race excepted, is the most respectable of animals.

The showman's description of his elephant's dimensions were probably fairly correct, but he had been tempted to double the quantity of food which the elephant actually consumed. For a 5 tonne elephant a good daily consumption, water included, would be just about 400 pounds.

Aristotle noted that an elephant could eat more than nine *medimni* at one meal, but that it should not have more than six or seven, or 'five *medimni* of bread and five *mareis* of wine', a *medimni* being about 47 kg and a *maris* about 1½ litres. So Aristotle's elephant could eat 423 kg of fodder and drink 8 litres of wine. Like the showman at Atkins's Royal Menagerie he had more than doubled the weight of food which an elephant could eat, although he admitted 'so large an amount is unwholesome'. As for the wine, 8 litres would not satisfy an elephant's thirst, but he goes on to say that an elephant had been known to drink right off 14 Macedonian *metretae* of water, equivalent to some 536 litres, whereas 100 litres is nearer the mark.

In more modern times, extrapolating from the estimated average weight of a trunkful of vegetation and the number of such trunkfuls taken in 24 hours, in the

Sengwa area an adult African bull consumed some 170 kg of fresh forage per day and the smaller cow about 150. This was similar to a number of other observations, such as the food taken by domesticated elephants in Zaïre, 150 kg per day, and the Asian elephant in Sri Lanka which took the same amount.

All told, 150 kg per day seems to be average, equivalent to about 60 of dry matter. Estimations from the weight of the stomach contents, assuming a mean turnover time of 12 hours and extrapolating from feeding rate and amount of time spent feeding per day, indicate a mean daily food intake of about 1.0–1.2% (dry matter to live weight) of body mass per day for bulls and non-lactating cows. Lactating cows take slightly more amounting to 1.2–1.5%.

Like Billy Bunter, elephants spend most of their time feeding but unlike the greedy Billy, are often only picking at selected items. At other times they consume large quantities of food in a relatively short space of time. Feeding is on a family basis; they copy one another and the kinds and amounts used by individuals within a family group are similar.

To obtain its 1% or more of body weight per day in dry food necessitated feeding for about 12–14 hours each day in Murchison Falls, the same amount of time as in the Sengwa area and that calculated for Asian elephants in Sri Lanka, but less than that reported for Queen Elizabeth Park where they spent three quarters of their time feeding. The Queen Elizabeth Park elephants had bigger stomach fills than the Murchison ones, even though they also had more protein in them, but the abundantly distributed water in the former area may have meant that this bigger fill was made up by more water.

In Sengwa the elephants took less than half of the number of trunkfuls of food per minute than did those in Uganda (although one bull did take in 14 a minute at one time) with an average of 2.5 per minute in the range 1.5–4.2, of an average weight of 75 g. The difference in rate between bull and cow in Sengwa was not significant but the slightly greater rate in the bull could mean on average an extra 20 kg of food taken in per day. The number of trunkfuls, whether browsing or grazing, was virtually the same; however, they took in more trunkfuls, that is they fed more rapidly, in the wet season than in either cold or hot seasons. Feeding was slowest in the hot season.

This rate of feeding compares with just over two per minute for the Asian elephant in Sri Lanka and the almost one per minute of another worker comparable to the observed rate in Malaya, calculated to take 150 g per trunkful. But these rates were much less than that in the Queen Elizabeth Park of almost six per minute.

The rate at which an elephant plucks vegetation with its trunk is much less than the biting rates of cattle and other herbivores. A mean ingestion rate of about 72 g of dry weight per minute, when compared with the biting rate of 55 per minute achieved by cattle, is approximately half. Thus the large trunkfuls taken by elephants do not compensate for the slower plucking rate and to achieve the same intake as cattle, elephants would have to feed for twice as long. But the daily food requirement of the elephant per unit of body weight is only about 55% of that of cattle and thus the reduced daily food intake almost compensates for the lower daily food requirement.

An amusing example of the elephant's alleged speed in eating was the case reported in *The Times* newspaper of the 1400 doughnuts. At a special performance of a circus in Vienna in 1937, 3000 children were to be given free doughnuts, but the elephant, named Jumbo but no relation of the famous London Zoo Jumbo, discovered the box containing them. Jumbo consumed 1400 of the delicacies before he was discovered. The case was taken to court, the circus authorities claiming that the pastry-cook should have guarded his doughnuts and the pastry-cook claiming that his men could not be expected to perform the duties of elephant trainers.

With ponderous levity a leading article in *The Times* stated:

> The proboscis must have settled down to work – one, two, two, box, mouth, box, mouth – with the rhythmical, precise, continuous, rotary motion only to be seen elsewhere in the concurrence of a high pile of spaghetti, a fork, and a hungry Italian.

In a letter the following week a dry don from Cambridge pointed out that they would not have been doughnuts at all, but Viennese *Krapfen*, and their consumption by the elephant should arouse envy rather than astonishment. Nevertheless it must have been a gargantuan gobble, for at a normal rapid feeding rate of up to five trunkfuls of food per minute it would have taken some eight hours for an elephant to consume 1400 individually seized items. We must suppose that Jumbo was not quite so delicate.

THE AUGEAN STABLES

The elephant's daily intake of forage means that it passes droppings about 14–20 times a day in the wet season and about ten in the dry. The bull passes about 14 times per day, compared with ten in the cow, at an average rate of 0.58 and 0.42 per hour respectively, most frequently in the late morning and during the afternoon, each adult defaecation weighing about 11 kg. Others have estimated 17 per day with a total weight of 136 kg, and the juvenile tame elephants at Tsavo passed about 16 times each day. The Asian elephant defaecates about 12–18 times a day.

In the woodland savannahs of the northern Central African Republic, the increased grass in the diet and greater overall intake in the wet season resulted in roughly a third as much increase in the dropping rate, just as it did for two areas in Tanzania, the Ruaha and Mikumi Parks. The Mikumi is mostly grassland and there was a significant difference in the wet season compared with Ruaha.

The total quantity produced per day amounts to about 150 kg wet weight or 35 kg dry weight, so when there was an estimated 35 000 elephants in Tsavo they were probably producing over 2000 tonnes of droppings per day. This could have represented some 22% of the vegetation being produced.

But not only elephants benefited from this consumption of forage, for a 1½ kg pile of fresh steaming yellow-green droppings, its smell reminiscent of the Augean Stables, was removed in the wet season in no less than two hours by a winged army of 16 000 dung beetles which weighed altogether almost ½ kg. These industrious beetles, among which is the scarab revered by the ancient Egyptians, roll away the dung in neat balls, burying it underground to feed their larvae. One beetle, *Drepanocerus coleoptera*, adopts a camouflage resembling in shape and colour coarse elephant dung particles.

At night, after the dung beetles have had their fill, like some science fiction horror countless termites swarm out from their subterranean channels, over 300 to the square metre. In one year, it is estimated, they can carry underground 9 tonnes of elephant droppings in every square kilometre, so elephants produce only a small fraction of what the termites are actually capable of removing. Without them the African countryside would become buried under elephant dung.

Elements important to plant growth such as nitrogen, phosphorus and potassium occur at higher concentrations in the droppings than in the forage so elephants play an important part, aided by the dung beetles and termites, in redistributing these chemicals.

THE FOOD THE ELEPHANT EATS

'The food of the elephant is so abundant that in eating he never appears to be impatient or voracious,' wrote Tennent of the elephant in Sri Lanka. To fill their capacious stomachs to 5–6% wet weight of their total body weight, elephants are opportunistic feeders and take a great variety of vegetation. African elephants will eat most tree species, the ones that they do not eat at all or only rarely include *Melia* (of which the fruits are poisonous) and *Protea* species. But as with the Asian elephant, although over 100 different species have been recorded as taken, the bulk of the intake is related to only a few.

In Hwange Park 87 species of browse plant, 42 of grass and 36 of forb have been recorded as eaten. In Uganda's Kibale forest, out of 255 species of plant growing there, 227 were eaten. Although nearly every woody plant in the forest was used to some extent, 30 species made up three quarters of the total taken. Some very common species were eaten simply because of their abundance, such as *Uvariopsis congensis*, giant diospyros and species of *Rinorea*.

The incidence of woody forage consumption was often as high and occasionally higher than that of herbaceous forage, but the total volume consumed was considerably lower. Leaf stripping of woody vegetation, which left the stem undamaged, was common. Some 80% of woody stems in the diet were from slender species of tree which rarely attained a diameter of more than ½ m at maturity.

Commonly eaten species of grasses range from short grasses such as the nitrogen-loving star grass, as well as taller species like red-oat grass, *Panicum*, *Setaria* and *Hyparrhenia*, while in Uganda elephant grass is the most commonly taken for want of something better. In the wet season flowers and leaves are taken but in the dry the leaf bases and roots of tussock grasses such as

Andropogon, *Cymbopogon*, *Hyparrhenia* and *Setaria* are selected. Tussocks are kicked free with a scuffing movement of the foot, the root bases bitten off and leaves and stems usually discarded uneaten, the elephant taking the carbohydrates stored in the roots.

In the Manovo-Gounda Park, in the wet season the dominant hyparrhenias were mostly taken but in the dry, where flood-plain grasses were available, these were concentrated upon. Species such as *Vossia cuspidata*, *Echinochloa colona* and *Phacelurus gabonensis* were taken.

Most grass eaten by the Asian elephant in Sri Lanka consisted of short species, entire plants being consumed. Short tussocks were kicked out of the ground with the foot as in the African species, the difference being that not only roots were taken. In the winter dry season tall swamp grasses were fed upon and the availability of fresh grass seemed to be the main factor controlling seasonal movements. A relatively large part of their time was spent in the transition zone between forest and grassland, perhaps to provide ready access to the forest for shade or concealment but also perhaps because a wider range of plants is found there. Open areas were preferred in the cooler hours of the early morning. At Ruhuna elephants made little use of evergreen forest vegetation, preferring the open scrub or scrub forest.

In Uganda woodlands were mainly used during the daytime for concealment and shade, not as a main source of food. Most use was where the forest was relatively open and there was an abundant understorey of herbaceous vegetation. Although elephants spent a considerable amount of time in woodlands in the dry season, woody vegetation formed a low percentage of their food intake. An examination of 71 elephant stomachs revealed that 99% contained mature grass, 56% young grass and only 35% a significant amount of woody vegetation, particularly the shrub *Combretum binderianum*, a favoured food in Uganda but also the commonest shrub occurring there. Species of combretum are also the favoured food in central and South Africa.

Combretums are usually the first trees to burst into new leaf after the dry season fires and thus are heavily browsed. Leguminous species such as acacias are also a favourite. In the semi-arid area of Ruaha, during the wet season the elephants ate mainly green grass and green browse and in the dry, after the grass had withered and the browse had disappeared, they consumed woody browse. In some months woody species formed an important part of the diet for both sexes, especially commiphoras and combretums, which sometimes formed more than a tenth of the diet.

Despite their arid dry season appearance, the Kalahari sands which reach from southern Africa into the Congo basin possess abundant food supplies in the shape of a great variety of browse species. Due to the loose nature of the sand, food in the form of roots, tubers and bulbs is available to elephants up to a metre underground. Roots of the large-fruited combretum, the variable combretum, the sickle bush, silver terminalia and the bloodwood tree in coppice form are much sought after. In the dry season after the leaf fall, the protein and carbohydrate content of roots is higher than that of any above-ground forage. In shallow soil areas the hard surface precludes digging by elephants.

1. The elephant's remarkable organ — the trunk.

2. (Left) *Hurrying to water after a hot day.*

3. *Drinking in the Chobe River, Botswana.*

4. (Above) *A suspicious cow stands guard.*

5. (Right) *A coating of mud helps heat loss.*

6. (Below) *Shade is very important in the heat of the afternoon.*

7. *The baby elephant suckles with its mouth, not the trunk.*

8. *Elephant calves are adventurous. This one wants to lead the way.*

9. *A calf of about 1 month of age.*

10. (Top) *Small calves are protected within the herd.* 11. (Above, left) *A calf sleeping while a young cow stands guard.* 12. (Above, right) *A unique study of a new species of Asian moth which makes an elephant cry and then drinks its tears.* Hypochrosis baenzigeri *from north Thailand.*

13. (Right) *Another of the extraordinary Asian moths from north Thailand,* Tarsolepis elephantorum.

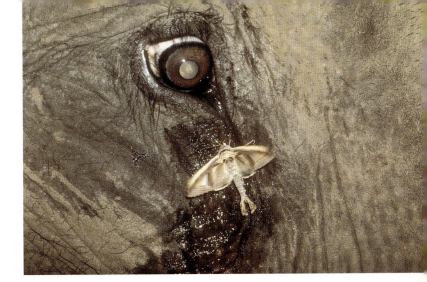

14. (Above, left) *The elephant demonstrates its remarkable reach in gathering food.*

15. (Above, right) *Fresh elephant droppings provide a rich habitat. Here Colotis spp. white butterflies seek its moisture and salts in Kenya.*

16. (Right) *An elephant prefers twigs to delicacies.*

17. *A desolate landscape. Savuti marsh, northern Botswana.*
Elephants are only partly to blame.

18. (Below) *Elephants destroying a baobab tree in Tsavo Park. Kenya.*

19. *The soft pith of the baobab is chewed.*

20. (Left) *Bark stripping by elephants of* Daniellia oliveri *in the Central African Republic.*

21. (Below) *Elephants as they were in Selous's time along the Chobe River in northern Botswana.*

22. (Left) *Parking, Hyderabad style.*

23. (Above) *The gentlest of creatures. An elephant with unconcerned impala.*

24. (Right) *Poached ivory at Bangassou, Central African Republic. The French soldier appears to be negotiating with the ivory collector.*

25. (Below) *Loading up the spoils. Bangassou.*

Remains of the succulent but stringy leaves of aloes and sansevieria, a plant like sisal, made up from one tenth to almost one third of the weight of food in some stomachs. In dry areas elephants chew these fleshy leaves for their moisture content then spit out the balls of fibrous 'chew'. Such balls were common in the dry areas of northern Kenya. Fronds of palms such as the raffia palm and the southern ilala are also chewed and the fibre spat out.

In the Malayan forest quick-growing pioneer species were mostly favoured and dominant *Dipterocarpaceae* trees rejected. Favoured feeding areas in the forest regions were the open glades bordering rivers. In Ruhuna Park the most favoured tree species was a thorny evergreen, *Feronia limonia*. Others were the milkberry and the Asian variety of the African sickle bush. The mustard tree, widespread in Tsavo, was also favoured. Thorny species were particularly liked and elephants returned repeatedly to the same individual tree.

In southern India during the early dry season until the onset of the pre-monsoon showers in April, elephants used the short grass areas, with species of acacia a favourite item of browse. In the first rainy season in May to August they occupied the deciduous forests with tall grass, but after the second heavier rains in September to December they moved into the short grass areas again.

During the summer season, including the south-west monsoon period, they browsed on bamboo, plantains (banana), tall grasses, reeds and lianas. With the retreat of the monsoon floodwaters they grazed on green grass in addition to continuing to browse on the former food types. In Bangladesh bamboo, plantain, reeds and lianas provide the staple diet of elephants all the year round. Bamboo was observed to be the favoured food in Bihar, clumps of which were pulled down and the whitish portion of the stem below the bark selected.

The elephant is the only animal which appears to make extensive use of papyrus, selecting only newly grown heads and ignoring the mature ones. In African swamps this provides a favoured food in some localities at certain seasons. When the above surface parts are dead, elephants wade in belly-deep and dredge up huge loads of matted roots on their tusks like the popular conception of prehistoric shovel-tuskers feeding. They eat only selected parts, probably the young roots. Before consuming them they wash the roots with a vigorous swishing back and forth in the water. In some areas they also feed heavily on the roots of *Phragmites* and other reeds.

Elephants particularly like cotton plants, especially when the bolls start to open, and they seem to know precisely when the time is ripe. This is a major cause of conflict between elephants and man wherever cotton is grown.

SOWING AS THEY REAP

Fruits and seed pods are eagerly sought by savannah elephants and the presence of such items seasonally guides their movements. Their seed dispersal role in dry forests was first reported from Uganda in the 1920s, where it was noted that such species as the umbrella thorn, the baobab, shepherd's bush, tamarind, nightshade, marula, *Grewia* species and the borassus palm were distributed in their own 'gro-bags' – a pile of elephant droppings. As many as 12 000 seeds of the umbrella thorn have been counted in a single dung bolus.

Elephants consume large quantities of fruits of the timber-producing white star apple tree, the seeds of which germinate in the droppings. Almost every dung bolus that I saw in Murchison Falls in the 1960s had a borassus seedling sprouting from it.

The hard seed coat of the apple-ring thorn tree softens on its passage through the elephant's gut allowing it to germinate immediately, instead of weathering for a long period at risk from rodents and boring beetles until water can penetrate the hard covering. The seeds of this species in elephant dung have a germination success rate of 75%, compared with only 12% for those straight from the pod.

Not only may seeds which have passed through the elephant's gut germinate more readily, the germination of three out of five West African trees showed a higher rate of germination than fresh seeds. Seeds such as that of the marula tree may be distributed in areas where there is a lowered risk of destruction by herbivores in the seedling stage.

The elephant's role as a seed disperser is probably of most importance in tropical rain forest where the forest elephants are fruit eaters as much as anything else, picking up most of it from the forest floor. In the Tai forest, of 37 species of forest tree seeds found in elephant droppings, 30 appeared to be distributed by elephants alone. The $2\frac{1}{2}$ cm long hard seeds of *Massularia acuminata* were found in elephant droppings all the year round. The heavy hard seeds of grey plum and *Sacoglottis gabonensis*, the former up to 5 cm in length and favoured by elephants as far away as in Uganda, although very numerous for only a part of the year could form up to half of the dry weight of elephant droppings. The seeds of these two latter species pass out intact so that it is unlikely that the elephant's stomach juices aid their germination in any way, but up to half of the seeds of *Massularia* are destroyed by digestion. Although up to ten different tree species germinate from a single elephant dropping, almost no herbaceous plants do so. Thus either the seeds of the herbaceous plants are digested or the seeding plants themselves are rarely eaten.

Elephants are at relatively low density in the Tai Forest, but almost one third of trees whose seed dispersal method is known was by elephants. Their role appears essential as a spreader of the seeds as the heavy fruits fall straight to the forest floor and will not germinate in the shade of the parent tree. Only the elephant scatters them far enough away that some may have the chance of germinating without competition. Daily ranges of elephants here were only up to 5 km, but there are longer seasonal displacements.

In the Ivory Coast forest of Banco, where there have been no elephants for 120 years, there is a marked absence of young trees of *Sacoglottis gabonensis* and *Panda oleosa*, both of which have large fruits, the former used in local gin-making. The extinction of elephants in these forests may thus mean the gradual disappearance of these large trees, but the decline would take two or three centuries and man will probably have cut them all down before it could be noticed anyway.

In one forest area of Ghana, prior to the main rains the seeds of *P. oleosa* were found in 26 out of 31 dung piles and comprised almost half of the seeds contained in them. Also common were the seeds of the grey plum and *Balanites wilsoniana*. In the region of the Bia Park elephants concentrate in the late wet season in the rainforest to the south where *Tieghemella heckelii* is fruiting. In the dry season they move into the forest in the Park when the grey plum is fruiting there, the fruits of both of these trees forming a major item of diet. Much feeding time is spent in clearings and open forest within the rainforest, where abundant browse is present but grass is rare or absent.

At the southernmost tip of Africa in the relict Knysna forest few tree seedlings germinate from the droppings of elephants. Most seeds which did germinate were of the ground flora. Here elephants are not important in forest tree seed dispersal, perhaps due to the fact that there are only three of them and they are a remnant savannah elephant population, not true forest elephants. But for most of Africa, elephants amply repay what destruction they may do to woody species by the role that they play in seed dispersal and germination. Many forest tree species may have evolved their particular seed dispersal mechanisms in concert with the elephant, as could have been the case with the extinct gomphotheres in South America and the now declining forest palm, *Scheelea rostrata*.

A LIFE OF EATING

When hunted, elephants change their routines, becoming creatures of the night, remaining in concealment as much as they can during the day and feeding intensively during darkness in open grassland. This rhythm does not differ markedly from a natural rhythm in hot climates, where from the middle of the day until 3 or 4 pm is spent resting from the heat in shade wherever possible, the elephants emerging into open areas in the evening and retiring again in the early morning.

But where conditions are not restrictive they show a triple peak in feeding, most of it taking place in the early hours of the day and in the late afternoon. In Uganda the most intense periods were midnight, the early hours of daylight and in the afternoon. There was a big drop in activity from 4 to 7 am, the main sleeping period, activity tailing off to a slow rate beforehand. On waking in the morning they then feed without a break for several hours until around midday when it begins to get hot and they rest again, but without sleeping. They feed for almost 18 hours in 24, at all hours. The decline in the evening is accompanied by increased walking, moving steadily in single file for some distance to a new feeding patch.

In Manyara they wasted a great deal of energy spending most of the morning walking down from the top of the escarpment to the woodlands below. At dusk they would move from the lakeshore to the woodlands and then often walk steadily in single file back up the escarpment to spend the night on the high ground in the Marang Forest, coming down again in the morning. Perhaps this movement is related to long ingrained previous hunting pressures on the low ground, the nearby village of Mto wa Mbu once having been an ivory trading centre.

The typical pattern of elephant feeding in grasslands is for an animal to spend long periods grazing while moving slowly but steadily along at a rate of about $\frac{1}{2}$ km an hour. But if it passes a thicket then it often stops to browse, browsing lasting for up to ten or 15 minutes. In the dry season, when much longer periods are spent browsing, an elephant will walk directly from bush to bush without stopping to graze. Much of the dry season grazing takes place at the periphery of thickets where the grass may remain green and elephants push back the branches with their tusks in order to reach the fresher grass, often toppling over shallow rooted species of bush to do so. This led to the destruction of thousands of square kilometres of commiphora bush in Tsavo, for the commiphora has low spreading thorny branches which conceal grass right up to its trunk.

At Sengwa it was estimated they fed for only $10\frac{1}{2}$ hours in every 24, but this assumed the same rate of feeding at night as observed during the day, no observations having been made at night. With hotter daily temperatures there they probably feed more intensively at night when it is cooler.

In the Manovo-Gounda Park the dry semi-deciduous woodland is interspersed with occasional riverine flood-plains whose grasses remain green, at least at their bases, the whole year round and which form an important source of food in the early dry season. Here elephants fed on the open flood-plains during the daylight hours, but after poaching escalated they changed their habits to drinking and feeding on the flood-plains at night, remaining in the comparative shelter of the woodland by day. Often waiting for nightfall in the trees adjacent to the plains, more and more groups joined together until herds of more than 1000 had gathered. Remaining together until about an hour after dark, they then broke into smaller groups of some 15 each as they fed over the plains, feeding intensity becoming highest near midnight. Just before daylight they reassembled into larger groups of up to 100 to leave the plains. Although they spent much more time grazing than browsing at night, even more so in the wet season, waiting in the woodland resulted in considerable pressure on the trees which would not have taken place had they moved straight onto the plains, even though in the dry season in the hot afternoon feeding was very perfunctory.

During a visit to the Ruaha Park I made the mistake of pitching my tent under a fruiting apple-ring thorn tree, so that I was constantly surrounded by elephants which came along to pick the fallen fruits from the ground. With their dexterous trunk tips they are able to pick up the smallest of fruits without getting the tip full of dust. With some species, such as the borassus or the tamarind, they butt the tree trunk with their foreheads, sending down a cascade of fruits. Much time is spent collecting up one by one tamarind pods which they knock down, an action equivalent to a man picking up hundreds-and-thousands one at a time on his fingertip and eating them.

THE MYSTERIOUS ELEPHANTS OF ELGON

In the miombo woodland of Africa the highest densities of elephants are to be found on the better soil types where the plants themselves have a higher mineral content, but sodium in plants is likely to be precarious and is more readily found in water or soil. In the dry season the elephants prefer to drink the cloudy grey, dirty-looking water that has soaked through the soil and thus contains more salts, rather than clear and cleaner looking water which has run off granite rocks or has been filtered through sterile sands.

Where sodium is deficient the soil that elephants eat generally has a high content and few elephants occur where it is deficient in either water or soil. An adult elephant requires 75–100 g of salt a day, so the most favoured waterholes are those with the highest content. Especially is this so in the dry season when more salt is required for the digestion of dry vegetation. Many years ago when I looked at the chemical content of samples from different salt-licks in Kenya, I found that although they contained different concentrations of a number of salts, the one that was always present, although not necessarily in the greatest quantity, was sodium. The same picture has emerged from the northern Central African Republic, where in the absence of leaching in flat terrain, termite mounds most frequently form the salt-licks when their sodium content reaches 320 parts per million. So although the presence of other minerals such as manganese may obscure the picture, it is sodium which the elephants are really seeking.

Earlier writers were intrigued by this habit of the elephant, some of the salt-licks in the more deficient areas being of striking appearance, forming great cliffs and even caves, dug out by elephants, rhinoceroses and buffaloes in their search. Just as we put salt on our food, so the elephant must have salt with his.

Some of the most interesting salt-licks known are the caves of Mt Elgon, which have been dubbed one of the wonders of the living world. Here, herds of up to 19 elephants, until the escalation of poaching in 1986, regularly entered up to 160 m deep inside a cavern, 50–100 m underground, feeling their way in total darkness into its depths.

In 1883 the explorer Joseph Thomson, as well as being the first European to cross Maasailand, was also the first to visit Mt Elgon's caves and romanticized that perhaps they had been dug out by the ancient Egyptians searching for gold and precious stones. None took Thomson's notion seriously, although it was agreed by subsequent visitors that they were at least partly manmade. Recently it has been suggested that some may have been the work of elephants seeking salt over countless generations. They prise off chunks of the cave walls with their tusks and eat the volcanic agglomerate which is high in sodium, digging further and further into the mountainside and ingesting several kilograms of salty earth at a time.

The elephants love their dark depths, spending up to six hours at a time inside, resting, bathing in the pools within, rubbing themselves on the rocks and younger ones playing. In the winter at night it is warmer in than outside the caves.

Geologists who examined the caves in some detail in 1960 came to the conclusion that they were partly waterworn and partly manmade. In the deeper recesses they found beautiful crystals of sodium salts growing on the walls. Where these crystals did not occur were the marks where they had been hacked off to be taken away as salt for cattle. All of the accounts at the turn of the century show that they were once inhabited and indeed one small cave has the earliest prehistoric cave paintings found in Kenya, once forming a frieze several hundred feet long, much removed now by weather and elephants with an itch on their backs. Although the 1960 expedition had a zoologist with it, no mention was made of elephants visiting the caves, apart from the destruction of the frieze. The many side grottoes of the undisturbed caves and the small gaps which open up into large galleries testify to their waterformed nature.

There were certainly elephants on Mt Elgon in the 1930s and a seasonal movement of four resident herds numbering together some 150–300 was reported to take place down the western slopes to the Bukedi plains in Uganda. The last record of Elgon elephants moving north into Karamoja was in 1935. By 1950 there were no longer any reports of elephants moving down the mountain and in 1959 there were only two small herds reported in the Suam and Bukwa valleys. However, by the early 1970s there were estimated to be 1700 elephants on the mountain.

Inhabited at the beginning of the century by people who preyed on passing caravans, the lack of elephants using the caves in 1960 suggests that their usage by elephants is a relatively recent phenomenon. The decrease to some 50–130 in 1987 suggests that the troglodytic elephants will also soon be a thing of the past.

'Chisel marks' in such caves, which give the impression that the roof has been dug out with pickaxes, are also the work of rhinoceroses, of which there are now none on Mt Elgon. I have seen only small caves of this nature but there is one of some depth on Mt Marsabit excavated by rhinoceroses and elephants.

At the famous Treetops in Kenya's Aberdare Mountains the formerly natural salt-lick is now maintained artificially because the elephants remove an estimated 5000 tonnes of soil per year from the wallow. But most of this is carried away sticking to their hides in the form of mud and is not ingested.

In Sri Lanka elephants have been known to exhume decomposed human bodies nearly reduced to skeletons, devouring them presumably for their mineral content. Captive elephants have been known to go further and try and bite people and there is one authenticated case of a young woman eaten by an Asian elephant known as Chang in Switzerland's Zurich Zoo. The woman was accustomed to feeding the elephant with loaves of bread because, as she put it, 'I find animals often are kinder than people'. One morning the keepers found blood on the floor and a human hand and toe in the elephant's straw. Later the woman's clothes, hat and handbag were passed in the elephant's droppings. Chang was not as kind as she thought.

A TRUNK FOR A HAND

With short grass which cannot be seized by curling the trunk around it, the elephant employs a scuffling, forward kick, first uprooting it. Then it sweeps it together with the trunk, picks it up with the 'fingers' at the end of the trunk and either bounces it on the ground several times or rubs it against the foreleg, before popping it into the mouth. The forefoot is also used to dislodge small trees and shrubs as well as tussocks of grass.

Unlike the African elephant, the Asian uses its forefeet to hold down branches and twigs while removing smaller pieces. When feeding on bark it breaks off large branches with its trunk and then holds them on the ground with the forefoot, breaking off smaller pieces which it grasps in its trunk and twists in its mouth between the teeth and, when present, against the tusks, stripping off the bark. To strip bark the African elephant uses a sideways pulling motion, dragging the bark over the anterior ridges of its teeth or, in the cases of monkeybread and *Detarium microcarpum*, it rolls a length of branch in its mouth while chewing on it, letting the branch fall when it has chewed off the bark. When feeding on the thorny yellow-fever tree the thorns are flattened between a tusk and the base of the trunk and the more prickly ends may be discarded.

In southern India the fresh grass which sprouts after the first rains in April is rich in protein and is eaten without uprooting. When it lengthens clumps are pulled up, carefully dusted by beating them against the leg, the fresh top portion bitten off and the rest discarded:

> . . . in eating grass the elephant selects a tussac (*sic*) which he draws from the ground by a dexterous twist of his trunk, and nothing can be more graceful than the ease with which, before conveying it to his mouth, he beats the earth from its roots by striking it gently upon his fore-leg.

wrote Tennent. Captive elephants, perhaps because they are sometimes fed medicines in their food, first crush fruits with the forefoot and transfer the scent to the mouth with the trunk before eating them.

The careful manner in which an elephant, Asian or African, always shakes off the soil first from a tussock before eating it may lead one to think that the elephant is a fastidious feeder, but up to 168 stones weighing together 3.6 kg have been found in an elephant's stomach.

When the famous elephant Jumbo, after he had been knocked down by a train, was dissected by America's leading taxidermist, Carl Akeley, his stomach was found to contain 'about a peck of stones and a hatful of English pennies', gold and silver coins, a bunch of keys, a police whistle, lead seals from railway trucks, trinkets of metal and glass, screws and rivets and pieces of wire. Of course, a captive elephant may have unnatural tendencies but when a dustbin-raiding bull which had become a nuisance was shot in the Queen Elizabeth Park in 1966, we opened him up and found his stomach to contain a similar collection of junk: broken drinking glasses with jagged edges, pieces of broken china

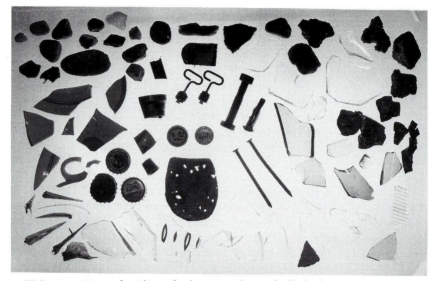

FIG. 9.1 *Not a fastidious feeder. Found in a bull elephant's stomach in Uganda.*

dinner plates, an old rubber heel of a shoe, the base of an electric light bulb, several 6″ nails, two bolts, coins, bottle tops and sundry other items. It is clear that when the elephant popped these items into his mouth from the dustbins and felt them there, he simply swallowed without first crushing them in his mighty molar teeth, just as we have the tendency to swallow sand in our picnic sandwiches.

The instinctive reaction was well expressed by Thomas Hardy in *Far From the Madding Crowd*:

> Don't ye chaw quite close, shepherd, for I let the bacon fall in the road outside as I was bringing it along, and may be 'tis rather gritty ... Don't let your teeth quite meet, and you won't feel the sandiness at all.

Chapter 10

THE GREAT DEBATE: ELEPHANTS AND TREES

The strength which he seemed to use in breaking down a tree may very fitly be compared to the force which a man exerts in order to knock down a child of three or four years old.

W. Bosman, 1705

CREATING HAVOC

'IN the green glens of many cliffs he stretches root and branch upon the ground, oaks and wild olives and the high-crowned race of palms, assailing them with his sharp tremendous tusks . . .' Thus did Oppian describe the feeding of elephants. Aelian, also in the early 3rd century, described them bending palm

FIG. 10.1   *Elephants laying waste a forest in Abyssinia (from Ludolphus, 1681).*

trees by butting with the forehead and that in India they first shook and tested a tree to see whether it was possible to overturn or not.

Job Ludolphus was to write 1400 years later in 1681 in his book *A New Historie of Ethiopia*, with an amusing illustration of elephants 'laying waste' a forest:

> But it is almost incredible to be told, what a havock they make in the Fields and woods: they will shake trees bigger than themselves in Bulk, so long, till either their Trunks break, or the whole Tree be torn up by the Roots, as with an Earthquake. Smaller Trees they snap off about a hands breadth from the Ground. As for shrubs and underwoods, and all sorts of fruit Trees, they either eat 'em up, or trample 'em under their feet.

For the next account of any detail we have to wait for Thomas Pringle, a missionary who went to the Cape in 1819:

> ... Immense numbers of these trees (acacia) had been torn out of the ground, and placed in an inverted position, in order to enable the animals to browse at their ease on the juicy roots, which form a favourite part of their food ... Many of the larger mimosas had resisted all their efforts; and, indeed, it is only after heavy rains, when the soil is soft and loose, that they can successfully attempt this operation.

The trigger-happy Roualeyn Gordon Cumming, hunting in eastern Botswana in 1848, wrote:

Almost every tree had half its branches broken short by them, and at every hundred yards I came across entire trees, and these the largest in the forest, uprooted clean out of the ground, or broken short across their stems. I observed several large trees placed in an inverted position, having their roots uppermost in the air ...

Having slept, they then proceed to feed extensively. Spreading out from one another, and proceeding in a zigzag course, they smash and destroy all the finest trees in the forest which happen to lie in their course. The number of goodly trees which a herd of bull elephants will thus destroy is utterly incredible. They are extremely capricious, and on coming to a group of five or six trees they break down not unfrequently the whole of them, when, having perhaps only tasted one or two small branches, they pass on and continue their work of destruction. I have repeatedly ridden through forests where the trees thus broken down lay so thick across one another that it was almost impossible to ride through the district.

In 1894 Frederick Jackson wrote:

It is difficult for a man who has never hunted elephants, or seen places where they have stopped to feed, to realize the tremendous havoc they play in those places which are much frequented by them, and the amount of wilful damage they do for no apparent reason. When hunting them I have often come across places where the herd I was following had stopped and scattered about to feed, and the amount of wreckage created in the short time before they had again moved on was astounding. Trees of various kinds had been broken down and uprooted in all directions for the sake of a few twigs and young shoots which could have been plucked off equally well whilst the trees stood; bushes had been pulled up and thrown on one side with scarcely a leaf off; branches of larger trees had been torn off without a twig or piece of bark having been eaten; wisps of long grass lay all round, pulled up by the roots, but otherwise untouched ... In fact, the whole place had more the appearance of a playground than of a feeding-place ... I have come across other places where an equal amount of damage has befallen the same kind of trees and bushes, but with every proof that the elephants really have fed. The trees have been well cropped of their branches and twigs; bushes that have been torn up have been devoid of leaves, and their stems well chewed; the upper part of the wisps of grass have been missing, and the branches of large trees and the trees themselves have been stripped of their bark ...

In 1931 Captain Pitman wrote of elephants along the Victoria Nile's south bank between L. Albert and Murchison Falls: '... the most striking feature in the landscape is the havoc wrought by elephants amongst the trees and bushes; this is carried to such an extent that not a single one is free from damage'. And in 1934 when Pitman conducted a study of the elephants of the Luangwa Valley, he noted that the elephants, whose numbers had assumed 'disquietingly large proportions', were addicted to bark chewing and large trees had been almost denuded of bark.

Pitman's earlier comments in Uganda were followed by those of an ecologist in 1943 who wrote:

The cumulative effect of the browsing habit of elephants on African vegetation must be very great; this deforesting effect may be strikingly seen in the Gulu elephant sanctuary which lies on the banks of the Nile ... an area from which the [human] population was evacuated thirty years ago on account of sleeping sickness. In this sanctuary are wide areas of almost treeless grassland and with little or no regeneration of the growth in spite of abundant rainfall; for most of the smaller trees are browsed back heavily and many are knocked down by the elephants in order that they may feed more easily; even the bark of the larger trees, whose branches are out of their reach, is scored by their tusks.

Today such remarks would elicit cries of 'overpopulation!', 'elephants are destroying their habitat!' and calls for cropping to reduce their numbers. Yet in Akagera Park, where there were no elephants at the time, I found huge swathes of acacia trees were felled during thunderstorms and lightning tore branches from them just as if they had been broken by elephants. So trees will be affected by the ravages of time, nature and the elements, whether elephants are present or not and the foregoing quotes show that tree destruction is not something which began in the 1960s.

THE ELEPHANTS' EFFECTS ON TREES

Elephants prefer to feed from 1 to 2 m above ground level, so preferred trees whose foliage is higher than this may be pushed over. Species not sought out for feeding tend to get pushed over according to their relative occurrence in an area – the more there are, the more get knocked down.

When browsing in the wet season elephants strip off leaves and break off branchlets to consume the soft growing terminal twigs of trees. From acacia trees the woody material ingested exceeds the foliage but this may relate to the rich protein content of the latter for, due to the amount of nitrogen which must be disposed of, too much protein is just as much of a problem to a herbivore as too little. In the dry season more bark, woody stems and roots are taken in.

Woody vegetation is affected in several ways according to the type of tree. Acacias and myrrh are easily pushed over by elephants; others, including acacias but also the bloodwood or 'fried-egg' tree (from the shape of its fruit) and the Prince of Wales's feathers, have their bark easily stripped off. Trees like the baobab and the tick tree have soft, pithy trunks which can be gouged out and yet others, such as the mopane tree, coppice from the stump and persist despite heavy browsing impact. When other food is in short supply elephants feed on the stems of such trees as the baobab and the chestnut, often destroying the entire tree.

Bark stripping is most noticeable at the onset of the rains, when the bark is rich in sap just before the trees flower or burst into leaf. In Ruaha Park it took place in the dry season prior to a tree coming into leaf but with the Tanganyika acacia it was just before flowering; the long-tail cassia both before and during flowering; and the umbrella thorn just before and during leaf production. The actual stripping of bark is coincidental. The elephant gouges the bark in order to prise off a mouthful or two and in pulling at it the bark strips off in some species in long lengths. More stripping took place during the drought of 1976 in Ruaha than in other dry seasons, but bulls ate bark throughout the year, whereas cows took it only occasionally. Debarking is light in forests where there is an abundance of herbaceous vegetation.

High elephant densities affect vegetation to the extent of considerably changing its appearance or composition, under extreme conditions transforming bushed or wooded savannah into open grassland with damage to the woody plants often being exacerbated by fire or drought. Thus the effects of elephant on vegetation depend upon the season, the length of time the elephants have their impact upon it, fire, drought cycles and the type of soil. On drier, fertile sandy soils, the felling of trees can lead to an increase of browse production of preferred species and maintenance of the preferred height by coppicing, thus improving the elephant's dry season food supply. In Asia the food available to elephants can be more than $2\frac{1}{2}$ times greater in secondary rainforest due to the regrowth than it is in the tall-tree primary rainforest. But on poor or clayey soils, the vegetation cannot respond quickly and trees tend to die out if felled or overbrowsed.

In East Africa, in a relatively dry climate without fire, large browsers or man's intervention, the natural succession is towards woody thickets, a process accentuated by cattle overgrazing. Elephants at low densities destroy mature trees; at higher ones they both destroy mature trees and prevent regeneration. A balance exists between trees and grass depending upon the soil structure, whether rocky and shallow, deep, clayey or sandy and so on, and rainfall. Thinning out of trees by elephants, or by fire and elephants, means that more moisture is available in the soil for grass and thus there is denser grass growth. This in turn means more fuel in the dry season and hotter fires which are more damaging to whatever woody vegetation still survives. Heavy grazing results in annual grasses which are less palatable.

Miombo is a type of dense fire-resistant woodland characterized by *Brachystegia* and *Julbernardia* trees, mostly msasa and munondo, forming the largest single vegetation type in southern Africa. In the miombo woodland of the Kasungu Park 13 tree species in 35 were most favoured. Analyses showed that it was the amount of protein in the browse which was the attractant, followed by sodium.

In mature miombo woodland elephant density is normally low because food availability is low, tied into the tops of the trees. As elephants move into or are pushed into such an area, they knock over trees to browse upon them. This results in a certain amount of coppice regrowth, fallen or broken trees sprouting from the base. At this stage selectivity begins to take effect between the favoured species and the less favoured. The favoured are constantly browsed and the coppice growth thus kept at the preferred feeding level. Many of the non-selected species, receiving less attention, may grow to canopy height. This causes them to thin out and so, in theory, we end up with a sort of elephant garden with an increased density of selected species held in the coppice phase of regrowth providing a favourable food supply for the elephants. But above about 300 trees per hectare elephant use levels off.

Although this sequence may conceivably take place in miombo woodland, in other areas such as northern Uganda and Tsavo this has not been the case and destruction of trees has led to open grassland.

The mopane woodland of southern Africa, characterized by a single dominant tree, reacts in different ways according to soil type. Occurring mainly in the more or less flat and wide valley bottoms of the large rivers and on the adjacent wide plains, woodlands on salty soils that promote coppicing may be more liable to changes than those on soils less favourable to mopane. With heavily browsed coppiced mopane almost total mortality of trees took place in the Luangwa valley when rainfall was 14% below average. Patches of coppiced woodland also appear to die out from nutrient exhaustion from continual foliage removal by elephants. But elephant feeding alone may not be the cause of such woodland changing to a more treeless grassland. On soils with more mixed woodland where mopane is limited, it is characterized by larger trees and recruitment is determined more by fire and other browsing species of animals which may affect seedling establishment.

In the Sengwa area riverine woodland, the originally dominant umbrella thorn and the donkeyberry shrub declined due to the former being felled or debarked and the latter uprooted. All tree felling was in the dry season when elephants were seeking fresh foliage. Bulls pushed over more trees than cows and ate less from them. A single bull pushed over nine trees a day in the dry season, with over three quarters of the bulls observed pushing over trees. It was estimated that 146 trees in every square kilometre were knocked down each year in an area of 390 sq. km, but this represented less than 1% of the total number of trees present.

In Ruaha bulls did more damage to baobabs than did cows because the latter tend to keep moving to keep up with the herd. The independent bulls can linger to their heart's content, smashing their way through a baobab until they tire of it. Perhaps because of their bigger stomach fill, they move from tree to tree less frequently than cows and therefore cause more damage to a species.

After heavy elephant removal, as in Gonarezhou, there has been abundant regeneration of umbrella thorn with trees growing to a height of 5–7 m in seven years. Under rainfall as little as 500 mm this species takes only 20 years to reach maturity. At Seronera the same tree was declining by 65% a year due to destruction by elephants, but saplings less than 1 m high were ignored. Here the yellow-fever tree was being destroyed at a rate of 5.5% a year and the three-thorned acacia at 2.6%. In Tsavo East umbrella thorn trees greater than 1 m tall declined in density by about 65% from 1970 to 1974, but regeneration of less than this height remained abundant. In Kruger Park and at Chobe and Tuli in Botswana, as well as at Sengwa and in the Luangwa, knob-thorn trees have been destroyed extensively by barking and felling. Along the Ruaha and Magusi rivers in Tanzania, apple-ring thorn trees declined in density by 15–25% over a period of 11 years due mainly to debarking. Yet in the Luangwa elephants felled some stands of this tree while leaving others only lightly affected, and at Mana Pools mature species have persisted with relatively little mortality since debarking was first reported 20 years ago, but regeneration has been prevented by elephants feeding on the saplings.

Once a woodland has been destroyed it could take 140 years to recover, for whereas a species like umbrella thorn can reach maturity in 20 years, the Prince of Wales's feathers takes 60 and Rhodesian teak 200. In the absence of elephants umbrella thorn grows in Zimbabwe at a density of 2500 to the square kilometre. If elephant density is one to the square kilometre, then there will be only 500 trees. And if elephant density is two, then tree density will be only 200. To maintain a balance between tree loss and tree regeneration requires an elephant density of not more than one to every 2 sq. km. Elephants can double in number in 12–14 years, whereas woodlands can take ten times as long to recover.

In southern Murchison Falls Park, *Terminalia glaucescens–Combretum binderianum* woodland was virtually eliminated in the central area, tree density declining from 1060 to 430 to the square kilometre in 1958 and 20 by 1967. Tree death followed debarking in the dry season and beginning of the rains, with damaged trees becoming infested by woodboring beetles. This leads to invasion by fungi, the trees eventually being killed by fire in the fierce annual grass fires which characterize the area. As the trees disappeared, because of the relatively high rainfall this gave way to dense elephant grass up to 10 m tall which created raging infernos in the dry seasons.

Although changes are usually associated with high elephant density, trees have also declined under relatively low densities. In Kruger Park with a mean density of 0.4 elephants to the square kilometre, bark damage and felling of species such as marula and knob-thorn was considerable. At Seronera reduction of umbrella thorn was caused by a local density of only 0.2.

In one Zimbabwe study 63% of the total tree population in three main vegetation types was killed or converted to shrubs in the space of seven years. But the elephants were attracted to areas of favoured riverine vegetation, preferring to browse on new regrowth coppicing from previously damaged mopane trees and damaging the adjacent mopane in the process.

More subtle effects may take place. The dominant tree of the Budongo forest, the Uganda ironwood, may result from elephants avoiding its seedlings and saplings and concentrating on its competitors. In high forest elephants may be responsible for the dominance of this tree over a very large area of Africa where both climate and soils favour its growth. Both African and Asian elephants may suppress shade tolerant climax trees in dense forests by creating open gaps which can be colonized by faster growing species.

Tropical forests are protected around their edges by thickets, and grass within the forests is scanty due to lack of light. High elephant numbers trample and feed on the thickets leading to replacement by grassland. Their disappearance lets light into the forest and grass invades, carrying the fire into the forest itself in the dry season. Eventually the fire-susceptible trees themselves are destroyed. Savannah trees in Africa are fire-resistant, resistance being provided by the corky bark. When a fire passes the bark is not even scorched but once the underlying wood is exposed it dries out and is easily burned. Even if not burnt it is attacked by fungi and woodboring beetles. What Dutch elm disease did for the countryside of Britain in the 1960s has been done for much of the countryside of Africa by elephants since the 1950s.

DESTRUCTION OF THE BAOBAB

Most spectacular has been the effect upon baobabs in Tsavo East Park where they were virtually eliminated over 8000 sq. km by 1974, less than 20 years after the first reports of damage. Hundreds were felled along the Tiva River by 1959 and many more in the drought of 1961. Some mature trees had healed scars, evidence of a former less disastrous cycle of elephant activity. In the Luangwa Valley elephants were reported as 'suddenly' beginning to eat and destroy baobabs in 1960, virtually the same time that they began their attacks in Tsavo more than 1000 km away to the north.

The baobab is known to Africans by the Lear-like name of the 'upside-down tree', because its huge swollen trunk with straggly branches, leafless for much of the year, makes it look as if its roots are pointing into the air. The distinctive growth rings of the baobab, the pith layered like an onion, have been correlated with radiocarbon dating as being of annual occurrence and in turn the girth of the tree has been related to age. But a constant rate of growth cannot be assumed; like all growth processes it is 's'-shaped, becoming slower as the tree gets older. During droughts the girth may actually shrink.

Adanson, after whom the baobab got its scientific name in the 18th century, believed that some veritable giants must be at least 5000 years old. A radiocarbon dating check on one of 4.57 m girth in Zimbabwe gave an age of 900–1100 years, fully suggesting that some might be several thousand years old although as a softwood it may well be generally a shortlived tree. A record 700 year old English oak has a girth of almost 13 m but probably this greater girth results from ancient coppicing.

In 1975 I measured the girths of a number of large baobabs growing actually out of the ruins of the ancient Arab city of Gedi, near Mombasa in Kenya, believed abandoned in the early 17th century. Extrapolating from the Zimbabwe tree, these had an average age of about 119 years, suggesting that they began growing about 1850. But as rainfall at Gedi is a third higher than where the Zimbabwe tree was measured, the Gedi trees may well be much younger.

At Ruaha baobab density declined from 72 to 40 to the square kilometre in 11 years, a mean rate of decrease of 3% per year. In Manyara elephants increased their attentions on baobabs from 1969, especially on younger trees, but mortality and damage rates have remained well below those of other areas, perhaps because of the proximity of the trees to the saline lake, if indeed minerals are the cause of the elephants' attentions. In the 1978 drought in this area acacia woodlands were reported as 'in ruins' and there was extensive destruction of aloes and myrrh bush, but the baobabs came off lightly.

Baobabs have suffered damage and decline in many other places, but none so complete as at Tsavo. Here also mature myrrh trees were reduced in density from a mean of 90 per hectare in 1970 to only five in 1974, with open savannah being created over an area of 4400 sq. km. Myrrh tree felling was first noticed in 1956 and was extensive by 1959.

Why do they do it?

Tree damage is not related to levels of chemical constituents in vegetation nor to those in the soil, except when low in sodium. It could result from one of three factors or a combination of them. First, ambling elephants casually stab at the nearest trees that they pass; given a high enough density of elephants then this will become destructive of trees. Secondly, they may be attracted to certain trees by smell and taste. Thirdly, it may be a learning process: one elephant starts it and the rest copy. Selection is relative to presence and they tend to concentrate on trees already barked, perhaps because of the smell of the exuding sap. But a certain species may be favoured in one area and not in others.

One theory is that woodland destruction is a feeding strategy leading to maintenance of a preferred stage of vegetation succession; that is, young coppice growth as opposed to mature trees. Extensive woodland destruction in dry savannah areas was caused by maladapted elephants, elephants attuned to a forest environment where their prodigality did not matter as rapid regeneration adequately repaired their ravages.

Could it be nutritional? A 3 tonne elephant cow pregnant or lactating needs about 60 g of calcium a day, which must be obtained from vegetation. But although bark is rich in calcium, so is grass and an elephant could obtain sufficient for its needs from grass alone. In Tsavo phosphorus may be a limiting factor for plant growth towards the end of the growing, or wet, season, in certain areas and in certain years. Production of vegetation is probably limited by phosphorus availability when rainfall is greater than 400 mm.

Only 7% of the amount of phosphorus available in the soil is accumulated in the woody biomass, tree bark containing about a third of the amount which grass does. But calcium may be five times higher in tree bark than it is in grass. The bark of *Terminalia glaucescens*, the tree selectively debarked in northern Uganda, is particularly high in calcium but the desert date in the same area, of which the bark is also high in calcium, showed little or no debarking.

Fat and carbohydrate do not vary significantly with season in the food; it is protein which shows most variation. Whereas a 1 tonne growing elephant needs about 300 g of protein a day, in the dry season its food will provide roughly 260 g and in the wet 600. But this dry season deficiency cannot be met from bark or woody vegetation, although it might be an inducement to feed on the crowns of trees which can only be made accessible by the elephant felling them. But in Murchison Falls the intake of essential fatty acids, vitamin F and linolenic acid decreased dramatically in the dry season in cow elephants feeding in grasslands. The intake of fat represented only 4.6% of the total calorific value of the elephants' diets and vitamin F accounted for only 0.2–0.4% of the total dietary calories, well below the 1% level necessary to prevent essential fatty acid deficiency in man. Whereas women desperately trying to slim might be envious of the cow elephant's deficiency, they may not be envious of the possibility that it may drive elephants to chew trees, for the woody pulp of *Terminalia* and baobab trees has higher concentrations of vitamin F than other types of forage. A deficiency of this vitamin may therefore drive elephants to attack these trees. But in Hwange Park, where there is no shortage of browse, elephants have relatively high levels of fatty acid in their blood, even in the dry season, indicating that they must be receiving enough vitamin F in their diet. Yet they still bark trees.

Perhaps the RSPCA Inspector was right and it may simply be to maintain a suitable protein to fibre ratio; in other words, like Jumbo and the lady's basket, to provide enough roughage to fill out the elephant's capacious stomach.

Sometimes tree destruction appears to be a displacement activity resulting from harassment by poachers. A herd of about 100 elephants in the Manovo-Gounda Park, after pursuit by poachers on horseback, were seen moving along the edge of a flood-plain and pushing down tree after tree as they fed, uprooting or breaking some 200 trees in 5 hectares. But the concentration of elephants after harassment, rather than a nervous disposition, may have resulted in a concentration of tree destruction. However, it has also been postulated that the knocking down of several species of mature acacia trees by middle-aged bulls in the Serengeti Park, which were then not fed upon, might have been a behavioural pattern resulting from disturbances to which the elephants had been subjected before entering the Park, invading it to escape persecution in Kenya.

In the Sengwa area, pushing over trees by bulls also appeared to be partly a social display of animals disturbed by hunting. Severe reduction of trees was already evident from air photos taken in 1958. In the Matusadona Highlands of the Zambezi escarpment, 60% canopy cover in 1959 was reduced to only 2% by 1973. Elsewhere on the escarpment there was no evidence of tree loss on 1966 air photos, suggesting massive losses may have taken place in just 5–7 years.

In one area in Zimbabwe the destruction of trees was clearly related to compression of the elephants at an unsupportably high density by settlement restricting their former range. Damage to Prince of Wales's feathers trees began in the mid-1960s and of 500 trees sampled almost 67% were dead within less than 10 years, just over 20% were damaged and only 13% alive and undamaged.

A PROBLEM IN ASIA?

Asian elephants occur at relatively low densities and although they affect the vegetation, lasting damage has not been reported. In one park in Sri Lanka some 8% of damage was tree felling, but bark stripping was rare because most Asian elephants lack tusks. Unlike the African elephant the utilization of woody plants in Sri Lanka was mainly by branch breaking, leaves and bark being stripped from the broken stem. Tennent had noted in 1859: '... where a herd has recently passed I have sometimes seen the bark peeled curiously off the twigs as though it had been done in mere dalliance'. Pushing trees over is also rare and again Tennent noted:

> In clearing an opening through forest land, the power of the African elephant, and the strength ascribed to him by a recent traveller [Gordon Cumming], as displayed in uprooting trees, have never been equalled or approached by anything I have seen of the elephant in Ceylon or heard of them in India.

But Captain Forsyth, writing in 1871 of the feeding of a herd of 50–60 elephants in India, described a scene reminiscent of that met with in Africa:

> I ... found the hillside completely levelled, bamboos torn down, crushed between their teeth, and many of their young shoots eaten away, and many trees of the *Boswellia* and other scantily rooted species overthrown and stripped of the tender bark of their top branches. The limit of their powers in overthrowing trees appeared, however, to be confined to those of not more than about eight inches in diameter, and my experience with trained tame elephants leads to a similar conclusion. Even these are not torn up by the roots but merely borne down by the application of their full weight, by means of the forehead and one foot ...

Captain Forsyth's observations apart, elephant feeding in Asia is not as destructive as it appears to be in Africa, trees suffering crown distortion but not being destroyed. Past elephant feeding activity, prior to 1969, was found to have been much greater in open scrub than in closed forest vegetation. Trees and shrubs of 2–5 m high showed extensive crown distortion in Ruhuna Park where elephants occurred at a density of 1.2 to the square kilometre. Such crown distortion has not been reported in African studies although many of the species involved have African counterparts. But the rainfall averaging 1100 mm in Sri Lanka is much higher than that of most of the African areas where destruction takes place and may permit more vigorous recuperation.

In southern India considerable amounts of bark were taken in the dry season but the effects upon trees seemed to be negligible. In Bihar the bark of such trees as the jujube, teak and *Bridelia retusa* was eaten, trees being uprooted as well as standing trees being stripped.

THE BENEFITS OF ELEPHANT TREE-BASHING

Some argue that elephant feeding is destructive but others stress that it creates coppicing and therefore a more productive vegetation capable of supporting more animals of all species. I recall that in the Aberdare Mountains elephants used to come by at regular intervals of several months, leaving an area looking as if a bomb had struck it, a tangle of trampled and broken bushes and white, skeleton-like branches stripped of their bark. But by the time that they came round again thicket had grown up once more and hidden the scars. Where elephants have been reduced or barriers set up to keep them out, recovery of vegetation has been remarkably rapid.

The breaking of stems of palatable species of trees results in the conversion of stands of tall trees offering little accessible forage to a dense shrubby regrowth which repeated browsing maintains in a favourable growth stage, like trimming a hedge. Examples of such beneficial transformations are stands of mixed msasa trees and others in Kasungu Park and of mopane in the Luangwa valley. Repeated heavy browsing of plants may also stress them to an extent where they do not produce so many deterrent chemicals, such as alkaloids and tannins, thus providing more palatable food.

Acacia trees inhibit seedling regrowth under their canopies so the destruction of mature trees accelerates seedling regeneration, as happened in the Serengeti. Elephants serve as major dispersal agents of the seeds of many trees, especially in primary rainforest where they consume large quantities of fruits. So many advantageous effects of the elephants' forestry activities can be hypothesized.

Predictions of elephant density and of the amount of tree canopy appear independent of the species of tree because the rates of damage to trees have an inverse relationship to the potential recovery rate of dominant trees. That is, trees which grow quickly to maturity are destroyed more quickly. This could imply that the habitats evolved in the presence of elephants but at lower densities than at present where destruction is taking place. Had elephants been absent from the evolution of these woodlands then one might have expected rates of recovery to be independent of elephant densities.

FIGHTING BACK

A remarkable discovery in recent years is that the woody plants themselves do not remain passive to the ravages of elephants or, for that matter, any other browsers but actively defend themselves against being eaten! Mopane particularly, which is greatly used by elephants, when browsed upon immediately increases the levels of phenols in its remaining leaves. The poorer the soil, and therefore the less quickly a plant can recover, the higher the level of tannins – derivatives of phenols.

Although we like tannin in our tea, too much is not good for one. Phenols are carbolic acids and, as naughty children used to learn if they swore and had their mouths washed out with carbolic soap, are not nice to taste. So the more an elephant browses on a plant like mopane, the less tasty it becomes and the elephant will move on to another. In several miombo species the tannin-C contents, or proanthocyanidins to give the phenols their proper scientific name, increase by as much as three times within an hour. After this some species continue to maintain a relatively high level for a couple of days. In the umbrella thorn, however, the level rapidly returns to normal so this chemical defence does not protect the plant entirely because the elephant can come back again later. But it does serve to give the tree a chance to recover a little and perhaps the elephant will not come back again for a long time, if at all.

Tree species growing on fairly fertile soils have low levels of phenols but if browsed they are able to respond with more vigorous growth to replace the losses quickly. Mature tree canopies also have relatively low levels so we can see why it is advantageous for an elephant to push over a tree to feed on the canopy, despite shorter species being within reach.

On infertile sandy soils where leaves cannot be replaced quickly, many herbaceous plants have indigestible chemical compounds in their leaves making them unpalatable in spite of a lush, rich appearance. The extreme case is the broad dark green leafed poisonous plant *mogau*, common in parts of northern Botswana. Adult elephants seemingly learn to avoid it but it is thought that it can be eaten with impunity if the elephant does not drink afterwards. Juvenile elephants, less wise, are often found dead near waterholes in the dry season showing no apparent cause of death, which is attributed to eating *mogau*. It causes many fatalities among cattle if they are allowed to graze in areas where it grows. It is an example of a plant which has perfected the ultimate deterrent.

Chapter *11*

THE ELEPHANT CASEBOOK: EXAMPLES OF OVERPOPULATION

... they are the favourite haunts and playgrounds of elephants that regard Toro and Bunyoro as their own special reserves. These mighty animals herd together in large companies, sometimes numbering hundreds, and absolutely disregard any claim or boundary that mere man may peg out for himself.

Mrs A.B. Fisher, 1911

THE UGANDA PROBLEM

NORTH Bunyoro is an area in Uganda bounded by L. Albert on the west and the Victoria Nile to the east. Although by 1955 the elephants which once occupied almost three quarters of Uganda had been restricted to less than one fifth of the land area, prior to the almost total destruction of its elephants in the mid-1970s this area had one of the most pronounced elephant overpopulations recorded in Africa. Even so, it is estimated that its population of 22 000 in 1946, and perhaps many more than that, had decreased to 7900 in 1967 but at the same time the elephant's range had been reduced by other land pressures to less than one half, from 6300 sq. km to 2800.

Already, by 1959 a number of populations had become completely isolated and by 1973 the elephant range in the whole of Uganda had shrunk to less than 13%. Due to overcrowding resulting from this constriction of range, with a density of almost three to the square kilometre and the deterioration of habitat in the Budongo Forest Reserve, age at puberty was delayed until 22 years and the average calving interval was almost eight. The population could therefore not replace the number of deaths with births and was in decline.

The high density of elephants in north Bunyoro, ranging from 2.8 to 3.5 to the square kilometre, was surpassed only by those of the Luangwa Valley and L. Manyara. Due to heavy use also by hippopotamuses and other animals such as buffaloes, up to within 3 km of the Nile the density was less than 1.5 per square kilometre, rising to almost two within 8 km. Density then increased rather abruptly inland to almost four, dropping again at about 17 km near the zone of human conflict.

Sir Samuel Baker tells us that in the 1860s to 1870s the area south of the Nile was well-inhabited and cultivated, a mosaic of forest interspersed with villages and cultivation. He referred to the 'parklike land that characterises Chobe and Bunyoro, the grass was above seven feet high . . .' North of the Nile he described as undulating prairie clear of trees, much as the southern area was to become in the next century.

Another famous traveller was Winston Churchill, who walked through the area in 1908 and described seeing much forest there. From the southern boundary of the present Murchison Park looking north, he wrote: 'In every direction spread a wide sea of foliage, thinning here into bush, darkening there into forest. . .'

In Churchill's time the area had already been depopulated due to an epidemic of sleeping sickness. Those who did not succumb to the disease were evacuated from the area in 1912 and by 1924 elephants had become a problem due to recolonization and expansion by human populations. Following expansion of the elephant population during the sleeping sickness epidemic and then compression in its aftermath, an excessive density of elephants ensued which led to the progressive destruction of the forest and woodland, turning it into open grassland dominated by 3 m high elephant grass.

Already begun by 1946 and in some places severe three years later, as the woody vegetation disappeared in north Bunyoro, the elephants were driven to feeding primarily on grass, particularly south of the Nile. From about 1946 the population inhabiting the area covering the Murchison Park and the Budongo Forest Reserve began to decline in numbers. Half of this decline resulted from a combination of control shooting and sport hunting, while natural regulation effected the rest. This natural control was through delayed maturity, reduced fecundity and increased calf mortality, resulting from the inadequate nutrition provided by an 80–90% grass diet. The decline was parallelled later, about 1957, north of the Nile.

Calf mortality doubled in the 20 years from 1946 to 1966 due to inadequate nutrition and lack of shade leading to heat stress. Added to this, deferred maturity and reduced fecundity on the part of cows led to a massive drop in recruitment. This meant that although by about 1967 the population size had been reduced by more than 60%, natural regulation alone was estimated to have been responsible for a decline from 16 000 to 7900. By 1971 there was only one third of the number of elephants present in 1946. But this resulted only in just over a 50% reduction in weight of live animals, so population stability was still not achieved as the reduced recruitment resulted in an ageing population with a preponderance of heavy older animals, and the average weight of an individual increased from just under 2 to $2\frac{1}{2}$ tonnes. Since the range of the animals had also been reduced by more than a half the effect was stalemate, as while the density of elephants decreased from 3.5 to 2.8 to the square kilometre, or by about one fifth, biomass actually increased from 6.6 to almost 7 tonnes per square kilometre. So the elephants continued to have the same destructive effect upon the habitat, continuing to change it at a rate influenced by the short-term rainfall cycles. In good years there was less lasting effect stemming from the elephant feeding and there would be some recovery, but in bad years this was reversed. Thus the range had contracted too rapidly to allow the elephants to adapt to it.

By virtue of their longevity, even without any increase in numbers the live weight of elephants per square kilometre would have continued to decline only slowly, giving no respite to the vegetation, had not events taken a different course with massive poaching intervening, beginning in 1973, to drastically reduce the population. Now with only a few elephants remaining, dense thickets have reinvaded the area, establishing without any doubt that elephants are the catalyst to destruction of woody vegetation by fire and not the other way around.

Some of the giant African and Budongo mahogany trees in the Budongo forest were believed to be well over 300 years old. These giants are characterized by buttresses and barking of the buttresses by elephants causes rot patches to develop due to invasion by fungi. The scars become grown over and when the trees are cut down an estimation of the years when the rot patches formed can be made by relating the scars to the number of tree rings covering them. This showed that there had been significant attacks by elephants beginning about 1780, possibly earlier. An apparent absence of scars follows from about 1810 to 1885 when the attacks then begin again.

This period could relate to that of intensive slaughter of elephants for ivory, causing them to shelter in the forest, until the imposition of controls in 1897. Coastal caravans did not penetrate Buganda until the 1880s, but the demand for ivory had begun well before that date.

An apparent marked drop in rot patches about 1935 to 1945 coincides with a sharp rise in ivory exports beginning in 1931 which peaked in 1936 and then declined somewhat, presumably related to control shooting which forced the elephants out of the forest.

Swynnerton estimated the 'Budongo herd' to number about 5000 head in 1923. In the 1960s it was estimated that the number of elephants resident in the Budongo forest was of the order of 300, while another 900 used it seasonally. The residents were of the forest elephant type, while the others were savannah elephants. The forest itself offers little in the way of food and it is used more for shelter than for feeding; thus even those elephants which are resident tend to feed outside its confines at night. But the more disturbance around the forest then the more time the elephants spend sheltering within it.

The reduction of the number of Murchison Park elephants to some 1200 by 1987 has amply shown how regeneration of woodland takes place in the continued presence of annual fires. At the time of the overpopulation when the effects of the elephants were at their height, the south-west of Budongo forest where there were few elephants was in a state of expansion and dense *Terminalia* was being colonized by a fast-growing forest tree known as musizi.

THE STORY OF TSAVO

In 1890 Lugard reported elephants along the Galana River, inside present-day Tsavo Park, yet at the beginning of 1894, A.H.Neumann, considered to be one of the greatest of elephant hunters, passed straight through Tsavo to hunt for ivory in Turkana with the remark 'The uninhabited (principally desert) country traversed previous to entering Ukambani has but little game . . .'. So the belief was perpetrated in the 1960s that elephants must have been formerly absent from the Tsavo area. When I visited Tsavo East in 1956 all that I saw in the thick bush which then clothed the area was one bull elephant near to the track. He departed as soon as I stopped. A noisy caravan of chattering people would have been even less likely to see elephants in the thick bush which characterized Tsavo East until the 1960s.

But Neumann went to Turkana because of the stories of vast quantities of ivory to be found there, which he found to be untrue anyway. He may well have believed that Tsavo was not worth the candle because of the earlier reports of the missionary Krapf, almost half a century before. In 1844 Krapf had written:

> There are said to be elephants in the Galla land, in the neighbour-
> hood of Emberria; but in the Wanika territories there are no longer
> any of these animals to be found, as they recede more and more into
> the large forests, and to the rivers of the interior, owing to their
> being so much molested since European commerce with Zanzibar
> has produced so great a demand for ivory. If it be true that yearly
> about 6000 elephants' tusks are brought to the Suahili coast, it can
> easily be understood how quickly these animals diminish, and why
> they recede ever further into the interior of Africa.

Krapf's colleague Rebmann, who journeyed to Kilimanjaro in 1848, reported:

FIG. 11.1   *Tsavo as it was in 1956. Contrast with the habitat shown in Fig. 6.3.*

> The wilderness between Teita and Chagga country [i.e. today's Tsavo West] appears to hold more elephants than to the east of Teita, where the animals have mostly disappeared or rather retreated into the interior.

But Krapf also noted in 1847, when referring to the Taru desert, a waterless stretch of 55 km between Taru and Maungu: 'We frequently saw footprints and dung of [elephants] ... that must have remained since the rainy season'. Krapf recorded other sightings above Lugard's Falls in 1850. Of Kisimani on the coast in 1844 he had written: 'Kisimani is said to have been a forest in which elephants lived. Nowadays one has to go three to four days into the interior until one finds elephants'. That is, to about the eastern boundary of present-day Tsavo East Park.

The inhospitable Tsavo East Park had been extensively populated in the precolonial period as numerous living sites and burial cairns testify. In the mid-15th century hunter–gatherers called Wambisha lived a Stone Age existence there, abandoning the area sometime before the second half of the 19th century. A remnant group lived on amongst the Teitas west of Voi until the turn of the century, having made contact with them in the mid-17th century. Short-term occupation by other tribes continued through the 19th, finishing with the elephant-hunting Waata or Waliangulo.

Intensive elephant hunting first took place in the coastal region dominated by the Wakamba from their headquarters at Ulu. By the early mid-19th century the coastal bush from around Kilifi to Shimba was largely hunted out and Krapf recorded in 1848 that elephant were 'much destroyed' in Ukambani.

Fitzgerald in 1891 recorded an account by his colleague Mr Foaker of large numbers a short way upstream of Sala in the Sobo area. The records suggest that there was at least one herd between Sala and Sobo and perhaps another centring on Lugard's Falls. Hobley in 1892 noted elephant south of Kasigau:

> The whole of this district (Kasigau-Kilibasi-Birikani) is the hunting
> ground of the Walangulo (sic) tribe, who live in the vicinity of Taro
> ... they are supposed to hand over to the Gallas half the ivory they
> kill ... they formerly lived in the jungle round Taro ...

In 1928 Kasigau, a hill to the south-west of Voi, was referred to as a 'favourite playground of the elephants'. Even so, the bush to the west of it was 'impenetrable and impassable'.

This was probably secondary thicket which had invaded former plantations, for up until the early part of the First World War Kasigau mountain was inhabited by the Kasigau people, a tribe numbering some 400 evicted due to alleged collaboration with the Germans.

Tsavo East is characterized by myrrh–acacia deciduous bushland, known locally as nyika. Myrrh is a 3 m high thorny bush with gaunt, twisted branches, which provides the aromatic myrrh of the Bible. The acacia, which comes in many forms, is also a thorny bush or large tree which provides the sticky resin of gum arabic. At one time dense bush dominated by these two species covered much of the area of 13 800 sq. km which, together with its surrounding ecosystem, totals 43 300. With an average rainfall of only 150–300 mm, the aridity of this area is compounded by the occurrence of periodic drought in approximately ten year cycles.

Until 1957, when poaching was at least temporarily controlled, hunting served to keep the elephants scattered throughout this vast, semiarid area. Where they are hunted elephants do not linger at water. They come in, drink quickly and get as much distance between the water and themselves as possible. But protection draws elephants to an area, added to which the construction in 1953 of a large permanent body of water in an otherwise waterless area, the Aruba dam, also attracted elephants to a point source.

In 1951 there were an estimated 5000 elephants in Tsavo, but the true number was probably nearer to 20 000. In 1965 a total of 20 300 was counted. This was unchanged in 1969 but thereafter the number increased dramatically and the elephants could now spend all the time that they wished in the green vegetation near to water.

Mature trees in the area are nearly eliminated when elephant density is greater than one elephant per square kilometre. Shrubs and the recruitment of trees are less affected. But if elephant density is 1.5 to the square kilometre then the tree cover will be only about 1%. Hence in Tsavo East for the reduction of trees to be noticed would have required a population of elephants of only 10 000–12 000. There would have had to have been some 30 000 elephants present in

1951 for the population to have stabilized in numbers at about 40 000 in 1976. But beginning about 1970 some of the surrounding area began to be settled and this undoubtedly drove many elephants into the Park, so it is unlikely that there were 30 000 in 1951.

In the years 1960–1961 came the first witnessed drought in the area. It was widely reported and the *Daily Mirror* newspaper carried headlines 'How about adopting a thirsty elephant?', a request for funds to construct more permanent water sources stating that 3000 elephants in Tsavo needed a drink. In fact the estimate was about 10 000 elephants at this time and the real number may have been three times this.

Elephants died but it was the black rhinoceros which suffered heaviest losses. Drought was followed by above average rain which created a remarkable profusion of springs, seepages and watercourses throughout what had previously been a near-desert, changing the face of Tsavo from one of famine to one of plenty.

But in 1970 and 1971 the rains failed again. Although springs and watercourses continued to flow the vegetation around them was eaten out and lack of rain created an even worse famine for the herbivores. Towards the end of 1970 the first elephant deaths occurred when about 300, mainly calves of 6–12 years of age, succumbed. The below average short rains in November gave a brief respite but the long rains in 1971 were a third below average and large scale die-offs began in August of that year. Once more the calves were the first to fall victim, to be followed this time by adult cows which stayed close to the water sources because their young could not range as far as the adults.

The major factor causing the deaths was the prolonged dry season with a very low rainfall and not the failure of the long rains in March to May. A rainfall of 235 mm is equivalent to a primary production of less than 200 g of vegetation per square metre, which is insufficient to support elephants at the numbers in which they occurred. Estimates of the primary production from January to November 1970 were less than 100 g per square metre. In some areas it was zero and these areas had the highest numbers of elephant deaths.

This low level of productivity continued into 1971 but the most important factor was the month-to-month production, not the total annual production. Food shortage is likely when two consecutive months fail to reach the monthly food requirements, four months results in severe handicap and five in death. The production required to sustain the maintenance level of all of the herbivorous animals in the Park was estimated at 107.5 g of dry matter per square metre per day, and this was only met from the total productivity of the area for 161 days out of a total dry season length of 180.

Bulls, which were not restricted like the cows, suffered much less but many died from staying for too long away from water. When they rushed to drink in a dehydrated state, the sudden influx of water into their systems knocked them down as if poleaxed. Some dropped dead in the water while drinking. This probably did not happen to those who drank from holes scooped into the sand of a river bed where they had to wait for the water to percolate through, and so took in a little at a time until their thirst was satiated.

FIG. 11.2 *Elephants which dropped dead in the Galana River after drinking when dehydrated.*

Altogether 5900 elephants are estimated to have died at this time, perhaps more, but mortality continued until 1975 so the total number of deaths was probably at least 9000. But this was still only one fifth of the estimated population and counts of the whole ecosystem in 1973–1974 revealed that there were as many elephants present then as before the drought. More must have moved in from outside the area once conditions became favourable again.

Past rainfall records suggest that the animals of Tsavo will suffer stress every five years on average and severe hardship every ten years. Superimposed upon this is a drought cycle of some 43–50 years when heavy mortality is likely to occur. Famines were recorded in the area in 1836 and 1887 and 1921 was the driest year this century. Poor years were 1949, 1960 and 1970, but it was not until 1960 that there are records of an effect upon the elephants. There were many more deaths in 1970–1971 than there had been in the previous ten year drought because of the much larger number of elephants present.

In 1974 it was estimated that there were 37 800 elephants and 12 000 had died. Counts in 1975 revealed a similar population but by 1976 there was significant poaching and two years later the number of elephants had been reduced to 20 000 by the onslaught. By 1980 the numbers were estimated at 11 000, mostly juveniles and subadults. Eight years later the total was down to 4900 for the whole ecosystem.

From 1975 to 1978 a study of the vegetation and soils in Tsavo concluded that it was unlikely that severe permanent damage could be done to either soil or vegetation by elephants and that all processes are reversible, given time. No one would dispute the latter; the question is, how long a period of time? In the case of Tsavo, predictions of irreversible change in a contemporary sense were made on the basis of the elephant population numbers which existed in the 1960s continuing to exert their effects upon the habitat for a good many more years. A taste of things to come occurred in 1975 when dust blown from Tsavo Park caused a dust storm over Voi which so obscured the sky that people thought it was an eclipse. Worse did not happen because of the reduction in elephant numbers, first by drought and then by poaching.

The destruction of woody vegetation did not seem to affect the soils. Usually the only effects are an increased filtration rate and a slightly higher organic carbon content of the topsoil due to better grass cover. Reversion to tree and scrub in the absence of elephants does not decrease the available nutrients much as the soils are rich enough and the amount of woody biomass that can be produced is limited by the arid climate. Thinning out of the woody vegetation by elephants or fire means that more soil moisture is available for grass growth and grass becomes more abundant. Nitrogen is not a factor limiting the growth of grasses in Tsavo, but phosphorus may do so towards the end of the wet season in some areas when rainfall is good.

A 3 km wide band of 'overuse' along the Galana River suggests that large concentrations of wild herbivores do not seem to have negative effects upon the soils and the strip was probably in equilibrium with the system. Such concentrations cause local enrichment of phosphorus in the soil. After 25 years the radius of the affected area around the Aruba dam was still only $\frac{1}{2}$ km, insignificant in the overall pattern. In the long run, however, wind and gulley erosion may have significant long-lasting effects in degrading a landscape from which the vegetative cover has been removed or reduced.

On the Galana ranch which abuts Tsavo East and suffered similar elephant problems, from 1963 to 1982 browsing species such as lesser kudus declined in numbers by 90%, gerenuks by 80% and giraffes by 40%. Black rhinoceroses also declined but there was heavy poaching of this species. Grevy's zebras, oryxes and Grant's gazelles allegedly increased. If these changes were due to elephants removing mature thicket trees, it is a puzzle why giraffes declined at a lesser rate than smaller browsers which would have found coppice regrowth. A two fifths increase in elephant numbers in Ruaha Park in 1973–1977 apparently caused declines in zebras, impalas, kudus and black rhinoceroses, while buffaloes and giraffes increased. Elephants may facilitate grazing for other species by opening up tall grass in valley grasslands but the removal of elephants resulting in dense woody coppice growth shading out the grass layer may create unsuitable conditions for some species.

THE SERENGETI STORY

At the beginning of this century elephants appear to have been absent from the Serengeti, although in 1882 the Venerable J.P. Farler drew up a map from descriptions given to him by Arab caravans, which referred to Wandorobo elephant hunters from the Seronera–Mbalangeti River area up to the Banagi–Grumeti River region. These hunters supplied the caravans with ivory. By the turn of the century elephants had been hunted out in this region and it was not until 1952 that the first elephants are recorded as having moved back into the area.

Damage to trees was noted three years later 50 km south of the Mara River in the north. Late in 1957 the first bulls were seen in the central Banagi area and by 1966 it was estimated that there were more than 2200 elephants in the Park. These were in two distinct populations: a south-west population which orginated from small groups of bulls moving eastwards along the rivers from the Maswa area, apparently attracted by the suppression of poaching; and another population in the north originating from south-west Kenya, driven out by settlement and deforestation. Together they began to attack the woodlands, destroying the yellow-fever trees along the watercourses and the umbrella thorn woodlands, destruction around Seronera beginning in 1963. Whole stands of magnificent trees were completely destroyed in 2–3 days, with trees up to 20 m tall being felled.

To the north the Mara was open grassland at the turn of the century but by the 1930s had become dense woodland. In the 1960s these woodlands declined rapidly and became open grassland again within 20 years. At the same time the elephants doubled in number from about 500 in the 1960s to an estimated 1000 in the 1980s. In the Serengeti the woodland continued to decline through the 1980s.

Thus yet another area seemed affected by what had become a continent-wide malaise, resulting from a tangle of elephant protection, increasing human population and, in some areas, an increase in the frequency of annual fires. The Serengeti–Mara woodlands suggest it was not elephants alone which were responsible for the conversion of the woodlands into open grassland. During the 1960s rainfall had been above average and the principal grazing animal, the wildebeest, was kept low in numbers by rinderpest disease. The removal of the woodland canopy allowed increased grass growth and thus increased fuel for the fires which became more frequent in occurrence with the increase in surrounding settlement. The fires, assisted by elephants, prevented seedling regeneration. With control of rinderpest in the surrounding cattle populations the wildebeest began to increase to a staggering one million head, a vast army of hungry animals marching through the grasslands, mowing them down with the regularity of a team of cricket groundsmen, removing the fuel for the annual fires. But browsing elephants then prevented the return to woodland, keeping the habitat in the state that it was believed to have been in prior to 1890, before the great rinderpest plague destroyed the grazing wildebeest and elephants had been hunted out of the area by the ivory traders, allowing the woodland to grow up unhindered.

But without annual fires assisting in the prevention of regeneration it is considered that elephants alone could not change the woodlands to grassland, for the destruction of the mature stands promotes seedling regeneration on a large scale. Now that the Serengeti elephants have been reduced by poaching to less than 500, we shall see whether the woodlands can recover or not.

INFLUENCE OF LAKE LEVELS

There are other areas where it is not elephants which have caused woodland decline. Amboseli is characterized by the saline dried-up bed of an ancient Pleistocene lake and around the lake much of the basin area until the mid-1950s was populated by attractive groves of mature, stately yellow-fever trees. Between 1950 and 1961, 11% of these trees was lost. By 1967 some 70% had gone and altogether 90% died, mainly between 1962 and 1972. But in the mid-1950s, after a bad drought, Amboseli suffered unusually heavy rainfall and from 1961 to 1964 the underground water table rose $3\frac{1}{2}$ m. Now the yellow-fever tree is a waterloving species but the rise in water table dissolved the salts in the very saline soil and concentrated them in the rooting layer of the trees. The result was 'physiological drought'. The roots were unable to take up water and the trees began to die. As fewer and fewer living trees were left, so the attention of the elephants became increasingly concentrated on the survivors and thus hastened the decline.

Meanwhile at L. Manyara in the 1960s a rise in lake level drowned much of the fringing umbrella thorn woodland, concentrating the elephants on the diminishing number of survivors. But here most of the elephants' daytime feeding was spent on the lake shore, where 80% of their diet was grass. When the lake level falls, more and more grassland is exposed, thus taking pressure off the woodlands. During 1975–1979 mature umbrella thorn was killed off at a rate of 8% a year and saplings at 3%, but recruitment by surviving saplings was adequate to maintain the tree population. After the end of a drought in 1976 there was a surge of acacia regeneration followed by about a quarter of the elephant population of some 500 dying, probably from anthrax, which further lifted pressure off the woodland. The cycle of elephants and trees here as witnessed in present times is of more regular and shorter wavelength than that in another area over 2000 km away known as the Savuti Marsh, where the cycle is influenced by much longer term climatic and also tectonic events.

An area of about 100 sq. km of open grassland, the Savuti Marsh in northern Botswana is bordered to the west by a woodland of mature camel thorn and Kalahari Sand acacia. Today a marsh only in name, when the Savuti River flowed into it until the late 1880s it was wet, then remained dry for 70 years until 1958 when the river flowed almost continuously again until 1981, filling the marsh. Once more it stopped flowing and the marsh dried out in 1983. The acacia trees were characterized by being uniformly mature, having grown up when the marsh first dried out, but many were then drowned by flooding in 1979. In the 1980s the survivors were dying due to dryness. The estimated 3000 elephants from the Linyanti region to the north which use the area in the dry season, together with a surrounding 100 sq. km, exert increasing pressure on the remaining trees at the periphery of the former marsh area, hastening their death by debarking. The diminishing number of trees concentrates the elephants on the survivors here as elsewhere, a tree being attacked in proportion to its abundance. Hence the forest of dead trees, as at L. Manyara, is only partially attributable to elephants. Regeneration here will take place only in a much wetter groundwater phase.

BOTSWANA – A SOUTHERN CASE HISTORY

Selous did not see many elephants although he was impressed with what he did see along the Chobe River front in northern Botswana in 1874. In spite of the tsetse fly and the remoteness of the area the ivory trade had already taken its greedy toll. Yet, in the early 1960s, in common with other areas in Africa, people began to report elephant 'damage' to vegetation along the riparian strip. Particularly affected were the luxuriant mature camel thorn trees, killed by ring barking. Beginning in 1980, aerial surveys suggested a population of 39 500 elephants in northern Botswana, using a total area of 80 000 sq. km and depending on the dry season lifeline of the Kwando, Linyanti and Chobe rivers which form a single tributary of the Zambezi. By 1989 the number had risen to almost 60 000, a mean estimated annual rate of increase of 5%.

The same pattern appeared to be repeating itself in southern Africa that had occurred elsewhere again and again in the past 40 years in Africa before poachers wreaked their toll; a huge increase of elephants in a safe refuge, beyond the limits the habitat could sustain.

Within recorded history the Chobe area has always been favoured by elephants. When he hunted from the Shinamba Hills in the south-east of the present Chobe Park in July 1853, Chapman found elephants to be very numerous, meeting one herd of 500 cows. But in January 1855 at Shinamba he reported:

> After travelling [eastwards] 30 miles over ground that two years ago was covered with spoor, I fell in with nothing … I continued … till March … Our search for elephants continued without success. They seemed to have all migrated into the tsetse country.

When Selous arrived at the Chobe River he found elephants but not apparently in large numbers and they appeared to be wary. He noted: 'This was one of the largest herds of elephants I had ever seen; I am afraid to say how many of them there were, but I think there must have been from 100 to 200 at least.'

There is little record of hunting after Selous's time for the great days of the ivory scramble were already over. In 1932 all game was protected in the Chobe district, this prohibition lasting until 1943. It appears to have been fairly effective, as contemporary references indicate.

The government Veterinary Officer reported in 1935 that elephants and buffalo were common in the thick bush about Kataba and Kasinka in the last year:

> This has not been the case for many years. There is no doubt that game has very largely increased in the last few years. Elephants were in large herds along the Chobe River all last winter as they used to be in Selous' time – the seventies.

The Resident Magistrate of the little border township of Kasane was driven to inquiring whether he could shoot an elephant in self-defence if needs be because of elephants on the road between Kasane and Kazungula (the ferry to Zambia across the Zambezi) in the afternoon. And:

> I got into Kasane … from Kachikau. There were elephants from Kabulabula to Kasane. They have dug the road to pieces and I could smell and hear them all the way.

A former resident of the area reported that in 1933 there was a well-known herd of 20–25 elephant between Kazungula and Kasane, but otherwise they were scarce along the river. This does not fit with the Resident Magistrate's reports, or was he making a fuss about only 25 elephants? Until about 1945 bushmen who had lived around the source of the Ngwezumba in the centre of the Chobe Park for several generations did not know of elephants in the area. Then within a single year the whole area to the north as far as the Chobe 'filled' with elephant which came from the direction of Masame to the east. One European who moved to Serondella in the north in 1946 did not see an elephant in the region until 1949. He recorded that the movement was from west to east.

The 1940s witnessed one of Botswana's worst recorded droughts. Summer rainfall along the Chobe River was very low in the 1930s, well below the long-term mean of 678 mm recorded from 1930 to 1954. But in 1945 rainfall was only 14.5% below the long-term average and in 1946 it was 17.8% above, so this may have accounted for an influx of elephants.

Little hunting followed the dropping of protection in 1943, relaxation of control being due to concern at the eastward spread of tsetse from the Okavango delta. In 1960 the Chobe Game Reserve was declared and in 1967 it became a national park. Local people living as far apart as Gweta, 250 km to the south, the fringe of the Okavango and the eastern Caprivi, asserted that the elephant population had increased very rapidly, especially since the late 1950s. But between 1947 and 1952 the 20 000 head of cattle along the Chobe River collapsed to virtually nil due to disease, opening up the area to occupation by elephants at a time of exploratory behaviour in good rainfall.

In 1966 elephants were reported for the first time in areas where they had not been known for many years. Rainfall for 1955–1981 was above average and may have accounted for movements from Hwange Park in the east. Elephants also increased on the Caprivi side if references to the numbers of 'garden raiders' shot are anything to go by, the number increasing rapidly from the end of 1962.

A bad drought in the 1980s had no visible effect upon the population, although the total amount of rain falling from 1978 to 1984 was one fifth less than that which fell between 1929 and 1935, a previous bad drought cycle.

Thus the population in this area increased relatively undisturbed from about 1914. Probably over 500 hunting licences a year had been issued prior to 1979, the number increasing in the 1960s, and from 1979 to 1982 a total of 1515 was issued. Hunting was stopped in 1983.

The present rate of increase of the population may be accounted for by reproduction alone, assuming that the maximum rate of increase has been sustained over a long period of time. A close fit to the observed population totals between 1981 and 1989 is obtained with an annual rate of increase of 7.1%. There is no necessity to invoke immigration from other regions, although that is not to suppose that there may not have been immigration from either Angola or Zambia or both. The destruction of trees close to the water front near Chobe, first noted in 1963, may have been due to compression along this sector resulting from settlement to the east of it, military operations in the Caprivi strip on the northern bank of the river forcing elephants across to the Botswana side in the 1970s, and immigration from wartorn Angola. Thus a complex of compression, protection, reproduction and possible immigration may all have contributed to an increase in numbers and consequent pressure on the riverine vegetation.

Left to increase it is unlikely that a Tsavo-type die-off would occur, although the effect of the severe periodic droughts which characterize this region cannot be overlooked. But the elephants at Chobe and Linyanti are supported in large measure in the dry season by extensive flood-plain grasses which remain green. Increasing competition for this food resource would more likely lead to a decline in reproductive ability and a slowing of population growth. In Tsavo's semi-arid ecosystem there was no food left close to permanent water. It seems likely therefore that a situation like that pertaining to Murchison Park might develop where, with overcrowding, population growth will slow up due to impaired nutrition. But as there, the population would age and continue to exert its effects upon the habitat for many years to come.

West of Chobe along the Linyanti River elephant density reaches up to four to the square kilometre in the dry season and much destruction of the riverine woodland is evident. But these fine camel thorn woodlands may reflect the reduction of elephants in the 19th century which allowed the trees grow up. Now the trees are ageing and more susceptible to overuse by elephants and also to wind throw, numbers are blown down in wind storms or their branches broken off. Elephants may be only contributing to the inevitable in aiding the disappearance of these mature woodlands, for large numbers of camel thorn trees are also dying where there are no elephants.

Up until 1991 the elephant population in northern Botswana was one of the few remaining populations in Africa still increasing in the absence of poaching and, with more than 6% of calves in the population, momentarily growing in numbers at its near-maximum rate. Limitations of habitat would eventually have come to bear on this rate of increase at density levels that we may suppose have been witnessed elsewhere in Africa, but this appears to have been averted.

FIG. 11.3   *Dead elephant calf. Tsavo 1971.*

With the cessation of hostilities in southern Angola and the lack of military presence in the Caprivi strip, the elephants have now been dispersing into these areas and the indications are that the population level appears to have stabilized, at least for the present. Unlike the situations which pertained in Uganda and Kenya, the Botswana problem seems to have been aggravated by military considerations, showing how complex and variable the contributing causes to elephant overpopulations may be.

Chapter 12

DID ELEPHANTS ONCE RULE AFRICA? POPULATION DYNAMICS AND PROBLEMS

... I am bound to admit that their method of hunting elephants is disgracefully unsportsmanlike ... There were eight elephants killed that day, but three burst through everything, sending energetic spectators flying, and squashing two men and a baby as flat as botanical specimens.

Mary Kingsley, 1897

DARWIN'S DEDUCTION

> The creation of the mammoth was a blunder of the Superior Being. In creating such an enormous animal, the creator did not take into consideration the size of the earth and its resources. One earth could not stand the weight of the mammoth and its vegetation was not sufficient to feed the mammoth race. The mammoth fed on tree trunks which he ground with his teeth, and in a short time the whole of North Siberia was deprived of trees. Hence is the origin of the northern tundra.

And hence runs the tradition of the Yukaghir natives of north-eastern Siberia as recorded at the beginning of this century. They might have been talking of the elephant in Africa today. But does the elephant's ability to break down trees in its seemingly careless manner lead to the destruction of its own habitat, as the Yukaghir thought happened with the mammoth? All over sub-Saharan Africa for the past 40 years we have seen the elephant laying waste its habitat and one ponders a past when man lacked firearms and was but an insignificant predator upon elephant numbers. Did elephants rule Africa? How is it that they did not increase in numbers until their habitat was destroyed, unlike what appears to happen today almost throughout the elephant's range?

Charles Darwin, in his 1882 edition of *The Origin of Species*, considered the elephant to be the slowest breeder of all known animals and that it was 'safest to assume' it began when 30 years old, bringing forth six young between then and the age of 90 and surviving 100 years. From this he deduced that after 740–750 years there would be nearly 19 million elephants alive descended from the first pair (the total would actually be reached in 652 years).

In fact the African cow elephant produces her first calf at about 12 years and thereafter one every 3–5 years during the next 40. The shortest recorded calving interval with the previous calf surviving is two years seven months, reduced to two years if the calf is lost at birth. This makes a total of ten calves in her lifetime and a possible 11, reproductive senescence setting in at about the age of 52, but it can be as late as 59. This is equivalent to an annual rate of increase of about 6%, and means that elephants can double their population size in 14 years.

A rate of increase greater than 6% per year could be sustained if a cow first conceived at eight years and gave birth at ten and if 0.5% of the adults died each year.

In the captive Asian elephant giving birth before the age of 12 is exceptional and the first calf is normally produced at 18–20 years. Observations in southern India suggest that in the wild the first calf is produced at 17–18 with an interval between each of about 4.7 years. These elephants would produce 8–9 calves in a lifetime if reproductive senescence sets in at about the same age as in the African elephant.

So we can see that the rate of reproduction is more than double Darwin's deduction, with ten young brought forth in 40 years in the African species, starting at about 14 and producing a total closer to 20 in 90 years. This means that at a rate of increase of 6% per year, and elephants can increase at up to 6.8% per year and possibly slightly more, Darwin's estimated total would be achieved in 277 years, equivalent to a density of about 0.64 elephants per square kilometre over the whole of Africa.

Not such an impossible thought and it has been calculated that based upon rainfall and vegetation the probable undisturbed elephant population potential for Africa would have been somewhere in the order of 14 million, a more recent estimate suggesting twice this number. But after 750 years there would be 18 *trillion* elephants, equivalent to 121 billion per square kilometre over all the land surface of the world! Since only 20 000 average elephants can fit into one square kilometre, they would be standing on top of one another far into outer space. But just as the sea is not full of oysters despite the million eggs that one oyster produces, so the surface of the world is not covered with elephants.

In the past man has been an insignificant predator on the elephant over much of its range, although exploiting it from earliest times, sometimes very effectively as Mary Kingsley discovered. In the 1920s the Banda in the Central African Republic killed as many as 100 at a time in ring fires. Other mass killing techniques that have been employed are stampeding elephants on steep hillsides, driving them into bogs and using pit falls. And the Nubians in the time of the ancient Egyptian pharoahs drove them into narrow defiles from whence they could not escape. But apart from the northernmost parts of Africa where man exterminated the elephant many centuries ago, hunting had little effect upon their populations. Indeed, man had no reason to kill large numbers. One elephant provided ample food for a native village for weeks.

But the advent of firearms and the Portuguese demand for ivory meant that elephants began to decline under this concerted attack at the same time that human populations began to increase due to more abundant sources of food. Firearms were used from the early 16th century when first introduced by the Portuguese, but probably not to any great extent until towards the end of the 17th. It was also at this time that the staple foods of the African as we know them today, introduced sometime after AD 1500, probably became common – maize, sweet potatoes and, introduced much earlier, plantains or bananas. Previous to this we may suppose that very little was grown, an existence being eked out with sorghums and other grains which perhaps elephants would not have sought out any more than other grasses. But the numbers of elephants may well have been the reason for the Africans' dependence on pastoralism rather than arable farming, for an elephant can destroy a season's crop in a couple of hours. A 1924 Uganda report describes 2 acres of bananas and a quarter of an acre of sweet potatoes being destroyed by four elephants in one brief foray.

LIVING WITH TOO MANY ELEPHANTS

In 1506 one Father dos Santos, attached to a Portuguese expedition which landed at Abassia in Ethiopia, reported:

> The number of elephants in this country is prodigious, so much so indeed that the inhabitants are obliged to pursue and make frequent hunting courses after them, to preserve from their ravage the lands they sow with rice and millet, in which lands these animals generally commit great waste . . .

A century later in 1609 another dos Santos wrote:

> Throughout this Kaffraria [south east Africa] there are many large and wild elephants that cause great damage to the plantations of millet and rice, which they eat and tread under foot to the loss of the Kaffirs. Besides this they do much harm to the palm groves by pulling down the trees to eat the small leaves . . .

Yet another century later in his description of the Guinea Coast, William Bosman, the chief Dutch factor at Elmina on the coast of Ghana, wrote in 1705:

> . . . the in-land countries of Benin . . ., Rio de Dalbary, Camerones, and several other adjacent countries, are so incredibly overcharged with these beasts, that it is to be admired how the inhabitants live there.

And in 1856 the hunter Chapman wrote:

> Where the elephant is not much hunted, or firearms are almost unknown, as at Linyanti [in northern Botswana], they come in herds to the cornfields in daytime and commit great depredations, to the terror and grief of the natives, who are often starved in consequence.

Conversely the Katikiro (Prime Minister) of Buganda in 1923 stated that before the advent of the Europeans elephants caused much less trouble because the human population was more concentrated and the elephants were hunted remorselessly whenever they came near to cultivation. Likewise old inhabitants close to the Selous Game Reserve state that there were no elephants near their villages until the 'Government of the English' arrived. But there had been many years of intensive hunting for ivory up to the end of the 19th century, while in Uganda sleeping sickness had greatly reduced the human population and cultivated fields became smaller, more scattered and less defensible against elephants.

In 1929 elephants occupied almost three quarters of Uganda and as a consequence much of Uganda's economic history for the first half of this century revolved around elephants. In 1923 the newly appointed Tanganyikan Game Warden, C.F.M. Swynnerton, was sent to Uganda to look into the problem of elephant conflict with native crops. As a result, in 1925 a Game Department was formed to control them, killing 587 in the first year. From 1925 to 1969 an estimated 94 014 were killed on control, with an average tusk weight of 6.4 kg, but the policy was to shoot the smaller animals. Over the same period in Kenya 56 787 elephants were killed with an average tusk weight of 9.1 kg and in Tanganyika over 40 years, 164 954 elephants were killed with an average tusk weight of 6.3 kg.

FIG. 12.1   *A rural scene in Uganda. A housewife hurries to pick up her drying maize before the elephant eats it.*

POPULATION DYNAMICS

The fastest rate of increase recorded for an elephant population is almost 7% per year since 1954 in the Addo Park, a fed herd now about 160 strong, within a 20 sq. km fenced enclosure. Previous to this it took 50 years to increase from 11 to 20 animals. In 1919 there were estimated to be 140 elephants in the Addo vicinity of which 120 were shot. In this population only one calf in every 15 now dies in the first year, whereas under extremely harsh conditions, such as in the Namib desert, the equivalent would be nine deaths, although the actual number is much less than this because fewer calves are produced.

The observed proportion of calves less than one year of age during a period of ten years in Addo was 7%, compared with other elephant populations where the average ranges from 6 to 8.5 and, in the combined totals of three areas in Sri Lanka for the Asian elephant, 6.5%. But single years may show anything from 2.4% to 10.4% due to the effects of rainfall on short term fertility.

Rates of increase higher than 7% in any population are due to immigration. The 20 000 sq. km Kruger Park had only an estimated ten elephants in 1905. In 1931 the warden who made the original estimate considered there were 135. If in fact there had been 70 in 1905 and not ten, a not unrealistic assumption since early assessments of elephant numbers were notorious underestimates, then natural increase at the rate of 5% a year could have accounted for the 995 estimated to be present in 1958, the estimates from 1947 closely matching the possible increase. Thereafter the number increased faster than could be accounted for by natural increase and the first helicopter census conducted in 1964 revealed a population of 2374. Increase in numbers became even faster after this, so that by 1967 the population was considered to total 6586, due to immigration from Mozambique. At this stage culling was introduced to prevent further increase, although by 1970 there were still almost 9000.

The recolonization process has been fairly well observed. As with many other animals young bulls were the first to move into empty areas where, if conditions were favourable, they remained and were later found by family groups. As these residents matured the youngest bulls would in their turn move out and colonize new areas, so that it took 30 years before the northern half of the park was recolonized and almost another 50 to complete the process. The first sightings of family groups were made in the extreme south-western corner in 1982, 150 years after the last elephants had disappeared from there.

In Namibia elephants recolonized the area of the Etosha Nat. Park in the 1950s after an absence of 70 years from 1880 to 1950. Although they occurred all around, this recolonization could not have been based upon memory associations but resulted from exploratory behaviour. Keeping track of elephants in Namibia by satellite, it was found that they moved about and mixed with other populations much more than was formerly supposed, casting doubt upon the supposed genetic isolation of populations.

The first game census in Africa, conducted in 1903, gave an estimate of 1500 elephants in the Luangwa Valley. Hunting was closed in the area from 1912 due to anti-sleeping sickness measures and in 1934 Captain Pitman noted that elephant numbers had assumed 'disquietingly large proportions' with an estimated 7000. He had probably underestimated by at least a half but at a rate of increase of 5% per year the 1903 estimate of 1500 would have produced almost 7000 by 1934 and 46 000 by 1973. In fact the estimated number from an aerial census in 1973 was 56 000, eight times Pitman's 'disquietingly large' number!

The highest densities of elephants are associated with well-wooded savannahs or shrublands with a rainfall of 450–1200 mm. Densities are relatively low in open savannah and in woodland with rainfall higher than this. Formerly in the Luangwa valley there were more than three per square kilometre, whereas local densities in north Bunyoro reached 5.5. In the dry season concentration area along the Chobe River and along the Luangwa River in the wet season, spot densities have reached seven to the square kilometre.

At Mkomazi in Tanzania, adjacent to Tsavo Park, where the density was just under one to the square kilometre, the age at puberty was 12 years and the calving interval only three, so the population was increasing. But at Manyara with a density of five, because of the rich habitat, puberty was being reached at 11 years and the calving interval was 4 years so the population was increasing there also.

Densities recorded for the Asian elephant are much lower and range from 0.5 to 0.8 to the square kilometre. In Malayan primary rainforest they are less than 0.1.

The higher densities recorded in Africa for an equivalent weight of medium-sized ungulates represent fewer animals per square kilometre. Species such as buffalo can be much higher. But in 1967 the average live weight of animals along the south bank of the Victoria Nile in Uganda was 28 tonnes per square kilometre, of which 16% was made up of elephants, 68% hippopotamuses and the remainder other animals such as buffaloes and hartebeests. Inland the weight of animals fell to just over 10 tonnes, but elephants rose to 84% of the total. Elephants were responsible for the consumption of 43–57% of the forage in more than nine tenths of the range.

IN BALANCE WITH NATURE

Elephants can exist without destroying their own environment. In the northern Namib Desert of south-west Africa, one of Africa's harshest deserts, the elephants have become true desert dwellers, remaining permanently in the desert and not migrating out seasonally. Although not a separate race, these desert elephants tend to be larger than others, bulls averaging 3.5–4 m tall, but the tusks are small and usually worn and broken from their usage among the rocks.

In this extremely arid region where rainfall ranges from only 19 mm in the west to 150 in the east, and where in parts it may not rain for five years at a time, they successfully exploit the environment by use of small group sizes and regularly moving long daily distances, home ranges covering as much as 10 000–15 000 sq. km.

There is no significant difference between distances travelled at night, when it is cooler, and those travelled during the day. The average is 27.5 km in 24 hours, of which 6–19 are travelled at night. Related to the quantity of green grass and the presence of waterholes, there is a significant difference between the daily distances travelled during wet and dry seasons, only 9 km in the dry compared to 17 in the wet. In the wet season the elephants move from one waterhole to another but in the dry they tend to stick to one and make daily sorties around it.

In the harshest region, that known as Kaokoland, the habitat is composed of sand and gravel plains in the north, while to the south it is rocky and mountainous. Here in the south the elephants have become adept climbers, making their own footpaths through the loose rocks and boulders by carefully moving the loose stones aside.

To survive in this unfriendly environment they are frugal feeders wasting scarcely a scrap of green vegetation and seldom break or push over the few scanty trees in their arid habitat. Along the dry Hoanib River where the largest concentration of these elephants occurs, almost one fifth of the huge old camel thorn trees had been killed by ring barking by elephants but a comparison of tree density in the 20 years between 1963 and 1982 showed that there had been negligible change, because regeneration more than compensated for the rate of attrition. Elephants play an important part in the regeneration because of their avid ingestion of the seed pods.

More than anything else they owe their success in this harsh habitat to their mobility, depending for their long-term survival on the habitat along the river courses. But most preferred are the flood-plains which are only available in the wet season. All other habitats are exploited only in a short-term, opportunistic manner.

The most preferred woody species – grey-leaved cordia, bottelboom and the round-leaved bushwillow – are taken irrespective of abundance or size, but since they are all at low density they contribute little to the elephant's diet. The great straplike leaves of the remarkable archaic plant *Welwitschia mirabilis* appear to be chewed just for their moisture content and the most important species in the diet are mopane, wild tamarisk and leadwood.

Food determines their habitat choice, not water. They trek great distances to seek out the stunted mopane trees which grow in the valleys, up to 70 km from water sources. They do not visit water pans where there is no food, travelling up to 100 km without watering and in drought periods drinking only every 3–4 days, moving at night as much as 70 km.

Their remarkable adaptability to this near-desert habitat was demonstrated in the drought of 1981 when four fifths of herbivores such as springboks, gemsboks, kudus and zebras died. But not one elephant is known to have done so.

THE MAGIC OF MIGRATION

It was formerly believed that such a large animal must necessarily undergo long seasonal migrations to satisfy its feeding requirements and already by 1929 constriction of its range was evident:

> ... the elephant in Africa claims territorial rights over very wide areas, from one part of which to another it travels, as a rule, regularly once a year, in accordance with the season and the supply of special food growing in each part of its territory at different times of the year. At the same time it is now, owing to the intrusion of settlers into its territory, constantly seeking new ground for feeding ...

Mungo Park had observed in 1799 that:

> There are certain seasons of the year when the elephants collect into large herds, and traverse the country in quest of food or water; and as all that part of the country to the north of the Niger, is destitute of rivers, whenever the pools in the woods are dried up, the elephants approach towards the banks of that river. Here, they continue until the commencement of the rainy season, in the months of June or July ...

In Tanganyika at the beginning of the 1920s it was considered that some elephants moved down the northern flank of the Usambara Mountains about April and spread almost to the coast 100 km away, the attraction being the ripe

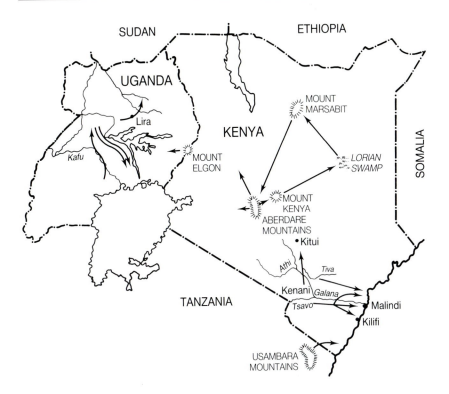

FIG. 12.2 *Some suggested former migration routes of elephants in East Africa at the beginning of the century.*

fruits of the doum palms. Others in Kenya came to the coast from north of the Galana River and haunted the coastal strip north and south of Malindi. Another herd was said to move east across the railway line near Kenani about 20 km north of the Tsavo River and across the Athi River into south Kitui. Some were said to cross the Serengeti plains (not to be confused with the Serengeti plains in Tanzania) to the south of Taita, going east to the Athi River and downstream to the Malindi–Kilifi area, crossing the Galana River near to Sala. Yet another herd was alleged to move each year from the Aberdare range to the Rift Valley. Others north of the Aberdares passed east of L. Baringo towards Mt Nyiro and those in the Mau Forest moved to high grass country in the lower Ngando Valley, others to a swamp at the foot of Gwai Mountain. The same road was followed almost to the month, and roads on each side of L. Ol Bolossat $2\frac{1}{2}$ m wide and another on the top of the Mau escarpment were at one time mistaken for ancient highways from Egypt to Zimbabwe, one of the fancied sites of King Solomon's Land of Ophir.

Apart from the annual movements associated with feeding grounds, 'breeding migrations' were also thought to take place. One was identified as across south Laikipia from the Aberdares to Mt Kenya, then north-east to the Lorian Swamp, from there north-west to Mt Marsabit, then south back to the Aberdares, making a round trip of 640 km which took three years to complete. The favourite breeding place was said to be Mt Marsabit. Animals left without young and came back with calves.

C.W. Hobley, formerly a geologist in East Africa and later an administrator, wrote:

> In Uganda this is not so marked for, owing to the climate, food supplies are more widely accessible. In Kenya and Tanganyika Territory the seasonal migrations are extensive.

But two administrative officers in Uganda at the beginning of the century considered that elephants migrated seasonally from north central Uganda across the Kafu River and north-westwards to the White Nile. They reported the existence of a remarkable well-defined elephant road, apparently used only during seasonal migrations, which ran east through Lira and on into Acholi country. It was smooth and hard and the best road in the whole country.

In northern Uganda in 1932 it was found that there were only four points within a 160 km frontier at which elephants crossed backwards and forwards between Uganda and the Sudan. It was claimed that in 1925 to 1935 there was a 'well-known migration' which began in late March at the onset of the rains, the elephants moving south-eastwards from the southern present-day Murchison Park along the southern edge of L. Kyoga, to return again in the early dry season of late October to early November. This was allegedly interrupted in the 1930s by control operations, but resumed again at the beginning of the 1950s.

At the onset of the rainy season in late March, large herds congregated above the escarpment preparatory to migrating to the Butiaba Flats adjacent to the shores of L. Albert below. By mid-April the migration was complete with herds of up to 100 elephants moving down together.

We should not be too ready to dismiss these supposed migrations, for there was undoubtedly much substance to them. Now in Kenya and Uganda any former routes have been completely disrupted, although they were probably not as extensive as indicated but rather composed of several movements. For example, the animals which appeared seasonally on Mt Marsabit had probably not come from as far away as south Laikipia but some much nearer locality.

There is one recorded observation in Kenya of a population of about 2000 elephants moving from the Tiva River in the north of Tsavo East Park a distance of 100 km to the Kenya coast. It has not been established that this is a regular annual movement although it is the same that Hobley referred to in the 1920s. Usually in Tsavo the elephants displace only 15–30 km from the Galana River in the wet season.

Where conditions are less favourable for year-round occupation elephants do undergo seasonal movements, loosely called migrations, just as do many other herbivores. The extent of these movements depends upon the habitat and they are not usually mass movements but family groups moving individually. In arid areas elephants must of necessity move farther than in well-watered regions. The Gourma elephants of Mali undergo the longest seasonal migrations known, 800 km in a round trip and up to 80 km in one day.

In northern Botswana tracking elephants fitted with radio collars showed that the average straight line distance moved by elephants dispersing from their wet season haunts was 73 km, with an average distance travelled of about 90. The longest straight line distance recorded was 200 km made by a cow travelling from the Nunga area south-east of the Chobe Park to the Linyanti River. Another cow moved 290 km, first eastwards 110 km to a forest (Kasuma) then back 180 km westwards to the Linyanti. Nineteen out of 23 of the collared elephants moved west, mainly north-west. Those which did this from the area known as the Shinamba Hills showed this to be of very long standing, for in 1855 Chapman reported that the elephants had all left the region, supposing them to have moved to the north-west. In the dry season, however, movements were restricted to the vicinity of the permanent water.

Some people question whether elephants can be shown to have ever migrated but this is largely a question of word meanings. Elephants are not known to gather together at certain seasons as if in response to some predetermined signal or long custom and displace *en masse* to another locality, returning at a later season – the familiar migration of birds. Neither do they undergo regular mass movements around their range like wildebeest in the Serengeti. And although it is still quoted that we shall never again see migrations on the scale that Sir Samuel Baker did at the beginning of the 19th century, Baker never witnessed a migration. All he saw was a large number of elephants together: 'It would have been impossible to guess the number as there was no regularity in their arrangement ...' Neither did he recall them as moving in any particular direction. This appears to have been early evidence of the gathering of a clan but not of a migration.

THE HOME RANGE

Where conditions are good elephants generally move little. The Manyara elephants' daily scramble up and down the escarpment apart, they are not ones for wasting energy. In the Luangwa Valley, out of 37 marked bulls, only one moved farther than 3 km from water in the dry season but there was widespread dispersal of all of them in the wet. In Namibia two cows each marked 60 km apart and then tracked by satellite, joined up together for some time and were probably both members of the same group, but another cow kept herself to a small home range in spite of the movements of other elephants in and out of it. Within the home range a family unit in Manyara has been observed to spend up to three days in one area and then march off determinedly for 15 km or so to another spot. This is probably the typical behaviour.

Studies in Tsavo of radio-collared elephants in 1971–1973 after the drought die-off, when patterns of dispersal may have radically changed, showed that in the dry season both bulls and cows occupied relatively small home ranges near to permanent water. At the first rain they moved out from these areas to where rain had fallen, detecting local rainstorms over considerable distances. This ability was confirmed by satellite tracking of elephants in north-west Namibia, with movements to areas of distant rainfall often a day or two before it actually fell. Individual bulls or cow family groups might make sudden movements of 30–50 km or more within a few days and appeared particularly attracted to areas of dense green grass where rain had fallen.

Such responses resulted in massive aggregations in Tsavo, mainly in open grassland, such as herds of 1100 as seen in May 1974. Intense mating activity took place in these large aggregations because many cows come into heat feeding on the fresh flush of grass, but this is an effect of the gregariousness and not the cause of it. Elephants do not join together for some gigantic orgy like a modern 'rave' party. They go there for the food, not the sex.

Although one could not predict exactly where elephants would move to because the rainfall in Tsavo was erratic in its spatial occurrence, most returned faithfully to the same dry season home range and it is only dry season ranges which become overused. Elephants always move away from permanent water in the rains.

There was no evidence of intergroup competition for the same dry season home range and wet season ranges were shared, thus there was much overlap between home ranges of both cows and cows, cows and bulls and bulls and bulls. Maximum recorded movement was 133 km, somewhat less than recorded in northern Botswana. In the better habitat of Tsavo West, greatest range was 75 km. Bull ranges here were greater than those of cows but in Tsavo East it was the reverse.

Thus bulls range in search of cows regardless of food availability and the cow's ranging is dependent upon food searching.

Whether in Asia or Africa, extensive fires also influence elephant movement, driving them away from burning areas but drawing them back again when the postburn flush of green grass occurs.

Home ranges in Tsavo varied from some 400 to 3700 sq. km, with averages of 750 in Tsavo West and 1600 in Tsavo East. Mean diameters were 51 and 73 km respectively. In the relatively lush conditions of Manyara Park the home ranges were as little as 14–54 sq. km.

Along the Zambezi River in northern Zimbabwe the comparatively small alluvial areas, comprising less than 5% of the area studied, supported approximately half of the elephant population for some four months in the dry season. But as soon as heavy rain falls inland the elephants which have congregated near permanent water immediately disperse. Only certain areas along the river attracted concentrations due to food preferences.

Elephants using flood-plain habitats show daily and seasonal patterns of movement, keeping to woodland during the day and moving out onto flood-plains in the evening in the dry season. As the dry season advances the herds move closer to the flood-plains where water abounds and food is still plentiful. Later there is the added attraction of the highly nutritious pods of the apple-ring thorn tree which ripen late in the dry season in August to October. But when the rains fall and the plains become waterlogged, then the elephants quit for higher and drier ground and can find their water from standing pools scattered in the woodland. Apart from lone bulls or small bull herds, no elephants were observed farther than 13 km from a water source.

At Amboseli, radio-collared elephants which inhabited the swamps were found to move up to 40 km away from them in the wet season but in the dry were always within 16. Once good rains came in 1977 they changed their pattern and remained in the basin in both wet and dry seasons up until 1981.

Mt Kilimanjaro to the south being a favourite hunting ground for ivory hunters at the end of the last century, the original Amboseli populations were probably shot or driven out. The elephants today are mostly colonizers and their offspring which invaded the area after the much drier 1950s. They do not move up into the Mt Kilimanjaro forests, the elephants inhabiting the mountain apparently being much smaller and leaner with hairy heads, wrinkled foreheads and little triangular-shaped ears. Although these forest creatures sometimes come down to the swamps they do not remain there, perhaps driven away by the Amboseli animals.

In India elephants moved along well-worn paths, considered as 'age-old' migration routes, in search of food, never remaining long in one place. Most are now blocked. But Sanderson implies only seasonal displacements, noting that the ranges were traversed with considerable regularity. During the dry months of January to April the elephants sought the vicinity of streams and shady forests. About June, after the first showers, they emerged to feed on the young grass until, in July and August when the grass becomes long and coarse on the higher ground, they descended to the lower woodlands, where they also visited the salt-licks. It was believed that they left the hills in the rains to avoid flies, mosquitoes and the elephant fly which was less numerous in the low country. About December, when the woodlands become dry and fodder scarce, then they retreated back into the hills and thick forests until the next rains. Perhaps related to the hilly nature of the habitat, unlike African elephants they usually moved from one place to another in single file.

> ... his [the African elephant's] inherited instinct impels him to wander annually; which is one of the reasons why, as settlers spread over the country, his future is becoming more and more precarious. Only recently [mid 1920s] serious inroads of elephants into culti-vated land have been reported in East Africa, and reprisals are sure to follow the damage they cause ...

IN CONFLICT WITH MAN

Between 1905 and 1908 there were 101 recorded deaths or serious injuries from elephants in the Toro and Buganda districts of Uganda. In India the man–elephant conflict is more serious than in Africa in spite of the smaller number of elephants, but then the dense human population is in much closer contact. An age-old problem, the *Gaja Sastra* referred to elephants devastating the kingdom of Anga sometime between 300 BC and AD 300, while the ancient Indian manual of statecraft, the 300 BC *Artha Sastra*, prescribed their eradication from river valleys but their strict protection in forests and on the borders of the kingdom. These 'sanctuaries' were to be patrolled by guards and poachers awarded the death penalty.

In the middle of last century in Asia, elephants which killed people were proscribed by government, meaning that the equivalent of a 'Wanted – Dead or Alive' notice was issued. In England, when Chuni killed one of his attendants at London's Exeter 'Change in 1825, the inquest found he was not guilty of intending to kill the attendant and he was fined the sum of one shilling as a deodand (a gift to God).

Instances such as that of 30 thatched huts being destroyed in 1987 by a herd of elephants in Bangladesh, with nine persons killed, are unknown in Africa. Eleven persons were killed in 1980 by elephants in north Bengal alone and in the 1970s more than 100. In the late 1980s a herd of 60–70 elephants from Bihar province began ravaging crops, knocking down huts and trampling people over a wide area including West Bengal. In Sumatra in recent years elephants were herded out of a forest to make way for settlement. Two years later the elephants came back and, as if in revenge, wreaked havoc on the plantations and huts. It is estimated that now some 100–150 people are killed each year in India, but this aggressiveness is usually due to the elephants suffering gunshot wounds. In the year 1875 only 61 people were reported killed by elephants and this was less than by any other animal. Most were killed by wolves with a total of 1061, followed by tigers with 828.

Crop raiders are most often solitary bulls above 25 years of age. The younger bulls, aged from about 15 to 25, usually get together in gangs of up to four to raid crops when they are plentiful. Cows are much less frequent raiders and the amount of crops taken contributes less than 2% of the total family herd requirements. But altogether the total loss suffered in southern India due to elephants is estimated to be as much as half a million American dollars. Some 15–40 elephants are killed in southern India each year either raiding or in defence of crops.

PRODIGAL OR PRUDENT PROBOSCIDEANS?

We can visualize how a balance between elephants and their habitats might have existed in the past. Starting with a woody thicket, such as existed in Tsavo East in the 1950s, elephants move in destroying the thicket and opening it up to fire. This forms a grassland with scattered trees and encourages grazing animals. These increase and cause overgrazing in dry years which results in a short grass savannah with scattered trees. At this stage the elephants move out because of the lack of grass and the area returns to thicket, when the cycle begins all over again. But the elephants do not move out until they have suffered loss and so the population of elephants tends to be regulated. The problem today is that the elephants cannot move out; they are hemmed in by settlement so that the cycle back to thicket cannot operate.

In some areas, concentrations of elephants removing thicket and woodland have locally eliminated tsetse flies, thus opening up the areas to occupation by man and cattle. But this is under *present* climatic conditions and cannot be inferred as a habitual role of elephants.

Before the rapid increase in human population Africa was probably a mosaic of habitats, each piece of the mosaic undergoing changes in human or elephant densities with consequent changes in the habitat. Overall the densities and vegetation were probably broadly stable over long periods of time, perhaps for centuries. But in any particular place cycles of woody vegetation–subsistence agriculture through shifting cultivation–bush or woodland–elephant increase–open habitat–elephant decrease–bush or woodland–human cultivation or pastoralism when the bush and woodland became open, were the norm. Then the distribution of human islands in a sea of elephants was reversed to islands of elephants in a sea of people, as human populations increased and became more settled, disrupting the cycle.

Charles Elton considered that instability of the environment would cause fluctuations in animal numbers:

> Whenever a group of animals or any one species is studied carefully over a series of years, it is found to vary in numbers in a more or less marked way.
>
> . . . it can be shown that animals as big as the Indian elephant are also subject to fluctuations in numbers, caused by epidemics; but at very long intervals, of seventy to a hundred years.

Elephants do not increase at the rate which Darwin postulated, nor even at their theoretical potential, due to limitations of food, drought, disease, accidents and living space. They probably are what the Reverend Thomas Malthus, the scholar–priest who shocked England in 1798 with his prognostications of the catastrophes attendant upon uncontrolled population increase (although he himself had 11 daughters), delicately termed 'irrational animals', '. . . impelled by a powerful instinct to the increase of their species; and this instinct is interrupted by no doubts about providing for their offspring'. That being so, is the destruction of woodland witnessed in various parts of Africa in the past 50 years the normal run of affairs? One theory proposes that it is and that there is no attainable natural equilibrium between elephants and forests or woodlands – at least not in eastern, central and southern Africa.

Elephants increase in number until they overshoot that number which the habitat can support, driven to destroying trees and bushes in their search for food. Giving the vegetation no time to recover, the elephants end up by destroying their own environment and starving to death, a population crash taking place. The numbers of elephants thus reduced, the woody plants have the opportunity to recover. The elephants then increase in numbers once more and the whole cycle is repeated, taking about 200 years.

The scientist who proposed this did so on the basis of what he saw as divided trunks in miombo woodlands in the Luangwa Valley. From examination of the tree growth rings he concluded that coppicing had taken place some 200 years before, caused by an overpopulation of elephants. What the theory failed to take into account was the effect of hunting for ivory which drastically reduced populations between 1850 and 1900. Sir Julian Huxley suggested in 1929 that elephants underwent periods of abundance followed by decrease in cycles of about 30 years. He also failed to appreciate that the scarcity reported 30 years before his deduction was due to hunting.

Nevertheless, building on this theory which is given the name of a stable-limit cycle, it has been suggested that elephant populations may behave in three different ways according to the type of habitat. The stable-limit cycle is seen as possibly operating in savanna woodland where, due to abundant food, the elephants have a high reproductive rate, early age at first calving and a short interval between one calf and the next. The populations crash relatively quickly and then recover relatively quickly, if you can call two centuries 'quick'. In deciduous forest in parts of India food is less abundant and consequently elephants are not as productive in biological terms. The same pattern takes place but the populations build up more slowly and reach much lower levels before they decline again, perhaps taking 400 years for a complete cycle. Thirdly, in the equatorial rainforests as in Malaysia, elephants exist at low density due to a limited supply of food but it is constant in occurrence and hence these elephants do not undergo cycles of increase and decrease at all.

The other principal theory advanced to explain the behaviour of elephant populations is the equilibrium hypothesis. This holds that the elephants increase to a certain level and then stabilize due to reduction in fertility caused by food limitation and perhaps social factors. As Malthus put it: '. . . the superabundant effects are repressed afterwards by want of room and nourishment'. The observations of delayed maturity and lengthened calving intervals in northern Uganda suggested that this reflected the equilibrium hypothesis, whereas in the Luangwa Valley it was claimed that the miombo trees showed evidence of high elephant pressures two centuries ago conforming to the stable-limit cycle.

Clearly a stable-limit cycle would have to include a stable climate. A comparison of tree destruction rates in the Kruger Park, the Murchison Park and along the eastern border of Botswana suggested that in general regular cycles, or stable-limit cycles, will not occur. Such cycles would be possible under certain limited conditions but the period of the cycles, about 800 years, would be so long that in practice they can be discounted.

Elephants are considered basically a forest edge ecotone species where the mixture of browse and graze they require in their diet is best found, but they can exploit a much wider range of habitat if they can move about freely. Those causing destruction are those trapped in areas where a long-term stable elephant–woodland balance is not possible.

No single theory can account for all of the examples of population increase in protected areas that have taken place since the 1960s, but compression may be a significant cause. In past times elephants conceivably regulated their numbers by dispersal, some being forced into less favourable areas and thus not surviving. The loss of range due to human presence provides a situation unrivalled over the past 10 000 years. Only tectonic Pleistocene upheavals could have produced effects of equal magnitude.

Some years ago I proposed that what we were really seeing in Africa was the explosion, or exponential rise to put it more correctly, of elephant populations recovering from the reduction at the end of the last century caused by hunting for ivory. This produced young populations which in the 1950s and 1960s entered an exponential rate of increase. What else, I asked myself, could cause this almost Africa-wide behaviour in elephants? The stable-limit cycle theory would imply that elephant population dynamics were synchronized to within about one generation throughout Africa. What we know *did* happen was that there was an almost universal onslaught on elephant populations in the last century. It was this, I argued, which disrupted population stability and resulted in the effects that we have been witnessing since the 1950s. The reprieve from mass persecution which elephants largely enjoyed from the beginning of this century until the onslaught of the 1970s could have resulted in the same pattern of response as shown by other mammal populations when heavy hunting pressure is removed. That is, an exponential rise in numbers.

Factors controlling rate of increase are defined as age distribution, sex ratio, fecundity and survivorship. In ivory hunting both older animals and bulls are selected, thus providing favourable conditions for increase. But the demand for ivory meant that all ages and both sexes were taken indiscriminately, thus reducing populations. In Tanzania in the ten years from 1966 to 1976 the mean tusk weight of 43 000 tusks declined from 8 to 4.8 kg, implying that much adult cow ivory was included from the most fertile sector of the population.

Scarcity of large tuskers in the 1970s was an obvious indication that elephants were young throughout most of their range and thus likely to be in an expanding phase. This repeated the pattern that had taken place before. By 1920 there were already reports of elephant problems in both Uganda and Tanganyika and shortly afterwards 'control' programmes were initiated in these countries, but served only to harass the elephants rather than exert any control on their numbers. In 1934 Pitman wrote of Zambia: '... elephant are increasing with alarming rapidity'. And in Kenya in 1948, Caldwell wrote: '... the elephant population is definitely rising'.

Added to this response, another possible factor is that today we have a climate which favours elephant increase by being not too dry, but on the other hand it is not sufficiently wet as it has been in some past eras to encourage vigorous vegetative growth and the expansion of rainforest. Wetter conditions are believed to have pertained in Uganda in AD 1400–1600, leading to expansion of forest, followed possibly by retrogression in a dry phase in the first half of the 19th century. This was followed soon after by an onslaught upon elephants for their ivory. An oscillation in elephant numbers with relation to rainfall cycles is the most likely explanation as to why elephants have not over-run Africa and eaten out their habitat in the past. At present we are witness to a phase of climate during which rainfall is not high enough to maintain vigorous vegetative regeneration in the elephants' savanna range but sufficient, despite periodic droughts, to maintain a high level of female fertility and calf survival.

There is yet another conceivable explanation for what we have witnessed. The Namib desert elephants show that it is possible for elephants to exist in balance with their environment. Is the destructive behaviour elsewhere therefore due to a loss of the learning process? Has the persistent destruction of matriarchs over the past 150 years led to a loss of acquired knowledge, a loss of experience which took countless years to acquire, learning how to feed prudently? Now that knowledge has been destroyed and elephants, knowing no better, lay waste their habitat with prodigal abandon.

Chapter *13*

IVORY, THE TEETH OF COMMERCE: THE STRUCTURE AND GROWTH OF TUSKS

The hatchet-men now advanced, and began to cut away his large ivory tusks, while the horsemen and soldiers in the most unfeeling manner attacked the dying creature with their swords. We can readily believe the writer, when he says the sight was very affecting. The noble animal still breathed, and breathed without a groan. He rolled his eyes in anguish on the surrounding crowd, and making a last effort to rise, expired with a sigh.

W. Hone, 1827

MIGHTY AS THE HEAD IS MIGHTY

NEVER has a creature on this earth been so persecuted as the elephant. The ancient Chinese had a saying for it, quoted in the *Tso Chwan* of 548 BC, that the elephant has tusks which lead to the destruction of its body because of their use as gifts.

Although tusks of other species such as the walrus have also found their way into commerce, it is the size that those of elephants attain which has so awed man, eloquently described by the ancient Greek Oppian as '... mighty as the head is mighty, even as the roots of the oak'.

So conspicuous in the elephant, tusks are rare phenomena in nature, confined to only a few orders of mammals. Formed of greatly lengthened upper second incisor teeth, like those of rats and rabbits they have persistent pulps allowing them to grow throughout life. All teeth, even human teeth, grow in a logarithmic spiral, that is, one side grows faster than the other, but the curvature which results is only evident in an excessively elongated structure.

Making their appearance in the African elephant at the age of 18 months to two years, tusks in the bull typically appear earlier than in the cow. They then grow at a constant rate in length throughout life, 11 and 8.5 cm a year in the bull and cow respectively in Uganda, so a bull African elephant would be capable of growing tusks up to 81 kg in weight and 550 cm in length in its lifetime. Due to wear and breakage they reach only some 61 kg and 250 cm at most. In the cow her potentials of just under 22 kg weight and 520 cm length reach only slightly over 9 kg and 155 cm at about 60 years. Although bull tusks can attain a weight almost seven times those of the cow, the potential weights are equal to 1.5% and 0.7% of the potential body weights respectively. In the bull the rate at which the tusks increase in weight accelerates as the pulp cavity fills.

By the age of 20 the mean weight of the bull's tusks has passed the maximum mean weight of the cow's. Each differs slightly in shape, the bull's more conical and only becoming cylindrical when well beyond the limits of cow growth. It is estimated that mammoth tusks underwent an intensive period of growth from 16 to 18 years up to 45–50, after which growth slowed.

The famous Ahmed of Mt Marsabit in Kenya, who died of old age in the 1970s, bore tusks weighing just over 67 kg each and measuring 2.85 and 2.97 m in length, left and right, not far different from what one would expect. In the Kruger Park one old bull which died in 1983 had tusks of 55.1 kg each with a length of 2.51 m, but like Ahmed he was not a large elephant, standing only 3.27 m at the shoulder. Another bull from the same area had long slender tusks, measuring 3.06 and 3.17 m in length at death, but weighing only 50.8 and 52.6 kg. Yet another had a tusk of 2.64 m in length and 58.1 kg in weight, the other being broken.

Now in London's Natural History Museum, the biggest pair of tusks for which we have a reliable record came from near Mt Kilimanjaro at the end of the last century. Well in excess of the potential weight they weighed 102.3 and 107.3 kg, with lengths of 3.11 and 3.17 m.

According to an early writer a tusk sold at Amsterdam in the 18th century weighed 159 kg, but perhaps this related to a pair, for in the 16th century Ludovico Barthema reported seeing a pair weighing 152.7 kg in Sumatra, a weight sometimes quoted as referring to a single tusk. Petri in his book

Elephantographia Curiosa (1715) notes a tusk in the possession of a merchant of Venice as 4.3 m long, perhaps a mammoth's tusk.

An East African ivory trader in the last century, Jumbe Kimemata, claimed to possess a tusk weighing 120 kg and three others each of 100, but after the Kilimanjaro pair the next biggest tusk is considered to be one from East Africa of 94 kg measuring 2.5 m in length, sold to Ludwig II the King of Bavaria.

Rowland Ward's *Records of Big Game* lists only 30 single tusks weighing 68 kg or more, although in 1927 out of 100 elephants shot on permit in Kenya, 46 had tusks weighing more than 45 kg. Between 1892 and 1935 most of the heaviest and the longest tusks are recorded as coming from Kenya, which would seem to have suffered less from the onslaught of the latter 19th century ivory trade than did neighbouring Uganda and Tanganyika. Only the Zanzibar tusks are reliably recorded as exceeding 100 kg, but no doubt many giant tusks were cut up by ivory traders for ease of carrying. A correspondent in the *The Field* reported seeing an 82 kg tusk sawn into two pieces in Gabon in 1887 and that some tusks were much heavier.

In the *SS Benin* of the African Steamship Company, which sank in 1881 in the English Channel on its return from West Africa, the 83 tusks it was carrying brought up from the sea bed in August 1990 weighed about a tonne. Some were as long as 2.5 m and weighed 41 kg.

The average adult Asian elephant bull produces less than $\frac{1}{2}$ kg of ivory each year, while growth may be up to 7.5 cm, less than half the rate of the African bull, but as this relates to trained elephants, diet and energy used in work may contribute to a slower growth rate.

The largest Asian elephant tusks come from a Siamese elephant and measured 3.0 and 2.74 m, but the weights are not known. Next come a pair weighing 73.1 and 72.7 kg, measuring 2.7 and 2.6 m, a gift to King George V. A pair from Orissa in India are said to have weighed 54.6 and 51.8 kg. These are followed by one from an elephant shot in 1863. The biggest tusk was 2.4 m in length and weighed 50 kg, the other being diseased and weighing only 27.

At the beginning of the 19th century it was considered that the largest Asian tusks came from Pegu in Burma and Cochinchina. Tusks of 68 kg were recorded from Pegu, Bengal tusks weighed little more than 33 and in Tipperah they did not exceeed 23. But clearly Asian elephants also at one time sported large tusks. Bull elephants with tusks were rare in Sri Lanka, Sir Samuel Baker estimating that only one in 300 carried them.

The cow Asian elephant is born with short, downwardly pointing tushes, rarely projecting more than 10 cm beyond the gum and usually broken off early in life. Those which are not broken off may be trimmed every 2–3 years, but little ivory is produced.

GROWTH AND STRUCTURE

Preceding the permanent tusks is a pair of milk tusks measuring less than 5 cm in length which have a solid, tapering root and a small cap tipped with enamel.

These cut the gum at about 5–7 months. In the African elephant, in which they are similar in shape and size to those of the Asian, the milk tusks are probably absorbed rather than shed. Those of the Siberian mammoth were of similar size, also erupting at 6–7 months.

The belief of Aelian in the second century AD that the elephant shed its tusks every ten years probably arose as an analogy with deer casting their antlers and the finding of fossil ivory.

Permanent tusks make their appearance on average in the African bull elephant at about 18 months and in the cow at 27. In the Asian elephant they appear at 15–18 months, as they did also in the Siberian mammoth. Prior to eruption the area becomes sensitive, the elephant squirting water and blowing air onto it. Often eruption of the tusks is preceded by a slight watery secretion.

Tusks of both bull and cow grow throughout life, albeit much more slowly in the latter. Thus it has been said that the most economical manner of harvesting ivory is when the animals have died of old age, for these will produce the heaviest. There is much variation in the rate of growth of the spiral, so that some tusks appear to be almost straight while mammoths possessed the most curved of all. Cow tusks grow long and slender, while those of the bull thicken as they lengthen, beginning to take on a noticeable curve at 10–12 years in the savanna elephant.

Tusk circumference rather than length is a better indication of age in older animals. Both African and Asian elephant tusks grow initially at much the same rate, for a rate of 16 cm per year was measured in a captive Asian elephant in 1926 compared with 17 in an African elephant in 1957, but in the Asian elephant the tusks often cease to extend beyond the gum. There is some doubt as to whether African bull and cow tusks grow at the same rate as one another to puberty, one opinion being that they do not and that growth is geometric or in a straight line for both sexes throughout life. Cow tusks are thinner than those of equivalent length in the bull, but the cow's body weight is much lighter. Whereas a cow with 6 kg tusks would have a body weight of some $2\frac{1}{2}$ tonnes, a bull with 6 kg tusks would weigh some 3 tonnes. Stress on the tusks is therefore proportional.

As nothing more than an extraordinarily modified tooth, three hard substances go into the make-up of a tusk: cementum, enamel and dentine. When a tusk first erupts it is completely covered by a layer of cementum under which is a small cap of harder enamel. As the softest substance the cementum quickly wears away, followed by the hard enamel cap, so that the tusk becomes a cone of dentine partially covered by a thin layer of cementum, known in the ivory trade as the 'bark'.

The pulp cavity is lined by odontoblastic or tooth-forming cells which produce dentine, the main substance of the tusk. Dentine is a mineralized connective tissue with an organic matrix of collagen, a fibrous protein which on boiling yields gelatine. The inorganic or mineral component consists of a substance formed of calcium, phosphate and carbonate, with the name of dahllite. Structurally dentine consists of microscopic tubules, known as dentinal tubules, which radiate outwards from the pulp cavity to the surface of the dentine. In elephant ivory these tubules are arranged in a wavelike pattern unique to elephants.

Unlike bone, dentine is without cells and it is denser, with only 18% of the collagen protein matrix compared with 25% in bone. But elephant ivory is much less dense than human dentine, with 40–43% organic matter compared to 25% in human teeth. This means that it can dry out significantly and the world record tusks in 1966 weighed 96.3 and 101.7 kg, a loss of 5.6% of their weight in 67 years. A tusk loses 0.9% of its fresh weight on initial storage, but dry ivory gains almost 15% of its weight if soaked in water.

Surrounding the dentine is the layer of cementum, a moderately calcified tissue softer than dentine and more like bone in structure, which is deposited in layers. Near to the gum region it can be 3–5 mm thick. Its main function is to anchor the tusk but as the tusk grows out of the socket so the cementum remains wrapped around it, becoming worn off at the tip and from the underside of the tusk.

Enamel, the hardest tissue found in animals, is formed by cells called ameloblasts which are lost after the enamel has been formed, so it does not continue to be laid down like dentine or cementum. It covers the tip when the tusk first emerges, but only $\frac{3}{4}$ mm in thickness it is quickly worn away. It is formed of highly calcified tissue of densely packed columns of prisms, arranged roughly at right angles to the surface. In the extinct *Phiomia* the prisms had a pronounced spiral arrangement, making the tusks tough and resistant like rodent incisor teeth. This persisted in *Gomphotherium* in a weaker form until in *Elephas* it had almost disappeared, leaving the enamel weak in structure.

The soft centre of the tusk is the tooth pulp, consisting of connective tissue and the dentine-forming cells. Although richly endowed with nerves it is not itself a nerve, although referred to as such by hunters.

In the 1880s during an attempt to saw off the end of the tusk of an Asian bull elephant in the Berlin Zoo, the saw touched the pulp, at which point it is recorded that the elephant, which up to that point had been perfectly quiet, began to cry piteously. It became so unmanageable that the operation could only be finished by striking off the end of the tusk by a blow with a heavy hammer. The exposed pulp was soon covered by secondary dentine and a dental surgeon, interested in the subject of the pathology of elephant tusks, six months later had a small piece sawn off to study its structure. Hardly surprisingly, the elephant remembered the previous operation and only with considerable difficulty could it be prevailed upon to submit.

The pulp cavity is always larger in the bull than in the cow. In the cow it increases in size up to the age of about 15 years when the tusk is 60 cm in length and then slows markedly in growth. In the bull it increases in size to at least 30 years of age and not until old age does it start to fill in. It is conceivable that it could fill in to the extent that in very old elephants the tusks would eventually drop out. Pliny wrote that when the tusks have fallen off, by accident or old age, the elephant buries them, another belief probably arising from the finding of fossil tusks.

The fractured tusk of an Asian elephant, which died two years later, was found to have grown in length at a rate of 3.3 mm per week, a rate which corresponds closely with that of the continuously growing incisor teeth of such creatures as the rabbit and porcupine. On average, tusks increase in weight at the rate of 2 g a day, but only half of this is calcium.

A 1 tonne elephant aged 5–6 years requires 8–9 g of calcium per day, of which 1 g is used by the growing tusks. A 30 year old 4–5 tonne bull would require 3 g a day for the tusks alone, although ivory has a poor degree of calcification due to its high collagen content. Normally the elephant's requirements are amply met by vegetation, the 1 tonne elephant obtaining about 13 g per day in the wet season and 38 in the dry. Calcium can also be obtained in drinking water, but in the wet season it is likely to be more diluted and at this season adult elephants may suffer shortage. Tusks sometimes show signs of deficiency and ivory known as tripy ivory, which has a mottled or speckled appearance, is probably due to this.

Growth depends upon both genetics and the chemistry of the place where the elephant lives. With a plentiful supply of calcium and phosphorus then tusks can grow faster and stronger.

ELEPHANTS AND DAISY PATTERNS

Elephant ivory is possessed of a characteristic structure in which it differs from all other ivory. Like other ivory, in cross-section it can be seen to be built up of layers of fine concentric rings superimposed upon which may be alternating light and dark bands, said to be most marked in ivory from Mali, possibly due to a more pronounced seasonal effect. But in addition to this concentric arrangement it is characterized by a pattern which gives it its unmistakable appearance. This is the 'engine-turned' appearance like that used to decorate the inside casings of pocket watches, caused by crossing elliptical or decussating lines formed by the dentinal tubules, providing a pattern of light and dark diamond-shaped areas.

This characteristic pattern, found in no other animal, appears to be related to the mass which the dentine may reach as it is present also in the dentine of the last three molar teeth. This may impart to ivory its elastic property, important to resist fracturing in such a large mass.

The lines, which are most distinct near the outer border of the tusk, have sometimes been referred to as Schreger lines, after the German anatomist Bernhard Schreger who first described them in 1800, distinguishing between incremental lines or contours due to differing rates of formation or mineralization of the dentine and lines caused by arrangement of the dentinal tubules. However, Schreger lines can be found in any dentine but not in the same alignment as in elephant ivory.

In mammoths the density of the dentinal tubules was almost $1\frac{1}{2}$ times that of mastodons and almost twice that of living elephants, crossing over at an angle consistently less than 90°, whereas in the latter ivory the angle is greater than

110°. This suggests that the ivory of mammoths and mastodons was more elastic but this is not surprising in view of the much greater size of the tusks, which would be subjected to much more leverage stress. This microscopic difference in structure has a practical use today in that it permits fossil ivory to be distinguished.

The characteristic microscopic structural pattern of elephant ivory is the gently undulating, radially oriented dentinal tubule with a superimposed incremental growth pattern. The dentinal tubules contain fine protoplasmic extensions of the dentine-forming cells lining the pulp cavity. These tubules are supported in a jellylike mass, the peritubular matrix. Fine collagen fibres are oriented in two distinct directions in the matrix surrounding the dentinal tubules and it is the optical effect caused by the reflection of light from these collagen fibres which produces the 'engine-turned' appearance in cross-section unmistakably diagnostic of elephant ivory. When the cementum covering is worn away near the tip of the tusk in older animals, this exposes the tubular pattern in longitudinal view as small cracks arranged in a herring-bone pattern.

The pattern in cross-section could be called 'the mathematical daisy' pattern, for it is the same as that produced by the florets of a daisy from fundamental mathematical rules. The tusk grows in a spiral, therefore the dentine within it must also be arranged in a spiral. The dentinal tubules thus radiate in a sequence known as a 'primary spiral', which in its turn generates 'secondary spirals'. These take the pathway of least resistance, forming 'Fibonacci spirals'. Fibonacci was an Italian mathematician who wrote the *Liber Abaci* or 'The Book of the Abacus' in 1202. In his book he posed a problem about the breeding of rabbits which resulted in a series of numbers, since known as Fibonacci numbers. Fibonacci numbers appear to be irregular but in fact have an almost exact ratio to one another known as the 'golden ratio' or 1.618034.

The most efficient angle for a primary spiral is 137.50776°, which divides each spiral from its neighbours either side by the so-called 'golden mean', an expression of Euclid's 'golden section', first enunciated about 300 BC. This angle most evenly and gradually divides a circle. If we could take one of the 'lozenges' in our ivory cross-section and trace it along the length of the tusk, we would find that it described a spiral of this angle.

Studies conducted by the United States National Fish and Wildlife Forensics Laboratory indicate that in mixed African and Asian elephant ivory, the mean angle at which the lines cross over is 124.15° ± 13.35°, the 13.35° being the standard deviation or that amount by which the angles varied either side of the mean. Add the two figures together and you get an answer of 137.45°, near enough to the 'golden mean' considering the difficulty of precise measurement. The difference between the mean and the 'golden mean' I believe to be due to a constant degree of shrinkage. In the extinct woolly mammoth the angle was 73.21° ± 14.71°. Add these two figures together and we get 87.92°, which relates to 137.50776° in the ratio 1.615, near enough to the 'golden ratio'. So in the mammoth the spirals, although following a Fibonacci series (if they didn't they would have produced a regular arrangement perhaps like a 45-pointed star), were closer than necessary and would have repeated themselves, producing gaps

FIG. 13.1   *Cross-section of an elephant tusk showing the 'mathematical daisy' or Fibonacci spiral pattern (polarized light).*

which can never be closed. Extant ivory therefore represents the perfect arrangement. Asian ivory is denser than African but the angle of the Fibonacci spiral appears to be the same.

Cuvier drew attention to the decussating pattern, noting that it was unique to elephant ivory and that it occurred in fossil elephant ivory as well. It appears first in the large upper tusks of *Gomphotherium* [*Tetrabelodon*] *angustidens*.

Some years ago I had the mechanical properties of elephant and hippopotamus ivory, buffalo horn, rhinoceros horn and red deer antler tested for me by the Department of Engineering Science of Oxford University. One of the difficulties of such an examination is that the prepared specimen, turned on a lathe, does not necessarily behave in the same manner as would the entire living structure, and its properties alter with drying. Nevertheless the elephant ivory appeared to be only moderately elastic, 9.7 GN/m²*, three times less so than buffalo horn. An earlier authority gives a figure of 13.6 for soft ivory and 17.2 for hard, possibly using much drier and therefore more inelastic material. A recent figure for Asian ivory, which is harder, was 12.5. Its elasticity is a reflection of the degree of mineralization, which is very low compared with substances such as bone or antler.

It is also a fairly weak substance. Its tensile strength, or the weight that it could withstand without breaking, is 56.5 MN/m²*, similar to horn and much less than hippopotamus ivory at 89.6. Rhinoceros horn was between the two. This test tends to produce much more variable results than the test for elasticity and the figure for Asian ivory is given as 110. Bone is a much stronger substance in this respect.

As regards brittleness or the amount of energy absorbed under impact, for example if hit with a hammer, at 5.7 joules it was almost four times more brittle than rhinoceros horn, probably five times as brittle as bone and only slightly less so than buffalo horn, which was 4.6. For Asian ivory the value was 8.7. Compared with the dentine of human teeth it is tougher but inferior in hardness.

The figures suggest that ivory as a substance is brittle, fairly weak and only moderately elastic, contrary to what is generally stated. Its medium qualities are probably what made it the most favoured material for billiard balls, although only East Indian ivory was used for this purpose originally as it had less collagen and did not shrink as much as other ivory. Nevertheless the contour of an ivory billiard ball is always changing and it tends to become ovoid, as well as contracting with cold and expanding with heat.

Billiard balls apart, its soft but fine close-grained texture makes it an excellent carving material and, according to Francis Buckland, son of the famous geologist William Buckland, ivory could be 'graded' for this purpose according to whether or not it was gnawed by rats. In the great Fauntleroy's ivory warehouse in London's Tooley Street, rats gnawed fresh African ivory but would not touch Asian ivory because of its lesser collagen content. The rats always chose ivory which was 'very transparent and of the finest quality'.

ELEPHANT FORENSICS

Ivory traders have long recognized differences in African ivory depending on where it came from. Eighteenth century traders considered that of elephants inhabiting swampy areas to be blue, spongy and knotty, which would indicate a calcium deficiency. The best was considered to come from elephants inhabiting hilly country or dry areas. Ivory merchants at the beginning of the 19th century

---

*Meganewtons (one million newtons) and giganewtons (one thousand million newtons) per square metre are the SI or Système International units which now replace pounds per square inch.

considered that east African ivory was far superior to that of the west, except that Ethiopian ivory had deep pulp cavities and thus was less esteemed. Later 19th century traders alleged that there existed an east–west gradient in hardness, the softest ivory originating from Somalia and eastern Kenya, the hardest from the equatorial forest regions. But in 1849 it was reported that the worst came from west of Lamu, the hinterland of Kenya, and the best from the region of L. Malawi, brought to Kilwa. Other regions produced only medium-priced tusks. The most easily recognized is that from Zaïre, referred to as 'hard' ivory, usually polished to a deep yellow patina with a comparative lack of small longitudinal cracks in the surface known as 'streamers', which must mean that the cementum is not worn away. 'Hardness' or 'softness' is a reflection of the mineral content, which is about 61% in soft ivory and 64% in hard.

Differences in hardness also existed in Asian ivory and an ancient Indian work, the *Brihat Sanhita*, in days when it was more abundant in India, proclaimed that ivory was the best material for constructing bedstead legs:

> In selecting ivory, about two thicknesses at the root of the tusk, which is hollow, should be rejected, if the animal from which it is taken comes from the plains; but if it be a mountain grazer, somewhat less ...

One of the most interesting recent developments relating to elephant natural history is the possibility that an elephant's origins can be determined from the microchemistry of its tusks. This is no new idea and Captain Pitman, when Chief Game Warden of Uganda, sent specimens of ivory from typical forest, savanna and grassland regions in 1936 to Sir Frank Colyer, the leading dental surgeon of the day, to determine whether differences relating to hard and soft ivory could be detected chemically. The analyses – specific gravity, colour and the amounts of magnesium, phosphorus and calcium – are what we would consider today as rather elementary and did not reveal obvious differences. In 1960 I conducted some experiments with hippopotamus ivory to determine whether different levels of minute traces of chemicals, called 'trace elements', could be detected. All that I was able to determine was that hippopotamus teeth were as near to pure calcium phosphate as one could hope to get.

More refined techniques are now available and researchers claim that the origin of tusks can be determined by the ratios of carbon and nitrogen stable atomic isotopes in the ivory's collagen base. These isotopes are types of atoms within an element with nearly identical physical and chemical behaviour but differing in their atomic weight. The carbon 12 isotope is lighter than carbon 13 and the ratio of one to the other in carbon dioxide in the air is altered during plant photosynthesis. Thus, the ratio of carbon 12 to carbon 13 in the animal's body reflects what the animal has been eating as, with few exceptions, these carbon atoms differ in quantity between grass and woody vegetation.

Trees and shrubs, and grasses which grow in dense forest shade, use the so-called C3 pathway in photosynthesis to convert carbon dioxide to sugars and other organic compounds. Tropical grasses use the more efficient C4 pathway – they have to be more efficient as they must replace their losses more quickly.

Carbon 13 is much lower in C3 plants than it is in C4 plants and animals which feed mostly on woody vegetation have lower levels of carbon 13 compared to carbon 12 in their tissues than do those which feed more on shrubs and trees, with ratios near to -21.5. More positive values, such as -15.5 to -17.2 in Tsavo for example, indicate more grass in the diet. But elephants from coastal forest areas such as Liberia and Sierra Leone have more negative carbon values than -22 because the carbon dioxide produced by the rotting leaf litter on the forest floor dilutes the carbon 13 content. A single exception to this is provided by the Addo elephants where there is much spekboom, a succulent plant with a unique chemistry of its own which produces carbon values of about -17 and also produces high nitrogen values.

In low rainfall areas levels of the nitrogen isotope nitrogen 15 are higher than those of nitrogen 14 apparently because it is stored in the tissues of animals stressed by drought, so one can use the ratio of nitrogen 14 to nitrogen 15 to determine whether the area in which the ivory was formed was dry or wet. Where rainfall is less than 400 mm a year the values are greater than 10, rising to 12.7 in Tsavo East and 15.4 in the desert conditions of the Kaokoveld. In wetter regions such as Kasungu and Knysna, the values fall to 3.5 and 2.4 respectively.

Likewise one can use the ratio of two strontium isotopes to one another to reflect whether the geology of the area is old or young, strontium being present in the calcium phosphate of which the tusk is composed. Soils derived from old granitic rocks have strontium 87 to strontium 86 ratios usually greater than 0.715, whereas soils of basaltic composition have lower ratios.

Thus the ratios of these three stable atomic isotopes of carbon, nitrogen and strontium reflect the vegetation, climate and geology of the area from which the ivory came. Elephants from Tsavo, for example, are claimed to have distinctly different ratios from those of elephants originating in the Shimba Hills only 150 km away, those from Addo differ from those in Knysna 250 km away, and different ratios can even be found within an area such as the Kruger Park. Thus it may be possible to build up an isotope map of African elephants to determine where any particular piece of ivory has come from.

The same can be done from an elephant's bones, but the value of the technique with relation to ivory is that it enables one to tell whether it has been illegally obtained or not.

DNA 'fingerprinting' can also be used on the collagen of ivory but to what extent different groupings of elephants can be distinguished has yet to be explored.

An Elephantine Dorian Gray

Tusks evolved in elephants as tools to dig with and there is no disputing their usefulness as a tool in younger living elephants. There may also have been selection for them in Pleistocene times as defences against predators such as the sabre-toothed tiger. If there was, it is a function they no longer require.

The probable explanation for the presence of large tusks which seemingly confer no practical benefits upon their bearers is that they were selected for in bulls to attain dominance in breeding. But when the period of their prime is past there is no selection against the tusks continuing to grow, since the bulls cease to play any role in passing on their genes. So like some distorted picture of Dorian Gray, the bull elephant must pay for the excesses of his prime by an encumbrance which becomes more and more of a hindrance to him. If the elephant could add another ten years onto its life span then its tusks would probably eventually fall out from complete occlusion of the pulp cavity.

But giant tusks are not entirely useless to such patriarchs, for their very size earns them the respect of other bulls and ensures that they are not molested in their old age. They play a real part in social dominance, as Sanderson noted:

> In the keddahs of Mysore we found the services of tuskers invaluable; we had two, amongst others, that were taller and with longer tusks than any wild ones we captured, and their presence was always sufficient to awe the most obstreperous wild male whilst the men were securing it ...
> ... our staunchest tame females shrank if any of the tame tuskers turned suddenly in their direction.

Daphne Sheldrick writes of her observations at a waterhole in Africa: 'Once again, I observed that the biggest tusker always had a right of way and that, as he approached others would stand aside, leaving a path for him.'

Trophy hunting is often blamed for the fact that today only some 10% of Indian elephants carry tusks, the tuskless gene allegedly selected for by man's hunting. A similar myth pertains in Africa where tusklessness is uncommon. Most frequent among cows, about 3% are tuskless. At Amboseli some 2% were tuskless, the trait tending to run in families, and 3% were one-tusked. Likewise in India the proportion varies enormously by area. In the north-east only half of the bulls are tuskless and in the south one tenth. In Sri Lanka only 6% carry tusks or 11% of bulls, and the Cambodian race is reputedly entirely tuskless.

Tusklessness cannot be due to man selectively shooting the largest tuskers as is sometimes alleged, because a trend towards tusklessness is present in all races of the Asian elephant. More probably it is due to endocrine factors, a continuation of the evolutionary process which began with the loss of the lower tusks in extinct forms. This process continues today in the upper tusks, the trunk having taken over their manipulative function.

Asian tuskless elephants are not incapacitated by this lack. One of the important functions of tusks in the African elephant is for digging holes in the sand of dry river beds to reach underground water in the dry season. The Asian elephant excavates the hole with a forward kicking motion of the forefoot.

The elephant can also make a narrow, pipelike hole with its trunk, and African elephants are known to plug them after use with a bunch of leaves or grass or even a ball of dried elephant dung.

J.H. Williams noted that tuskless bulls developed much more powerful trunks, so strong in fact that in fighting they could smash off an opponent's tusk with them, but such a difference is not apparent in the tuskless cow. Sanderson was of the opinion that tuskless bulls were better developed than tuskers because they were allowed to suckle the mother for longer, the mother rejecting offspring whose tusks begin to protrude and stick into her. On the other hand he noted that in captivity they were generally much ill-treated by the tuskers and might become very timid as a consequence.

About AD 170 a Roman named Amyntianus wrote a book called *Concerning Elephants* which, although lost, we know correctly stated that both male and female 'Ethiopian and Libyan' (that is, African) elephants have tusks but the Indian female does not. What a pity that this is all we know of this work.

CONJURING TRICKS OF NATURE

From time to time multiple tusks and even spiral tusks have been reported and there is more than one case of a tusk curving round on itself. Spiral tusks are the result of disease or injury on one side of the root causing the tusk to grow more slowly on that side. The oldest specimen in the Odontological Museum of the Royal College of Surgeons is a spiral tusk described by Nehemiah Grew in 1681:

> A spiral or wreathed tusk of an elephant. Presented from the Royal African Company by Thomas Crispe, Esq. It is twisted and wreathed from the bottom to the top with three circumvolutions standing between two straight lines. 'Tis also furrowed by the length. Yet the furrows surround it not as in the horn of the Sea Unicorn, but run parallel therewith. Neither is it round as the said horn, but somewhat flat. The tip very blunt.

In the region of Uele-Shari in central Africa, four-tusked elephants were not unknown in the 1920s and in 1926 a correspondence on them ensued in *The Times* newspaper. While multiple tusks, spiral and curved tusks can always be attributed to injury at the base of the tusks causing irregular growth, double tusks on both sides are probably genetic due to a divided tooth germ. This is simply a chance mutation and not a throwback to some ancestral form. A four-tusked elephant has also been reported from Sumatra, and from Sumatra also came a remarkable double tusk consisting of one tusk twisted around the other.

Multiple tusks, on the other hand, with as many as eight small ones growing in a bundle have always been shown to result from injury at the base and have been recorded from both Asian and African elephants. An early record of multiple tusks occurring on both sides in an elephant shot about 1856 was reported by Thomas Baines. It had five on the right and four on the left.

Sometimes tusks grow in slight corrugations. I have occasionally seen such tusks in Africa but never paid much attention to them. In Burma this is considered to be an extreme rarity giving the elephant the name of Kyan Zit, which the Burmese consider to be a king of elephants to whom all other elephants do obeisance in terror of his strength.

Ivory curiosities form a common feature of dental museums and collections, one of the reasons being that they present examples of dental lesions, especially of the pulp, on a gigantic scale. Also, until the advent of vulcanite about the middle of last century, ivory was much used for making artificial teeth, although hippopotamus ivory was the most favoured for this purpose because of its greater hardness, followed by walrus which was cheaper. No doubt the dealings between the ivory-carving dentist of the day and the ivory carvers who, to their chagrin, discovered musket balls embedded in tusks, provided the channel through which so many such specimens found their way into odontological museums.

In 1870 Britain's great anatomist Richard Owen remarked that the presence of foreign bodies in solid ivory had long ceased to be a source of wonder, yet despite Owen's pragmatism they remain a source of fascination to this day. Such curiosities intrigued many other notable people besides dental surgeons, one of whom was the famous German poet and natural philosopher Goethe. Some time before 1798 Goethe described 13 preparations of abnormal ivory, seven of which contained musket balls. He obtained his specimens from ivory comb-makers who would leave them aside 'to sell to interested scientists'. In a later passage probably dating from 1823, Goethe mentions that specimens had become less easy to obtain because the trade in ivory had diminished. More likely it was because guns were becoming more effective for the ivory trade was in its ascendancy at that time.

In 1887 a dental surgeon by name of Sudduth examined several thousand pieces of pathological ivory and in 1890 another named Miller examined 58 examples of tusk lesions, most of them being in the dental institute of the University of Berlin. Of this total, 44 were iron musket balls, one was a flat rectangular iron body, seven were leaden balls, round or cylindrical, one was a copper ball, two were iron cylinders and three were spear-points broken off in the ivory. In four cases there were two iron balls side by side. On one occasion even a gold ball was found by a London ivory shop.

Musket balls were frequently found lying loose inside tusks without any discernible point of entry nor were the balls flattened in any way, much to the puzzlement of those who cut the tusks open, such as a Sheffield cutler in 1767 who found an iron ball. This conjuring trick of nature is explained by the bullet having entered through the thin ivory at the root of the tusk and gradually moving down with the pulp as the tusk grows, the wound in the gum healing over.

One can imagine the astonishment these musket balls caused and the number of such specimens in the Hunterian collection shows that this phenomenon had intrigued the great surgeon John Hunter, who collected a number of examples in the second half of the 18th century.

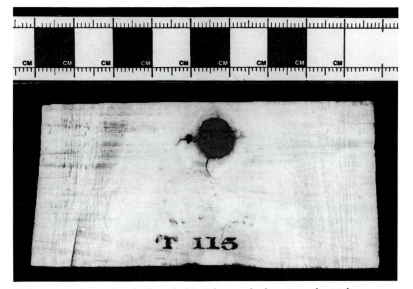

FIG. 13.2   *A musket ball sealed inside an elephant's tusk. 19th century.
Royal College of Surgeons of England, Hunterian Museum T115.*

Fired from muzzle loaders, the balls had very little penetrating power;
witness the 300 plus rounds which Bosman recorded were needed to collapse an
elephant and still did not kill it. And the 152 balls fired by soldiers at close range
into the hapless Chuni at Cross's Menagerie in London. One 1826 report states:
'It is not until after the discharge of a hundred or perhaps double the number of
rifles, that the elephant is slain in India . . .'

If an iron musket ball passed into the unfortunate elephant's pulp, then, due
to the metal oxidizing, an irregular coating of ivory was laid down around it by
the pulp, the ball lying free in the casing so formed. If the ball was lead then a
much closer and less irregular coating was formed. The observation of this
phenomenon in elephants' tusks resulted in lead being used in some of the
earliest teeth implantations about 1888, prompting a Cambridge dental practi-
tioner, George Cunningham, to use it in experiments in the implantation of
tooth substitutes in the jaws of dogs and monkeys at the same period.

Albrecht von Haller, a Swiss physician who produced one of the most
important early textbooks on the physiology of the human body, is generally
credited with having first indicated the occurrence of such secondary dentine
formation in 1766, although Ruysch had depicted examples in 1715. In
describing the growth of the body and age changes in teeth, Haller wrote:

> . . . even the fibres of ivory in the elephant's teeth have quitted their
> places, and surrounded on each side in curve[ed] lines a leaden
> shot . . .

FIG. 13.3   *A spearhead lying loose inside an elephant's tusk. 19th century, Royal College of Surgeons of England, Odontological Museum G126.1.*

But the rarest and most remarkable specimens are not musket balls but complete spearheads lying loose in the pulp cavity. They probably found their way there as weighted spears, dropped from above when the unsuspecting elephant ambled under the tree from which the spear was suspended; with his tusks pointing downwards, the spearhead pierced the base of the pulp cavity.

The first example was described by Charles Combe of Exeter College, Oxford, in 1801 in a communication to the Royal Society. Mr Combe obtained it from Mr Pope, 'an eminent manufacturer at Birmingham', who had bought the tusk in an ivory sale at Liverpool. The tusk weighed 22.7 kg and measured 1.8 m in length. On being shaken there was a rattling noise about $\frac{3}{4}$ m from the base and, opening the tusk, it was found to be caused by a 19 cm long iron spearhead. The spearhead pointed downwards in the tusk and there was no exterior sign of injury. At least two other examples of this remarkable phenomenon are known.

Another person to become interested in elephant tusk abnormalities was Sir Frank Colyer in the 1920s–1930s. He came to the conclusion that multiple tusks or spiral tusks were not throwbacks to some ancestral monster but in most cases were due to injury of the pulp cavity, usually by an ill-placed musket ball. Thomas Baines's five tusks on one side and four on the other were simply due to the splitting of the tooth germ by a misplaced shot on each side. As many as eight tusks on one side may be created in this way, sometimes as bundles of

FIG. 13.4 *How the spearhead finds its way into an elephant's tusk (from Bland-Sutton, 1910).*

small separate tusks, sometimes fused together towards the base. With the use of high velocity rifles such curiosities have become much rarer, but one was recovered in Tanzania in the early 1970s, probably caused about 1920.

Balls have also been found embedded in the roots of molar teeth, distorting the lamellae. Such examples are less common because teeth did not appear in trade, as well as the fact that it was more difficult for a musket ball to penetrate the maxilla or mandible. Furthermore, due to the forward progression of the teeth, unless it was lodged in the sixth molar it was likely to be pushed out of the mouth during life. One may well have cause to wonder at the recuperative powers of elephants, for even a 40 cm long hardwood stake, more than 10 cm thick at the base and bearing an iron spearhead, has been found in the abdominal cavity of an elephant which appeared to be perfectly healthy. It had been there for several years and was marked only by a small discharge to the exterior.

The great Renaissance zoologist at Bologna, Ulisse Aldrovandi, provides the first report of *catarrhus elephanti lapidescens* or 'elephant catarrh stones', published posthumously in 1616 a century and a half before Ruysch and Haller's observations. Aldrovandi figured an example of an acicular pulp nodule, the cause of which is irregular growth of the dentine rather than any form of injury:

> Among other rather rare exhibits which I have in the museum, is a fragment of an elephant's tooth [tusk], but of a much harder material, and in colour not, like other teeth, white, but almost boxwood. It was the gift of a worthy man, and one who has published some very learned works on medicine, the very famous D. Joannes Cecchius, a public professor in this kindly school, and a very authoritative medical specialist, who stated that it was not part of a tooth, but a catarrh, changed into so hard a substance when it fell down from the head of an elephant, suffering from a discharge, into the hollow of a tooth (for where the tooth fits in the head, it is hollow) and these drippings in their changed form are not unlike those excrescences which we see hanging from roofs in winter, and I and others, who are not ignorant of the different effects of catarrh, are easily persuaded that this is so, and the picture itself points it out to those who look at it.

But by far the earliest example of a 'catarrh' is from a mammoth's tusk. This was a smooth-surfaced pulp nodule shaped like a drawn-out egg and about the size of a hen's egg, bearing a small protuberance at one end through which a hole had been bored and the nodule worn as a pendant by a Stone Age man or woman in Aurignacian times. It was found in 1912 in a cave at Paviland in South Wales. Egg-shaped nodules of similar size are known from African elephant tusks. No less remarkable about this example was that Dr William Buckland had found the exact piece of tusk from which it came in the same cave in 1823, almost a century before. Philip Powell of the Oxford University Museum, which holds the pendant, kindly had it X-rayed for me in the hope that we might find a flint arrowhead embedded in it! But the X-ray revealed nothing enclosed within the ivory, confirming it as a pulp nodule.

Found also in the cave were parts of a delicate slender ivory bangle cut by

FIG. 13.5   *An early example of an odontome in an elephant's tusk (from Aldrovandi, 1616).*

FIG. 13.6 *The Paviland pendant. A pulp nodule from the tusk of a mammoth worn as a pendant by a Stone Age man in Wales about 18 000 years ago.*

Aurignacian man from a mammoth's tusk. The decorative properties of ivory have made it coveted by man from his earliest origins, long before gold, silver or jewels became objects of adornment. The fate of the elephant was sealed even before that ancient Welshman proudly suspended the Paviland pendant around his neck just before the glacial advance over 18 000 years ago.

MAMMOTH IVORY

Ivory from Africa and India was not the only ivory used in modern times. In the year 1611 an English sea captain, Jonas Logan, brought the first Siberian mammoth tusk to London: 'One would not have dreamed of finding such a thing in that cold and remote corner of the world,' he wrote. In 1644 Mikhail

Staduschin explored the arctic coast of north-east Siberia and verified reports current among the Yakuts of 'large islands rich in great elephant bones'. But it was not until the mid-18th century that the trade in fossil mammoth ivory from Siberia developed on a considerable scale. This was as a result of the rich stores discovered in 1750 by a Russian fur-trader, Liakhov, after whom two of the islands are named, Bolshoi Lyakhovskiye and Malyy Lyakhovskiye, which some claimed were almost built of mammoth remains. This encouraged others to follow him into the frozen wastes of Siberia in search of fortune far north of the Arctic Circle and induced the Russian government to conduct further exploration in 1775, leading to the discovery of the also mammoth-rich more northern New Siberia Is. The ivory was 'often as fresh and white as that from Africa'.

An indication of the amount contained in these incredible deposits is given by the facts that in 1809 one searcher brought back $4\frac{1}{2}$ tonnes and in 1821 another 9 tonnes, each tusk averaging 54.6 kg. Eighteen tonnes were sold annually at Yakutsk and between the years 1825 and 1831, from 27 to 36 tonnes. Together with other trading centres, it was calculated that not less than 50 tonnes went to market each year about 1840, representing at least 100 mammoths. Others quite rightly thought this estimate to be far too low; perhaps 400 would be closer to the mark.

In 1872, 1635 'very fine' mammoth tusks were sold in England and the following year 1140, weighing from 63 to 73 kg each. Of the tusks recovered, it was calculated that about 14% were good, 17% could be made use of, 54% were bad and 15% wholly decayed and useless. At the beginning of this century those tusks collected in the extreme north mostly went to America, whereas those from the district of Okhotsk went mostly to Japan, the total output from north-eastern Siberia being estimated at over 32 tonnes. Yakutsk alone was said to average 30 tonnes a year in 1900, equivalent to about 200 mammoths, each pair of tusks averaging more than 100 kg and each tusk being up to almost 5 m in length. Between 1660 and 1915, a total of some 50 000 mammoth tusks are estimated to have been recovered in Siberia.

Up to the First World War there was no diminishing of the trade and the United States alone imported 40.8 tonnes in 1914. But most went to Europe, particularly Hamburg, forming an inexpensive substitute for the then rare and more costly African and Indian ivory.

In 1929, 6000 tonnes of fossil ivory were said to be in circulation worldwide, but in 1934 it suddenly ceased to appear on the Moscow market. Recently the mining of ivory in Siberia has once more increased. The official news agency Tass announced in July 1982 that it was starting a new export business in mammoth ivory from the Arctic coast, which it anticipated could raise up to £1 million per year. However, in 1986 India imported only 5 tonnes and in 1989 Japan less than 2.

Formerly there had been, at least in the mid-18th century, a considerable trade with China. The traveller Avril who crossed Russia in 1685 stated that most Siberian ivory went to China where it was highly prized, but the Persians and the Turks also valued it more highly than Indian elephant ivory as it was whiter. More than 50 years later in 1738, von Strahlenberg, a Swedish officer in the service of Charles XII, taken prisoner in Siberia, reported, 'A great many of these teeth (mammoths' tusks), which are white, are carried for sale to China'.

In 1818 it was noted that ivory collectors had been collecting from the west side of Liakhov Is. for 80 years without any apparent diminution in the supply. What might now be done to these vast hoards with modern earthmoving equipment?

Perfectly preserved mammoth tusks have sometimes been found in Britain; one was discovered in Scotland in the middle of the 19th century in 'such preservation that it was sold to an ivory turner for £2. Before it was rescued . . . it had been sawn asunder for the manufacture of chessmen'. There had been no change since Aurignacian times. What other substance has maintained its appeal for 18 000 years?

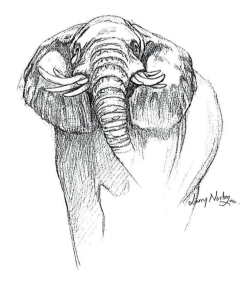

Chapter 14

THE MASSACRE OF THE GIANTS: THE IVORY TRADE

Major Rogers, ... is said to have applied the value of the ivory obtained ... towards the purchase of his successive regimental commissions, and had, therefore, an object, however disproportionate, in his slaughter of 1400 elephants.

Sir Emerson Tennent, 1867

The luxurious tastes of man are inimical to the existence of the elephant.

Anon, 1852

FOUR THOUSAND YEARS OF SLAUGHTER

*E*BURATUS is a Latin word meaning 'adorned with ivory'. Well might the Romans coin such a word for, copying the arts of the ancient Greeks, they used more ivory than anyone else in history until exceeded in modern times by the avaricious rapacity of the Japanese. Caligula built a stable for his horse from it replete with ivory manger, and the ivory seated colossus of Jupiter at Olympia was over 17 m high (although it probably had a hollow wooden base). Ivory was mentioned in ancient Greece long before the elephant itself. In 420 BC it was reported, 'Libya supplies ivory in plenty for trade'. The father of the ancient Greek Demosthenes (384–322 BC) was an ivory dealer and wholesaler who owned a factory for making cabinet ware, knife handles and walking stick handles for gouty old Greeks.

Ancient Egyptians had used ivory even earlier, perhaps before 6000 BC. A noble of the 6th dynasty (2475–2025 BC) relates in his tomb inscription how, on return from an expedition to the south, he sent the king a 1.5 m tusk and kept one of 3.0 m for himself. In Tutankhamen's tomb, *circa* 1352 BC, there was a casket inlaid with 45 000 pieces, a solid ivory jewel casket with gold fittings and a solid ivory bowl 16.5 cm in diameter.

The ancient Greeks knew also of fossil mammoth ivory. Theophrastus (371–287 BC) wrote of ivory embedded in the soil, the tusks recovered by the Chinese who referred to them as 'dragon bones'. But in the 12th century *Ta–Kuan-pen-Tsao* they were thought to be the bones of huge fish collected during the spring floods at 'Dragon's Gate'. Some authorities believed this to be a reference to walrus tusks, but the locality is also referred to as the home of *fyn-shu*, and at the beginning of this century in India an antique substance known traditionally as 'fish tooth' was found to be mammoth ivory.

In the 15th century BC the ancient Egyptian pharoah Thutmose III killed 120 elephants on a tributary of the Euphrates 'because of their tusks'. Mercilessly hunted for their ivory since ancient times, elephants are the oldest known animal to have been exploited for reasons other than food or clothing and records of the ivory trade extend back farther than those of any other natural product.

Many properties were attributed to ivory by the ancients and in the 19th century it was believed that ivory shavings (they sold at sixpence a pound in 1855), boiled into a jelly with water, had the same medicinal properties as hartshorn (ammonia or smelling salts) and the same restorative qualities. Perhaps the calcium content served as an anti-indigestion cure but it was also favoured as a sort of 'calf's foot jelly': 'when properly boiled, and otherwise treated, [it] makes the finest, purest, and most nutritious animal jelly that we know of'. The recipe for this delicacy was:

> In a brown stewing-pan with a cover, put 1lb of ivory-dust, and three quarts of water; let it gently simmer for twelve hours, or until it is reduced to one quart; then put it away to cool, and take the clear jelly off. Add wine and sugar *ad libitum*.

Well, I like the wine and sugar bit.

Another ancient belief was that it was a febrifuge or fever dispelling substance. The Chinese, as well as using mammoth ivory for medicinal purposes, believed that the meat of frozen mammoths served as a febrifuge.

Burnt ivory, termed 'black velvet' by the French, was used to maintain a youthful appearance by men wishing to disguise their grey hairs. It was also used in the manufacture of black artists' paint and black ink.

In Europe ivory shavings were believed to be an emetic. I can well believe it but I would have thought that there were plenty of other things that one could make oneself sick with without resorting to ivory dust, even in the 19th century.

Clearly the poet Gerard Manley Hopkins, writing in *Once A Week* in July 1860, did not subscribe to the supposed beneficial qualities of elephant remains:

> Our inquiries as to the fate of the 'mammoth bones' which formed the ossuary of All Saints, West Ham, are unsuccessful. Three things may have happened. They may have been decently interred in the churchyard before it was closed for sepulture; or they may have been crushed to manure the corn-lands of that parish; or they may have entered more immediately into our cereal food by being ground and mixed with flour.

Tu Li Shin, Chinese envoy in 1712–1715 to a tribe inhabiting the Volga area, noted that the tusks of mammoths had more practical uses: 'The Russians collect the bones of this animal [the mammoth], in order to make cups, saucers, combs, and other small articles'.

But it is not for these utilitarian reasons that ivory is mainly sought. It has primarily always been coveted for its artistic qualities, first exploited by Stone Age man etching pieces of mammoth ivory and carving figurines such as the 25 000 year old Venus of Brassempouy, an exaggerated female figure. Later carved ivories have been found over a wide range of the Mediterranean region. Highly prized and skilfully worked in Minoan and Mycenean times, ivory was already regarded as a luxury object by 1450 BC. But there came a lull until 900–800 BC when contact between the East and Greece was re-established. The Phoenicians became the great ivory carvers of this period and first drew on the local Syrian elephants for their supply, but soon had to turn to India. But by 700 BC India had become a diminishing source and the Greeks turned to Libya for supplies. One hundred years later India was importing ivory from Africa and the Phoenicians were importing from north Arabia ivory probably of Ethiopian and Somalian origin.

The ancient Egyptians had obtained ivory from Syria, Sudan and Somalia, ivory being brought down the Nile from at least 1580 BC and probably from Somalia, the fabled Land of Punt, by sea, from whence Egypt imported 700 tusks in 700 BC.

With the rise of the Roman Empire demand for both African and Indian ivory exceeded all bounds, so that Pliny wrote in AD 77: '... an ample supply of tusks is now rarely obtained except from India, all the rest in our world [i.e. North Africa] having succumbed to luxury'. The Romans also captured elephants for the circus and there was a demand for eating elephant's trunk among gourmets, who appreciated 'the taste of its trunk's rind, with no other reason I think, than because one thus pretends to eat the ivory itself', wrote Pliny.

Pliny's remark is the first reference suggesting over-exploitation of the resource, the demands of the Roman Empire having exhausted all but small tusks from African sources and they had to turn to India which had seemingly recovered as a source of supply.

About AD 100, 'a great quantity' of ivory was being exported from East Africa but the trade was probably a comparatively modest one at this time. In the 3rd century the African trade was renewed and the demands, not only for ivory but for elephants for the Roman circus as well, resulted in the extinction of the Syrian elephant leading in the 4th century to the gradual decrease of elephants in North Africa and their virtual disappearance by the 7th.

The Arab al-Mas'udi wrote about AD 915 that the inhabitants of East Africa killed elephants for their ivory: 'The Zanj do not use them for war or anything else, but only hunt and kill them [for their ivory]'. Some tusks weighed 23 kg or more: 'They usually go to Oman, and from there are sent to China and India. This is the chief trade route, and if it were not so, ivory would be common in Muslim lands'. The 9th century Arab writer Suleiman noted that ivory was imported to Canton.

A Chinese trade, possibly relating to mammoth ivory or elephants in the north of China, dates back to at least 50 BC, and perhaps 500 BC with Siberia. At first the Chinese would have used their own elephants. The earliest known Chinese ivory carvings date from the Shang-Yin period of 1783–1123 BC and already show a high degree of accomplishment, ivory being greatly valued for religious and ceremonial articles. From about 206 BC to AD 906 the bulk probably came from countries of the Far East, particularly Borneo, Java, Burma and India. From the 10th century onwards, probably until the 18th, the chief importers were Arabs who traded it from the Malay Peninsula, Java, Borneo, Sumatra, India and East Africa. A 12th century account states that the tusks imported from Africa weighed from 23 to 45 kg, while those from Tonkin and Cambodia only 5–13. About the year 1100 tusks weighing around 16–20 kg imported into China had to be disposed of in the official market. As the price was lower there the merchants cut the larger tusks into pieces of 2 kg or less so that they could sell them where they pleased. Much later, in 1226, in *A Description of Barbarous Peoples*, Chau Ju-Kua wrote that tusks obtained from the Somali coast sometimes weighed more than 60 kg. Kublai Khan (AD 1214–1294), ruler over China and much of the Far East, founded an ivory carving workshop in Beijing which in 1263 employed 150 workmen. In the 14th century Tonkin, Siam, Burma and India were still sending ivory to China.

Its decorative qualities were not unappreciated in Africa itself and ivory bangles have been found in early Iron Age sites dating from AD 815 and possibly earlier. At Mapungubwe at the junction of the Shashi and Limpopo rivers in the northern Transvaal, there are many pieces dating from 970 to 1150 AD. These show signs of being sawn with a saw-toothed instrument as well as drilled and in some cases simply carved. The presence of a complete tusk together with cowries and beads suggests that not only was the ivory worked at these sites but it was also traded with the coast. Much later, in 1589, an English trader brought from Benin 'spoones of Elephants teeth very curiously wrought with divers proportions of foules and beasts made upon them'. But by that time design could have been influenced by the Portuguese.

Four hundred years before the date of the earliest known African ivory bangles, from the 5th to the 7th centuries Saxon women were being laid to rest in rural cemeteries in England and on the continent accompanied by ivory rings of 10–15 cm in diameter. Archaeologists believe them to have been ladies' 'bag rings', rings from which a leathern bag was suspended to keep its mouth open. Why so rare and valuable a material for such a mundane use? They are comparatively common in Saxon graves yet are not found in those of the more noble Franks. Further mystery surrounds the rings' provenance. Was ivory still being traded with Britain? It was brought there by the Romans and there was still contact with Rome. That they are the only ivory objects of the period suggests that the finished rings alone were imported. Radiocarbon dating shows they are of recent and not fossil ivory. All we can say is that even Saxon women valued ivory.

AFRICA'S APPALLING ACELDAMA

At the beginning of the 17th century ivory exploitation, encouraged by the Portuguese trading on the west coast, began to intensify over a wide area of Africa. When the Portuguese captain Azurara first visited the mouth of the Senegal River in 1450 he noted that elephant 'bones' (tusks) were not used in any manner, but he had learnt that in the Levant and on the Mediterranean coast they were very valuable, traded by the Arabs from the Orient and from East Africa.

After the Islamic expansion of the 7th and 8th centuries it was the Arabs who kept the ivory trade alive following the decline of the Roman Empire. When ivory began to reappear in northern Europe it was used almost wholly for religious purposes and carving became important in north-east France in the 9th and 10th centuries. But ivory was to remain scarce for a further four centuries or so, that which reached Europe coming from Byzantium, until in the later 13th and 14th centuries French and Flemish ports began to import it direct. After the sacking of Constantinople in 1204 Byzantine sources probably declined due to the severing of Arab trade routes, and it was rarely used in Renaissance Europe in the mid-14th to mid-16th centuries. Its revival probably stemmed from its being made available once more by the Portuguese.

In 1469 the King of Portugal granted to a Lisbon merchant, Fernao Gomes, the exploration of the Guinea coast for five years on condition that he paid an annual rent, discovered 100 leagues of new coast a year and sold to the crown all the ivory that he could obtain from the natives at a price of 1500 reis (about 31p) per 51 kg. Thus began the great ivory scramble, such that John Ogilby was to write in 1670 that such a great abundance of ivory had been brought from the Congo since the early part of the century that the supply had already begun to diminish.

The seed of the English trade which was to swell to such monstrous proportions was sown in 1530 when William Hawkins, mayor of Plymouth whose son was to sail with Drake, 'not contented with the short voyages commonly then made onely to the knowne coasts of Europe,' voyaged from Plymouth to Brazil, stopping at Guinea and buying 'Elephants teeth'.

The amounts brought back in the 16th century varied. In 1540 William Hawkins's ship brought only 12 tusks. In January 1557 one ship's master records taking '5 small Elephants teeth'. The third day 'we tooke 5 more'. On the fourth day, together with a French admiral, they took 15 'small teethe'. Not content with this they then decided to seek their own elephants:

> This day wee tooke thirtie men with us and went to seeke Elephants, our men being all well armed with harquebusses, pikes, long bowes, crossebowes, partizans, long swordes, and swordes and bucklers; wee found two Elephants which wee stroke divers times with harquebusses and long bowes, but they went away from us and hurt one of our men.

Obviously it was not as easy to do it yourself as they thought. Describing a voyage to Guinea in 1554, Sir George Barnes wrote:

> They brought from thence ... about two hundred and fifty Elephants teeth of all quantities. Of these I saw and measured some of nine spans in length [2 m], as they were crooked [i.e. measured along the curve]. Some of them were as bigge as a mans thigh above the knee, and weyed about forescore and ten pound weight a peece. They say that some one hath bin seene of an hundred and five and twentie pound weight. Other there were which they call the teeth of calves, of one or two or three yeeres, whereof some were a foot and a halfe, some two foot, and some three or more, according to ye age of the beast.

Already the scramble was on for tusks of any size.

In 1562 William Rutter took 166 tusks weighing a total of 800 kg, a mean weight of 4.8 per tusk, while in 1590 one ship records taking 150 on a voyage to Benin. The Portuguese at this time were probably taking about 68 tonnes a year from Mozambique and in the late part of this century India was importing 272 tonnes per year. Writing of Zaïre in 1591, Filippo Pigafetta noted: '... ivory was not accounted valuable till after the Portuguese began to trade in these regions'.

There are few records of the amounts traded in the 17th century, although the Portuguese were probably still taking about 68 tonnes a year from Mozambique. We learn that 18 tonnes could be traded from Senegal in 1689. In 1703 its trade was estimated at 125 tonnes. In the latter 1720s it was estimated that France was importing some 50 tonnes annually but in 1763 Britain was taking only an estimated 15–30.

Altogether from 1500 to 1700 in the region of 100–200 tonnes per year may have left Africa. In the next century this could have exceeded 200 tonnes a year, while from 1800 to 1850 it exceeded 400 and in the latter half of the 19th century, 700.

Figures for 1879–1883, after the peak in the ivory trade had passed, give some idea of the spread of the trade in Africa. During these years Europe was importing an average of 848 tonnes each year divided as follows: Niger and Benue 89; Cameroon and Gabon 64; Congo 86; Ethiopia and Somalia 26; Benguela 26; South Africa 29; Mozambique 142; Egypt (Khartoum) and Tripoli 171, and Zanzibar 196.

WHERE DID IT ALL GO TO?

From 1771 to 1799 a total of approximately 1857 tonnes was imported into Britain, an average of 66 per year, mainly from south east Africa. About 1830 the average annual import into Great Britain was 210 tonnes per year. It was not until 1836 that Britain imported ivory directly from East Africa, all previous supplies having been channelled through India. India had been an important entrepot for African ivory. Garcias ab Horto alleged that 272 tonnes were imported annually in the 16th century, although this was probably an overestimate. In 1831 she re-exported 110 tonnes to London just before Britain began to import directly from East Africa. In 1883–1884 Bombay imported 210 tonnes, almost half of which was re-exported, particularly to London. From 1840 to 1850 total British imports averaged 266 tonnes a year and from 1850 to 1890 they rose to 521. One 1859 reference gives the import as averaging 254 tonnes when in fact it was twice this amount. In 1875 imports reached an all-time high of 800. For the nine years 1873–1881 a total of 5542 tonnes was imported, comprising at least 300 000 elephants with an average tusk weight of just over 9 kg each side.

Livingstone calculated that between 1860 and 1870 Britain received about 550 tonnes of ivory annually (it was actually 600). Of this annual total, 160 came from Zanzibar and Bombay (Bombay obtaining it from Zanzibar); 180 from Alexandria and Malta; 140 from the west coast; 50 from the Cape and 20 from Mozambique. In 1874 the mean weight per tusk was about 6 kg.

From 1853 to 1879 a single Dutch merchant, H.A. Meyer of Antwerp, imported an average of 137 tonnes per year from Khartoum. From 1888 to 1913 the total annual tonnage imported to Antwerp rose from 6.4 to 351, the highest being in 1902 with 370. In 1889 and 1890 the average tusk weights were 12.5 and 10.9 kg respectively, weights not subsequently equalled. In 1901 it was 8.4. The Antwerp market averaged 18 500 elephants per year between 1895 and 1906, while Khartoum's export was equivalent to about 2500 in 1905 with an average tusk weight of only 4 kg. Well might General Gordon write in 1875, 'What a number of poor beasts have died for this ivory! It is of slow growth, and there are numbers of very little tusks of little elephants'.

In 1887 Stanley sent 6 tonnes from the Congo for sale in Britain which were bought by the leading cutlers of Sheffield, Messrs Rodgers and Sons, who were estimated to use the ivory from 800 elephants a year for making knife handles.

In 1863 the first plastic, celluloid, was invented, probably in the search for a cheap substitute for ivory, but although it was used as such it did nothing to

TABLE 14.1 *Ivory imported into Great Britain 1771 to 1918 (from Sheriff, 1987, and other sources).*

Year	Tonnes	Year	Tonnes	Year	Tonnes
1771	34	1821	187	1871	630
1772	34	1822	100	1872	552
1773	34	1823	160	1873	658
1774	34	1824	265	1874	657
1775	34	1825	297	1875	800
1776	34	1826	220	1876	576
1777	66	1827	165	1877	637
1778	66	1828	177	1878	662
1779	66	1829	214	1879	451
1780	66	1830	270	1880	545
1781	66	1831	260	1881	555
1782	66	1832	148	1882	432
1783	66	1833	248	1883	606
1784	66	1834	332	1884	474
1785	66	1835	256	1885	446
1786	66	1836	320	1886	406
1787	66	1837	287	1887	426
1788	66	1838	240	1888	516
1789	105	1839	253	1889	480
1790	73	1840	266	1890	372
1791	184	1841	281	1891	430
1792	129	1842	309	1892	486
1793	119	1843	263	1893	456
1794	113	1844	256	1894	628
1795	111	1845	309	1895	436
1796	57	1846	259	1896	495
1797	97	1847	310	1897	467
1798	44	1846	225	1898	454
1799		1849	359	1899	451
1800	117	1850	451	1900	449
1801		1851	297	1901	400
1802		1852	446	1902	491
1803		1853	490	1903	419
1804		1854	433	1904	410
1805		1855	403	1905	479
1806	111	1856	456	1906	447
1807	109	1857	474	1907	489
1808		1858	590	1908	424
1809		1859	496	1909	524
1810		1860	518	1910	508
1811		1861	535	1911	406
1812	129	1862	547	1912	556
1813		1863	448	1913	516
1814	135	1864	548	1914	495
1815	182	1865	493	1915	372
1816	136	1866	584	1916	430
1817	102	1867	502	1917	486
1818	116	1868	482	1918	250
1819	128	1869	682		
1820	152	1870	592		

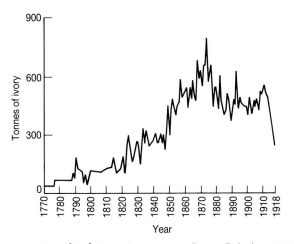

FIG. 14.1 *Graph of ivory imports to Great Britain 1771–1918.*

reduce the demand. Nor did the development of subsequent imitations, such as that in 1887 made by boiling potatoes in sulphuric acid:

> This artificial ivory can be dyed and turned in the lathe, and applied to any of the uses for which real ivory – now becoming so scarce – is usually employed. It remains to be seen whether this imitation ivory will answer for many purposes as well as celluloid.

The result was simply to enable the less well-off to buy cheap imitations, leaving the demand for real ivory unabated.

In 1911 Europe still took 600–800 tonnes per year, of which Britain was probably using 265, continuing to do so until after 1918 when the figure was 250. The London market alone was still taking about 255 tonnes per year in 1933, with an average tusk weight of 6.4 kg (20 000 elephants).

In 1889–1893 the average uses to which ivory was put were knife handles 34%; piano keys 31.6%; combs 17.7%; billiard balls 9.6%; and miscellaneous (prayerbook covers were a favourite) 6.6%. This consumed 513 tonnes. In addition India consumed another 121 and China 13, making a grand total of 647. Great Britain was the largest maker of knife handles, using 143 tonnes for this purpose or 76% of its imports. The United States was the biggest manufacturer of piano keys, using 62 tonnes for this or 53% of its imports, closely followed by Germany. In 1913 the weight of ivory used in the United States for making piano keys rose to 198 tonnes.

AN AFRICA OVERVIEW

West Africa

A West African trade in ivory was in existence from at least 350 BC, and from the time of their arrival in the 15th century until the middle of the 17th, the

FIG. 14.2   *The Antwerp Ivory Room before an auction, 1897.*

FIG. 14.3   *The London Ivory Room before an auction, 1892.*

Portuguese reported ivory as common. But after 1830 the trade declined and by 1850 the supply was exhausted, to be replaced on the world market by East African ivory.

Not only were the Portuguese involved but the British were quick to vie with them for the trade, and between 1608 and 1612 the Dutch also were exporting 23 tonnes a year from Loango (Pointe Noire). The introduction of firearms about 1635 intensified hunting and by 1642 the Vili, a tribe of elephant hunters, were hunting as far east as Stanley Pool. In the next century the trade diminished but at the beginning of the 19th the Portuguese turned their attention back to ivory once more.

In 1705 William Bosman had written that the greatest number of elephants was found before one came to Ghana, i.e. in Liberia and the Ivory Coast, 'several elephants being daily killed in the said places'. He reported them coming every day to the seashore in Ghana and:

> In the tract of land betwixt Ante and Accra, there are a few, though not so many as in the former countries, because this place hath long been reasonably well peopled, except the country of Fetu, which for five or six years past, hath lain almost waste; wherefore there is a much larger number of elephants there at present than formerly.
>
> A great part of the country about Accra lying waste and uninhabited, a great quantity are annually killed here. In the year 1697, one of an uncommon magnitude was killed near Accra, just by our fortress, and no doubt but that he was full-aged, his two teeth weighing two hundred and twenty pounds; from which you may infer that he was not very light himself.

FIG. 14.4   *Ivory hunting tribes and places in precolonial Africa. The names of tribes are underlined.*

A century later, when Mungo Park explored the Gambia in 1795–1797, he found the Africans unable to comprehend the white man's desire for ivory:

> Nothing creates a greater surprise among the Negroes on the sea coast, than the eagerness displayed by the European traders to procure elephants' teeth; it being exceedingly difficult to make them comprehend to what use it is applied. Although they are shown knives with ivory hafts, combs and toys of the same material, and are convinced that the ivory thus manufactured, was originally parts of a tooth, they are not satisfied. They suspect that this commodity is more frequently converted in Europe, to purposes of far greater importance; the true nature of which is studiously concealed from them, lest the price of ivory should be enhanced. They cannot, they say, easily persuade themselves, that ships would be built, and voyages undertaken, to procure an article, which had no other value than that of furnishing handles to knives, etc. when pieces of wood would answer the purpose equally well.

The greater part of the ivory sold on the Gambia and Senegal rivers, Park asserted, came from the hinterland, elephants being very numerous and gunpowder scarce in present-day south-west Mali. But:

> The quantity of ivory collected in this part of Africa, is not so great, nor are the teeth in general so large as in the countries nearer the Line [equator]: few of them weigh more than eighty, or one hundred pounds...'

In 1832 Luanda exported 1.36 tonnes, rising to 47.7 in 1844 and 85.86 in 1859. By 1854 the Cokwe, a tribe of elephant hunters existing in present-day Lunda, had virtually eliminated elephant from the north and east of their district and were hunting as far east as the Zambezi headwaters. By the mid-1860s there was no ivory left in the region and the Cokwe acted as middlemen for the ivory of Lunda further east. This source was also soon exhausted and the trade moved to the north-east.

In the 1850s a weight of 6.8 kg was considered to be a fair average for a tusk from Gabon which was estimated to be exporting not less than 80 tonnes a year at that time, principally to England, France and America. In 1855–1856 the average weight of the tusk was 7.7 when the price had doubled over that in 1851–1852, mainly on account of the French traders and the high increase in the cost of trade articles.

In spite of the decline in Angola, plenty was now being taken from the Congo. Between 1888 and 1909 this region exported an average of 352 tonnes per year and in 1898, 243 tonnes of the total African export of 555 tonnes came from here. In 1899 it was 388 tonnes with a mean tusk weight of 30 kg. Between 1889 and 1950 the estimate that 585 000 elephants were killed in the Belgian Congo was based on ivory exports, but if we deduct natural deaths the figure would be more like 550 000.

From 1896 to 1905 the German Cameroons exported 45.2 tonnes per year, described as being 'chiefly young elephants'.

These figures indicate but a fraction of the trade from West Africa and the Congo until the decline at the beginning of the 20th century. Later, as elsewhere, there was a revival. In 1925 the Congo exported 2.64 tonnes through the East African market, rising to 22.8 in 1962. In 1979 this was to rise to over 160 tonnes from Zaïre and a total of over 683 in the ten years up to 1988.

The eastern coast

The East African ivory trade is of far greater antiquity than that of West Africa. The lost city of Rhapta (possibly Kilwa) traded it in the 1st century and it may go back a staggering 2000 years before this, a total history of 4000 years.

East of L. Malawi and south of the Rovuma River in Mozambique, the area known as Yaoland, inhabited by the Yao ivory traders, was a great centre of exploitation due to its abundance of elephants, still 'fairly numerous' at the beginning of this century. The Portuguese dominated its trade from the 16th until the 19th century, when it was wrested from them by the Arabs in East Africa.

Angoche, south of Mozambique, flourished on gold and ivory from 1505 to about 1530. These products from present-day Zimbabwe had already been the staple items of Kilwa trade for more than two centuries before 1500 but in 1511 a report to the King of Portugal noted that only a little ivory came from Kilwa and much from Sofala. At this time the Portuguese obtained what they considered to be 'a lot' from Mombasa. From 1512 to 1515 they exported some 69 tonnes from Beira and in 1544 reported 'great quantities' could be obtained at Delagoa Bay. By 1680 the English had bought up all of the supplies reaching this port so that there was 'virtually none left in the country'.

Before the middle of the 16th century there was almost no call at Kilwa for ivory from the interior, but by the end of the 17th a well-organized trade had developed between it and Yaoland. During the first half of the 18th century the Yao channelled most of their trade to Mozambique, which emerged as a major centre of the ivory trade and by the middle, the Yao trade was at its height, taking about 100–120 tonnes to Mozambique each year. Estimated to be 65–70% of all the ivory entering there, it had an annual turnover of 150–180 tonnes.

The following century was to see extensive hunting out of elephants in the coastal hinterland. Figures for ivory exported from Mozambique between 1759 and 1761 could suggest a total of 11 500 elephants killed in the three years, assuming an average tusk size of 20 kg for 'large and average', and 10 kg for 'small and small made large'. But the number could have been almost twice this, for the average tusk weight in 1679 is given as 16.36 kg, falling to 6.89 in 1852.

An important and regular trade involving the Yao, Maravi and Lenje tribes began to flourish between Luangwa and the coast after 1760. The principal hunting ground of the Chewa, known as the Malambo, was located around the middle and lower reaches of the Luangwa. They took their ivory to Kilwa and in 1770 it was reported that more ivory was brought there than to Mozambique. From about 1785 the demise of the Mozambique trade set in and was completed about 1810, Kilwa and Zanzibar taking over. This was due to an artificially low price imposed by the Portuguese so Yao traders took their ivory to the north. By the year 1780 the Yao were bringing no more than 25–32 tonnes per year to Mozambique and by 1795 this had dropped to scarcely 7–10. About 1770–1780 the Yao penetrated northern Malawi where ivory had no trading value and by the end of the 18th century three routes were established across L. Malawi.

In 1793 the Portuguese lowered their re-export duties and as a result exports reached an 18th century peak of 189 tonnes, falling to not quite half of this in 1801 and 107 in 1809. By 1817 it had fallen to 58. Most of this ivory came from other ports. Inhambane exported 40.4 tonnes in 1802 with an average weight of 9.9 kg per tusk and in 1806 Quelimane exported 64.3.

By the end of the first decade of the 19th century all of the trade north of the Zambezi was going to East Africa, particularly that from Kazembe, and this period saw the increasing subordination of the ivory trade in Surat to that of Great Britain. Hitherto the main demand had come from India, which prior to 1830 re-exported some 40% of her imports to China. For the next 20 years this was to average no more than just under 6%.

The Portuguese had abandoned Mombasa in 1698, but before an organized ivory trading structure was in place in the 18th century there is little evidence of contact between the East African coast and the interior, although an early 16th century Portuguese account tells of a mid-15th century trade caravan reaching Malindi from 20 days' march up the Galana River, that is, the region of Machakos. It has been postulated from archaeological evidence that a regular trade existed between the hinterland and the coast from 1300 to 1600. By the 15th century ivory hunted by hunter–gatherers and traded with other tribes was coming from a considerable area of the interior, until by the 18th nearly all of the East African interior was being exploited.

By 1800 the Wakamba began to expand throughout the interior and in 1825 Wakamba traders visited Mombasa. Coastal merchants began to make contact with tribes in the hinterland in the first decade of the 19th century, but it was nearly the end of the century before they were able to penetrate northern Kenya. The few Arab caravans which had tried to enter Maasailand in 1882–1883 were wiped out. The Maasai, who monopolized the trade in their area, obtained 1000–1500 tusks a year mostly from the Waboni on the southern bank of the Galana River.

In 1859 Zanzibar exported 221 tonnes of which exactly half went to India. Mozambique was exporting about half of the amount that Zanzibar was until, in the early 1860s, the figure almost trebled to about 600 tonnes due to the opening up of the country between Inhambane and Laurenço Marques. It is reported that 137.7 tonnes were exported from Beira in 1852, equivalent to '10 000 elephants', but in 1927 only 3.95 tonnes came from there, representing 333 elephants. In 1929 it was a mere 27 kg, and in 1930 it was 129.

Further north, Ethiopia had been exporting ivory to India from the 6th century BC, while early in the Christian era the Galla tribe originally brought ivory to Pate and then to Barawa north of Pate. Even so, this old-established east coast trade was probably of moderate proportions until the revival of Arab interest when the Omani capital was moved to Zanzibar in 1840.

The trade reached its peak between 1830 and 1856. In 1843, 71% of the total value of Zanzibar's exports was from ivory and in 1849 the quantity totalled 297 tonnes. By the middle of the 19th century the average annual export from East Africa was estimated to be greater than 300. One contemporary observer estimated that this represented some 26 000 elephants, but the average tusk weight at the time imported into Bombay suggests 19 000 as nearer the mark.

By this date coastal caravans were already making regular trips to Usagara in Tanganyika and Maasailand and Kikuyu in Kenya, at first collecting ivory from the tribes who had in turn traded it from the hunter–gatherers.

Except for a brief ten years from 1800 to 1810, demand always exceeded supply and by the middle of the 19th century Mombasa was exporting 45 tonnes a year, Tanga 32 and Pangani some 16, although in 1856 the total annual East African export was put at 385. The 6000 tusks per year that Krapf believed were being brought to Mombasa would probably have weighed more than 45 tonnes. Burton reported in 1856: '... tusks weighing 100lb each are common, those of

175lb are not so rare ...' But by 1894 a tusk of over 55 kg was reported as sufficiently rare to attract attention.

During 1859–1860 an 'unprecedented' number of firearms entered East Africa and there was a steady high input thereafter. In 1856–1857 there had been a sharp rise in the price of ivory which caused a rush of Arab traders into Urua and other inland regions. Zanzibar exported 222 tonnes in 1859, followed by an annual export of about 180 until the end of the century. In 1893 the amount was 19 931 tusks weighing 169 tonnes and in the first 11 months of 1894, 21 059 tusks weighing 182. In 1909 it was exporting about 317 tonnes a year.

Tabora in Tanganyika had been established as a major ivory centre between 1850 and 1860, the Wanyamwezi becoming important elephant hunters. About 1855 a marketing centre was established at Kafuro in Karagwe and another at Kitangule about 1860. By 1863 the explorer Speke wrote that the area (Karagwe) was '... formerly stocked by vast herds of elephants; but since the ivory trade had increased these animals had all been driven off ...' By 1880 the country east of Ujiji was '... long since denuded of ivory' and by 1890 the Wanyamwezi hunters were seeking it as far north as near L. Edward in Uganda. In 1894 it was reported that elephants were probably completely absent from 'Karagwe, Urundi and the whole eastern shore of Tanganyika'.

The infamous ivory trader Tippu Tip, who journeyed from Bagamoyo to the Manyema country between 1871 and 1881, recorded: 'At one time there were great herds of elephant around Itawa ... Countless numbers were killed'. This was midway between L. Mweru and the southern tip of L. Tanganyika. He stayed nine months at L. Mweru, but there was little ivory in Urua and he obtained only about 4 tonnes. Irande he recorded as heavily populated, with no sign of elephants and no ivory, but at Kassongo Rushe's in two weeks he collected 200 tusks totalling 5958 kg; an average weight of 29.8 kg per tusk. One chief gave him five tusks averaging 30.2 kg each.

Although he traded initially for small ivory because it was cheaper, he soon came to dominate the trade. An agent at Tabora brought in 3.9 tonnes, while one expedition out of Stanley Falls brought in 32 and another nothing. At Kassongo he obtained 14.3 tonnes. Yet when he returned to Stanley Falls after 1885 to assist the Belgians, he considered that the number of tusks which were being brought in to the Belgian company was 'staggering'.

In 1874 ivory had been described as 'abundant and cheap' in Kavirondo but 20 years later the supply was exhausted. Many elephant populations still existed in scattered localities and in 1882 even on caravan routes, but there was constant pressure on them. As the elephants disappeared from the coastal regions so the Wakamba hunters searched farther and farther inland, until in 1890 they were operating almost as far as 500 km north and 1000 km south of Ulu. They traded as well as hunted for ivory with the Kikuyu, with tribes near to L. Baringo, in Samburu, Turkana, East Kilimanjaro and south to Songea. At the southern end of Lake Rudolf they met the domain of the Arbore elephant hunters from the north of L. Stephanie, who combed the whole area to the lower Omo.

In 1900 the travellers Grogan and Sharpe wrote:

> In the greater part of Africa the elephant is now a thing of the past; and the rate at which they have disappeared is appalling. Ten years ago elephant swarmed in places like British Central Africa, where now you will not find one.

This did not apply to parts of Uganda. Grogan and Sharp estimated that there must have been 15 000 elephants in Toro. The reason for their abundance here, especially in Bunyoro, was the fact that ivory traders from the north did not penetrate as far south as Bunyoro and trade eastwards was strictly controlled by Buganda.

Sporadic ivory trading had taken place in the 18th century in Buganda and about 1800 Bugandans were organized into guilds of elephant hunters, but it was not until 1877 that a coastal caravan reached Bunyoro. In 1872 the young king Kabarega, ruler of Bunyoro, strictly prohibited on pain of death the free trade in ivory which Samuel Baker endeavoured to establish. But in 1877 two Arab traders reached the Bunyoro capital and succeeded in initiating a trade to the Tanzanian coast, bypassing Buganda.

Some ivory did leave Bunyoro down the Nile until the Mahdist rebellion in the early 1880s, and the trader Stokes obtained some from Buganda having helped restore the Kabaka Mwanga to power in 1888.

The first visit of an ivory trader to Turkana in the north-east of Uganda is believed to have been in the early 1880s and by 1896 the district had become well known. At this time trade was small and restricted and in 1897 one Swahili trader considered himself lucky to get about 10 tonnes as no other trader had been there for three years. The area centring on TshudiTshudi, halfway between Loyoro and Mongole, was also raided by Ethiopians from the north. By 1900 Harry Johnston reported the destruction of elephant as 'shocking' in a Foreign Office communiqué.

The Ethiopians began a big firearms trade and coupled with the use of firearms by the traders, this rapidly destroyed the herds. Between 1900 and 1910 the area was reported as cleaned out, a few survivors moving to the remote northern mountain ranges so that after 1910 they could be found only around Moruakipi and Mt Zulia. But this was the country of which the elephant hunter Bell wrote in 1902: 'Here [west of Kadam] we were face to face with such a gathering of elephants as I had never dared to dream of even. The whole country was black with them'. Ormsby, the administrator at Mbale, reported: 'I have seen herds on the plains below Save [Sebei] in which the total number of elephants would well reach 2000'. In a six months trip Bell obtained 354 tusks and on one day 665 kg of ivory from nine elephants at Moruakipi. Although the limit was two elephants, there was no one to enforce the law and by the time that the government took action in 1911 clearing the ivory traders out of Karamoja, it was already too late.

The Ethiopian centre was Maji, and traders with Uganda licences took their bull ivory to Mbale but the cow and immature tusks to Maji as these were illegal in Uganda.

The protection eventually imposed had effect. In the ten years 1979–1988

TABLE 14.2 *Annual export of raw ivory from Africa 1950 to 1988 (data from Barbier* et al. *(1990)).*

Year	Tonnes	Year	Tonnes
1950	204	1970	564
1951	318	1971	488
1952	254	1972	573
1953	295	1973	878
1954	305	1974	573
1955	313	1975	598
1956	348	1976	934
1957	329	1977	738
1958	259	1978	882
1959	380	1979	950
1960	412	1980	1164
1961	282	1981	912
1962	348	1982	900
1963	319	1983	1040
1964	459	1984	798
1965	403	1985	913
2966	371	1986	805
1967	468	1987	331
1968	532	1988	142
1969	620		

over 424 tonnes of ivory were exported from Uganda, 131.5 tonnes from Kenya and over 697 tonnes from Tanzania, quantities which would never have been thought possible at the turn of the century.

North Africa

Another major region of exploitation was the Sudan and north-west Uganda, from where ivory was channelled through Khartoum. At the same time that the Arabs penetrated from the east, the Khartoumers came from the north, up the Nile to L. Albert. By 1860 intensive ivory exploitation had begun and from 1853 to 1879 an average of 148 tonnes per year was exported from Khartoum to a single ivory house. Few ivory merchants remained on the Nile by 1879 due to the Mahdist rebellion, but the supply of ivory was soon to fall anyway. Emin Pasha wrote in 1883:

> If the supply of ivory has been plentiful up to the present, we must not forget that it is due to the trade established with the south and western countries far beyond Egyptian territory; nevertheless, for some years there has been a considerable decrease in its supply.
> The Equatorial provinces send about 700 cwt [35.6 tonnes] of ivory per annum to the markets, of the average value of £30 000. It is difficult to say how much is supplied by the territory of Bahr-el-Ghazal, as the greatest part of the ivory sent from thence to

> Khartoum is not the actual annual production, but the remnants of
> the old stock of proprietors of zeribas... The day will soon come,
> therefore, when the supply of ivory will not be sufficient to meet
> the heavy charges.

Nevertheless Emin collected 85 tonnes at Wadelai from the Equatoria region between 1886 and 1887 and claimed that he could have collected double this by 1889 if he had continued.

Output had already dropped to a fraction of that of the 1870s, but Emin's belief that much of this was stored ivory was incorrect. Many elephants were destroyed by ring-firing; Schweinfurth (1873) commented on their destruction and Gordon in 1875 noted that many small tusks were collected. In 1888 Khartoum's output was 42 tonnes and by 1905 it had fallen to 20.

Channelling ivory from the Central African Republic and northern Zaïre, as well as marketing its own, in recent times Khartoum once more came into prominence as an ivory entrepot, exporting over 1451 tonnes in the ten years from 1979.

Southern Africa

South Africa's elephant populations were eroded over a longer span of time. In 1652, when the first Dutch colonists landed at the Cape, elephants had been common in the vicinity of Table Mountain but by 1761 could not be found south of the Oliphants River in the west, and in the east by 1775 they could not be found west, of Port Elizabeth. They remained plentiful in the eastern regions of Cape Colony and Kaffraria until 1820–1830, when they became scarce. This was probably due in part to the Austrians offering twice the price the Portuguese were paying for ivory, brought to the east coast from several hundred kilometres inland of present-day Natal.

By 1897 there were only 150 elephants left in the Cape, of which descendants survive in the Knysna and Addo forests today. In 1889 South Africa's export was only some 4 tonnes, having fallen from an estimated average of 50 per year between 1850 and 1875. In 1855 over 90 tonnes were estimated to have been exported from the Transvaal.

By 1855 elephants were scarce in eastern Botswana and were already being hunted in Ngamiland and towards the Zambezi. With the decline of elephants in the south by the early 19th century, particularly along the Molopo and Limpopo Rivers, hunters ventured north in the wake of Livingstone. He recorded that in the first year following his discovery of L. Ngami in 1849, 900 elephants were killed near there. By 1890 there was only one small troop left, later wiped out. But the lake had dried out in 1881 perhaps causing the majority to move north to the Okavango delta, although Thomas Baines wrote in 1864 that:

> The Botletle [the Boteti river 175 km to the east which still flows]
> only a few years since swarmed with elephants, and the deserted
> and desolate plains we have passed over were alive with everything.

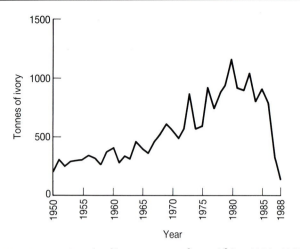

FIG. 14.5   *Graph of ivory exports from Africa 1950–1988.*

By 1860 Botswana had seen its best days as far as elephants were concerned. Only four years before in an address to the Royal Society of Arts, Livingstone stated that elephants to the north of the Zambezi were so numerous that he 'could hardly imagine their ever becoming extinct'. Yet they had become extremely scarce in Mashonaland by 1885 and in 1890 few were left in the country. But again according to Livingstone, in 1859 they were plentiful in Elephant Marsh on the lower Shire valley, also on the Bura River south-west of L. Malawi and in the Luangwa river valley. By 1903 elephants had practically ceased to exist south of the Cunene and Zambezi rivers, their disappearance having been effected in the space of 60–70 years. The last elephant in Zululand was shot in 1890.

Between 1979 and 1988 South Africa exported almost 336 tonnes of ivory with annual exports as high as they had ever been, but much of this probably came from Mozambique and Angola.

ASIAN IVORY

Within recorded history Asia never experienced the same holocaust. This was due to the large number of tuskless elephants, cultural reasons, Hindu religion forbidding the taking of life; and the fact that elephants had a practical use. Megasthenes recorded in the 4th century BC that no private person in India was permitted to keep an elephant, possession being a royal privilege. In Sri Lanka the penalty for killing an elephant was whipping, confiscation of property or banishment. Although India was using some ivory for carving by at least about 2500 BC, its wider use is considered to be recent, stemming from the demands of British occupation, particularly in the 19th century. Cultural reservations were not observed by everyone, and in the early 19th century tribes in Upper Assam hunted elephants both for ivory and meat.

From about 1880 to 1910 a small but constant supply of 5–10 tonnes of Indian elephant ivory was exported to Japan per year. From 1918 to 1939 this totalled about 1 tonne per year. Between 1875 and 1877, 4–8 tonnes per year were exported, some of this from live tusks, the ends of the tusks of domestic elephants being cut usually every 8–10 years. In the late 19th century Sri Lanka and Sumatra exported an estimated 2 tonnes per year, of which half came from Sumatra.

Today about 100–150 elephants are killed each year in southern India, half by poachers. The average weight of the poached tusks is 9.5 kg, showing that they go after the larger bulls.

THE CRASH

Overall it has been estimated that at least a million elephants were killed between 1830 and 1930 in Central, East and West Africa. In fact 10 000 a year is not a large number and it was probably five times this. The estimate around 1880 was 60 000–70 000 a year; for 1894 it was 65 000 and from 1895 to 1900 at least 40 000 a year. If in 1894 Zanzibar was supplying the same proportion of the total of African ivory as it was in 1879–1883 (about 20%), then the annual elephant crop would have been about 75 000, not 65 000, based on an average tusk weight at Zanzibar for that year of 8.5 kg. In 1889 Europe had already received 100 tonnes less of ivory, and 1899 saw a further marked drop with Mombasa's export falling to 46. But in 1909 Zanzibar was still exporting around 317 tonnes a year.

Figures often differ because, taking Britain as an example, some authors give the imports to London as the figure for a particular year, yet Liverpool imported some 15% of the total, at least between 1889 and 1909. Also the total British imports were about 25% greater than those recorded for London and Liverpool alone, although this included some Asian and fossil mammoth ivory. From 1880 to 1900 Anvers in Belgium and London in Britain were the main markets, but other ports of import, in addition to Liverpool, were Le Havre, Bordeaux, Marseille, Hamburg and Constantinople, let alone the eastern and American markets. And there were other channels which may not have touched Europe.

Seven-tenths of the ivory received in Europe was reported in 1891 as 'worthless for industry', which suggests most of it was weathered or found ivory. There is little justification for the belief that this was because vast amounts were stored by local people. Although large quantities of found ivory could mean very large elephant populations with many dying naturally each year, the considerable amounts of 'worthless' ivory recovered before the 1940s more probably testify to the inefficiency of the muzzle-loader as a killing weapon. Most of the luckless beasts were only wounded, to die later and their ivory found subsequently. Ivory can weather quickly on the ground, especially on acidic soils. It was also reported in 1870 that 'people at home have little idea of the tear and wear ivory is subjected to in its transport'. The market value was seriously affected by the ivory becoming cracked from the 'intense heat which tusks from Central Africa are subjected to in crossing the Nubian Desert on camel back'. To prevent or lessen this drying out, some tusks were packed together in fresh bullock's hide which dried out around them and thus afforded some protection. Even having reached its final destination, it was not immune to damage. At the beginning of the century explosions were sometimes heard 'as loud as pistol shots' from ivory stored at the London Docks as it cracked in response to a sudden change of temperature.

Regulations to control the killing were passed in 1822 in South Africa and in India and Burma in 1879. Further control was mooted in 1891 and regulations introduced in German East Africa in 1896. These made it illegal to possess tusks under 6.35 kg weight. (The average weight of tusks from Tanzania passing through the ivory room between 1962 and 1970 was 6.3 kg, and of those from Uganda between 1959 and 1967, 6.4 kg.) Others were introduced into Uganda and the East African Protectorate in 1897 which forbade the shooting of cows and the possession of tusks below 4.6 kg. In 1905 the minimum weight was raised to 13.6 kg, and lowered again in 1933 to 5 kg.

As in the current conflict surrounding the ivory trade, there were dissenters to the opinion that elephants were threatened. Dr Cuthbert Christy, who had much experience of hunting elephants, wrote in 1924 that:

> In many parts of tropical Africa elephants still exist in enormous numbers. If a census should be taken I should not be surprised to learn that their actual numerical decrease during the last thirty years has been very little. [He continued] The great herds of several hundred animals once common enough are now rarely met with ... the large herds have been scattered, their feeding-grounds restricted, and individuals and family parties kept perpetually on the move, or confined to uninhabited areas. The result is that the decrease in numbers is more apparent than real.

However, he then went on to say that the number of big tuskers with ivory over 34 kg in weight had decreased greatly and medium tuskers with over 23 kg to a lesser extent. He considered that in 1902 in Uganda tusks of about 68 kg had been comparatively common.

The introduction over much of Africa at the end of the last century of the legislation controlling elephant hunting, helped by a fall in the price of ivory and a drop in demand following the First and Second World Wars, allowed populations to recover substantially over much of central, eastern and southern Africa, but not in the West.

From about 1936 the annual Zanzibar ivory returns showed a steady rise to 1962, increasing from 62.5 tonnes to 230. The average for the last five years of this period reached former levels of exploitation: over 197 tonnes compared with 196 for 1879–1883. This changed suddenly in the early 1970s, when probably the general level of affluence rather than world financial instability greatly increased demand and exports rose quickly to pre-1914 levels. Harvesting had progressively accelerated from 1950 or even before, passed the maximum sustainable level by the early 1960s and was then reducing the population below its reproductive ability so that elephants could be brought to virtual extinction by the year 2015, and in East Africa 20 years sooner. The continental population had possibly declined by 45% in the ten years 1979–1988.

It was not the first time that extinction was predicted. It had been said repeatedly in the 19th century and in 1938 the *News Chronicle* newspaper reported a Dr Kirkman as stating:

> Africa is killing off the elephant … Soon it will have none left …
> Elephants (he said) were being killed off at the rate of 36 500 a year,
> greatly in excess of their reproductive capacity.

Elephant control and poaching were blamed by Dr Kirkman; the former he alleged was conducted by game departments to balance their budgets. The American Committee for International Wildlife Protection, promulgating the American approach of sustainable use, had stated in 1933 that 'the elephant is in no danger of extermination in British East Africa. The problem there is to keep the number within bounds'.

But the demand for ivory meant that all ages and both sexes were indiscriminately taken, reducing populations. Peak fertility in females occurs at 30–40 years, when the individual tusk weight is no more than 6.3 kg. The populations in East Africa in the 1970s were much younger in age structure than those which were exploited in 1840–1890. The average age of legally hunted elephants in Uganda declined by about six years during a period of 32. In Tanzania in the ten years from 1966 to 1975 the mean tusk weight of 43 000 tusks declined from 8 kg to 4.8, implying that much cow ivory of the most fertile sector of the population was being included.

North Bunyoro apart, populations showed the type of survival curve associated with heavy adult mortality or increasing population size, the hunting pressure to which elephants have been subjected in recent history suggesting that the populations have been depressed at a young age structure rather than being in an expanding phase. As populations become younger, so their numbers should be replaced more quickly, but as the price of ivory rises and tusk size declines, so pressure on the remaining animals increases.

If there was evidence to suggest that elephants increase in number without restraint until the size of the population exceeds the carrying capacity of the environment and the population then crashes, leaving a few survivors to repeat the pattern, then such cycles of abundance and scarcity would have been masked in the last three centuries by the intensity of hunting. Cycles which may have taken place in different areas are unlikely to represent more than phases of overexploitation, followed by population recovery when hunting in an area was no longer profitable.

Between 1925 and 1969 it is calculated that some 500 000–600 000 elephants were killed in East Africa for their ivory, and between 1981 and 1988 almost 200 000. The 1950s saw a resurgence of elephant poaching with the ivory trade averaging just over 200 tonnes per year. In 1956 it was estimated that 600 elephants had been poached in the Tsavo area and the adjacent coast province, but the following year more than 3000 elephants were believed to have been killed in the Tsavo area alone and a concerted effort had cleared the Tsavo Park of poachers 'for the first time in its history'. In a strip of land 40 × 32 km between the Galana and Tana rivers more than 1280 carcases were seen from the air, of which 1 in 5 still had tusks. A total of 444 tusks was recovered from them weighing more than 4 tonnes, an average of some 18 kg per elephant.

From 1925 to 1939 the annual increase in ivory offtake was approximately 3%, but rose to almost 6% in 1950–1973 and may have been as high as 7%. By the early 1960s the annual offtake, assuming a high natural rate of increase of 6% per year, had exceeded the annual replacement so that the standing crop of elephants was being reduced. It was believed in 1959 that there were 200 000 elephants in Africa and that 30 000 a year were being killed. If this was so, reproducing at the greatest possible rate of 7% a year, the population would have been extinct within ten years. For there to have been 1.3 million in 1979 as estimated, then there would have had to have been about 650 000 present in 1959. In fact the number of elephants killed each year was rising all the time from 1925 through the mid-1980s. From 204 tonnes of ivory in 1945, it had risen to 380 in 1959, was 412 in 1960, 564 ten years later and about 1000 in 1980; an average increase per year of 10% including natural mortality of 3%. The population in 1959 must therefore have been of the order of at least 1.15 million and more probably was 1.5 million.

Between 1979 and 1988 some 7625–7955 tonnes were exported altogether, peaking in 1983 with the equivalent of 700 000–800 000 elephants of an average tusk weight of 9–10 kg each side. But in 1979 1 tonne of ivory represented approximately 54 dead elephants, mostly bulls, with an average tusk weight of 9.3 kg each side. By 1987 the average weight was 4.7 kg, so that 1 tonne of ivory now represented about 113 dead elephants. Not only were many of these cows, it has been calculated that a further 55 calves would be orphaned and die. Thus in 1987 almost the same number of elephants was being killed as in 1979, to supply one third of the amount of ivory.

Whereas a sustained harvest of 750 tonnes a year could be obtained from a population of one million elephants, this falls to 400 if the selection is for large tusks. Calculating from the 1950 production of ivory the amount traded will be negligible by the year 2015 and the African elephant extinct five years later because harvesting has progressively accelerated. Although the production of ivory continually increased, elephants declined outside protected areas and although the massacre almost stopped in 1990 but resurged again the following year in southern Africa, the populations are unlikely to ever recover 1950 levels due to contraction and fragmentation of their range.

The estimated population of 1.3 million elephants in the late 1970s is estimated to have declined to 609 000 in 1989. In East Africa alone, where ivory exports rose at about 6.4% per year, elephants declined by up to 92% compared with 1973 levels. Eighty percent of the ivory traded in this holocaust was illegal.

WHY NOT KILL ELEPHANTS?

Pragmatists argue there is no difference between killing an elephant and killing any other animal, therefore why all this fuss? They must be used. They must pay for the land they occupy or let us have it for other purposes. The difference lies in the fact that when a mature elephant is destroyed an information base is also destroyed which has taken, say, five times as long to accumulate as that of a wildebeest. The destruction of these stores of information or knowledge, leaves the young survivors often almost helpless. This was shown when young elephants were released into the Pilanesburg Park in Bophutatswana. They just did not know how to look after themselves until adult cows were introduced which taught them to forage systematically.

Our own knowledge stores are of similar age to those of elephants but in human warfare we sacrifice our young men first, thereby guarding the accumulated knowledge of the older men and enabling us to rebuild using their experience whatever warfare may have destroyed. By killing off the oldest first we deprive elephants of that essential for successful survival.

But ivory is only one side of the coin, some have argued. The competition is between man and elephants for living space and food, not for ivory. In East Africa elephants inhabited some 87% of the country in 1925 but by 1950 this had fallen to 63% and by 1975 to 27%, due to increase and expansion of settlement of the human population. The doubling time of the population of Africa is now only 18 years, so in another 18 years another 670 million people will want a place to live unless disease, famine and war limit population growth.

Thus one school of thought claims that an increase in elephant deaths has resulted from range compression caused by an expanding human population and not a demand for ivory fuelling high prices. Others discount this because the weights of elephant tusks which are traded are not random, as one would expect them to be if the elephants were being killed simply to control them. On the contrary, selection is for the larger tusks. The increase in elephant deaths in recent years is also much greater than the increase in human population in Africa or the rate at which land has been taken under cultivation. In countries such as the Central African Republic, elephants have been massacred in virtually uninhabited areas, and there is little competition for land in the tropical rainforest. In East Africa the worst declines have taken place in national parks and the slaughter is often by foreign nationals, Sudanese in the Central African Republic, Somalis in Kenya.

A former American ivory trader, E.D. Moore, claimed in 1931 in his book *Ivory, Scourge of Africa*, that the 50 000 tonnes of ivory coming out of Africa from about 1840 to 1895 did not represent elephants killed in those years, but largely the collection of ivory stored by Africans who used it for fences, doorposts and other mundane requirements or simply left it lying around. The story of tusks being used for doorposts and partitions goes back to antiquity. Pliny reported Polybius, who wrote in the 2nd century BC, as having it on the authority of a Numidian chieftain that:

> ... in the outlying parts of the province where it marches with Ethiopia, elephants' tusks serve instead of doorposts in the houses, and partitions in these buildings and in stabling for cattle are made by using elephants' tusks for poles.

But by Pliny's time, of course, ivory was scarce in northern Africa.

Two thousand years later we still hear the same story. An Arab ivory trader El Zubeir, who visited Dar Tikma in the Niam-niam country in 1859, reported that the chief's compound was surrounded by a palisade of 3000–4000 tusks. El Zubeir asked to trade them but the chief did not understand how the Arabs could set such store by ivory. El Zubeir told him that they simply converted it into powder. Returning the following year in the hope of buying up this vast amount, he found that all of the tusks had been burnt, the chief fearing that El Zubeir wanted to cheat him (as he did). Thus was the precedent set for burning ivory to prevent it from entering the ivory trade, 130 years before Kenya publicly burned a similar number of tusks amounting to 12 tonnes of ivory!

But when exposed in a tropical climate ivory does not last for many years, added to which the Portuguese had been avidly pursuing the trade from the 16th century. It was only demand for the product beginning about 1825, particularly from Britain, which encouraged the ravishing of the interior of East Africa by the more intrepid Arab traders. These actively encouraged the killing of as many elephants as possible.

This traditional view of the East African pattern has been questioned, postulating that the huge amounts traded in the 19th century were the result of a cumulative effect, or compound growth, which took place over the preceding 300 years. European demand and Arab activity were also considered to be less important than were changes in the Indian national economy, many Indian entrepreneurs entering the trade.

THE GRAVEYARD OF GREED

Between 1979 and 1989, 691 000 elephants died in Africa. Standing trunk to tail they would have stretched for 1800 km, almost from London to Venice. From these 691 000 elephants 8000 tonnes of ivory were recovered to fuel the insatiable demand of the Japanese, although only 1800 tonnes of this went directly to Japan and over 2800 went to Hong Kong. This horrific greed has now led to the threatened extinction of the elephant.

Chief Tshekedi Khama of the Bamangwato tribe in Botswana stated in 1938:

> In my territory there are many elephants at present, but they are not hunted because of the law of the Chief. There are so many of them that they destroy crops but they have been protected. This protection was effected by the original owners of the country who had in mind their children ...

It is a sobering thought that children born after the year 2000 may never see an elephant in the wild.

In 1897 Stanley wrote in his best-selling book *In Darkest Africa*:

> Every tusk, piece and scrap of ivory in the possession of an Arab
> trader has been steeped in human blood. Every pound weight has
> cost the life of a man, woman, or child; for every five pounds a hut
> has been burned; for every two tusks a whole village has been
> destroyed; every twenty tusks have been obtained at the price of a
> district with all its people, villages and plantations. It is simply
> incredible that, because ivory is required for ornaments or billiard
> games, the rich heart of Africa should be laid waste at this late year
> of the nineteenth century, and that native populations, tribes,
> and nations should be utterly destroyed. Whom does all this
> bloody seizure enrich? Only a few dozens of half-castes, Arab
> and Negro ...

Stanley's eloquence fell on deaf ears and the amount of ivory imported into
Britain rose dramatically in the following years, just as it did in the United
States. If people took no notice then, regardless of the appalling price being paid,
why should they take any more notice today, when at most only a handful of
poachers and game guards die as a result of the trade?

Knife handles, billiard balls and piano keys were more important then than
human life, items which could be construed as marginally more useful than
those which ivory is used for today.

Stanley could not stop it and neither could the King of Egypt 2150 years
before him. When Ptolemy II desired to capture elephants in Ethiopia for
training as war elephants from the region which supplied Egypt and the Middle
East with ivory, he urged the hunters to refrain from slaughtering them in order
that he might have them alive. The ancient Greek writer Agatarchides records
their reply:

> Although he promised them many wondrous things, he not only
> did not persuade them but he heard their reply was that they would
> not exchange his whole kingdom for their present way of life.

Chapter 15

Anachronism or Wasted Asset? The Domestication of Elephants

The Dog is man's companion; the Elephant is his slave.

Sir Samuel Baker, 1890

You don't shoot elephants, you ride them – you might as well shoot your charger.

King George V

An Ancient Arms Race

ARISTOTLE tells us that the ancient Egyptian pharoahs hunted or captured elephants in the Nile valley, the Nubians driving herds into a narrow gorge where they slaughtered the adults and then roped the young, and it has been said that in India the military use of elephants is 'as old as civilization'. More precisely, the Dravidian Indus Valley civilization is believed to have domesticated the elephant as early as 3000 BC, well before the invasion of the Greeks. Some 2000 years after the ancient Egyptians may have tamed them, a tomb inscription of the 12th Dynasty (2000–1788 BC) notes that the owner of the tomb had captured a live one, suggesting that this was an exceptional feat and a curiosity. A later painting of tribute from Nubia in the tomb of Thutmose III (1504–1450 BC) shows tusks and a live elephant calf, but nowhere are they figured on the monuments of ancient Egypt and they do not occur in Egyptian mythology. The later Egyptians first encountered war elephants in the Asiatic elephant wars with Syria about 1500 BC.

The Assyrian king Tiglath Pileser I tells us about 1100 BC that he:

> brought down ten immense bull elephants in the region of Harran [on the Euphrates], and on the banks of the Haber. I took four elephants alive. The skins and tusks, as well as the live elephants I sent to my city Asshur.

Much later, about 400 BC, elephants were important in the Meroitic culture centred on Meroe south of Aswan in Egypt, where they were apparently ridden by kings.

At this time the ancient Greeks learned of the practice of using them in warfare from Ctesias in his 4th century BC history of India, but were first confronted with them at the battle of Gaugamela in 331 BC when Alexander the Great defeated Darius III of Persia. Darius had a few backed up by some 15 belonging to the Indians who joined forces with him. Having captured these, Alexander went on to capture others and eventually amassed a force of 126. But after taking 30 more he gave those to another general, obviously considering that 126 elephants were enough to handle.

Alexander fielded these in his invasion of India in 326 BC, when he defeated the Indian king Porus in the battle of Hydaspes at the Jhelum River in present-day Pakistan.

Their value in war so impressed itself upon the mind of Alexander's general Seleucus that they became the first arms in an ancient arms race. After the death of Alexander a few years later and the division of his empire among the generals, Seleucus obtained Persia and the East and instituted a monopoly on the supply of Asian elephants. Used in war with 'castles' on their backs manned by 2–4 soldiers armed with 4.5 m long pikes and dressed in armour plating, the Carthaginians adding iron points or spears to the elephants' tusks, they became ancient forerunners of the tank.

The arms race began when in 303 BC Seleucus I ceded to Chandragupta, the first ruler of all northern India, the Macedonian conquests bordering India in exchange for 500 elephants. Because Asian trained elephants had become almost a Seleucid monopoly, Ptolemy II (282–246 BC), the Macedonian king of Egypt and Carthage who had inherited a small number of Asian elephants captured by his father Ptolemy I at Gaza, nervous of the growing might of Ptolemy his repudiated elder brother, and the Seleucids whom this brother now ruled, decided to obtain and train his own war elephants from Africa. Hitherto African elephants had been known only as a source of ivory. This led to his undertaking an exploration of the Red Sea coasts and Ethiopia about 280 BC, particularly for the capturing of elephants for use in war. He obtained them from the head-waters of the Atbara River, from Eritrea and the borders of Abyssinia. Brought to the coast of the Red Sea to ports near modern Massawa and Suakin, they were shipped in specially constructed boats to Red Sea ports further north and from here marched overland to the Nile to the main elephant stables at Memphis. By the mid 240s BC the estimated herd of 300 was big enough for Ptolemy III (246–222 BC) to use effectively in his Asian campaign.

Under this Ptolemy and his successor Ptolemy IV (222–205 BC), elephant hunting continued on a reorganized basis and in new areas. More and more expeditions operated not in Aithiopia, an area south-west of the Red Sea hills, but in Trogodytice, the hinterlands of the Red Sea coasts of Eritrea, Ethiopia and even Somalia. A new port with access to important hunting grounds was founded at Adulis, modern Massawa, and under Ptolemy IV additional hunting stations were established along Somalia's northern coast. The intensity with which the search for new hunting grounds south of Ptolemais near present Port Sudan was conducted under these two Ptolemies, indicates that the Aithiopian hunting grounds must have been seriously depleted.

But then suddenly the reason for Ptolemaic activity in the Red Sea for almost three quarters of a century ceased, when Ptolemy IV's largest elephant field force of 73 was defeated by the 102 Asian elephants of Antiochus III of Syria, at the battle of Raphia near Gaza in Palestine in 217 BC.

In the only account of a battle in which the Ptolemaic elephants were used, Ptolemy's elephants were apparently afraid to face the Asian elephants of Antiochus and retreated onto his own army, a common hazard of using them, added to which they were often roused for battle by giving them wine to drink.

At the same time that African elephants were being captured by Egypt in the north-east, by 277 BC in the north-west Carthage was making use of a much nearer supply. The countries of Numidia and Mauretania, present-day Algeria and Morocco, had numerous elephants in the forests at the foot of the Atlas Mountains. Among the Berber tribes were people who proved themselves capable of both capturing and training them. Allegedly, stables for 300 were built into the walls of Carthage.

These elephants played a prominent part in the Mediterranean warfare of the times, beginning with the first Punic war and ending with Caesar's victory at Thapsus in 47 BC.

Use of elephants simply as showpieces against people who had never seen them before was often their most effective role in battle. The savage Gauls were driven out of Asia Minor in 275 BC initially by 16 elephants. When the victorious Macedonians crowded round their leader Antiochus I, hailing him as 'glorious in victory', he reproached them with the words:

> Shame, my men, whose salvation came through these sixteen

beasts. If the novelty of their appearance had not struck the enemy with panic, where should we have been?

Asian war elephants obtained from the Seleucids were first used in Europe by Pyrrhus in 280 BC at the battle of Heraclea in southern Italy. At first perturbed, the Romans captured a number and paraded them in Rome. They then learned how to use them themselves, so that in the first Punic war in 262 BC, when the Carthaginian general Hanno took 50 to Sicily to try and raise the siege of Agrigentum by the Romans, the latter were ready for them and ended up by capturing most of the elephants.

Seven years later at the battle of Tunis the tables were turned when the Carthaginian elephants almost annihilated the Roman army, which made the mistake of facing the elephant charge in closed ranks. But then five years after this at the battle of Palermo the Carthaginian general Hasdrubal, brother of Hannibal, made the mistake of using his elephants to attack a fortified position and the elephants turned tail before the onslaught of missiles. This time it was the Romans who won, killing 26 elephants and capturing 104. The captured elephants were taken to Rome and paraded in the circus by the triumphant general, Metellus, after which they were all slaughtered. Savage as this seems its object was probably to show how easily elephants could be killed, in order to boost the confidence of the Roman soldiers.

They do not appear again in major warfare until Hannibal's famous use of them in his invasion of Italy by way of the Alps from Spain in 219 BC. He left Spain with 40 elephants. Three had died by the time that he reached the Alps, crossing with 37 used as pack animals. Then, in 218 BC after the battle of Trebia River where they were used with great effect against the Roman cavalry, all but one died of cold or starvation after crossing the Apennines. Only Hannibal's survived, which he rode into Arno in triumph. Later Hannibal imported 40 more from Carthage through southern Italy and used them successfully at the battle of Capua in 211 BC, but little more is heard of them.

Three years later Hasdrubal crossed the Alps with 15 more to join his brother Hannibal, using them at the battle of the Metaurus where the Carthaginians were finally and decisively defeated in Italy by the Romans. At this battle the elephants got out of hand and ranged to and fro through the ranks but, now experienced in the disadvantages of using them, Hasdrubal had provided each rider with an iron spike and a mallet, with instructions to kill the elephants by driving the spike into the spine at the base of the skull if they became uncontrollable. Six were killed in this manner, more than the number killed by the Romans.

The Carthaginians continued to use them and Hannibal again fielded 80 against Scipio at Zama in 202 BC, the final battle near Carthage of the second Punic war. The battle ended in complete victory for the Romans by using skirmishes against the elephants instead of meeting them in closed ranks.

In dictating his peace terms to the Carthaginians, Scipio required that all of their trained elephants be handed over and they refrain from training any more. Those which he captured were taken to Rome and used occasionally during the next ten years, the last time in any major war being the battle of Pydna in 168 BC, where Perseus king of Macedonia was defeated, African and Asian elephants being used together.

The final appearance of the African elephant in any numbers on the battlefield was at the battle of Thapsus in 47 BC when 64 were used against the Roman army commanded by Julius Caesar, half of which number had been sent from Numidia and were only partly trained. These were routed by the Romans because Caesar had had the foresight to have some sent over from Italy before the battle to teach his soldiers familiarity with them and how to kill them, as well as habituating his cavalry. Caesar was not in favour of war elephants because he considered that long years of training were necessary and then they were uncertain, just as liable to harm one's own troops as to harm the enemy.

CLASSICAL CONTROVERSIES

Classical scholars have gone to great lengths to try to prove that Hannibal crossed the Alps with African elephants. Although some Carthaginian coins of Catagena picture African elephants, a 3rd century BC Etruscan coin depicts an Asian. Some have carried it further by claiming that African forest elephants must have been used by the Carthaginians and the Romans because their elephants were allegedly smaller than Asian elephants.

It was an ancient belief that the Asian elephant was larger than the African. Megasthenes wrote about 300 BC:

> India also breeds elephants both in the greatest numbers and of the largest size, providing them with sustenance in abundance; and it is because of this food that the elephants of this land are much more powerful than those produced in Libya . . .

Polybius had written of the battle of Raphia which had taken place 37 years earlier, before he was born:

> Most of Ptolemy's elephants shirked the fight, as is the way of African elephants. For they cannot stand the smell and trumpeting of the Indian elephants; moreover, *so it seems to me* [my emphasis], they are taken aback by their great size and strength, so that they turn tail before getting to close quarters.

Another translation reads: 'terrified *I suppose* [my emphasis] by the great size and strength of the Indians . . .' Thus enlarging upon this conjecture Pliny was to write almost 300 hundred years later: 'African elephants fear Indian, because the Indian is bigger'. But he also wrote: 'Ethiopia produces elephants that rival those of India, being 30 feet high . . .' This observation has seemingly been dismissed because of the exaggerated height, but who knows if Pliny actually wrote 30 feet or if the scale of measurement was misinterpreted? Perhaps some later scribe considered that a little extra emphasis was needed.

Nevertheless, that Asian elephants were bigger than African became the accepted view until almost the end of the 19th century. In 1926 a distinguished classicist, Sir William Tarn, dismissed the idea that the African elephants were of a smaller race, based on the weight of 34 tusks which Ptolemy Auletes, father of Cleopatra, gave to the great Temple of Apollo at Didyma about 55 BC. These had an average weight each of 14.4 or 18.1 kg (depending upon which ancient measure is used). Sir William Gowers, a former Governor of Uganda who had hunted elephants, challenged this idea on the basis that the tusks were not large enough for such a purpose – one offered nothing but the best to the gods. If the Ptolemies had for centuries a monopoly on all of the ivory obtained from northeast Africa then the royal storehouse at Alexandria would have been filled with the finest tusks procurable and 18 kg would have been small by East African standards. But Ptolemy Auletes had been in exile and this gift was probably one of his bribes in his attempt to regain power. As an exile he would not have had the best resources at his disposal.

Gowers argued that African elephants used by Carthage and Egypt must have been of the small forest race and also, he claimed, the Belgians found the larger bush elephant was intractable. He proposed that the forest race once extended to the Red Sea and the Gulf of Aden. I would concur with Tarn and if the African elephants *were* smaller and feared the Indian elephants, then it was because they were young elephants insufficiently trained. No doubt the Ptolemies and Carthaginians rather than waiting some 20 years for them to grow, used the young ones as soon as they were trained. The slow rate of growth may have led them to believe that they would not grow much bigger, whereas from long use the Asian elephants were mature and fully grown. In this respect the comment by Filippo Pigafetta in 1591 is of interest:

> When in our time, in Portugal, Italy or Germany, these animals are found much smaller in size [than wild African ones] it is because they are young ones, and were taken to those countries at an early age in order to domesticate them.

Much of our knowledge of who, in antiquity, used what race of elephants comes from coins. Classical scholars have pretended to identify, often from a single coin, whether an elephant was African or Indian. On some coins the image is clear enough, but even so no credence whatsoever can be given to the interpretation that the elephant commemorated on a coin indicated the type of elephant used. The artist designing the coin would model the only elephant that was available to him or that he knew from memory, so if he had at some stage seen an African elephant, then he would portray an African elephant. We can surely have no faith in what coins struck more than 2000 years ago depicted.

ANCIENT SKILLS

The most remarkable facts to emerge from these accounts of yore are that the ancients were able to train elephants, which are nervous animals, to warfare. Just as importantly, they successfully overcame enormous logistics of transporting such huge numbers of them, over both land and sea, and of keeping them fed.

Clearly an abundance of skill and knowledge has long been lost to mankind although, as J.H. Williams has shown in his remarkable book *Elephant Bill*, elephants can be trained to put up with almost anything, especially if they have confidence in their handlers.

The end of the use of war elephants by the Romans was not universal; they continued to do battle in Asia for another 1500 years, playing a part in the conquests of the great Mongol tartars. It was the introduction of gunpowder which finally spelt their demise as weapons of war.

There are no reliable records of the ancient Chinese having trained elephants, although the animal was numerous in their country and was kept in zoos in the second millennium. The Chinese knew in the 2nd century BC that elephants were domesticated in Thailand and in 128 BC one Chang K'ien reported that war elephants were used in India, Persia and Cambodia. A clay figure of a draped elephant from the T'ang period (AD 618–907) (page 40) suggests that domesticated elephants were used at that time, although they may have been imported. In Yunnan in AD 860 they were used for ploughing and in Canton they were used for putting criminals to death up until the 10th century.

Marco Polo wrote that the great Kublai Khan, founder of the Mongol dynasty in China, had employed war elephants since 1272 and was borne into battle in a castle carried by four elephants. In 1277 he captured 200 from the Burmese. Marco Polo claimed the Khan had 5000 and the Burmese 2000, but these were probably exaggerations. About AD 1340 the Delhi Sultanate had 3000 but only 750–1000 were actually battle elephants, the others being young animals or what the army today would classify as 'not battleworthy'. When the Sultanate was overthrown by Timur in 1398 the number of war elephants had fallen to only 120.

In 1588 King Raja Sinha I attacked the Portuguese fort at Colombo with 2200 elephants while much later, at the taking of Delhi in 1739 by Nadir Shah of Persia, 300 war elephants were captured. The numbers were habitually exaggerated for tactical reasons or simple flattery and whereas the Mogul Emperor Aurengzeb was said to have 3000–4000, a doubting French traveller in 1679, Jean Baptiste Tavernier, confirmed that there were actually only 80–90. However as recently as the 1930s the King of Nepal fielded up to 315 elephants on a royal hunt.

Elephants were on the strength of the Royal Engineers in the Indian Army from a very early date up until 1895, when Daisy the last and oldest pensioner died. In the war against Tipu Sultan in 1799, 1500 elephants were used under the command of Captain Sandys. They were used again in war in 1867, when 44 were shipped from Bombay for the carriage of artillery in the Abyssinian campaign. Nineteen were required to carry the four 12-pounder 'Armstrong' cannons, the barrels of which alone each weighed almost a ton. With all of the bits and pieces, some elephants were carrying almost 2 tons. Others bore the 8" mortars. Sir Robert Napier, the British Commander in Chief rode on one to impress the Abyssinians, terrifying them. The care with which these elephants were looked after is borne out by the fact that 39 were returned safely to Bombay after the successful conclusion of the campaign, the five which died

FIG. 15.1   *Military elephants in India, 1879.*

being believed to have done so from malnourishment. The expedition often had difficulty finding the elephants sufficient food.

In the Second World War after the Japanese overran Malaya, an Elephant Company attached to the XIVth Army was formed in Burma, which played an important part in the war. The elephants' role was summed up by Field-Marshall Sir William Slim in his foreword to J.H.Williams' book *Elephant Bill*:

> They built hundreds of bridges for us, they helped to build and launch more ships for us than Helen ever did for Greece. Without them our retreat from Burma would have been even more arduous and our advance to its liberation slower and more difficult. We of the XIVth Army were – and are – proud of our Elephant Companies.

ELEPHANTS IN BRITAIN

The first elephant to be seen in Britain since prehistoric times was perhaps not that presented by the King of France in 1255 to Henry III, who ordered the Sheriff to 'cause without delay, to be built at our Tower of London one house forty feet long, and twenty feet deep, for our elephant', but one brought by the Romans in their invasion in 54 BC.

It is alleged that the defending Briton Cassivelaunus was confronted by an elephant clad in a coat of mail by the aid of which the crossing of the Thames near Brentford was effected. Some classical scholars consider this a doubtful tale as it was not mentioned by Caesar in his account. Perhaps he never mentioned it because, unlike Antiochus I, he preferred to give all of the credit to his legionnaires, rather than admit that the Britons fled in panic at the sight of a single elephant as one Roman writer alleged. It is a remarkable thought that the Roman conquest of Britain may have been achieved by a single elephant.

Henry III's lived for 12 years. Perhaps he obtained it after hearing the account of his brother Richard, Earl of Cornwall, who, travelling in Italy some ten years before, had been met at Cremona by an elephant carrying a band of musicians on its back. They were not uncommon pets in Europe in the 16th century and in 1741 Thamas Kouli Khan sent 14 as gifts to the Russian Emperor at St Petersburg. Because she coveted it so much, one was presented to Queen Elizabeth I by Henry IV of France, glad to rid himself of such an expensive luxury. In 1623 another was sent to James I by the King of Spain, which 'cost the King as much to maintain as a garrison'. By 1865 it was reported that from one to eight were being imported into Britain every year.

THE MYTH OF INTRACTABILITY

In *Back to Africa*, Moore and Munnion aptly explode the myth that African elephants are not tractable and cannot be trained like their Asian counterparts. The American trainer 'Slim' Lewis asserts that African circus-trained elephants respond to a command much more quickly than do Asian elephants and, indeed, for this reason you have to be more on your toes when dealing with them. All of the evidence available also indicates that it is the Asian elephant which is the more aggressive.

The famous London Zoo elephant Jumbo was a 3.32 m high 6 tonne 24 year old African elephant, considered completely tractable although he had had ungovernable fits of temper from about the age of 20. After his death his fifth upper molars were found to be malerupted which may have been the cause of his temper, suffering a giant toothache. He met an untimely death by being run into by a train in the United States. An adult African bull elephant Jumbo II was the star attraction in the US Cole Brothers Circus in 1935. Bull elephants, whether African or Asian, are considered by elephant handlers to be much more predictable than cows, but they are less often used in circuses because of the great size they grow to, which poses problems of feeding and transportation.

So how the belief originated that African elephants could not be trained, no-one seems to know. It may even be an ancient myth enshrined for millennia dating from the defeat of Ptolemy IV's African elephants by Asian ones.

Overlooked also has been Carl Hagenbeck's bet. Hagenbeck related how in the 1870s he trained five young African elephants in 24 hours as a boast. The animals had been newly imported to the Berlin Zoological Gardens and were each about 1.7 m high, that is, about five years old. Hagenbeck trained them to accept riders and carry loads first by having the riders keep climbing onto their backs. All except one were immediately shaken off. The elephants were then fed titbits and quietened down and the process repeated. Within five hours three of them had accepted their riders and the following morning the other two followed suit. Filled sacks were then hung on their backs which, by constant encouragement and bribery with titbits, they came to accept by midday. As he put it: '. . . the wild elephants [were] changed into domestic animals after a few hours' schooling'.

Sanderson alleged there was no Asian elephant which could not be easily subjugated, whatever its size or age. A 1658 Sri Lankan account states that captured elephants obey their keepers after eight days. It takes a month or so to train a Burmese timber elephant caught in the wild, depending upon its temperament. Then for the first four or five years they are used as baggage animals and only when they are 25–30 years old are they considered strong enough to be skilled timber elephants, becoming veterans by the age of 40 or so.

ACCIDENTS WILL HAPPEN

Although for many years after the conquest of India by the British, elephants continued to be employed by the princes and nobles, in the latter half of the 19th century their use was prohibited in Calcutta because of the many accidents caused by them frightening horses. Asian elephants have occasionally caused problems elsewhere. One broke loose in Venice at the beginning of the 18th century and was killed by a cannon shot 'after it had committed considerable ravages in that city'. Mindful of this, when one became intractable at Geneva in 1820 and chased its attendants, it was enticed into an enclosure and two holes made in the wall through which two cannons were sited. The elephant was then shot at point-blank range with one of them, the cannon ball passing through the head behind the right eye and out behind the left ear, to hit a wall at the other side of the enclosure. Hardly surprisingly, the elephant died almost immediately and thus suffered a better fate than poor Chuni at Exeter 'Change:

> At this time he had from a hundred and ten to a hundred and twenty balls in him . . . Cartmell thrust the sword into his body to the hilt. The sanguinary conflict had now lasted nearly an hour; yet, with astonishing alacrity, he again rose, without evincing any sign that he had sustained vital injury . . .

He was eventually brought down by firing point blank into his ear. *The Times* newspaper reported:

> No less than 152 bullets were expended before he fell to the ground, where he lay nearly motionless, and was soon despatched with a sword, which after being secured upon the end of a rifle, was plunged into his neck. The quantity of blood that flowed from him was very considerable, and flooded the den to a considerable depth.

The post mortem examination showed that he had a large abscess at the root of one of his teeth which may have been the cause of his paroxysms of rage.

The worst recorded incident was that of the great Munich Elephant Panic in 1888 when eight Asian elephants in the Hagenbeck Circus street procession

FIG. 15.2   *How to shoot an elephant, Geneva style (1820).*

created havoc amongst the crowds, countless numbers of people being seriously injured and at least one woman killed. The elephants were alarmed by a traction engine disguised as a dragon which suddenly began to move and spurted steam at the hindmost elephants, causing them to rush forward. Hagenbeck desperately tried to bring them under control and would have succeeded in doing so but for the swarming mass of excited onlookers which attacked them with sticks, umbrellas and knives, driving them down the street. They were then driven back by the Light Horse Dragoons, but turned into a narrow side street, broke through the crowd and, according to the press reports, a frightful panic ensued with everybody fleeing screaming. Horses bolted and the police and military broke ranks. In a flash hundreds of spectators were pushed over, the rest fell over them as they ran away and countless broken bones were the result. The commotion in the city was reported as indescribable. Had the public remained calm, the elephants would not have panicked.

In 1893 a 'monster bull elephant' named Jim, which belonged to George Sanger's circus, said to be 75 years old and presumably an Asian, ran amok in Finsbury Park when being taken for a walk. Although not seriously injuring anyone, it created mild havoc, charging and damaging a band-stand, wrecking various gardens, smashing down seven walls, walking through closed gates, wrenching down iron railings and eventually calming down in a field near Tottenham, where his keeper was able to hobble his front legs after 4½ hours of freedom.

In 1930 four took part in London's Lord Mayor's Show and were involved in an accident in which 30 people were injured, two seriously. The elephants reacted angrily to a red replica of a lion held aloft by students. Trumpeting, the biggest elephant seized the mascot and threw it on the ground and all trampled on it. They then continued their stately march as if nothing had happened, but as in Munich, the crowd stampeded in fright. A correspondence followed in *The Times* newspaper as to why the elephants should react to a rather shoddy imitation of a lion.

In 1973 the Corporation of London refused to allow an elephant to take part in the same show although it was not aware of this precedent, the grounds for refusal being that it had never occurred before! In fact elephants had taken part in the show in 1876 without incident.

In 1979 there was almost as much consternation as the 1930 rumpus when a young bull elephant charged towards the Royal box at a circus charity performance attended by Princess Anne and Captain Mark Phillips. The *Daily Telegraph* newspaper reported:

> A bull elephant charged towards the Royal box at a gala circus performance in London last night, narrowly missing Princess Anne and her husband, Captain Mark Phillips.
> After the three-ton elephant, named Maxie, lumbered past, Princess Anne, looking shaken, commented: 'I'm glad they have good eyesight'.

It transpired that a special entrance had been made for Princess Anne, which the 13 year old Maxie saw and made for to reach the stables after being upset in the ring by a cow elephant.

Circus elephants running amok, or trying to, is not unusual. In 1922 William Hornaday wrote:

> So many men have been killed by elephants in this country [America] that of late years the idea has steadily been gaining ground that elephants are naturally ill-tempered, and vicious to a dangerous extent.

In 1889 an elephant exhibited by The People's Palace and Aquarium Company in Scarborough took a sudden dislike to a former detective in the Leeds police force. Along with some friends, he threw down a penny for the elephant to pick up. The elephant was approaching the penny when it suddenly gave a scream and rushed at the man, hitting him in the chest with its trunk, crushing his chest and breaking several of his ribs. The unfortunate ex-detective took the company to court for damages. It was suggested that he must have done something to the elephant beforehand and the jury's verdict was that the elephant was not an animal dangerous to man. On appeal the judge ruled:

> It cannot be doubted that elephants as a class have not been reduced

to a state of subjection; they still remain wild and untamed, though
individuals are brought to a degree of tameness which amounts to
domestication. A person, therefore, who keeps an elephant, does so
at his own risk ...

More recently, in 1970, a young African elephant which roamed freely in a
safari park in Zimbabwe knocked over an elderly lady because she didn't have a
sweet for it. The lady broke her wrist in the fall and sued the park's owners. In
this case the judge was moved to comment:

> Courts have had enough difficulty in speculating on the behaviour
> of 'the reasonable man', without having the additional burden
> thrust upon them of speculating on the motives of 'a reasonable
> elephant', and it relieves me to be able to find that I am not asked to
> shoulder this burden.

Close managing of elephants in captivity requires a great deal of courage and
understanding on the part of the handler and fatal accidents to handlers are
relatively common. What these accounts show, however, is that the Asian
elephant does not have such a spotless record in captivity, yet it is the African
which gets the blame for intractability.

The continually-on-guard circus handler and his charge would seem to have a
very different relationship from the close contact of the Burmese oozie and his
timber elephant which lives in relative freedom amongst its companions when
not working during the day. The Asian working elephant's obedience and
gentle nature are indeed surprising considering the cruelty to which some of
them are, or used to be, subjected at capture. It is one thing that the elephant
does seem to forget.

USING AFRICAN ELEPHANTS

The Negus of Ethiopia in AD 533 received the Emperor Justinian's envoy while
seated in a chariot drawn by four elephants. In AD 571 he is said to have sent an
army of Africans with 13 elephants to destroy the Kaaba at Mecca in retaliation
for the desecration of the Christian church that he had built at Sanaa. The attack
was defeated by the Prophet's grandfather (the invaders are believed to have
actually succumbed to smallpox), an event recorded in the Qu'ran and still
commemorated today in the Muslim calendar. In modern times, this was to have
surprising and disastrous repercussions for the Iraqui leader, Saddam Hussein,
said to have based his belief that he would win the 1991 Gulf War against the
Americans on the fact that the emblem of the American President's Republican
Party is the elephant. 'When I heard of it I was completely surprised. I said,
"Praise be to God, praise be to God".' But he was not fated to be as successful as
the Prophet's grandfather.

In AD 797 an African elephant was presented by Harun al Rashid to the
Emperor Charlemagne, but in more recent history the first record of domestication of an African elephant comes from South Africa, where Peter Kolb

reported in 1719 that an elephant was harnessed to a ship as a test of strength and demonstrated its ability to haul the ship along. One deduces that it must have been tame and accustomed to harness!

Filippo Pigafetta had advocated using African elephants in 1591: 'The natives do not know how to tame these animals, of whom so much use might be made in transporting merchandise, and in many other ways'.

Andrew Sparrman, reporting on his visit to the Cape in 1772–1776, thought that elephants could be castrated and domesticated. He acknowledged the difficulty of feeding such a large animal and doubted whether many private people could keep them but 'it certainly would be very proper for government to endeavour to tame these animals, and use them in its service'.

Yet where was the source of the African elephants reported in 1763 to be 4.1 m high at the shoulder and worth £900, as opposed to those from Ceylon being worth four times that sum?

THE GREAT ELEPHANT EXPERIMENT

The next introduction of Asian elephants into Africa after Napier's Abyssinian campaign was not so fortunate. The Germans had proposed using them in 1873 to explore the Congo but it was not until 1878 that the Bombay government presented four to the King of the Belgians, for use in training African elephants in the Congo. These, standing over 2.4 m high and therefore some 30 years old, were landed at Msesani on the Tanganyika coast in January 1879 and marched to Dar es Salaam. On 3rd July they set out with their Indian mahouts to march west across Tanganyika to the Congo, the first staging post to be Mpwapwa, 400 km distant. Three of the elephants carried packs and one carried the expedition leader, Captain Carter, and another. The large bull, Sundar Gaj, had a very bad temper and decided that he didn't like it at all, taking to frequently bolting until his legs were chained and spiked anklets fitted. Unlike the Abyssinian expedition's experience, the natives seemed very little in awe of them and raised angry scenes demanding compensation for the elephants trampling through their crops.

> Yet amid their many real trials of strength, difficulties, and occasional danger, as they clambered up and down, over boulders and tree-trunks, across treacherous bogs and shifty, stony torrent-beds, and up hills which made them pause, look round for help, and trumpet with remonstrance – amid all this these noble beasts at all times exhibited unfailing judgement, patience and willingness. Their pluck under their too great labours compelled an admiring pity for them. I mention these facts to show the splendid qualities of these grandest of 'weight-carriers'.

So wrote the missionary Rankin who accompanied the party.

They arrived at Mpwapwa 33 days later on August 3rd, having covered the distance at an average rate of 12 km a day compared with the recommended 28 for a pack elephant. Here they were obliged to remain for a month awaiting their

Belgian counterparts. Captain Carter immediately sent off an enthusiastic message to King Leopold: 'The elephant experiment has now been proved a complete success'.

This 'complete success' he attributed to the facts that the elephants had now been exposed for 23 days to the tsetse fly without effect; they had maintained themselves upon the food of the country and they had shown themselves to be able to cover all types of ground with up to double the recommended weight of baggage. Furthermore, the cost of keeping them for the 33 days, including the reparations paid for damaged crops, was less than £2, about £49 at today's value.

Unfortunately Carter had been too hasty. Ten days later Sundar Gaj suddenly died and the death of a second elephant soon followed. Rankin spent two days dissecting Sundar Gaj but, hardly surprisingly in view of his lack of veterinary expertise, could find nothing wrong. The heart had no appearance of disease (it weighed 14 kg and was 40 cm long, its weight being what one would expect to find in an adult cow African elephant of just under 3 tonnes so he was not a very large elephant). But by then the elephants were very thin and their backbones 'stood up six or seven inches from their flanks', which Rankin attributed to them not having been adapted to foraging for themselves as in India they had been stall fed on white bread and other foods. Only a little corn and rice had been given as a supplement. Coupled with this they had been overloaded, carrying 545 kg, 680 and at one time, 770, against a probable maximum of 550.

On 28th October the remaining two arrived at Tabora 700 km distant from Mpwapwa and still 200 km from the shores of L. Tanganyika, having kept similar time. One elephant then died shortly after arrival and the other, left at Tabora, after living for some months, was reported as having 'wasted away and died of nostalgia'.

As a result of this misfortune the experiment was abandoned. Captain Carter himself was murdered on his return march. Rankin laid much blame on the mahouts who showed little concern for the elephants and also made no attempt to teach the Zanzibar Arabs, who were supposed to take over from them, how to manage the elephants. Nonetheless he considered that the aims of the exercise were still possible:

> I have not the shadow of a doubt that there is yet a great future in
> Africa for the elephant, especially when the stage of capturing and
> taming the native species has been reached.

Two years after the failure of Captain Carter's expedition six Asian elephants were sent by the Khedive Ismail from Cairo to Gordon in the Sudan. They travelled 3200 km to Makraka, south-west of Lado, swimming the Nile six times. By Christmas Day 1881 only half of the number was still alive and they were scarcely used for transport as there was nobody to look after them. Emin Pasha, governor of the province, stated that Gordon, 'for the sake of a few guineas', had sent back the attendants which came with them from India without first obtaining any replacement handlers (Captain Carter's Indians had each cost 1.2p per day, or 31p at today's value). The aim had been to obtain young

Africans for handlers but, hardly surprisingly, none were produced by the local chiefs despite their promises to do so. Emin Pasha wrote: 'I have no doubt that, with sufficient care and a trained staff for the purpose, elephants would save us much of the continued annoyance from porters'. It seems the remainder died, for we hear no more about them.

Then in 1899 much publicity was given in the French press to a young orphaned African elephant that had been trained to do simple tasks by missionaries of the mission of the Holy Spirit at Gobo in the Congo. King Leopold therefore decided to try again without using Asian elephants and charged Commandant Laplume with the task of setting up a domestication centre. This Laplume did at the confluence of the Uele and Bomakandi rivers, and by 1910 had collected a herd of 35 young elephants. This was not achieved without some difficulty. Baron Fallon, who reported on the experiments, noted: 'Many valued assistants were killed ...'

By the end of 1902 Laplume had caught four young ones which he began to train. He then adopted another method in which some 20 hunters fired guns to stampede the herd. A number of rope carriers, with ropes wound around their bodies, then flung themselves onto the desired elephants, quickly roped a hind leg and tied it to a tree. The hunters then stood over the roped elephant and fired at the mother if she attempted to save it, shooting her if necessary. Once other elephants were trained the captives were taken back to camp by pairs of trained elephants which quickly subdued any resistance.

The method was only applied to elephants of 1.5–1.8 m height; larger than this, they were too powerful to handle or train, while smaller ones were not easily reared.

At first they took many years to train until in 1918 a fresh team took over the task, and in 1919 imported seven Sri Lankan mahouts to teach them elephant handling. The mahouts did not stay for long, nervous of the rumours of the cannibalistic tendencies of some of the Congolese tribes, but their assistance reduced the period for complete training to eight months. This was still much longer than Carl Hagenbeck's 48 hours, taking more than a month before a man could mount one.

By 1935 the station had about 50 elephants, some of which were 30 years old, and a second station had been set up in 1927 at Gangala na Bodio near to the Garamba Park, where there were another 40. A number of private concerns began capturing and training so a law was passed controlling capture.

Baron Fallon gave the following comparisons: one trained elephant could do the work of 50 men in clearing land, was equivalent to four carthorses, 12 oxen or one Fordson tractor (1930s model).

Captain Keith Caldwell, seconded from the Kenya Game Department to Uganda to set up a game department there, in response to the criticisms of the 'wholesale slaughter' of elephants in East Africa and the clamour for domestication measures to be adopted, visited the station in 1925 with a view to seeing whether or not he could set up such a centre. His reaction was to produce as many arguments against domestication as possible, not least that it would be impossible to find work for the thousands of elephants involved.

FIG. 15.3   *Elephant capture in India, circa 1920. Tame elephants entering the stockade.*

He considered that as far as the Belgian project was concerned, the Burmese keddah or stockade system should be introduced for capturing. An elephant spent an average of ten years in the school before being strong enough to work and early attempts to work them at a younger age had led to heavy mortality.

When Caldwell visited the station he reported only half a dozen mahouts or cornacs having been killed and this was due to their own fault: 'There has never been a case of an elephant having to be destroyed for vice or even becoming habitually bad-tempered,' he wrote.

In 1948, E.H. Peacock, a former director of forestry and former game warden in Burma, who was also familiar with the Burmese keddah method of capture, likewise paid the station a visit with a possible view to creating a training school in Northern Rhodesia. He came to the same conclusion as Caldwell, that the method of capture and training was uneconomical and the Burmese method should be tried. Neither report was taken further.

In 1993 only four elephants remained of an average age of 38 years and only one was a trained 'monitor'. Despite Belgian claims the project was never a great success because there was no real use for the elephants in that part of the world. They were used simply as farm animals, harnessed to ploughs or drawing carts to transport timber and other commodities to the railway. In later years they were just kept as a curiosity and by 1960 their numbers had declined to 15. No-one else took up the idea.

Superior to a tractor as they were, better success would have been attained had the large savannah elephant been used, which could then have carried the loads on its back instead of pulling them in carts. It *was* successful in proving

FIG. 15.4 *Tying up the captured elephants.*

conclusively that African elephants could be used just as well as their Asian counterparts. Now the hope is that the survivors of this experiment will be trained to carry tourists on safari as is done in Botswana with savannah elephants.

There is a belief that they require excessive attention when young to the extent that the keeper must virtually live with them and that they only accept one keeper, with instances of replacements being killed through jealousy. This may be true if the young elephant is kept isolated as a prisoner, but unlikely to be so if more than one are reared together and they are allowed a certain freedom of movement, beyond the grim confines of an 'elephant house' in a zoo.

AN INVALUABLE ANIMAL

In Burma it was found that elephant calves born in captivity could be trained much more easily than captured wild elephants. So successful was this that eventually the timber extraction Bombay Burma Corporation's strength of 2000 was able to balance its deaths from births and only rarely was it necessary to capture new stock.

Prior to the war some 6000 elephants had been used by the British in Burma to work in the jungles and at the ports, but the tonnage of teak logs extracted was half of that in 1982 and mechanical extraction was practically unknown. With double the extraction volume now taking place mechanical extraction had to be used as the sources of timber became more and more remote, added to which only one third of the number of elephants was in use. But timber elephants are

FIG. 15.5   *A big bull recently captured.*

still required for selective exploitation and difficult terrain, and attempts were being made to build up the herds again by capturing from the wild. Although some capture is now by use of immobilizing drugs, still the majority is by the keddah method and the method of enticing with trained elephants. Over a period of seven years ending in 1981 the target was 200 wild elephants a year, although the actual number reported caught was roughly half of this.

The value of the Asian elephant in forestry in Asia is too well known to elaborate upon. In 1861 every village in one area of Thailand had 50–100 tame elephants for transport purposes. In 1878 the lowest price for an Asian elephant was £150 for a young one. Good working cows were £200–£300 and the best quality bull tuskers were up to £2000. In today's terms that would represent £3750 up to £50 000.

In Kandy in Sri Lanka, elephant capture was an annual event. Each year the headmen would be called into council by the chiefs to report where damage to crops had occurred. Instead of shooting the elephants as had once been done, plans were then laid to capture them where they were the most numerous. In India it was the Indian-born Englishman, Sanderson, who first introduced the Burmese keddah method of capture. The Muslim conqueror of Mysore, Hyder

FIG. 15.6 *Chit Sayah, 'the biggest elephant in Burma', circa 1920. The original description continues: 'Height 9ft 6ins, girth 14ft 7ins, at his best. He is now an old elephant and was much overworked by his former owner and has never fully recovered'.*

Ali, had tried unsuccessfully to use it in the mid-18th century and in 1867 a Colonel Pearse also failed. Sanderson, who had been in the Canal Engineering Department, used 800 men and captured 55 at his first attempt.

The average pace of a laden elephant on good level ground is slightly more than 5.6 kph, fast animals doing 6 kph. The maximum march is five hours, for the back does not stand up to heavy loads for long periods, causing sores on thinskinned animals. They are capable swimmers, Sanderson reporting a batch which swam for six hours and, after a rest on a sandbank, continued for another three, not one elephant being lost. A speed of up to 2.7 kph has been recorded and a non-stop distance of 50 km. This record distance was achieved in America in 1856 by an Asian elephant lost overboard from a ship coming into port in a heavy gale, which swam to shore in Mt Pleasant Harbour, South Carolina. Two young bull African elephants spent about 30 hours swimming 35 km across L. Kariba.

There are few places that an elephant cannot go.

A USE FOR AFRICAN ELEPHANTS

Clearly, as Pigafetta foresaw, the future of the African elephant is as a transport animal. If there were people with the courage and ability of Randall Jay Moore to initiate training, and he has also trained Africans as handlers in a matter of months, then the benefits to Africa, let alone the elephant, would be incalculable.

Presently thousands of square kilometres of Africa north of the equator come to a standstill for six months of every year, not on account of the tsetse fly but because of 'black cotton' soil, a greyish-black hard clay which becomes a soft glutinous sticky mess as soon as it rains. The elephant, with its dinner-plate feet, travels over it with ease and fords, or swims if needs be, the streams which have grown overnight from tinkling rivulets no more than 10 m wide to $\frac{1}{2}$ km wide rushing torrents. Such conditions occur over great parts of the southern Sudan, the Central African Republic, Chad, Nigeria, Niger, right across to Senegal, a vast area that can only be penetrated year-round by railways or hard road, both of which are prohibitively expensive to construct on this type of soil. The elephant, on the other hand, could open up this vast untamed area with ease, at no other cost than that required to train it.

In the Central African Republic, as soon as the rains arrive no lorry transporter leaves the capital Bangui in the south on the 1500 km journey to El Fasher in the Sudan with his loads of timber and other merchandise. He must wait patiently for six months until the roads dry out again. But anyone with a pack of trained elephants could continue trading throughout the year, for the elephants would require no petrol or diesel oil and would feed themselves on the way. Not only that, they could travel as the crow flies, shortening the journey by some 250 km. Such advantages over wheeled transport would far outstrip the few dollars' worth of ivory that they carry and double the economic tempo for a whole range of industries.

Extrapolating from the recommended loads for Asian elephants, one medium-sized cow elephant of about 30 years of age standing 2.5 m high at the shoulder and weighing some 1.8 tonnes could carry almost half a tonne on her back in addition to the gear (chain hobbles and harness) which would weigh about 200 kg. A bull of the same age could probably carry three quarters of a tonne in addition to his gear. So one would need nine grown bull elephants for every 7 tonne truck, or 13 for every 10 tonne truck. Obviously a large bull would be able to carry far more.

Some put an Asian elephant's load at only one tenth of the animal's weight and consider that one adult elephant carries what six small ponies can. Writing of elephants in the former Indo-China, Bazé considered that:

> Transport of goods by elephants is not an economical proposition. The animal cannot go for long without water, eats several hundred pounds of fodder a day and requires frequent rests ... thirty miles a day is the average ...

I haue rid vpon an elephant since I came to this Court, determining one day (by Gods leaue) to haue my picture expressed in my next Booke, sitting vpon an Elephant,

FIG. 15.7   *Tom Coriate 'Traveller for the English Wits: Greeting' (1616).*

But its value depends upon what the alternative is. In this part of Africa there is no alternative and fodder and water are not problems in the wet season. Time also has never been considered to be of the essence in Africa.

Previous ideas on the use of African elephants have related to areas where they have no advantage over more conventional alternatives. The economic importance of the elephant in maintaining year-round trade in this vast area of Africa has gone unimagined. Joining north and south of this area throughout the year the African elephant could become the linchpin to a new opening-up of Africa. Rather than spending money on trying to save the elephant by protecting it in national parks and game reserves or on gimmicky research like tracking its movements by satellite at the cost of a quarter of a million dollars, money should be put to a strategic training programme for transport animals, with as many centres as possible set up *north* of the equator, providing careers for redundant circus hands by enlisting elephant trainers, not scientists, to operate them.

In 1859 Tennent postulated the demise of elephants as transport animals:

> ... there may be a question on the score of prudence and economy.
> In the wild and unopened parts of the country, where rivers are to
> be forded, and forests are only traversed by jungle paths, their

> labour is of value, in certain contingencies, in the conveyance of stores, ... But in more highly civilized districts, and wherever macadamized roads admit of the employment of horses and oxen for draught, I apprehend that the services of the elephant might, with advantage, be gradually reduced, if not altogether dispensed with.

Those conditions are not likely to occur in many parts of Africa in the foreseeable future.

With wider vision than Tennent, it was also in 1859 that the King of Siam offered to send to Abraham Lincoln, President of the United States, a number of pairs of elephants which he considered could be released in the forests:

> ... and, if the climate should prove favorable to the elephants, we are of opinion, that, after a while, they will increase till there be large herds, as there are on the continent of Asia, until the inhabitants of America will be able to catch them and tame them, and use them as beasts of burden ... since they can travel where carriage and other roads have not been made.

When President Lincoln was asked what should be done with the elephants if they came he replied that he did not know, unless 'they were used to stamp out the rebellion'. So the offer was declined.

We need greater foresight than President Lincoln to save this great beast which Pliny said possesses virtues rare even in man. The beast of which the poet Donne wrote, '... foe to none, suspects no enemies.' Of which Sanderson wrote, 'Amongst all created creatures the elephant stands unrivalled in gentleness'. And the Old Testament: 'He is the chief of the ways of God'.

COMMON AND SCIENTIFIC NAMES OF PLANTS MENTIONED IN THE TEXT

Scientific name	Common name
Acacia albida	Apple-ring thorn tree
Acacia erioloba	Camel thorn
Acacia luederitzii	Kalahari Sand acacia
Acacia nigrescens	Knob-thorn
Acacia senegal	Three-thorned acacia
Acacia tanganyikensis	Tanganyika acacia
Acacia tortilis	Umbrella thorn
Acacia xanthophloea	Yellow-fever tree
Adansonia digitata	Baobab tree
Arundinaria spp.	Bamboo
Baikiaea plurijuga	Rhodesian teak
Balanites aegyptiaca	Shepherd's bush or desert date
Balanites wilsoniana	—
Borassus aethiopicus	Borassus palm
Brachystegia spp.	Msasa
Brachystegia boehmii	Prince of Wales's feathers
Cassia abbreviata	Long-tail cassia
Chrysophyllum albidum	White star apple tree
Colophospermum mopane	Mopane
Combretum binderianum	—
Combretum collinum	Variable combretum
Combretum imberbe	Leadwood
Combretum wattii	Round-leaved bushwillow
Combretum zeyheri	Large-fruited combretum
Commiphora spp.	Myrrh
Cordia sinensis	Grey-leaved cordia

Cynometra alexandrii	Uganda ironwood
Detarium microcarpum	—
Dichrostachys cinerea	Sickle bush
Diospyros abyssinica	Giant diospyros
Entandrophragma angolense	Budongo mahogany
Ericaceae spp.	Giant ericacea
Euclea pseudebenus	Ebony tree
Feronia limonia	—
Grewia spp.	Grewia
Grewia flavescens	Donkeyberry shrub
Hagenia abyssinica	Hagenia
Hyphaene natalensis	Southern ilala palm
Hyphaene ventricosa	Raffia palm
Hyphaene coriacea	Doum palm
Julbernardia globiflora	Munondo
Khaya anthotheca	African mahogany
Maesopsis eminii	Musizi
Manilkara hexandra	Milk berry
Massularia acuminata	—
Melia volkensii	Melia
Musa spp.	Plantain
Pachypodium lealii	Bottelboom
Panda oleosa	—
Parinarii (excelsa) holstii	Grey plum
Piliostigma thonningii	Monkeybread
Portulacaria afra	Spekboom
Protea spp.	Protea
Pterocarpus angolensis	Bloodwood or fried-egg tree
Rinorea spp.	Rinorea
Saccoglottis gabonensis	—
Salvadora persica	Mustard tree
Scheelea rostrata	—
Sclerocarya birrea	Marula
Sterculia spp.	Chestnut
Sterculia africana	Tick tree
Strychnos pungens	Nightshade
Tamarindus indica	Tamarind
Tamarix usneoides	Wild tamarisk
Tectona grandis	Teak
Terminalia sericea	Silver terminalia
Tieghemella heckelii	—
Uvariopsis congensis	—
Ziziphus xylocarpa	Jujube
Cymbopogon spp.	Lemongrass

Cynodon dactylon	Star grass
Panicum spp.	Wild cereal
Pennisteum purpureum	Elephant grass
Setaria spp.	Love grass
Themeda triandra	Red-oat grass

GAZETTEER OF PARKS AND RESERVES

Addo	Addo Elephant National Park, South Africa
Akagera	Akagera National Park, Rwanda
Amboseli	Amboseli National Park, Kenya
Bia Park	Bia National Park, Ghana
Chobe	Chobe National Park, Botswana
Etosha	Etosha National Park, Namibia
Gal Oya	Gal Oya National Park, Sri Lanka
Gonarezhou	Gonarezhou National Park, Zimbabwe
Hluhluwe	Hluhluwe Game Reserve, South Africa
Hwange	Hwange National Park, Zimbabwe
Kasungu	Kasungu National Park, Malawi
Kruger	Kruger National Park, South Africa
Luangwa Valley	Luangwa Valley National Park, Zambia
Mana Pools	Mana Pools National Park, Zimbabwe
Manyara / Lake Manyara	Lake Manyara National Park, Tanzania
Manovo-Gounda	Manovo-Gounda-Saint Floris National Park, Central African Republic
Mara	Maasai-Mara Game Reserve, Kenya
Mikumi	Mikumi National Park, Tanzania
Mkomazi	Mkomazi National Park, Tanzania
Murchison / Murchison Falls	Murchison Falls National Park, Uganda
Queen Elizabeth	Queen Elizabeth National Park, Uganda
Ruaha	Ruaha National Park, Tanzania
Ruhuna	Ruhuna National Park, Sri Lanka
Selous	Selous Game Reserve, Tanzania
Sengwa	Sengwa Wildlife Research Area, Zimbabwe
Serengeti	Serengeti National Park, Tanzania
Tai Forest	Tai National Park, Ivory Coast
Tarangire	Tarangire National Park, Tanzania

Tsavo
Tsavo East   } Tsavo National Park, Kenya
Tsavo West
Tuli   Tuli Private Game Reserve, Botswana

SELECT BIBLIOGRAPHY

An extensive literature exists on elephants and to list all references consulted would require another book. For those whose interest takes them further most references are in the works given here. Often I pay more attention to older references as these can be harder to trace than recent ones, usually referred to in modern works. A lengthy bibliography is given in Sikes (1971) and a running bibliography appears in *Elephant*, the journal of the Elephant Interest Group of Wayne State University.

GENERAL

Bosman, P. & Hall-Martin, A. (1986) *Elephants of Africa*. Capetown: C. Struik.

Carrington, R. (1958) *Elephants*. London: Chatto & Windus.

Eltringham, S.K. (1982) *Elephants*. Poole: Blandford Press.

Jeannin, A. (1947) *L'Eléphant d'Afrique*. Paris: Payot.

Holder, C.F. (1886) *The Ivory King. A Popular History of the Elephant and Its Allies*. London: Sampson Low, Marston, Searle & Rivington.

Kunz, G.F. (1916) *Ivory and the Elephant in Art, in Archaeology, and in Science*. New York: Doubleday, Page & Company.

Sanderson, G.P. (1878) *Thirteen Years Among the Wild Beasts of India*. Edinburgh: John Grant.

Sanderson, I.T. (1963) *The Dynasty of Abu*. London: Cassell.

Sikes, S.K. (1971) *The Natural History of the African Elephant*. London: Weidenfeld & Nicolson.

Sukumar, R. (1989) *The Asian Elephant: Ecology and Management*. Cambridge: Cambridge University Press.

Tennent, J.E. (1867) *The Wild Elephant and the Method of Capturing and Taming it in Ceylon*. London: Longman, Green & Co.

Williams, J.H. (1950) *Elephant Bill*. London: Rupert Hart-Davis.

CHAPTERS 1 AND 2 EVOLUTION AND CLASSIFICATION

The most up-to-date treatments of elephant evolution are those of Shoshani (1986) and Maglio (1973). I have also drawn on the contributors in Maglio & Cooke (1978), Kingdon (1979) and Martin & Klein (1984). Howorth (1887) still provides one of the most exhaustive accounts of mammoths.

Agenbroad, L.D. (1984) New World mammoth distribution. In *Quaternary Extinctions*, P.S. Martin & R.G. Klein (eds). Tucson: University of Arizona Press.

Allen, G.M. (1936) Zoological results of the George Vanderbilt African expedition of 1934. Part II. The forest elephant of Africa. *Proc. Acad. Nat. Sci. Philadelphia* **88**: 15–44.

Bryden, H.A. (1903) The decline and fall of the South African elephant. *Fortnightly Review* **79**: 100–108.

Deraniyagala, P.E.P. (1955) *Some Extinct Elephants, Their Relatives and the Two Living Species*. Colombo: Government Press.

Digby, B. (1926) *The Mammoth and Mammoth-hunting in North-east Siberia*. London: H.F. & G. Witherby.

Douglas-Hamilton, I. (1979) *The African Elephant Action Plan*. IUCN/WWF/NYZS Elephant Survey and Conservation Programme.

Harris, J.M. (1975) Evolution of feeding mechanisms in the family *Deinotheriidae* (*Mammalia: Proboscidea*). *Zoo. J. Linn. Soc.* **56**: 331–362.

Haynes, G. (1986) Spiral fractures and cut mark-mimics in noncultural bone assemblages. *Curr. Res. Pleistocene* **3**: 45–46.

Haynes, G. (1991) *Mammoths, Mastodonts and Elephants*. Cambridge: Cambridge University Press.

Howorth, H.H. (1887) *The Mammoth and the Flood*. London: Sampson, Marston, Searle & Rivington.

Janzen, D.H. & Martin, P.S. (1981) Neotropical anachronisms: the fruits the Gomphotheres ate. *Science* **215**: 19–27.

Jochelson, W. (1909) Some notes on the traditions of the natives of North-eastern Siberia about the Mammoth. *Am. Naturalist* **43**: 48–50.

Kingdon, J. (1979) *East African Mammals: an Atlas of Evolution in Africa. Vol. IIIB*. London: Academic Press.

Krause, H. (1978) *The Mammoth in Ice and Snow?* Stuttgart: Self-publisher.

Krause, H. (1986) *Elephants at the Arctic Sea*. Stuttgart: Self-publisher.

Lydekker, R. (1907) The ears as a race character in the African elephant. *Proc. Zool. Soc. Lond.* **1907**: 380–403.

Maglio, V.J. (1973) Origin and evolution of the *Elephantidae*. *Trans. Amer. Phil. Soc.* **63**: 1–149.

Maglio, V.J. & Cooke, H.B.S. (eds) (1978) *Evolution of African Mammals*. Cambridge, Mass.: Harvard University Press.

Martin, P.S. & Klein, R.G. (eds) (1984) *Quaternary Extinctions. A Prehistoric Revolution*. Tucson: University of Arizona Press.

Noack, T. (1906) A dwarf form of the African elephant. *Ann. Mag. Nat. Hist.* **17**: 501–503.

Olivier, R. (1978) Distribution and status of the Asian elephant. *Oryx* **XIV**: 379–424.

Owen-Smith, N. (1987) Pleistocene extinctions:the pivotal role of megaherbivores. *Palaeobiology* **13**: 351–362.

Pfizenmayer, E.W. (1939) *Siberian Man and Mammoth*. London: Blackie & Son.

Shoshani, J. (1986) On the phylogenetic relationships among *Paenungulata* and within *Elephantidae* as demonstrated by molecular and osteological evidence. 2 vols. PhD thesis. Wayne State University, Detroit, Michigan.

Sollas, W.J. (1911) *Ancient Hunters and their Modern Representatives*. London: Macmillan & Co. Ltd.

Vartanyan, S.L., Garutt, V.E. & Sher, A.V. (1993) Holocene dwarf mammoths from Wrangel Island in the Siberian Arctic. *Nature* **362**: 337–340.

Vereshchagen, N.K. & Tikhonov, A.N. (1987) A study of mammoth tusks from permafrost of northeastern Siberia. *Curr. Res. Pleistocene* **4**: 120–122.

Wood, S.V. (1872) On the climate of the Post-glacial period. *Geol. Mag.* **10**: 153–161.

CHAPTERS 3 AND 4 ANATOMY AND PHYSIOLOGY

The most modern treatment of the anatomy of an elephant is that in Grassé (1955), but even this is only partial and a compilation of fairly early work. In spite of its title, the book by Mariappa (1986) refers only to parts of the anatomy. Benedict (1936) still stands as the most comprehensive account of the physiology of an elephant.

Baldwin, H. (1975) In *Among the Elephants*, I. Douglas-Hamilton and O. Douglas-Hamilton. London: Collins.

Benedict, F.G. (1936) *The Physiology of the Elephant*. Washington: Carnegie Institute.

Blair, P. (1710) Osteographia Elephantina, or a full and exact description of all bones of an elephant, with their several dimensions, etc. *Philos. Trans.* **27**: 51–168.

Corse, J. (1799) Observations on the Manners, Habits, and natural History, of the Elephant. *Philos. Trans.* **1**: 31–55.

Corse, J. (1799) Observations on the different species of Asiatic elephants, and their mode of dentition. *Philos. Trans.* **1**: 205–236.

Cresswell, R. (trans.) (1907) *Aristotle's History of Animals in Ten Books*. London: George Bell & Sons.

Fatti, L.P., Smuts, G.L., Starfield, A.M. & Spurdle, A.A. (1980) Age determination in African elephants. *J. Mamm.* **61**: 547–551.

Grasse, P-P. (1955) *Traité de Zoologie, Anatomie, Systématique, Biologie. Vol.XVII(1)*. Paris: Masson et Cie.

Hiley, P. (1984) How the elephant keeps its cool. *Nat. Hist.* **75**: 34–41.

Jachmann, H. (1988) Estimating age in African elephants: a revision of Laws's molar evaluation technique. *Afr. J. Ecol.* **26**: 51–56.

Lang, E.M. (1980) Observations on growth and molar change in the African elephant. *Afr. J. Ecol.* **18**: 217–234.

Laws, R.M. (1967) Eye lens weight and age in African elephants. *E. Afr. Wildl. J.* **5**: 46–52.

Lewis, G.W. & Fish, B. (1955) *Elephant Tramp*. Boston: Little, Brown & Co.

Mariappa, D. (1986) *Anatomy and Histology of the Indian Elephant*. Michigan: Indira Publishing House.

Mizukami, H. & Bartnicki, D.E. (1986) Unusual myoglobin of elephant. *Elephant* **2**: 80–81.

Mullen, A. (1681) *An Anatomical Account of the Elephant Accidentally Burnt in Dublin, on Fryday, June 17. in the Year 168[1]*. Dublin?: S. Smith.

Pigafetta, F. (1881) *A Report of the Kingdom of Congo and of the Surrounding Countries Drawn out of the Writings and Discourses of the Portuguese Duarte Lopez*. London: John Murray.

Schmidt-Nielsen, K. (1972) *How Animals Work*. Cambridge: Cambridge University Press.

Short, R.V. (1962) The peculiar lungs of the elephant. *New Sci.* **316**: 570–572.

Shoshani, J. (1982) On the dissection of a female Asian elephant (*Elephas maximus maximus* Linnaeus, 1758) and data from other elephants. *Elephant* **2**: 3–85.

Smith, F. (1890) Histology of the skin of the elephant. *J. Anat. & Phys.* **24**: 493–503.

Van Hoven, W., Prins, R.A. & Lankhorst, A. (1981) Fermentative digestion in the African elephant. *S. Afr. J. Wildl. Res.* **11**: 78–86.

Western, D., Moss, C.J. & Georgiadis, N. (1983) Age estimation and population age structure of elephants from footprint dimensions. *J. Wildl. Manage.* **47**: 1192–1197.

White, P.T. & Brown, I.R. (1978) Haematological studies on wild African elephants. *J. Zool. Lond.* **185**: 491–503.

Whitehill, N. (1979) Suggested mechanical model of elephant trunk muscle tissue and its sheer conjecture. *Elephant* **1**: 34–35.

Wright, P.G. (1984) Why do elephants flap their ears? *S. Afr. J. Zool.* **19**: 265–269.

Wright, P.G. & Luck, C.P. (1984) Do elephants need to sweat? *S. Afr. J. Zool.* **19**: 270–274.

Chapters 5 and 6 Reproduction, Reproductive Behaviour, Growth and Death

Most of what we know about the reproductive physiology of elephants is based on the work of Laws, who developed the earlier studies of Perry. There are several early studies on the reproductive anatomy of the Asian elephant. For reproductive behaviour I have drawn mostly upon the work of Cynthia Moss, Joyce Poole and Anthony Hall-Martin.

Conybeare, A. & Haynes, G. (1984) Observations on elephant mortality and bones in water holes. *Quat. Res.* **22**: 189–200.

Corfield, T.F. (1973) Elephant mortality in Tsavo National Park, Kenya. *E. Afr. Wildl. J.* **11**: 339–368.

Craig, G.C. (1984) Foetal mass and date of conception in African elephants: a revised formula. *S. Afr. J. Sci.* **80**: 512–516.

Douglas-Hamilton, I. & Douglas-Hamilton, O. (1975) *Among the Elephants.* London: Collins.

Eisenberg, J.F., McKay, G.M. & Jainudeen, M.R. (1971) Reproductive behaviour of the Asiatic elephant. *Behaviour* **38**: 193–225.

Jones, R.C., Bailey, D.W. & Skinner, J.D. (1975) Studies on the collection and storage of semen from the African elephant, *Loxodonta africana. Koedoe* **18**: 147–164.

Jones, R.C., Rowlands, I.W. & Skinner, J.D. (1974) Spermatozoa in the genital ducts of the African elephant, *Loxodonta africana. J. Reprod. Fert.* **41**: 189–192.

Laws, R.M. (1967) Occurrence of placental scars in the uterus of the African elephant (*Loxodonta africana*). *J. Reprod. Fert.* **14**: 445–449.

Laws, R.M. (1969) Aspects of reproduction in the African elephant, *Loxodonta africana. J. Reprod. Fert.* **6 (Suppl.)**: 193–217.

Laws, R.M. & Parker, I.S.C. (1968) Recent studies on elephant populations in East Africa. *Symp. Zool. Soc. Lond.* **21**: 319–359.

Lee, P.C. (1987) Allomothering among African elephants. *Anim. Behav.* **35**: 287–291.

Lee, P.C. & Moss, C.J. (1986) Early maternal investment in male and female African elephant calves. *Behav. Ecol. Sociobiol.* **18**: 353–361.

Leuthold, W. & Leuthold, B. (1975) Parturition and related behaviour in the African elephant. *Z. Tierpsychol.* **39**: 75–84.

Moss, C.J. (1983) Oestrous behaviour and female choice in the African elephant. *Behaviour* **86**: 167–196.

Moss, C.J. (1988) *Elephant Memories.* London: Elm Tree Books.

Perry, J.S. (1953) The reproduction of the African elephant, *Loxodonta africana. Phil. Trans. B.* **237**: 93–149.

Poole, J.H. (1989) Mate guarding, reproductive success and female choice in African elephants. *Anim. Behav.* **37**: 842–849.

Poole, J.H. (1989) The effects of poaching on the age structures and social and reproductive patterns of selected East African elephant populations. In *The Ivory Trade and the Future of the African Elephant. Vol. 2.* Technical Reports, Ivory Trade Review Group, Oxford.

Powell-Cotton, P.H.G. (1904) *In Unknown Africa.* London: Hurst & Blackett.

Sheldrick, D. (1966) *Orphans of Tsavo.* London: Collins.

Short, R.V. (1966) Oestrous behaviour, ovulation and the formation of the corpus luteum in the African elephant, *Loxodonta africana. E. Afr. Wildl. J.* **4**: 56–68

Short, R.V., Mann, T. & Hay, M.F. (1967) Male reproductive organs of the African elephant. *J. Reprod. Fert.* **13**: 517–536.

Smith, N.S. & Buss, I.O. (1973) Reproductive ecology of the female African elephant. *J. Wildl. Manage.* **37**: 524–534.

Sparrman, A. (1786) *A Voyage to the Cape of Good Hope towards the Antarctic Polar Circle, and Round the World: but Chiefly into the Country of the Hottentots and Caffres, from the Year 1772, to 1776.* 2nd. edn. 2 vols. London: G.G.J. & J. Robinson.

Watson, P.F. & D'Souza, F. (1975) Detection of oestrus in the African elephant (*Loxodonta africana*). *Theriogenology* **4**: 203–209.

CHAPTER 7 DISEASES, PARASITES AND SYMBIONTS

For internal parasites the most up-to-date treatment is by Bauer and Stoye (1985), unfortunately in German. A number of papers is scattered in veterinary journals, mostly dealing with parasites of the Asian elephant.

Bänziger, H. (1988) The heaviest tear drinkers: ecology and systematics of new and unusual notodontid moths. *Nat. Hist. Bull. Siam Soc.* **36**: 17–53.

Bauer, C. & Stoye, M. (1985) Endoparasiten beim afrikanischen und asiatischen Elefanten. *Praktische Tierarzt.* **66**: 55–60.

Clay, T. (1963) A new species of *Haematomyzus* Piaget (Pthiraptera, Insecta). *Proc. Zool. Soc. Lond.* **141**: 153–161.

Domrow, R. & Ladds, P.W. (1984) A new ear mite from the Indian elephant (Acari: Anoetidae). *J. Nat. Hist.* **18**: 759–764.

Eloff, A.K. & van Hoven, N. (1980) Internal protozoa of the African elephant *Loxodonta africana* (Blumenbach). *S. Afr. J. Zool.* **15**: 83–90.

Evans, G. (1910) *Elephants and their Diseases.* Shillong: Government Printer.

Fain, A. (1983) Notes sur les genres *Loxanoetus* Fain, 1970 et *Otanoetus* Fain et Zumpt, 1974. (*Acari, Anoetidae*). *Rev. Zool. Afr.* **97**: 846–851.

McGaughey, C.A. (1962) Diseases of elephants. Part V. Internal parasites. *Ceylon Vet. J.* **X**: 61–64.

Rothschild, M. & Clay, T. (1952) *Fleas, Flukes and Cuckoos.* New Naturalist Library. London: Collins.

Sikes, S.K. (1969) Habitat and cardiovascular disease: observations made in East Africa on free-living wild animals, with particular reference to the African elephant. *Trans. Zool. Soc. Lond.* **32**: 1–104.

Zumpt, F. & Wetzel, H. (1970) Fly parasites (*Diptera: Oestridae* and *Gasterophilidae*) of the African elephant *Loxodonta africana* (Blumenbach) and their problems. *Koedoe* **13**: 109–121.

CHAPTER 8 SOCIAL BEHAVIOUR

The main sources for this chapter are Cynthia Moss (1988), Douglas-Hamilton (1975) and the papers of Joyce Poole. Also important in relation to musth is the work of Anthony Hall-Martin.

Barnes, R.F.W. (1982) Mate-searching behaviour of elephant bulls in a semi-arid environment. *Anim. Behav.* **30**: 1217–1223.

Bazé, W. (1955) *Just Elephants*. London: Elek Books.

Buss, I.O. (1990) *Elephant Life. Fifteen Years of High Population Density.* Ames: Iowa State University Press.

Fernando, S.D.A., Jayasinghe, J.B. & Panabokke, R.G. (1963) A study of the temporal gland in an Asiatic elephant. *Ceylon Vet. J.* **11**: 108–111.

Hall-Martin, A.J. (1987) Role of musth in the reproductive strategy of the African elephant (*Loxodonta africana*). *S. Afr. J. Sci.* **83**: 616–620.

Hall-Martin, A.J. & van der Walt, L.A. (1984) Plasma testosterone levels in relation to musth in the male African elephant. *Koedoe* **27**: 147–149.

Heffner, R. & Heffner, H. (1980) Hearing in the elephant (*Elephas maximus*). *Science* **208**: 518–520.

Heffner, R., Heffner, H. & Stichman, N. (1982) Role of the elephant pinna in sound localization. *Anim. Behav.* **30**: 628–630.

Home, E. (1823) On the difference of structure between the human Membrana Tympani and that of the elephant. *Philos. Trans.* 23–26.

Hone, W. (1827) *The Every-Day Book and Table-Book*, etc. London: Thomas Tegg.

Jainudeen, M.R., Katongole, C.B. & Short, R.V. (1972) Plasma testosterone levels in relation to musth and sexual activity in the male Asiatic elephant. *J. Reprod. Fert.* **29**: 99–103.

Kittenberger, K. (1929) *Big Game Hunting and Collecting in East Africa 1903–1926*. London: Edward Arnold & Co.

Kurt, F. (1974) Remarks on the social structure and ecology of the Ceylon elephant in the Yala National Park. In *The Behaviour of Ungulates and its Relation to Management*, Vol. 2. V. Geist & F. Walther (eds) pp. 618–634. Morges: IUCN.

Moore, R.J. & Munnion, C. (1989) *Back to Africa*. Johannesburg: Southern Book Publishers.

Poole, J.H. (1987) Rutting behaviour in African elephants: the phenomenon of musth. *Behaviour* **102**: 283–316.

Poole, J.H. (1989) Announcing intent: the aggressive state of musth in African elephants. *Anim. Behav.* **37**: 140–152.

Poole, J.H. & Moss, C.J. (1981) Musth in the African elephant, *Loxodonta africana*. *Nature.* **292**: 830–831.

Poole, J.H., Payne, K., Langbauer, W.R. & Moss, C.J. (1988) The social contexts of some very low frequency calls of African elephants. *Behav. Ecol. Sociobiol.* **22**: 385–392.

Rasmussen, L.E., Buss, I.O., Hess, D.L. & Schmidt, M.J. (1984) Testosterone and dihydrotestosterone concentrations in elephant serum and temporal gland secretions. *Bio. Reprod.* **30**: 352–362.

Ruggiero, R.G. (1990) The effects of poaching disturbance on elephant behaviour. *Pachyderm.* **13**: 42–44.

Tabler, E.C. (ed.) (1971) *James Chapman, Travels in the Interior of South Africa 1849–1863*. Cape Town: A. A. Balkema.

Wheeler, J.W., Rasmussen, L.E., Ayorinde, F., Buss, I.O. & Smuts, G.L. (1982) Constituents of temporal gland secretion of the African elephant. *J. Chem. Ecol.* **8**: 821–835.

CHAPTERS 9 AND 10 FEEDING AND EFFECTS ON TREES

There are many scientific papers on feeding in elephants, most dealing with the African elephant. Some are given here.

Alexandre, D-Y. (1978) Le role disseminateur des eléphants en foret de Tai, Cote-d'Ivoire. *La Terre et La Vie* **32**: 47–72.

Anderson, G.D. & Walker, B.H. (1974) Vegetation composition and elephant damage in the Sengwa wildlife research area, Rhodesia. *J. S. Afr. Wildl. Mgmt. Ass.* **4**: 1–14.

Anderson, J.M. & Coe, M.J. (1974) Decomposition of elephant dung in an arid, tropical environment. *Oecologia* **14**: 111–125.

Barnes, R.W. (1980) The decline of the baobab tree in Ruaha National Park, Tanzania. *Afr. J. Ecol.* **18**: 243–252.

Barnes, R.W. (1982) Elephant feeding behaviour in Ruaha National Park, Tanzania. *Afr. J. Ecol.* **20**: 123–136.

Bristow, C. (1961) The mystery caves of Elgon. *East African Annual 1960–61*, pp. 16–21. Nairobi: East African Standard Ltd.

Buechner, H.K. & Dawkins, H.C. (1961) Vegetation change induced by elephants and fire in Murchison Falls National Park, Uganda. *Ecology* **42**: 752–766.

Buss, I.O. (1961) Some observations on food habits and behaviour of the African elephant. *J. Wildl. Manage.* **25**: 131–148.

Coe, M. (1972) Defaecation by African elephants (*Loxodonta africana* (Blumenbach)). *E. Afr. Wildl. J.* **10**: 165–174.

Coe, M. (1977) The role of termites in the removal of elephant dung in the Tsavo (East) National Park, Kenya. *E. Afr. Wildl. J.* **15**: 49–56.

Croze, H. (1974) The Seronera bull problem. I. The elephants. *E. Afr. Wildl. J.* **12**: 1–27.

Croze, H. (1974) The Seronera bull problem. II. The trees. *E. Afr. Wildl. J.* **12**: 29–47.

Cumming, R.G. (1850) *Five Years of a Hunter's Life in the Far Interior of South Africa.* 2 vols. London: John Murray.

Dublin, H.T., Sinclair, A.R.E. & McGlade, J. (1990) Elephants and fire as causes of multiple stable states in the Serengeti–Mara woodlands. *J. Anim. Ecol.* **59**: 1147–1164.

Field, C.R. & Ross, I.C. (1976) The savannah ecology of Kidepo Valley National Park. II. Feeding ecology of elephant and giraffe. *E. Afr. Wildl. J.* **14**: 1–15.

Guy, P.R. (1975) The daily food intake of the African elephant, *Loxodonta africana* Blumenbach, in Rhodesia. *Arnoldia* **7**: 1–6.

Guy, P.R. (1976) The feeding behaviour of elephant (*Loxodonta africana*) in the Sengwa area, Rhodesia. *S. Afr. J. Wildl. Res.* **6**: 55–63.

Guy, P.R. (1982) Baobabs and elephants. *Afr. J. Ecol.* **20**: 215–220.

Jachmann, H. & Bell, R.H.V. (1985) Utilization by elephants of the *Brachystegia* woodlands of the Kasungu National Park, Malawi. *Afr. J. Ecol.* **23**: 245–258.

Jackson, F. (1894) The elephant. In *Big Game Shooting. Vol. I*, C. Phillips-Wolley (ed.) The Badminton Library. London: Longmans, Green, & Co.

Kalemera, M.C. (1987) Dry season diurnal activity of elephants in Lake Manyara National Park, Tanzania. *Afr. J. Ecol.* **25**: 255–263.

Koen, J.H. (1983) Seed dispersal by the Knysna elephants. *S. Afr. For. J.* **124**: 54–58.

Laws, R.M., Parker, I.S.C. & Johnstone, R.C.B. (1975) *Elephants and their Habitats. The ecology of elephants in North Bunyoro, Uganda.* Oxford: Clarendon Press.

Malpas, R.C. (1977) Diet and the condition and growth of elephants in Uganda. *J. Appl. Ecol.* **14**: 489–504.

McCullagh, K.G. (1969) The growth and nutrition of the African elephant. I. Seasonal variations in the rate of growth and the urinary excretion of hydroxyproline. *E. Afr. Wildl. J.* **7**: 85–90.

McCullagh, K.G. (1969) The growth and nutrition of the African elephant. II. The chemical nature of the diet. *E. Afr. Wildl. J.* **7**: 91–98.

McCullagh, K.G. (1973) Are African elephants deficient in essential fatty acids? *Nature.* **242**: 267–268.

Mertz, G. (1981) Recherches sur la biologie de nutrition et les habitats préfères de l'elephant de forêt, *Loxodonta africana cyclotis* Matschie. *Mammalia* **45**: 299–312.

McKay, G.M. (1973) Behaviour and ecology of the Asiatic elephant in south-eastern Ceylon. *Smithsonian Contrib. Zool.* **125**.

Pitman, C.R.S. (1931) *A Game Warden Among His Charges.* London: Nisbet & Co. Ltd.

Pringle, T. (1834) *African Sketches. Part II. Narrative of a Residence in South Africa.* London: Edward Moxon.

Redmond, I. (1982) Salt-mining elephants of Mount Elgon. *Swara* **5**: 28–31.

Ridley, H.N. (1930) *The Dispersal of Plants Throughout the World.* Ashford: L. Reeve.

Short, J.C. (1981) Diet and feeding behaviour of the forest elephant. *Mammalia* **45**: 177–185.

Short, J.C. (1983) Density and seasonal movements of forest elephant (*Loxodonta africana cyclotis*, Matschie) in Bia National Park, Ghana. *Afr. J. Ecol.* **21**: 175–184.

Swart, E. (1963) Age of the baobab tree. *Nature* **198**: 708–709.

Thomas, A.S. (1943) The vegetation of the Karamoja District, Uganda. An illustration of biological factors in tropical ecology. *J. Ecol.* **31**: 149–177.

Thomson, J. (1885) *Through Masai Land.* Sampson Low, Marston, Searle & Rivington.

Thomson, P.J. (1975) The role of elephants, fire and other agents in the decline of a *Brachystegia boehmii* woodland. J. S. Afr. Wildl. Mgmt. Ass. **5:** 11–18.

Weir, J.S. (1969) Chemical properties and occurrences on Kalahari sand of salt licks created by elephant. *J. Zool. Lond.* **158:** 293–310.

Weyerhaeuser, F.J. (1985) Survey of elephant damage to baobabs in Tanzania's Lake Manyara National Park. *Afr. J. Ecol.* **23:** 235–243.

Williamson, B.R. (1975) The condition and nutrition of elephant in Wankie National Park. *Arnoldia* **7:** 1–20.

Wing, L.D. & Buss, I.O. (1970) Elephants and forests. *Wildl. Monogr.* **19:** 1–92.

Wyatt, J.R. & Eltringham, S.K. (1974) The daily activity of the elephant in the Rwenzori National Park, Uganda. *E. Afr. Wildl. J.* **12:** 273–289.

CHAPTERS 11 AND 12 POPULATION DYNAMICS AND OVERPOPULATION

The main source for Uganda is Laws, Parker & Johnstone (1975) (see page 300).

Baker, S. W. (1866) *The Albert N'yanza Great Basin of the Nile and Explorations of the Nile Sources.* London: Macmillan & Co.

Bosman, W. (1705) *A New and Accurate Description of the Coast of Guinea, divided into the Gold, the Slave and the Ivory Coasts.* London: James Knapton.

Brooks, A.C. & Buss, I.O. (1962) Past and present status of the elephant in Uganda. *J. Wildl. Manage.* **26:** 38–50.

Buechner, H.K., Buss, I.O., Longhurst, W.M. & Brooks, A.C. (1963) Numbers and migration of elephants in Murchison Falls National Park, Uganda. *J. Wildl. Manage.* **27:** 36–53.

Calef, G.W. (1988) Maximum rate of increase in the African elephant. *Afr. J. Ecol.* **26:** 323–327.

Caughley, G. (1976) The elephant problem – an alternative hypothesis. *E. Afr. Wildl. J.* **14:** 265–283.

Churchill, W.S. (1908) *My African Journey.* London: Hodder & Stoughton.

Corfield, M. (1974) *Historical Notes on Tsavo.* Nairobi: Kenya National Parks.

Corfield, T. F. (1973) Elephant mortality in Tsavo National Park, Kenya. *E. Afr. Wildl. J.* **11:** 339–368.

Elton, C. (1927) *Animal Ecology.* London: Sidgwick & Jackson Ltd.

Foaker, Mr. In Fitzgerald, W.A.A. (1898) *Travels in the Coastlands of British East Africa and the Islands of Zanzibar and Pemba.* London: Chapman & Hall Ltd.

Krapf, J.L. (1860) *Travels, Researches, and Missionary Labours During an Eighteen Years' Residence in Eastern Africa.* London: Trubner & Co.

Lamprey, H.F., Glover, P.E., Turner, M.I. & Bell, R.H.V. (1967) Invasion of the Serengeti National Park by elephants. *E. Afr. Wildl. J.* **5:** 151–166.

Leuthhold, W. & Sale, J.B. (1973) Movements and patterns of habitat utilization of elephants in Tsavo National Park, Kenya. *E. Afr. Wildl. J.* **11:** 369–384.

Lindeque, M. & Lindeque, P.M. (1991) Satellite tracking of elephants in northwestern Namibia. *Afr. J. Ecol.* **29:** 196–206.

Melton, D.A. (1985) The status of elephants in northern Botswana. *Biol. Cons.* **31:** 317–333.

Neumann, A.H. (1898) *Elephant-hunting in East Equatorial Africa.* London: Rowland Ward Ltd.

Phillipson, J. (1975) Rainfall, primary production and 'carrying capacity' of Tsavo National Park (East), Kenya. *E. Afr. Wildl. J.* **13:** 171–201.

Pitman, C.R.S. (1934) *A Report on a Faunal Survey of Northern Rhodesia with Especial Reference to Game, Elephant Control and National Parks.* Livingstone: Government Printer.

Selous, F.C. (1881) *A Hunter's Wanderings in Africa.* London: Richard Bentley & Son.

Sheldrick, D. (1973) *The Tsavo Story.* London: Collins.

Simpson, C.D. (1978) *Effects of Elephant and Other Wildlife on Vegetation along the Chobe River, Botswana.* Occasional Papers, Museum Texas Tech. Univ. No. 48, pp. 1–15.

Spinage, C.A. (1990) Botswana's problem elephants. *Pachyderm* **13:** 14–19.

Swart, J.H. & Duffy, K.J. (1987) The stability of a predator–prey model applied to the destruction of trees by elephants. *S. Afr. J. Sci.* **83:** 156–158.

Swynnerton, C.F.M. (1924) *Report on the control of elephants in Uganda.* Entebbe: Government Press.

Thorbahn, P. F. (1979) The precolonial ivory trade of East Africa. PhD dissertation, University of Massachusetts.

Tyrrell, J.G. (1985) Distribution of elephants in the Tsavo region during the late 19th century. *Afr. J. Ecol.* **23:** 29–33.

Van Wijngaarden, W. (1985) *Elephants-Trees-Grass-Grazers. Relationships between Climate, Soils, Vegetation and Large Herbivores in a Semi-arid Ecosystem (Tsavo, Kenya).* Enschede: International Institute for Aerospace Survey and Earth Sciences (ITC).

Watson, R.M. & Bell, R.H.V. (1969) The distribution, abundance and status of elephant in the Serengeti region of northern Tanzania. *J. Appl. Ecol.* **6:** 115–132.

Western, D. & van Praet, C. (1973) Cyclical changes in the habitat and climate of an East African ecosystem. *Nature* **241:** 104–106.

CHAPTER 13 IVORY STRUCTURE AND GROWTH

Many dental works describe briefly the structure of elephant ivory, for example Tomes (1904). Descriptions are also given in most books on ivory carvings.

Aldrovandi, U. (1616) *De Quadrupedibus Solidipedibus Volumen Integrum.* Bologna: Victor Benatius.

Baines, T. (1864) *Explorations in South-west Africa*. London: Longman, Green, Longman, Roberts & Green.

Bland-Sutton, J. (1910) The diseases of elephants' tusks in relation to billiard balls. *Lancet* **2**: 1534–1537.

Colyer, F. (1926) The pathology of the teeth of elephants. *Dental Record* **XLVI**: 73–98.

Colyer, F. & Miles, A.E.W. (1957) Injury to and rate of growth of an elephant tusk. *J. Mammal.* **38**: 243–247.

Combe, C. (1801) Account of an Elephant's Tusk, in which the Iron Head of a Spear was found imbedded. *Philos. Trans.* 165–169.

Dixon, R. (1981) The mathematical daisy. *New Scientist* **107**: 792–795.

Espinoza, E.O & Mann, M-J. (1991) *Identification Guide for Ivory and Ivory Substitutes*. Washington: WWF.

Espinoza, E.O., Mann, M-J., LeMay, J.P. & Oakes, K.A. (1990) A method for differentiating modern from ancient proboscidean ivory in worked objects. *Curr. Res. Pleistocene* **7**: 81–83.

Humphreys, H.F. (1926) Particulars relating to the broken tusk of a wild Indian elephant. *Brit. Dent. J.* **47**: 1400–1407.

Miles, A.E.W. & Grigson, C. (eds) (1990) *Colyer's Variations and Diseases of the Teeth of Animals*, 2nd edn. Cambridge: Cambridge University Press.

Miles, A.E.W. & White, J.W. (1960) Ivory. *Proc. Roy. Soc. Med.* **53**: 775–780.

Miller, W.D. (1890–91) Studies on the anatomy and pathology of the tusks of the elephant. *Dental Cosmos* **XXXII**: 337–348; 421–429; 505–526; 673–679; **XXXIII**: 169–175; 421–440.

Miller, W.D. (1899) Some very rare cases of gunshot and spear wounds in the tusks of elephants. *Dental Cosmos* **XL**: 1239–1244.

Owen, R. (1856) The ivory and teeth of commerce. *J. Roy. Soc. Arts* **V**: 65–73.

Perry, J.S. (1954) Some observations on growth and tusk weight in male and female African elephants. *Proc. Zool. Soc. Lond.* **124**: 97–105.

Rajaram, A. (1986) Tensile properties and fracture of ivory. *J. Materials Sci. Lett.* **5**: 1077–1080.

Tomes, C.S. (1904) *A Manual of Dental Anatomy, Human and Comparative*, 6th edn. London: J. & A. Churchill.

Van der Merwe, N.J., Lee-Thorpe, J.A., Thackeray, J.F. *et al.* (1990) Source-area determination of elephant ivory by isotopic analysis. *Nature* **346**: 744–746.

Chapter 14 The Ivory Trade, Historical and Modern, and the Destruction of Elephants

There is no comprehensive work on the ivory trade. Very general treatments are Moore (1931) and Wilson & Ayerst (1976). St Aubyn (1987) provides a comprehensive survey of ivory as an art form, updating Maskell (1905).

Quantities for ivory come from many sources and few agree with one another. Parker (1979) provides extensive modern documentation and a comprehensive worldwide review of recent ivory trading is provided by the ITRG report. Many recent developments are covered in Anon (1989) and Douglas-Hamilton & Douglas-Hamilton (1992).

Alpers, E.A. (1975) *Ivory and Slaves in East Central Africa*. London: Heinemann.

Anon (1989) *A System of Extinction. The African Elephant Disaster*. London: Environmental Investigation Agency.

Barbier, E.B., Burgess, J.C., Swanson, T.M. & Pearce, D.W. (1990) *Elephants, Economics and Ivory*. London: Earthscan Publications Ltd.

Beachey, R.W. (1967) The East African ivory trade in the nineteenth century. *J. Afr. History* **8**: 269–290.

Brooks, A.C. & Buss, I.O. (1962) Trend in tusk size of the Uganda elephant. *Mammalia* **26**: 10–34.

Caughley, G. (1988) *A projection of Ivory Production and Its Implications for the Conservation of African Elephants*. CSIRO: Australia Consultancy report to CITES: Gland.

Christy, C. (1924) *Big Game and Pygmies*. London: Macmillan & Co. Ltd.

Douglas-Hamilton, I. & Douglas-Hamilton. O. (1992) *Battle for the Elephants*. London: Doubleday.

Gray, R. & Birmingham, D. (1970) *Pre-colonial African Trade. Essays on Trade in Central and Eastern Africa before 1900*. London: Oxford University Press.

Grogan, E.S. & Sharp, A.H. (1900) *From the Cape to Cairo*. London: Hurst & Blackett.

Laufer, B. (1925) *Ivory in China*. Chicago: Field Museum of Natural History.

Martin, E.B. (1985) *The Japanese Ivory Industry*. Tokyo: WWF, Japan.

Maskell, A. (1905) *Ivories. The Connoisseur's Library*. London: Methuen & Co.

Myres, J.N.L. & Green, B. (1973) *The Anglo-Saxon Cemeteries of Caistor-by-Norwich and Markshall, Norfolk*. Reports of the Research Committee of the Society of Antiquaries of London, No. XXX. London: The Society of Antiquaries of London.

Park, M. (1799) *Travels in the Interior Districts of Africa: Performed under the Direction and Patronage of the African Association, in the Years 1795, 1796, and 1797*. London: W. Bulmer & Co.

Parker, I.S.C. (1979) *The Ivory Trade*. 3 vols. Nairobi: Wildlife Services Ltd.

Pilgram, T. & Western, D. (1986) Inferring hunting patterns on African elephants from tusks in the international ivory trade. *J. Appl. Ecol.* **23**: 503–514.

Sheriff, A. (1987) *Slaves, Spices and Ivory in Zanzibar*. London: James Currey.

Sowerby, A. de C. (1936) China and ivory. *China J.* **25(3)**.

Spinage, C.A. (1973) A review of ivory exploitation and elephant population trends in Africa. *E. Afr. Wildl. J.* **11**: 281–289.

St Aubyn, F. (ed.) (1987) *Ivory: A History and Collector's Guide*. London: Thames & Hudson.

Voigt, E.A. (1982) Ivory in the Early Iron Age of South Africa. *Transvaal Museum Bull.* **18:** 17–20.

Whitely, W.H. (trans.) (1966) *Maisha Ya Hamed Bin Muhammed El Murjebi Yaani Tippu Tip*. Nairobi: East African Literature Bureau.

Williamson, G. C. (1938) *The Book of Ivory*. London: Frederick Muller Ltd.

Wilson, D. & Ayerst, P. (1976) *White Gold. The Story of African Ivory*. London: Heinemann.

CHAPTER 15 ELEPHANT DOMESTICATION

The use of elephants by the Carthaginians is taken mostly from Burstein (1989) who provides the most up-to-date analysis. Other texts are Scullard (1974) which updates the Roman sections of Armandi (1843); and Rankin (1826). A number of books deal in a general manner with the modern use of working elephants, such as Stracey (1963).

Armandi, P. (1843) *Histoire Militaire des Eléphants Depuis les Temps les Plus Reculés Jusqu'à l'Introduction des Armes à Feu*. Paris: Librairie d'Amyot.

Burstein, S.M. (1989) *Agatarchides of Cnidus*. Cambridge: Hakluyt Society.

Fallon, Baron. (1935) Inspanning the African elephant. Successful experiments in the Belgian Congo. *African Observer* **2:** 32–39.

Gowers, W. (1947) The African elephant in warfare. *African Affairs* **46:** 42–49.

Gowers, W. (1948) African elephants and ancient authors. *African Affairs* **47:** 173–180.

Hagenbeck, C. (1909) *Beasts and Men*. London: Longmans, Green & Co.

Offerman, P.B. (1953) The elephant in the Belgian Congo. In *The African Elephant in East Central Africa*. W.C.O. Hill (ed.). London: Rowland Ward.

Rankin, J. (1826) *Historical Researches on the Wars and Sports of the Mongols and Romans: in which Elephants and Wild Beasts were Employed or Slain and the Remarkable Local Agreements of History with the Remains of Such Animals Found in Europe and Siberia*. London: Longman, Rees, Orme, Brown, & Green.

Rankin, L.K. (1882) The elephant experiment in Africa: a brief account of the Belgian elephant expedition on the march from Dar-es-Salaam to Mpwapwa. *Proc. Roy. Geog. Soc.* **V:** 273–289.

Scullard, H.H. (1974) *The Elephant in the Greek and Roman World*. London: Thames & Hudson.

Stracey, P.D. (1963) *Elephant Gold*. London: Weidenfeld & Nicolson.

Tarn, W.W. (1926) Polybius and a literary commonplace. *Class. Quarterly* **20:** 98–99.

Index

Aardvark 3,4
Abyssinian campaign 270–1
Adamson, George 110
Addo 255
    elephants 30, 201
Aelian 169, 218
Afghan campaign 114
African elephant 5, 17
    biggest 100
    decline 32–33
    decline in South Africa 33
    growth 100–101
    poaching of 28
    population 28
    range 27–28
    and rainfall 27
    races, naming of 30
    shoulder height 100
    subspecies 28, 30
    type locality 26
    war 266
    weight 100
African horse sickness 114
Agatarchides 45, 263
Ageing population 184
Aggregations 208
Aggression at waterholes 106–7
Ahmed 108, 216
Aixinjuelo Xuanhua 13
'Ajax' 102
Akagera Park 172
Akbar 80
Aldrovandi, Ulisse 232
Alexander the Great 102, 265
'Alice' 102
Alimentary tract 56–7
    size 56
    utilization rate 56

Al-Mas'udi 240
Altruism 132
Amboseli 103, 105–6, 129, 132, 192,
        209
Amebelodon 11
Ameloblasts 219
America 10, 11, 12, 22
American Committee for International
        Wildlife Protection 259
    Indians 16
    mastodon 12
Amyntianus 227
Anaemia 112
Anancus kenyensis 16
Anaplasma 115
Ancient Egyptians 238, 239, 265
    Greece 238
    Greeks 265
Andean mastodon 6
Andes 6
Angola 100, 195–6, 249
Anoplocephala manubriata 117
Anoplura 123
Antarctica 10
Anthrax 114, 192
Antiochus I 266–7
Antwerp market 243
Arboviruses 113–4
Arctic Circle 69
Aristotle 27, 41–2, 45, 49, 54, 56, 59, 74,
        77, 79, 80, 81, 83, 86, 102, 112,
        113, 156, 264–5
Armenian mammoth 13
Arms race 265–6
Arsinoitherium 7
Arteriosclerosis 113
Artha Sastra 210
Aruba Dam 187, 190

Asian elephant 3, 5, 17, 34–40
  a browser 155
  birth season 82–3
  bull tusk growth 217
  density 202
  captive 36
  capture 37
  cow tusks 217
  decline, causes of 37–8
  distribution in India 37
  grass intake 155
  numbers 35, 36
  races 34–5
  and rainfall 38
  range 35–8
  shooting of 37
  shoulder height 100
  sizes 34
  value 282–3
  war 267
  war numbers 270
Assurbanipal 25
Atkins's 'Royal Menagerie' 156
Augustine, Saint 4
'Aunties' 97
Aurignacian man 232
Australia 10
Avril, Father 235
Azurara 241

Babesia 115
Bag rings 241
Baines, Thomas 228, 230, 255–6
Baker, Sir Samuel 43, 183, 207, 253
Balance of elephants and habitats 210
Bänziger, Dr. 127
Barnes, Sir George 42, 242
Barthema, Ludovico 216
Barytheres 9
Barytheroidea 5
Baobab 172, 174, 176–7, 178
  age 176
Bark chewing 171
  stripping 172–3, 178
Basal heat production 64
  metabolic rate 64
Basle Zoo 149
Bastard elephant 40
Bathmostomum sangeri 116
Bazé, William 128, 284
Behemoth 12

Belgian Congo 249
  domesticated elephant centre 279
Benedict, Francis 51, 61, 62, 63, 64, 73
Benedict's breathalyser 69
Benin 240
Behaviour when meeting 134
  in rain 97
Beresovka mammoth 21
Berlin zoo 219, 272
Bhutan 38
Billiard balls 223
Birth 89–90
  behaviour of mother at 90, 91
  behaviour of calf 90
  time of 82
Bishop St. James 120–1
Biting flies 121
Bivitellobilharzia 117
Blair, P 42
Blood cells 67–8
  circulation 66–7
  thickening 113
  volume 66
Blumenbach 26
Body temperature 62
Bombay Burma Trading Co 101, 281
Bone arrangement 45
  structure 45
Boney Springs, Missouri 19
Borneo 39, 40
Bosman, William 76, 200, 229, 247
Bot, black elephant stomach 119
  blue elephant stomach 120
  green elephant stomach 120
  throat 119
Bots, mammoth 120
Botswana 2, 64, 192–6, 255–6, 262, 281
  radio-tracking 207
Boucher de Perthes 4
Brain anatomy 74–5
  size 74
Breathing rate 63
Breeding 'migrations' 206
  prediction of 82
  season 82, 143
Britain 250
  elephant imports 272
  ivory imports 242–3, 245, 257, 263
Browne, Sir Thomas 45
Browse 154, 155
  plants eaten 159, 160
Browsing wet season 172–3
  species decline 190

Brihat Sanita 224
Bruce, D 115
Brumptia 117
Buckland, Francis 223
    Rev. Dr. William 9, 232
Bryden, H.A 33
Budongo Forest 183, 185
    herd 185
Buganda 253
Bull areas in Kruger Park 137
    behaviour 86–7
    calf, age driven from family 97
    calf, investment in 97
    encounters 142
    group size 133
    imbalance from poaching 98
    independence 131, 133
Bunyoro 135
    North 182–3
Burma 36, 38, 39, 68, 82, 92, 94, 104,
        118, 281
Burmese timber elephant 273, 281–2
Burton, Sir R.F 251–2
Burying objects 109–10
Bush elephant races 30–1
Byzantium 241

Caesar, Julius 266, 268, 272
Cainozoic era 6, 16
Calcium absorption 47
    requirements 220
    in vegetation 177
Caldwell, K 213, 279–80
Calf behaviour 93–96
    carrying 91–2
    dependence on mother 94
    disciplining 95–6
    distress calls 95
    feeding 94
    first 198
    mortality 97, 103, 184
    play 96
    protection 95
Californian coast 21
Caligula 238
Calls, contact 147
    greeting 146–7
Calves at waterholes 94
Calving interval 85, 183, 198
Camel thorn woodland 195
Camper, Petrus 71
Caprivi Strip 195–6

Captain Mark Phillips 275
Carbon monoxide sensitivity 68
Cardio-vascular abnormality 113
Carter, Captain 277–8
Carthage 266
Carthaginian elephants 267
Cassivelaunus 271
Castration 84
Cattle population 194
Cave drawings 13
Caves 166
Celluloid 243
Cementum 219
Census, first 202
Central African Republic 284
Central America 12
Central Kalahari Game Reserve 137
'Chang' 166
Chang K'ien 270
Chapman, James 129, 132, 193, 200,
        207
Charging 151
Charlemagne, Emperor 276
Chau Ju-Kua 240
Chester Zoo 26
Chewa 250
China 16, 22, 38–9, 40, 235–6, 240
Chinese 12, 215, 238, 270
Chobe River 2, 193
Christy, Dr. Cuthbert 258
Chrysomia bezziana 122
Chuni 42–3, 145, 210, 229, 273
Churchill, Winston 183
Ciliates 124
Circus elephants 275
Clan 132, 134, 135–6
Clans in Kruger Park 136
    in Sri Lanka 136
Classification of elephants 8
Climate 25, 213
    change 20, 21
Clive, Lord 101
Clovis culture 18
Cobboldia russanovi 120
Columbian mammoth 19
Coins 268–9
Cokwe 249
Collagen fibre pattern 221
Colyer, Sir Frank 224, 230
Combe, Charles 230
Combretums 160
Competition 261
Compression 178, 195, 212, 261

Conception 85
   age at first 89
Condylarth 3
Control 213
   killing 200
Coprophagy 125
Copulation, mode of 79–80, 81–2, 86
   rarity of 80
   successful 87
Corpora lutea 84
Corrugated tusks 228
Corse, John 49, 50, 80, 129, 148
Costa Rica 11
Cotton plant 161
Courtship behaviour 87–8
   difference in African and Asian 88
Creation theory 4
Crop raiders 210
Cross, Mr. 42–3, 145
Crown distortion 179
Ctesias 83, 265
Culicoides loxodontis 122
Cumming, Roualeyn Gordon 170
Cumulative effect of ivory trade 262
Cunningham, George 229
Cuvier, Baron 3, 4, 5, 11, 26, 55, 75, 222
Cuvieronius 12
   andium 6
Cycles of increase 211

Dahllite 218
Daily digestible protein 154
Daily Mirror 188
   Telegraph 108, 275
'Daisy' 270
Daisy pattern 221
Darwin, Charles 80–1, 137–8, 198–9
Death 102–3
   causes of 104
   from dehydration 188
   by elephants 209–10
   of wild elephant 108–9
Deaths in Tsavo 188–9
Decline of trees 174
Defaecation 158–9
Deinotherium bozasi 9
   giganteum 9
Deinotheroidea 5
Demosthenes 238
Densities 165
Density 183
   Linyanti River 195

Dentine 218–9
Dentinal tubule density 220
   tubules 218
Deodand 210
Department of Engineering Science
      Oxford University 222
Deraniyagala 34
Desmostylia 7
Destruction of huts 210
Dichapetalum spp 104
Digby, Bassett 15
Digestibility 73
Digging for water 227
'Diksie' 100
Dinocerata 8
Dinosaurs 2, 3
Dinothere tusks 9
Dinotheres 8–9
Dipetalonema 117
Displacement activity 178
Display 151
Dissections 42–3
Distances travelled 206–8
Distribution maps, oldest 39
Diurnal rhythm 163
DNA 'fingerprinting' 225
Dollman, G 31
Domestication 265
Douglas-Hamilton, Dr. I. H 109, 138
Dravidian civilization 265
Drepanocerus coleoptera 159
Drinking 70, 106–7
Droppings 51
Dropsy 115
Drought 19, 105–6, 154, 188, 204
   in Botswana 194–5
   periodic 187
   in Tsavo 189, 207
Dung 122
   beetles 159
Durbar 101
Dutch 247
Dwarf stegodont 21
   woolly mammoth 21, 22

Ear mite 123–4
   signals 150–1
Ears, area 66
   flapping 66
   blood circulation 66–7
   and temperature regulation 62, 64–6

East Africa 240
  African ivory trade 249–54
Eating bodies 166
Eburatus 237
Economic importance 285
Effects on vegetation 173
Egrets 127
'Eleanor' 94
Eleph 17
Elephant, Asian and African compared
      43
  capture 282–3
  deaths 262
  distribution 16
  drugs 112
  dwarf 21, 26, 31–2
  fossils 4
  population in Africa 260
  shot by cannon 273
  survival 21
  training programme 285
Elephant Company 271
Elephant Preservation Act 37
Elephantidae 5, 9, 10, 12, 17
Elephantinae 17
Elephantoloemus indicus 118–9
Elephants killed 257, 259–60
Elephas 33, 219
  antiquus 2, 12
  falconeri 26
  maximus 26
  indicus 26
  iolensis 25
  melitensis 26
  namadicus 26
  recki 25, 26
  evolution 17, 18
  extinction 22
  extinction in Africa 18, 25
  in Africa 22
Elton, Charles 211
El Zubeir 262
Embrithopoda 7
Emin Pasha 254–5, 278–9
Enamel 219
Energy absorption 62
Energetic cost of walking 46
Encysted bullets 113
English trade 241–2
Equilibrium hypothesis 212
Essential fatty acids 177
Ethiopia 251, 253
Etosha Park 114

Eurasia 6, 10, 13
Eocene 6, 10, 17
Evans, G.H 80, 84, 119
Evolution 17
  rates 17
Extinctions 23
Exponential increase 213
Eyeball 76

Faecal contents 155
Fallon, Baron 279
Families, origin of 6
Family, basic unit 130, 132, 133
  splitting 133
Famine in Tsavo 189
Farler, Ven. J.P 191
Fasciola jacksoni 117
Fatty acids 154
Fauntleroy's ivory warehouse 223
Fazl, Abul 70
Feeding, of Indian 167
  method 167
  pattern 164
  rate 157
  time 157
  times 163
Feet, damage to 54
  estimating height from 53
  structure of 53
Fenykoevi elephant 100
Fermentation of food 56, 73
Fernao, Gomes 241
Fibonacci, Leonardo 221
  spirals 221–22
The Field 217
Fighting 89, 143–4
Filariid worms 116–7
'Fingerprinting' from blood 30
Fire 184, 191, 208
Firearms 22, 199, 252–53
Fire-resistance of trees 175–6
Fitzgerald, W.W.A 187
Flatulence 113
Flea, strength of 78
Fluid in gut 56–7
Flukes 117
Foaker, Mr. 187
Food consumption 156–7
  intake 71–2
  quality 154
  requirements 73
Foot-and-mouth disease 114

Foot fly 120
Forefeet in feeding 167
Forest elephant 28–9, 100, 185, 269
  groups 132
  races 31
  tusks 28
Forest palm 11
Forestry 282
Fossil ivory 221
Fossils 5, 6
Forsyth, Captain 117, 179
Found deaths 107
  ivory 257
Four-tusked elephants 227
France ivory imports 242
Franssen, Lt. 32
Friesenhahn Cave, Texas 19
Fusion of bones 46
Fyn schu 12, 238

Gabon 249
Gaja Sastra 34, 36, 210
Galana Ranch 190
  River 185, 190, 206, 251
Galen, Claudius 41–2
Gall bladder 59
  stones 59
Game theory 144
Gangala-na-Bodio 279–80
Gatherings 134–5
Gaugamela 265
Genetic relationships 30
Geneva 273
Geological time scale 7
Gestation length 81
Gilchrist, W 112
Goethe, Johann W. von 228
Gomphothere extinction 16
Gomphotherium 219
  angustidens 11, 222
Gomphotheres 10, 11
Gomphotheroidea 5
Gordon, General Charles G 243, 255,
  278–9
Gourma elephants 207
Gowers, Sir William 269
Grammocephalus clathratus 116
Grass in diet 155
  species eaten 159–60
Grasses, C3 20
  C4 20
Graveyards 107–8

Great Lakes 20
Grew, Nehemiah 227
Grogan, E.S. and Sharpe, A 252–3
Group size 131
Guinea Coast 241–2
Gut capacity 72
  fluid 124

Habitat choice 204
  mosaic 211
  preference 136–7
Haematobia 121
Haematomyzus elephantis 123
  hopkinsi 123
Haematopinus phacochoeri 123
Haemoglobin 3
  types 30
Hagenbeck, Carl 32, 272–3, 273–4
Hair 52
Haller, Albrecht von 229
Hannibal 267–8
Hanno 27, 267
Harderian gland 76
Hasdrubal 267
Hawkesius hawkesii 117
Hawkins, William 241
Hawthorn 2, 11
Hearing range 148–9
Heart beat 67
  elephant with two 67
  shape 67
  size 67
Heat avoidance 62
  output 64
  stress 107
Heat, oestrus 80, 84, 85
  behaviour 86
  chasing by bulls 87
  signs of 86
  suppression 88
Henry III 271–2
Hepatitis 117
Herd leader 129
Herodotus 17
High density areas 202
Hippopotamus 117
Hluhluwe Game Reserve 22
Hobley, Charles W 187, 206
Hodson, Arnold 31
Holotrichs 124
Home, Sir Everard 71, 148–9
Home range 131, 135–7, 207–8

Hookworms 116
Hopkins, Gerald M 239
Hornaday, William 75, 275
Hot Springs 19
Howorth, H 19
Human population 22
Hunter, John 229
    William 11
Hunting elephant 186–7
    licences 31, 195
Huxley, Sir Julian 212
Hwange Park 194
Hybrid elephant 26
Hypothermia 68–9
Hyrax 3, 4, 7

Ice Age landscape 21
Ice retreat 20
Ides, Evert Ysbrand 13
Illegal ivory trade 260
Immigration 201
Immunological tests 12, 26
Incontinence 139
India 250–1, 239–10, 243, 256–7, 273
Indian Army elephants 270
    ivory exports 257
Indofilaria pattabiramani 117
Infrasound 147–8
Intelligence 75
Iron Age sites 240
Islamic expansion 241
Islands, Mediterranean 21
    south-east Asian 21
Ivory, ancient properties 238–9
    brittleness 223
    carving in India 256
    carving workshop 240
    characteristic structure 220
    chemical analyses 224
    demand 259
    differences 223–4
    drying 219
    elasticity 223
    'engine-turned' appearance   221
    exports 184
    graded by rat gnawing 223
    hunters 19, 184, 209
    hunting 212–3
    imports to Europe 243
    scramble 241
    tensile strength 223
    trade 40, 193

    uses 245
    wear and tear 257–8
    weight loss 219
    yield 28

Jackson, Sir Frederick 171
James I 272
'Jap' 61, 63, 64, 67, 69–70, 73, 77
Japan 257
Japanese 238, 262, 271
Java 40
Jaw 48
    movement 49
'Jim' 274–5
Judges' rulings 275–6
'Jumbo' 272
    dissection of 167
Jupiter 238

Kaokoland 203
Kaokoveld 27
    elephants 62
Karagwe 252
Kasane 194
Kasigau 187
Keddah system 280, 282
Kenya ivory burning 262
    tusks 217
Khartoum 254–5
    ivory exports 243
Killing elephants 261
Kilwa 250
Kimemata, Jumbe 217
King of Persia 120–1
    of Siam 286
Kipling, Rudyard 6
Kirgiljach River 14
Kirk, Dr. James 119
Kirkman, Dr. 259
Kisimani 186
Kittenberger, Kalman 135
Knife handles 245
Knowledge 131
    store 261
Knysna 27, 255
    forest 163
Kolb, Peter 276
Krapf, J. L 185–7, 251
Kruger Park 30, 91
    bulls 216
    population 201–2

Kublai Khan 36, 240, 270
Kyan Zit 228

Lactation 85
Laden elephant 283
Lake Manyara 28, 66
  level 192
  woodlands 192
Laplume, Commandant 279
Laws, Dr. Richard 136
Learning 75
Leech 111–2
Legislation 258
Leiperenia moreli 116
Leopold, King 277–9
Leptospirosis 115
Le Vaillant 26
Lewis, Slim 76, 272
Liakhov Islands 235–6
  Ivan 235
Libya 239
Lice 122–3
Lifespan 101–2
Lifetime production 198
Limb movement 46
Lincoln, Abraham 286
Linnaeus, Carl 26, 33
Linolenic acid 154, 177
Lion 104
Liver 59
Livingstone, Dr. David 243, 255–6
Loads 284
Logan, Jonas 234
London Zoo 156, 272
Lord George Sanger 116
  Mayor's Show 275
Loss of learning process 214
Louse 123
Loxanoetus bassoni 124
  lenae 123
Loxodonta adaurora 24–5
  africana 25
  africana africana 28
  africana cyclotis 25, 28
  atlantica 25
Loxodonta 26
  evolution 17
  radiation 25
  survival of 22
  tooth structure 25
Loxodontofilaria 117
LSD and elephant 61

Luangwa Valley 211–2
  population 202
Ludolphus, Job 170
Lugard, F.D 185
Lungs 57, 59
Lung volume 67
Lydekker, Richard 35
Lyell, Sir Charles 14
Lyperosia 121, 124

Maasai 251
Macnaghten, H 101
Mahogany tree 184–5
Maintenance level 188
Mali 207
  ivory 220
Mallophaga 123
Malthus, Rev. Thomas 211–2
Mammalian societies 129
Mammonomonogamus indicus 116
  loxodontis 116
Mammoth 198
  bone marks 18
  dung 21
  extinction 23
  food 21
  imperial 13, 16
  ivory 238–9
    markets 235–6
    quantities 235
  lifespan 102
  milk tusks 218
  remains 5, 18–9
  tusk 217, 234–6
    found in Scotland 236
    growth 216
  tusks 15–6
  woolly 2
Mammoths 4, 5, 12–6, 18–9
  extinction 16, 21
  frozen 12–4
Mammut americanum 12
Mammuthus 26
  evolution 17–8
Mammuthus armenicus 13
  imperator 13
  meridionalis 23
  primigenius 13
Mammutidae 11
Mammutoidea 5
Man, role in extermination 22
  as predator 199

Management in captivity 276
Manovo-Gounda Park 135, 164, 178
Manyara 163–4, 202
  deaths 104
Mapungubwe 240
Mara 191
Marco Polo 270
Mass mortality 19
  killing 199
Mastodon 11–2, 18–9
  age at death 12
  food 20
  hair 52
  North America, in 20
  remains 20
Maternal bond 93–4
  investment 89
Mating by highest ranking bull 89
  competition for 89
  effectiveness of 89
  pandemonium 87
Matriarch 128–9
  age of 129
Mauretania 27
Megasthenes 137, 256, 268
Mehemot 12
Meroitic culture 265
Metabolic rate 61, 67
Metellus, Lucius Caecilius   267
Methane production 74
Meyer, H.A 243
Midges 122
Migration 204–7
  in Kenya 204–6
    Tanganyika 204–5
    Uganda 206
Military 196
Milk analysis 93
  production 89
Minoan times 239
Miocene 5, 6, 7, 10, 24
Miombo woodland 165, 173–4, 211–2
Mkomazi 116, 202
Mnesitheus 59
Moeritheres 7
Moeritheroidea 5
Moeritherium 6
Mogau 104, 181
Moghul emperors 36
Mombasa 250–1
Moore, E.D 261
Moore, Randall 76, 284
  and Munnion 150, 272

Mopane woodland 174, 180
Mortality rate 102–3
Mosquitoes 113
Moss, Cynthia 129
Moths 125–6
Mount Kilimanjaro 216
  Marsabit 108
Mount Elgon caves 165–6
  elephants 166
Mounting frequency 86–7
Movement patterns 131, 208–9
Mozambique 242, 250, 256
Mpwapa expedition 277–8
Mullen, Dr. A 42, 54
Munich elephant panic 273–4
Murchison Falls Park 107, 154, 183
  elephants 113
  tree elimination 175
Murshidia murshida 116
  omoensis 116
Musket balls in ivory 228–9
  in molar teeth 232
Musth 80, 89, 137–46
  in Asian and African elephant 145
  bull posture 139–40
    movements 142
  control of 145–6
  rumble 140–1
  seasons 141
  suppression 142
  theories 143
Mycenean times 239
Mycoplasma 113
Myoglobin 68
Myrrh tree 177, 187

Nairobi 33
Namib Desert elephants 203–4
Natural control 184
Natural History Museum, London 100, 216
Negus of Ethiopia 276
Nematode worm 116
Neocuterebra squamosa 120
Neumann, A.H 185
Neumann, Dr. Oscar 119
New Siberia Islands 19, 235
New World 5
News Chronicle 259
Nile 183, 203, 239
Nitrogen limiting growth 190

North African elephants 240
 ivory trade 254–5
North America 13, 18
 vegetation 20
Northern Rhodesia 280
Nubians 199

Odontoblastic cells 218
Oestrid flies 117–8
Ogilby, John 241
Olduvai Gorge 25
Oligocene 6, 7, 10, 11, 12
Once A Week 239
Onescritus 34
Oppian 54, 99–100, 148, 169, 216
Orphan calves 92, 94
Osborn, Henry Fairfield 5
Otanoetus wetzeli 124
Ovaries 84–5
Overpopulation 183
Owen, Prof. Richard 43, 71, 228
Oxford University Museum 232
Oxygen transport 67–8

Paenungulates 3
 earliest 6
Pachyderms 51
Palaeocene 6
Palaeomastodon 10
Palmitic acid 154
Papyrus 161
Park, Mungo 204, 248–9
Passage time of food 73–4
Paviland cave 232
 pendant 232, 234
Peacock, E.H 280
Pelvis 45
People's Palace and Aquarium
 Company 275
Perrault, C 52, 81
Perry, J.S 82
Petri, Dr. Georgio C 216
Pharoah's elephant 31
Pharyngobolus africanus 119
Phenacodus 3
Phenols 180
Phiomia 10, 219
Phoenicians 239
Phoresis 124
Phosphorous limiting growth 190
 in vegetation 177

Physiological drought 192
Piano key maker 114
Piano keys 245
Piapiac 127
Pig water loss 63–4
Pigafetta, Filippo 242, 269, 277
Pitman, Captain C.R.S 171, 202, 213,
 224
Plant growth elements 159
 species eaten in India 161
  in Malaya 161
Platybelodon 11
Platycobboldia (Cobboldia) loxodontis
 119–20
Pleistocene 2, 12, 13, 16, 18, 20
 extinctions 22
 glaciation 14
Pliny 40, 75, 111–2, 219, 239, 261–2, 268
Pliocene 7, 13, 17, 18, 20, 24
Pneumatic osteolysis 47
 sinuses 47
Poaching 37, 98, 184, 187, 189, 192
Poisonous plant 159, 181
Polybius 268
Polydinium mysoreum 124–5
Polyperchon 154
Poole, Joyce 139
Population decline 259
 increase in Botswana 195
Portuguese 240–2, 247, 249, 250–1, 255,
 262
 and ivory 199
Porus 102, 265
Potatoes, boiled 245
Powell, Philip 232
Powell-Cotton, P.H.G 108
Poisons 73
Pox, elephant 113
Predmost 18
Primary spiral 221
Primelephas 5, 17
Primitive features 44
Princess Anne 275
Pringle, Thomas 170
Proanthocyanidins 180
Proboscidea 5, 18
Proboscidean ancestral line 7
Proboscideans 3
Progesterone 84–5
Protection from hunting 193–4
Protein content 154
 requirement 177
Protofasciola (Distomum) robusta 117

Protozoan fauna 124–5
  parasites 115
Pseudoentodinium elephantis 124
Ptolemy Auletes 269
Ptolemy II 263, 265–6
Puberty 81
  bull 84, 133
  cow 85
  delay 183
Pulp cavity of tusk 219
  nodule acicular 232
    from mammoth tusk 232
Pydna 268
Pygmy elephant 31–2

Queen Elizabeth I 272
Qu'ran 276

Radiation of elephants 16
Rainfall in Botswana 194
  effect on fertility 105
  influence of 137
  movements 208
  in Tsavo 189
  variation 105
Ralph of Coggeshall 4
Rami, King 36
Rancho La Brea tar pits 19
Rankin, L.K 115, 277
Range reduction 183
Raphia 266, 268
Rate of increase 198–9, 201, 213
  in Botswana 195
Ray, John 33
Rebmann, J 185–6
Reck, Hans 25
Recolonization of Etosha Park 202
  in Kruger Park 202
Red Sea elephant hunting grounds 266
Regeneration 174–5
Reproductive life 85
  senescence 198
  tract of bull 83
Resident Magistrate's report 194
Rhapta 249
Rheumatoid arthritis 112–3
Rhinoceros 116, 118, 188
Rhynchotheres, beak-tusked 10
Right-handedness 76
Rinderpest 191

Ring fires 199
Roman army 267
  empire 239
  occupation of Britain 4
Romans 237–8, 241, 267, 271
Rome 80
Rome Zoo 132
Roots eaten 160
Rot patches 184
Rotterdam Zoo 123
Roughage 156
Roundworms 116
Rowland Ward 217
Royal Society 230
Ruaha Park 190
  deaths 105
Ruttenia (Cobboldia) elephantis 119
  loxodontis 118
Ruysch, F 229

Sabre-toothed tiger 225
Saddam Hussein 276
Salmonella 76, 114–5
Salt-lick 117, 165
'Samson' and rhinoceros 96
Sanderson, G.P 37, 75, 86, 92, 100, 107,
  129, 131, 136, 146, 147–8, 209,
  226–7, 273, 282–3
Sanger, Lord George 274
dos Santos, Father 199
Savuti marsh 192–3
Sawing off tusk 219
Saxon women 241
Scheelea rostrata 11, 163
Schreger, Bernhard 220
  lines 220
Science 148
Scipio 267–8
Screw-worm 122
Sebaceous glands 52
Seed dispersal 11, 161–3, 180
Seeds in dung 162
Seleucus 265
Selous, F.C 2, 193
Semiothisa elephantedestructa 126
  inaequilinea 127
Senegal 242
  River 241
Sengwa 174, 178
Serengeti Park 108, 178, 191–2
Sexual anatomy 81–2
Shade seeking 107

Sheldrick, Daphne 94, 96, 226
   David 96
Shen-i-king 12
Shinamba 193, 207
Shooting, reaction to 129
Short, Dr. Roger 57
Shoulder height of calf 89
Shovel-tuskers 10, 11
Siberia 13, 19, 235, 240
Sikes, Sylvia 146
"Silent heat" 84
Sindbad the Sailor 107
Sirenia 3
Size advantages and disadvantages 62
   limit 43
Skeleton 44
   behaviour towards 109
   sent to Britain 43
Skin 51–2
   maggot 118
   sensitivity 52
Skull 47–8
Sleep 77
Sleeping sickness 183
Slim, Sir William 271
Slime mites 124
Slym, M 112
Smith, F 52
   Prof. J. Maynard 144
Smithsonian Museum 100
Social bonds 133
Sodium 165, 177
Soil, effects on 190
   damage to 190
Sound location 148–50
Sounds made 146–50
South African ivory exports 255–6
South America 10, 11, 12
Sparrman, Andrew 70, 77, 81, 277
Spear heads in ivory 230
Species' duration 17–8
Speed of elephant 43, 46
Speke, J.H 252
Sperms 83
Spiral tusks 227
Spiroid worms 116
Spirotrichs 124
Sri Lanka 34, 39, 82, 91, 256, 282
   activity 65
   calf percentage 201
SS Benin 217
Stable atomic isotope ratios 224–5
   limit cycle 212–3

Staduschin, Mikhail 235
Stanley, H.M 243, 263
Steel, J 112, 115
Stegodonts 6, 16, 40
Stegomastodon 11
Stegotetrabelodontines 24
Stephanofilaria assamensis 117
Sterility 81
Stomach contents 167–8
   fill 159
Stomoxys 121, 124
Stone Age man 5, 13, 18, 22, 107, 232–3,
   239
Stones in stomach 167
Stored ivory 255, 261–2
Strahlenberg P.I von 236
Strongylid worms 116
Stylohyoidean bone 7
Straight-tusked elephant 2, 16
   in Essex 19
Strength 78
Stress 68
Succulent plants 161
Suckling by calf 92–3
Suction power of trunk 57
Sudduth, W.X 228
Sukumar, R 131
Sumatra 216, 257
'Sundar Gaj' 277–8
Surra 115
Sweat glands 52
Swimming 284
Swynnerton, C.F.M 185, 200
Sydney Zoo 102
Symbionts 124
Synchronized mating 82
Syria 265
Syrian elephants 239–40

Tabanid flies 115
Tabora 278
Tai Forest 162
Tail 46–7
Ta-Kuan-pen-Tsao 238
Tamyr Peninsula 14
T'ang elephant 270
Tapeworm cysts 117
Tarangire Park 98
Tarn, Sir William 269
Tarsolepis elephantorum 126
   remicaudata 126
Taru desert 186

Tear-drinkers 125–7
Tears 76
Teeth 10, 11, 48–51
    action of 51
    cementum 49
    chronology of 50
    of elephants 16
    enamel covering 49
    enamel organ 49
    germ 49
    grinding surface 51
    lamellae 49
    laminae 49
    laminary index 50
    of *Loxodonta* 17
    of mammoth 13
    nerve 49
    pulp 49
    shearing-index 16
    of stegodonts 16
    structure 49
Temperature changes 66
    low 69
Temporal gland 134, 138–9
Tennent, Sir, E 70, 102, 134, 159, 167,
        178–9, 285–6
Terminalia glaucescens 177
Termites 159
Testes 83
Testosterone level 141–2
Tetrabelodon 11
Tethys Sea 6, 7
Thapsus 266, 268
Theileria 115
Theophrastus 238
Thomson, Joseph 165
Threat display 151–2
Throat 59
Thut 115
Thutmose III 238, 265
Tick birds 127
Ticks 115, 122
Tiger 92, 104
Tiglath Pileser I 265
The Times 43, 101, 158, 227, 273, 275
Timofeyevitch, Y 23
Tippu Tip 252
Toes, elephant 52–3
    mammoth 53
Tooth abscess 51
    eruption pattern 16, 49–50
    implants 229
    seventh 50

structure 5
    wear 102
Topsell, E 74
Trade in mammoth ivory 235
Tradescants 42
Transport animal 284
Tree cover and elephant density 187
    damage causes 177
Treetops 166
Trichostrongyle 116
Triplets 89
Trunk 54–5, 62
    in display 151
    in feeding 167
    'fingers' 55
    greeting with 55
    hydraulic system 55
    muscles 55
Trypanosoma brucei elephantis 115
    evansi 115
Trypanosomiasis 115
Tsavo Park 96, 98, 185–90, 260
    deaths 103–5, 108, 153–4
    drought 71
    East Park 107, 176, 185, 187, 210
    East Park human population 186
Tsetse fly 115–6, 121, 193–4, 211, 278
Tshekedi Khama, Chief 262
Tso Chwan 215
Tu Li Shin 239
Tundra 14
Turkana 108, 185, 253
Turnover rate 17
    time 157
Tushes 217
Tusk 122
    appearance 218
    appearance African 216
    breakage 107
    composition 218–9
    growth 216, 218
    growth rate 220
    persistent pulp 216
    potential length 216
        weight 216
    pulp cavity 218
    uneven wear 75–6
    weight average 200, 213
        decline 259
Tusklessness 226–7
Tusks 48
    biggest African 216
    biggest Asian 217

Tusks—contd.
  in display 151
  mammoth 15–6, 20
  milk 217–8
  multiple 227–8
  selection for defence 225
    dominance 226
Tutankhamen 238
Twins 89, 91

Uganda 97, 183, 200
  breeding in 82
  elephants 30
  ironwood 175
  parks 107
United States 272
  ivory imports 263
United States National Fish and
      Wildlife Forensic Laboratory 221
University Museum Oxford 42
Urine loss 139
  sampling 145
  trails 139
Uterine scar 85

Vegetation 20
  damage 190
Venice 273
Venus of Brassempouy 239
Vertebrae 44
Very low frequency sound 147–8
Veterinary Officer's report 194
Vienna 158
  Zoo 119
Vietnam 135
Vili 247
Visual discernment 76
Vitamin F 154, 177–8

Wakamba 251–2
Wakawaka 32
Wallowing 63–4
Wallows 123
Wambisha 186
Wandorobo hunters 191
Wanyamwezi 252
Warble fly 117–8

'Warren Hastings' 101
Warthog louse 123
Water elephant 32
  loss 69–70
    through skin 62–3
  store 70–1
Waterhole 19
Weight at birth 82, 89
Welwitschia mirabilis 204
West African ivory trade 245–9
Wet season 82
Whale communication 150
White elephants 35
Wildebeest 191
Williams, J.H 91–2, 146, 227, 270
Willow 14–5
Woodland/elephant evolution 180
Woodland recovery 175
  use 160
Woolly mammoth 13–4, 119
  calf 14
  digits 14
  distribution 14
  in Essex 19
  fat 14
  hair 14
  heart 67
  heat retention 14
  migration 15
  skin 14
  trunk 14
Wood, S.V 22
Wrangel Island 14, 16, 21, 22

Yakutsk 235
Yala Game Reserve 91
Yao 249
Yellow-fever tree 192
Yukaghir 198

Zaïre 28
Zambezi River 119
Zanzibar 251–2, 257–8
Zimbabwe 18, 19, 21
  breeding 82
  deaths 106
  drought 106
Zurich Zoo 166